The European Union and its eastern neighbourhood

Manchester University Press

The European Union and its eastern neighbourhood

Europeanisation and its twenty-first-century contradictions

Edited by
Paul Flenley and Michael Mannin

Manchester University Press

Published by Manchester University Press
Altrincham Street, Manchester M1 7JA
www.manchesteruniversitypress.co.uk

British Library Cataloguing-in-Publication Data
A catalogue record for this book is available from the British Library

ISBN 978 1 5261 0909 5 hardback
ISBN 978 0 5261 0910 1 paperback

First published 2018

Typeset
by Toppan Best-set Premedia Limited

Contents

List of figures and tables	*page* vii
List of contributors	ix
Preface	xi
Acknowledgements	xii
Abbreviations	xiii

Introduction   *Paul Flenley and Michael Mannin*   1

Part I   Concepts and frameworks
  1 Europeanisation as a past and present narrative
    Michael Mannin   9
  2 Defining contemporary European identity/ies
    Nora Siklodi   25
  3 The limitations of the EU's strategies for Europeanisation
    of the neighbours   *Paul Flenley*   38

Part II   Country/Area studies
  4 Europeanisation and Russia   *Tatiana Romanova*   57
  5 'Bounded Europeanisation': the case of Ukraine
    Nadiia Bureiko and Teodor Lucian Moga   71
  6 Belarus: does Europeanisation require a geopolitical choice?
    Kiryl Kascian   86
  7 Relations between Moldova and the European Union
    Kamil Całus and Marcin Kosienkowski   99
  8 Value-oriented aspects of EU-isation: the case of the Balkans
    Monika Eriksen   114
  9 Turkey: identity politics and reticent Europeanisation
    Dimitris Tsarouhas   126

Part III   Issues and sectors
 10 New member states' economic relations with Russia:
    'Europeanisation' or bilateral preferences?
    Martin Dangerfield   141

11 EU energy security policy in the eastern neighbourhood:
    towards Europeanisation?   *Edward Stoddard*   155
12 The EU and the European Other: the Janus face of
    EU migration and visa policies in the neighbourhood
    Igor Merheim-Eyre   167
13 'Neighbour languages': Europeanisation and
    language borders   *Maria Stoicheva*   181
14 Security and democratisation: the case of the South
    Caucasus   *Kevork Oskanian and Derek Averre*   195

Conclusion   *Paul Flenley and Michael Mannin*   210

Bibliography   219
Index   260

Figures and tables

Figures

5.1 'Bounded' Europeanisation   *page* 73
5.2 Which foreign policy direction should be a priority
    for Ukraine? (2002–15). Authors' own representation
    according to data provided by Razumkov Centre (2015b).   78
5.3 Do you consider yourself European? Authors'
    own representation according to data provided
    by Razumkov Centre (2014).   81
5.4 The relevance of Ukraine's future development for
    different age groups. Authors' own representation
    according to the compiled data provided by
    the project 'Region, Nation and Beyond:
    An Interdisciplinary and Transcultural
    Reconceptualization of Ukraine' (University of
    St Gallen, 2013).   82
5.5 The relevance of Ukraine's future development
    depending on the place of study/work. Authors' own
    representation according to the compiled data provided
    by the project 'Region, Nation and Beyond' (University of
    St Gallen, 2013).   83
15.1 The nexus of EU/neighbourhood relations   211

Tables

1.1 Historic Europeanisations   14
1.2 Europeanisation and its contemporary manifestations
    (adapted from McCormick, 2010)   24
2.1 Defining European identity/ies: A conceptual framework   37
5.1 Preferences for foreign policy direction of Ukraine.
    Regional parameters   77

5.2 Native language in Ukraine   78
5.3 Positive attitude towards the monuments   79
5.4 Positive attitude towards the historical events in the
    history of independent Ukraine   80
5.5 Self-identification   81
11.1 The macro and meso structures of the EU's energy
     governance matrix in the Caspian   162
13.1 Proportions of titulars, ethnic Russians and L1 Russian
     speakers in Soviet republics in 1989 and in post-Soviet
     countries in 1999–2004 (USSR census and respective
     post-Soviet censuses)   187

Contributors

Derek Averre is reader in Russian Foreign and Security Policy and former Director of the Centre for Russian, European and Eurasian Studies at the Department of Politics and International Studies, University of Birmingham, United Kingdom.

Nadiia Bureiko is head of Europeanisation Studies at the Foreign Policy Council 'Ukrainian Prism', Ukraine. Since 2014 she has been a post-doctoral researcher at the Center for Governance and Culture in Europe, University of St Gallen, Switzerland.

Kamil Całus is an expert on Moldova at the Centre for Eastern Studies, Warsaw, Poland.

Martin Dangerfield is Professor of European Integration and Jean Monnet Chair in the European Integration of Central and Eastern Europe at the University of Wolverhampton, United Kingdom.

Monika Eriksen is doctoral candidate at the Institute of European Studies, Jagiellonian University, Krakow, Poland.

Paul Flenley is Subject leader in Politics and International Relations at the School of Social, Historical and Literary Studies, University of Portsmouth, United Kingdom, and managing co-editor of *The Journal of Contemporary European Studies*.

Kiryl Kascian is Editor-in-Chief at *Belarusian Review*. He is an expert in inter-ethnic relations, human rights, constitutional law, security issues and regional development.

Marcin Kosienkowski is Assistant Professor at the Institute of Political Science and International Affairs, John Paul II Catholic University of Lublin, Poland.

Michael Mannin is Jean Monnet Chair in European Politics (*ad personam*) and Director of the Jean Monnet Centre of Excellence for Studies in

Transnational Europe at the School of Social, Historical and Literary Studies, University of Portsmouth, United Kingdom.

Igor Merheim-Eyre is doctoral researcher at the University of Kent, United Kingdom and a visiting scholar at Katholieke Universiteit Leuven, Belgium.

Teodor Lucian Moga is Assistant Professor at the Centre for European Studies, Faculty of Law, 'Alexandru Ioan Cuza' University of Iasi (UAIC), Romania, and a post-doctoral researcher at the Center for Governance and Culture in Europe, University of St Gallen, Switzerland.

Kevork Oskanian is lecturer at the Department of Political Science and International Studies (POLSIS), University of Birmingham, United Kingdom.

Tatiana Romanova is Associate Professor, Jean Monnet Chair and Director of the Jean Monnet Centre of Excellence at St Petersburg State University, Russia.

Nora Siklodi is lecturer in Politics and European Studies at the School of Social, Historical and Literary Studies, University of Portsmouth, United Kingdom.

Edward Stoddard is lecturer in International Relations at the School of Social, Historical and Literary Studies, University of Portsmouth, United Kingdom.

Maria Stoicheva is Professor, Jean Monnet Chair at the Department of European Studies, Sofia University 'St Kliment Ohridski', Bulgaria.

Dimitris Tsarouhas is Associate Professor at the Department of International Relations, Bilkent University, Turkey.

Preface

This volume is part of the output of a much larger project, associated with the Jean Monnet Centre of Excellence for the Study of a Transnational Europe (CESTE) and funded by the European Commission from 2013 to 2016 at the University of Portsmouth. CESTE and its several activities were based on the prior research of several of its contributors including the editors, Paul Flenley and Michael Mannin, in the fields of East European/ Russian studies and the EU and Europeanisation, respectively. The associated research activities led to three conferences that brought together colleagues from a Europe-wide collection of universities, whose interests complemented our own questioning of the relevance and success of the EU as a progenitor of political and socio-economic change (Europeanisation) among its Eastern neighbours.

This field of study and its associated controversies have paralleled, and been partly obscured by, other recent challenges to the EU – economic, political, strategic (with the Trump election) and existential issues (in the case of Brexit). However, the EU and its Eastern neighbourhood relationships remain a part of the more familiar internal dilemmas that the EU faces in relation to free movement, migration, external security, energy futures, EU-Russian relations, notions of identity and the balance of power between member states and community institutions. All of these are reflected in the problems of EU–Eastern neighbourhood relations and are discussed in the following chapters. We hope this will make a contribution to the analysis of the dilemmas that the EU faces as it adapts to its changing role in twenty-first century regional and world politics.

Paul Flenley and Michael Mannin
Portsmouth, 2017

Acknowledgements

On behalf of the contributors, the editors would like to thank the EU, national officials and political and societal actors who gave their time and expert advice in the development of this volume. We also wish to praise the major contribution to the presentational editing of this volume that Andrew Waterman, postgraduate researcher at the University of Portsmouth, has made to its completion. We thank the Centre for International and European Studies Research (CEISR), University of Portsmouth for its financial support in the final stages. We would also like to thank the anonymous reviewers of the book proposal and draft for their comments. Finally, we must fully acknowledge that this project has been funded with support from the European Commission. This publication only reflects the views of the authors and the Commission cannot be held responsible for any use which may be made of the information therein.

Abbreviations

AA	Association Agreement
ACAA	Agreements on Conformity Assessment and Acceptance
AKP	*Adalet ve Kalkınma Partisi* (Justice and Development Party (Turkey))
ATP	autonomous trade preferences
BMD	Ballistic Missile Defence
BSS	Black Sea Synergy
BUMAD	Belarus, Ukraine, Moldova Anti-Drugs Programme
CBC	cross-border cooperation
CEE	Central and East European
CEEC	Central and Eastern European Countries
CEFTA	Central European Free Trade Agreement
CEN	*Comité Européen de Normalisation* (European Committee for Standardization)
CFSP	Common Foreign and Security Policy
CHP	*Cumhuriyet Halk Partisi* (Republican People's Party (Turkey))
CIB	Comprehensive Institution Building
CIS	Commonwealth of Independent States
CMEA	Council for Mutual Economic Assistance
COEST	Council of the European Union's Working Party on Eastern Europe and Central Asia
C-RICEISC	Czech-Russian Intergovernmental Commission for Economic, Industrial and Scientific Cooperation
ČSSD	*Česká strana sociálně demokratická* (Czech Social Democratic Party)
DCFTA	Deep and Comprehensive Free Trade Area
DCI	Development Cooperation Instrument
DG	Directorate General
DPT	Democratic Peace Theory

EaP	Eastern Partnership
EC	European Community
ECSC	European Coal and Steel Community
ECT	Energy Charter Treaty
ECU	Eurasian Customs Union
EEAS	European External Action Service
EEC	European Economic Community
EED	European Endowment for Democracy
EEU	Eurasian Economic Union
EIDHR	European Instrument for Democracy and Human Rights
EITI	Extractive Industry Transparency Initiative
ENI	European Neighbourhood Instrument
ENP	European Neighbourhood Policy
ENPI	European Neighbourhood and Partnership Instrument
EP	European Parliament
EU	European Union
EUBAM	EU Border Assistance Mission
EUJUST/THEMIS	EU Rule of Law Mission to Georgia
EURODAC	European Dactyloscopy
EUROSUR	European Border Surveillance System
EUSR	European Union Special Representative
FCNM	Framework Convention for the Protection of National Minorities
FDI	foreign direct investment
FYROM	Former Yugoslav Republic of Macedonia
GDP	Gross Domestic Product
GSP	generalised system of preferences
H-RICEC	Hungarian-Russian Intergovernmental Commission on Cooperation in the Economy, Science and Technology
HR	High Representative
INOGATE	Interstate Oil and Gas Transport to Europe
ITGI	Interconnector-Turkey-Greece-Italy
MFA	Multiannual Indicative Programme
MID	Министерство иностранных дел Российской Федерации (Ministry of Foreign Affairs of the Russian Federation)
MOU	Memoranda of understanding
MSZP	*Magyar Szocialista Párt* (Hungarian Socialist Party)
NATO	North Atlantic Treaty Organization
NGOs	Non-governmental organisations
NIS	newly independent states

NITG	National Integration and Tolerance in Georgia
NKR	Nagorno-Karabakh Republic
ODS	*Občanská demokratická strana* (Civic Democratic Party (Czech Republic))
OSCE	Organization for Security and Co-operation in Europe
PCA	Partnership and Cooperation Agreement
PCRM	*Partidul Comuniştilor din Republica Moldova* (Party of Communists of the Republic of Moldova)
PDM	*Partidul Democrat din Moldova* (Democratic Party of Moldova)
PHARE	Poland and Hungary: Assistance for Restructuring their Economies
PL	*Partidul Liberal* (Liberal Party (Moldova))
PLDM	*Partidul Liberal Democrat din Moldova* (Liberal Democratic Party of Moldova)
Rosstandart	Росстандарт (Federal Agency for Technical Regulation and Metrology (Russia))
SARIO	*Slovenská Agentúra pre rozvoj investícií a obchodu* (Slovak Investment and Trade Development Agency)
SDKÚ-DS	*Slovenská demokratická a kresťanská únia – Demokratická strana* (Slovak Democratic and Christian Union-Democratic Party)
SEA	Single European Act
SEECP	South East European Cooperation Process
SMER-SD	*Smer–sociálna demokracia* (Direction-Social Democracy (Slovakia))
S-RICCEST	Slovak–Russian Intergovernmental Commission on Cooperation in the Economy, Science and Technology
TACIS	Technical Assistance for the Commonwealth of Independent States
TANAP	Trans-Anatolian pipeline
TAP	Trans-Adriatic pipeline
TEU	Treaty on European Union
TNCs	Transnational corporations
USSR	Union of Soviet Socialist Republics
V4	Visegrad Four
VLAP	Visa Liberalisation Action Plan
WTO	World Trade Organization

Paul Flenley and Michael Mannin

Introduction

The publication of this volume comes at a time of existential crisis for the European Union (EU). Internally it is faced by the Eurozone crisis, the rise of anti-EU populism and 'Brexit'. In its immediate neighbourhood it is confronted by a range of challenges and threats. The Arab revolutions have not turned into the hoped-for promise of democratisation and have instead degenerated into civil war in the case of Libya, Syria and Yemen. The direct impact of this on the EU is illustrated by the migration crisis which has reinforced tensions at the heart of the EU itself. In the Eastern part of the neighbourhood, a resurgent Russia has not only provided an alternative pole of attraction but also appears to directly challenge the values of the EU. According to some commentators, Russia's political model is being projected as an alternative, not only for some neighbours but also for certain member states of the EU itself. Through the annexation of Crimea and support for the rebels in Donbas, Russia also seems to be challenging some of the basic assumptions of the post-Cold War era in Europe. The EU's response to this in the form of sanctions also exposes tensions between the member states of the EU.

In the Balkans the path to stability and democratisation is still not assured. In the past, the EU's traditional approach to instability in the neighbourhood has been to rely on the power and attractiveness of its pull as a normative power. There appeared to be no alternative to the pursuit of democracy and economic modernisation epitomised by the EU. However, the capacity of the EU to exert such external influence appears to be limited for the time being by its preoccupation with the internal crises within the EU itself and the strength and attractiveness of countervailing forces both domestically and externally in the neighbourhood countries. The context is further complicated by the uncertainties placed over the nature of future EU–US–Russia relations posed by the Trump administration.

The term applied to the process of the EU seeking to influence the neighbourhood is 'Europeanisation' or 'EU-isation' – the focus of this volume. Most books and articles on the subject of Europeanisation in the Eastern neighbourhood have concentrated largely on the process of policy transfer and the foreign policy aspects of relations (see Weber, Smith and Baun, 2007). There have been several effective studies of the European Neighbour-hood Policy (ENP) in particular (for example, Korosteleva, 2012; Noutcheva, Pomorska and Bosse, 2013). This volume differs in that it seeks to explore the problems which the EU has had in projecting EU-isation onto its Eastern neighbourhood by focusing on the way in which interests, values and iden-tity interact with each other in the neighbourhood and between the neigh-bourhood and the EU itself to shape the nature of EU-isation. In doing so the volume takes as its focus countries in the Eastern neighbourhood which, in one way or another demonstrate, a European perspective as part of their identity. The latter does not necessarily mean that they seek to be members of the EU and it may be that a European identity is internally disputed and a cause of conflict. The volume therefore considers not only the countries that are part of the ENP, but also looks at Russia, Turkey and the Balkans. What these countries all have in common is that the concepts of Europe, European identity and Europeanisation are key elements in their politics and identity. They may be interpreted in different ways and be interacting with different values and interests. A key theme of this volume is to show how these interactions affect the ways in which EU-isation occurs.

In order to facilitate this approach this volume is divided into three parts. Part I consists of three chapters which set out the key parameters and frameworks which inform the discussions in the following chapters. Michael Mannin explores the origins of the term 'Europeanisation' and the way in which its contemporary iteration – EU-isation – has become associated with the normative power of the EU. He argues that alternative interpretations and traditions of Europeanisation contest the EU-dominated version. This is a key factor in shaping reaction to the EU's influence in the neighbour-hood countries such as Russia. Nora Siklodi discusses the concept of Euro-pean identity, indicating that there are different levels of identity of which a European consciousness can be just one. She explores the particular approach the European Commission has taken in articulating the notion of European identity. This EU perspective on European identity can be a source of fundamental problems when it confronts other identities and approaches to being European, such as in the Balkans and Russia. Paul Flenley provides an overview of different mechanisms which the EU uses to promote EU-isation in the neighbourhood and discusses the limits of conditionality when membership is not on offer. He considers the lack of symmetry between the interests of the EU and its neighbours, the lack of a resonance with the interests of domestic elites, the impact of a powerful alternative pole in the Eastern neighbourhood (namely Russia) and, finally, the way effective EU-isation is undermined by divisions within the EU itself.

In Part II the themes and concepts discussed in Part I are examined in more detail through a number of country/area specific chapters. Tatiana

Romanova's chapter powerfully states the salience of Russia in establishing an alternative geopolitical pole to the EU. Russia asserts that its European identity is not dependent on approval from the EU. Romanova shows that Russia has an alternative interpretation of Europeanisation and European values based on its history and culture. Any EU-isation in Russia is instrumental and Russia is keen to limit its effect in the shared neighbourhood. Nadiia Bureiko and Teodor Lucian Moga's chapter on Ukraine is the first of three chapters which consider the position of those states which are 'in-betweeners' – that is, pulled between the EU and Russia. They depict a country that is divided over its future direction, attempting to pursue a multi-vector foreign policy out of necessity and which contains differences over its adherence to European identity. For the authors, the experience of being an 'in-betweener' is a key limitation on the effectiveness of EU-isation. Kamil Całus and Marcin Kosienkowski's study of Moldova reveals similar constraints for EU-isation of another 'in-betweener'. In this case the chapter reveals the way 'Europeanisation' can actually mean 'modernisation'. However, in reality there has been a lack of reform in such areas as corruption. The presence of Russia in the form of the Eurasian Economic Union appears to play the role of being not only an alternative economic pole but also a way of preserving traditional conservative values in contrast to the uncomfortable challenges of EU-isation.

Belarus is also an 'in-betweener' country apparently caught between the choice of EU and Russia. Kiryl Kascian, however, shows that this is not a choice which the Belarusian authorities wish to make – they instead seek a relationship with both the EU and Russia. Belarus provides perhaps the starkest example of the limitations of the EU's values-based approach to its neighbours. Belarus's domestic political system and its prioritisation of the relationship with Russia mean that the EU lacks any real impact. Belarus does, however, seek a more pragmatic, interest-based relationship in contrast to the EU's values-based approach which appears to be going nowhere. The chapter also raises the problems of the perception of European identity promoted through EU-isation. While Belarus considers itself European and at the centre of a wider Europe, EU-isation, as it is currently configured, relegates it to the periphery. This theme of differing perceptions of European identity and the consequences of the narrow application of EU-isation recurs across the chapters and is re-addressed in the conclusion of this volume.

The Balkans' and Turkey's reception of EU-isation is not affected by the experience of being in-betweeners. However, here issues of identity are also still important in affecting the success of EU-isation. In the case of the Balkans, Monika Eriksen shows us that EU-isation is dependent on how far it accords with domestic narratives. Croatia and Serbia experience it differently to other Balkan states, for example. This chapter raises the question of how far EU-isation can fundamentally change values and promote an EU-defined European identity when it confronts other local identities such as Balkan identity. Identity politics is also at the heart of Dimitris Tsarouhas's chapter on Turkey. Turkey's key role in contributing to the security of the EU is shown by the migration crisis. However, over a long period certain member states of the EU have questioned Turkey's suitability for EU membership on the basis of identity and values. In the case of Turkey therefore, the tensions between interests, identity and values which concern this volume are being played out most starkly.

Part III goes on to examine the issue of EU-isation and the relationship between values (norms), interests and identity from the point of view of various sectors/themes which cut across different neighbours and are core elements in their relations with the EU. In sectors such as energy, migration, security and trade, the EU often finds that its commitments to values/norms are challenged when it is confronted by the need to pursue its interests in the neighbourhood. One way round this has been to try to promote EU structures and principles of governance externally so that both values and interests can be aligned. However, the chapters in this part reveal the contradictions in this approach. Martin Dangerfield examines the ways in which EU-isation, in the form of a coherent approach to Russia in the sphere of politics, is not fully reflected in the bilateral approach based on interests preferred by member states when it comes to trade. Interestingly, he shows that the apparent alignment of values and interests of member states such as Hungary vis-à-vis Russia is not what it seems. The growing illiberal politics in countries such as Hungary and Poland has more to do with internal dynamics than any attraction of alternative norms coming from Putin's Russia. Trade relations with Russia have long been interest-based and not pursued as a reflection of shared norms. Edward Stoddard also shows that while there may be EU-isation in terms of a common approach to the structures of energy governance, EU-isation breaks down when it comes to 'pipeline politics'. Here and elsewhere in this book we see how values/norms can be Europeanised, but when it comes to the pursuit of interests in the areas of security, migration and energy, member states usually prefer bilateralism.

Igor Merheim-Eyre examines an area where EU values and interests appear to be currently in real tension – migration. Once again, while the EU institutions themselves may wish to promote values, individual member states are protecting their interests. He examines the ways in which the development of the single market and internal free movement has led to the need for greater control of the EU's external borders. In this context the neighbours are seen as having a responsibility to help protect the EU from migration from further afield. In acquiescing in this they are promised visa-free access. We see the application of conditionality by the EU, referred to in several chapters, used not to just to promote norms and values but to defend the EU's security interests. The EU may wish Turkey to be EU-ised but more immediately it needs Turkey to stop migration into the EU from Syria.

In the chapters on the Balkans and Ukraine, identity is also tied to language use. Maria Stoicheva's chapter on language policy and Europeanisation examines an area which is overlooked in the studies of Europeanisation. She considers the ways in which the status of languages such as Russian changed in the Eastern neighbourhood after the collapse of the Soviet Union. The 'Return to Europe' and Europeanisation have implications for language policy. Europeanisation may mean promoting English instead of Russian or moving from Cyrillic to the Latin script. The fact that Russian language speakers in Ukraine, for example, do not necessarily identify themselves as ethnic Russian and may have a Ukrainian and/or European identity raises the possibility that language use is being replaced by territorial divisions as the indicator of identity. Thus, her chapter shows that the relationship between geopolitics, policymaking and identity is played out at a much more profound level – that of language.

Finally, Kevork Oskanian and Derek Averre explore the relationship between security and democracy in the promotion of the EU's norms and interests. Their case study of the countries of the South Caucasus – Armenia, Azerbaijan and Georgia – provides a useful additional insight into neighbourhood countries which do manifest a European perspective but with different degrees of intensity. In the context of discussing the relevance of Democratic Peace Theory and the EU's perception that conflict resolution and security on its borders are best resolved through democratic governance, their chapter raises the question as to whether conflict is actually more likely when democratisation is incomplete and when there are variations between neighbouring countries between authoritarian systems and near-democracies. This seems to apply to conflicts in the South Caucasus, including the Russo-Georgia war, and indicates a clear limit to EU-isation as a means of ensuring stability and security on the EU's borders.

In the course of investigating the relationship between values, interests and identity and how this affects EU-isation, the chapters in this volume raise a range of common, cross-cutting themes. We note, first, the different interpretations and uses of Europeanisation throughout the neighbourhood. EU-isation in particular is often used by the neighbours for very different purposes to fulfil their own ends. Second, and connected to this, it becomes apparent that much of the reception of EU-isation is primarily instrumental – what is often referred to as 'thin' Europeanisation. There would seem to be a reluctance to engage in deeper, so-called 'thick' Europeanisation, which would have a more fundamental socialising dimension and perhaps produce real shifts towards a common European identity and the sharing of common European values with associated political consequences. Third, we see that one of the major obstacles to effective EU-isation is that it confronts entrenched domestic interests and networks. These domestic concerns may not just be in the form of practices such as corruption, but may concern much more existential threats to the neighbour such as the attempted coup in Turkey and fragmentation of the state itself as in Ukraine. These are likely to preoccupy the neighbour more than adhering to the niceties of EU norms and values. Fourth, EU-isation confronts the immutable certainties of geopolitics in the neighbourhood. Eastern neighbours often have their own external constraints whether it be the imperative of engagement with Russia or – in the case of Turkey – dealing with the destabilising effects of the civil war next door in Syria. Finally, while the volume concentrates mainly on the neighbourhood and relations with the EU, EU-isation is affected by the extent to which the EU itself can operate as a coherent international actor. Divisions between member states and EU institutions also undermine the coherence and effectiveness of EU-isation.

The chapters raise two fundamental questions for consideration by both the EU and its Eastern neighbours. First, given the political, cultural, social, economic and strategic obstacles in the path of EU-isation as a transformative normative project, should the EU resign itself to a more instrumental, interest-based approach to neighbours? Second, an EU-led notion of European identity is (and perhaps always has been) challenged by competing notions of what it is to be European. How far should the EU reconstruct its notion of Europeanness in a way that facilitates the Eastern neighbourhood being included as 'core Europe' rather than as a transforming 'other'? These and other issues are examined in the following chapters.

PART I

Concepts and frameworks

1 Michael Mannin

Europeanisation as a past and present narrative

This chapter has two objectives: first, to serve as a conceptual and definitional reference point distinguishing between the related terminologies used in the complex field of Europeanisation; and second, to discuss the premise which recurs in subsequent chapters – that 'the past is our present reality'. This means that our apparently objective view of what seems contemporary and obvious is actually a construct of the past conceptions of what Europe has been (Flockhart, 2010).

The chapter commences with a discussion of this historical-constructivist approach and then proceeds to examine the prevailing notion of Europeanisation as 'EU- isation'. It then explores the significance of the Enlightenment and the emergence of, on the one hand, the contemporary paradigm of 'Europeanism' and, on the other, the existence of competing interpretations of Enlightenment values that remain to explain what Europe was/is. These interpretations are then explored through an examination of historic periods of Europeanisation. Events in the post-Cold War period have exposed competing legacies of the past and interpretations of Europe's future. The chapter therefore concludes with a summary of the current dilemmas for the EU and its near neighbours that are to some considerable extent a product of these persisting and varied interpretations of Europe's past.

Europeanisation through time and space

A historical constructivist approach brings with it a shifting perspective of what Europe was and is, and thus what it is to be a European today. It also involves a similarly shifting view of what a European 'other' comprises (Flockhart, 2010; Giesen, 2003). This means departing from a narrow focus on Europeanisation as EU-isation towards one that exposes causal relationships and diffused patterns of Europeanisation behind its present reality. These can be identified not only within EU Eastern neighbourhood relations, but also as the internal dialogue and division within the EU itself. There are a number of reasons why such an approach is pertinent to the aims of this book. Assumptions about the inevitability of Europeanisation as EU-isation have been challenged by several contemporary circumstances. Internally, the EU has suffered several economic and political shocks in the second decade of the twenty-first century that have not been conducive to deepening and widening its reach. Economic uncertainty and perceived weakness in response to security problems on its Eastern and Southern borders have resulted in a re-evaluation – by new neighbours – of the EU's attractiveness as a pole of security. This has also emerged as an existentialist debate in 2016 following the 'Brexit' referendum.

In effect, alternative potentials for Europe's future have emerged and, in order to appreciate the nature of these challenges, an examination of historic Europeanisation as well as observations of national, sub-national, ethnic and cultural memories are salient to an understanding of the present reality of the region. Thus, what Schimmelfennig (2001) characterises as 'thin Europeanisation' – that is, the pragmatic acceptance of the constituent rules of the EU – is no longer sufficient to sustain Brussels's impact on the political and economic choices within its new neighbourhood. Without an established set of 'thick EU values' involving acceptance of prior norms (i.e. a universal European values set), there is always room for alternative pathways to modernisation, well-being, cultural preservation and societal stability. An alternative pole to the East, Russia, and the growing ambivalence towards a Turkish/EU European destiny, presents a dilemma to other near neighbours when evaluating where their own European futures lie. This is reinforced by the evident lack of any hope of EU membership for near neighbours in the foreseeable future. To complicate matters further, at sub-state level, minority nationalist groups can undermine nation states in seeking the EU as a strategic partner (for example, Ukraine, Moldova, Georgia, Turkey, the Balkans). These problems are explored further in Part II.

In light of these factors, a turn to prior experience, to history and its role in the social construction of the present, would seem imperative in the understanding of 'present reality', especially for policy makers and consumers. In a 2015 UK Institute of Government publication, understanding historical viewpoints of those involved and affected by policy, an appreciation of how and why mythologies build up, and 'getting outside of the now' were all seen as contributing to 'historically informed instinctive [*sic*] analysis' (Haddon et al., 2015: 6–7). With specific reference to Russia's intervention in Georgia, Crimea and Ukraine, UK Foreign Office officials were conscious of the limitations of knowledge which is based solely around post-Soviet history. They considered that perspectives from the Cold War and earlier were necessary to appreciate how Russia reviewed its own history. For one UK Foreign Office official, 'the good news is history back on the agenda – though using it strategically is still a challenge.' (Haddon et al., 2015: 6).

The contemporary idea of EU-isation rests for its integrity on prior notions of Europeanisation. When examined, each of the periods referred to later, primarily rest on an elite-led selection of values that have both internal and external origins. Each period also brings with it a social construction of a European 'we' and a dominant 'other' (Mead, 1929). This provides a vista of changing values, rather than a boundary of political geography, of what Europe is today. Europeanisation is thus considered across time and space (Flockhart, 2010) with its norms subject to translation between past and present (Giesen, 2003).

Europeanisation as EU-isation

The concept of Europeanisation has dominated the analysis of the EU and its political systems since the mid-1990s, first, in relation to the deepening of the EU and its influence over domestic member state institutional and policy change during the 1990s following the Single European Act (SEA; 1986) and the Treaty on European Union (TEU; 1992), and more latterly, in observing and evaluating the 'return to Europe' of post-Soviet Central and Eastern European countries (CEECs), culminating in the enlargements of 2004 and 2007 (Blavoukos and Oikonomou, 2012; Featherstone, 2003). Use of the term *EU-isation* as a distinct version of Europeanisation (Wallace, 2000) coincided with a period of EU triumphalism mirroring notions of the 'liberal triumph' of the West after the events of 1989–91 (Fukuyama, 1992). For many, 'the hour of Europe' had arrived (Sakwa, 2015). Thus, it was to the EU that the West – and particularly the USA – looked for the consolidation of a liberal market model for the future of Europe (Mannin, 1999; Sedelmeier and Wallace, 1996).

Such assumptions are reflected in a 'unilinear' conceptual framework of EU-sation (Beichelt, 2008). Whether perceived as 'uploading, downloading or a transversal mechanism', the EU-isation process starts with an assumption of EU-centricity, with the strategic dominance of the EU as either originator or mediator of domestic and, in some instances, external policy changes for existing and aspirant member states (Börzel, 2002). Thus, our definition of Europeanisation follows that of Ladrech (1994) or Radaelli (2004) and is extended to include the near neighbourhood:

> EU-isation is the process of ideational, institutional and policy transformation within EU members and other European states whose major force emanates from the EU as a centre of political discourse ... directed towards the achievement of EU core values and political objectives. (Bretherton and Mannin, 2013: 15)

Radaelli's (2003) identification of three domains for analysis – policy, polity and politics – and its associated vocabulary has become an accepted part of the subject's analytical frame. By far the biggest research focus has been on EU-ised policy and its processes (Radaelli, 2003). This has given the subject the now familiar vocabulary of 'uploading and downloading', 'fits and misfits', 'veto points', 'absorption transformation', 'inertia' and so on. However, as Radaelli states, explanations of the emergence and consequences of a Europeanised member state policy sector cannot be disassociated from polity (institutions) and politics (ideas) that make up the EU and its member states as a composite political system (Radaelli, 2004: 36). Thus, a historical dimension and the significance of cultural diffusion underscores Radaelli's search for an adequate conceptual research bandwidth (Featherstone, 2003).

With these caveats in mind, the main thrust of the most used analytical approach in the field is based on an assumption that EU exported values can be measured against the fairly specific criteria of the *acquis communautaire* and, more generally, an adherence to a political–legal value set. These are the benchmarks contained within the Copenhagen Criteria (1993) and Agenda 2000 (1998) that shaped the progress of Central and Eastern European states towards membership, which achieved quasi-constitutional status in the Treaty of Lisbon (2007). EU-isation, therefore, creates conditions to be met and a process to be evaluated by EU actors, based on half a century of growing and complex interdependence among an increasingly complex membership underpinned by an assumption of shared, predetermined and measurable values.

When observing the practice of EU-isation, especially in the application of policy, observers have acknowledged the possibility of a variety of outcomes dependent on a number of variables that challenge the immediate unilinear nature of the process (Börzel, 2005; Cowles and Risse, 2001; Héritier, 2001). Transformation of policies and associated institutional processes are one outcome, others may be adaption or absorption into existing political behaviour. Other responses result in political and bureaucratic inertia and thus nominal or non-compliance and, in some cases, outright rejection of EU-isation and its direction of travel. However, while there is room within the application of the concept for the possibility of multiple outcomes for member states and for candidate members, the penalties for non-compliance are expensive for both member states – either through Commission/European Court of Justice intervention – or for candidates – through delays in gaining access to the EU club itself. Financial or political penalties, together with the assessment of the overall net advantage of membership/compliance to participants have been factors that have sustained this uneven path towards EU-isation. In the longer term, the expected trajectory for those who seek club membership remains unilinear in its outcome.

There are, however, factors that combine to confound this assumption of EU progression throughout the broader region. First, the incentive for membership seems much less likely in the foreseeable future for the new neighbours than it was for the CEECs in the 1990s. Second, the multiple and mutual economic advantages of membership/association have been challenged by the tribulations of the Eurozone since the start of the financial crisis from 2009 onwards. Third, the migration crisis, internal insecurity and self-doubt within the EU have resulted in an internal and external questioning of the value and validity of the EU project itself. In turn, this has led to the emergence of other perceptions of Europe and European futures rather than the inevitability of EU-isation. Identification with the EU as 'Europe' and as the only source of regional economic, social or strategic security for neighbour states, is challenged and historic European identities re-emerge as other futures outside of the EU are considered.

The EU and Europeanism: a complex narrative

Before considering the particular historic circumstances that complicate EU–near neighbour relationships, it is worth exploring the contemporary and normative assumptions that underpin EU-isation contained within another concept: Europeanism. Writing before the economic sclerosis of 2011–15, McCormick concludes that the post-Cold War period has led to a 'rediscovery of Europe', making a distinction between the European Union and Europe 'increasingly meaningless' (McCormick, 2010: 63). The possibilities for a hegemonic notion of Europeanism are also evident in Bjorn Hettne's earlier post-Soviet perspective of 'the elimination of extremes' (Hettne, 1995: 219).

Europeanism may be perceived as a paradigm that is 'a universally recognised scientific achievement that, *for a time*, provides model problems and solutions to a community of practitioners' (Kuhn, 1970: 12; my emphasis). Its characteristics provide a frame of reference within which current European values and norms may be identified. As a starting point, McCormick points to Habermas and Derrida (2003), who described a 'common European mentality' composed of seven values: secularisation; trust in the state; sceptical perceptions of the market; a realistic (limited) expectation of the value of progress through technology; welfarism; limited belief in the use of force; multilateralism and internationalism for external problem solution. McCormick's more detailed characteristics of Europeanism – 'the political, economic and social values that Europeans have in common' – in the first decade of the twenty-first century run to seventeen constituent qualities (McCormick 2010: 217; and Table 1.2).

These qualities reflect Europe's 'civilisational constellation' (Delanty and Rumford, 2005), that are not delineated by state borders but by association with norms and values. The EU has attached itself to these aspirations, not least in its explicit reference to historic values in the preamble to the Lisbon

Table 1.1 Historic Europeanisations

Historical era	Stage of development
to AD 700	Pre-Europe
700–1450	Europe as Christendom
1450–1700	The Europeanisation of New Worlds
1700–1919	Enlightenment and modernisation
1919–1989	Europeanisation and ideological division
1989–present	The EU-isation of Europe

Treaty. In its preamble the treaty drew 'inspiration from the cultural, religious and humanist inheritance of Europe, from which have developed universal values of inviolable and inalienable rights of the human person, freedom, democracy, equality and the rule of law'. The ubiquity of these characteristics are discussed in relation to the elusive notion of a European identity in Chapter 2 and are further explored in the conclusion. But, as a paradigmatic frame, Europeanism serves as an entry point to the themes of the book in that, by observing the extent to which it is accepted as a contemporary summary of pan-European values, the reader achieves a broader understanding of EU–near neighbour relationships and the transformational possibilities of the EU in the region, as well as its limits as an interpreter and universal teacher of European norms (Phinnemore, 1993).

The Enlightenment as a foundational narrative?

Europe's 'civilisational constellation' is conventionally attributed to the Enlightenment and its thinkers whose ideals seemed to represent the triumphalism of 1989. As Fukuyama declared 'the end of history', the removal of the final impediments to a global liberal capitalist democratic hegemony was hailed as the apotheosis of Enlightenment thinking, fulfilling eighteenth-century ideals of a European-led 'humanitarian revolution' (Singer as quoted by Grey, 2015; see also Delanty and Rumford, 2005: 38). Notions of tolerance, reason, scientific rationality, the organisational forces of the state and its bureaucracy, capitalism and resultant technological innovation, had social and political outcomes. The secular state, republicanism, national and social solidarity and the conditions for modern democratic practice manifest themselves as Enlightenment progress (Delanty and Rumford, 2005: 38).

But their global spread, the 'Westernisation' of the eighteenth and early nineteenth century through European imperial ventures, and the region's domination of world trade was neither uniform nor always compatible with these superior values. A clear example of the various interpretations of Enlightenment values is evident in the notion of Americanism that emerges as both a cousin of, and 'other', to Europeanism. As Table 1.1 illustrates, though originating from a shared Enlightenment source, European, American and, as we include later, Russian interpretations and the ordering/prioritisation of these values has led to a markedly different mix of social norms and expectations for individuals and societies in each of the regions. In effect, it is an example of differing social/historical constructions of the past.

There is not just the possibility of differing social constructs of Enlightenment values but also evident contradictions in their historic application, which have presented challenges to the positive notion of a European civilisation mentioned here. Thus, 'imperialism, militant nationalism and racism when combined with bureaucratic and technological superiority, Christian values and social Darwinism, produced dubious rationalisations for the European Empires of British, French, Dutch, Belgian, Italian, German and eventually a US variety' (Mannin, 2013: 6; also Flockhart, 2010; Headley, 2008; Zielonka, 2006). Similarly, rationalism, scientific method and an unquestioning belief in technological progress as a basis for the material good, when mixed with the post-Great War European nationalisms and ideologies, combined to produce vividly different interpretations of Enlightenment, culture and contemporary progress, manifested in the twentieth century in the form of fascist and communist movements that permeated the region. These movements, together with the development of inter-war democratic politics increasingly influenced by the USA in terms of self-determination and internationalism, competed for a hegemonic status within and around the European region as ideological frameworks for European and world futures for more than half a century (Davies: 1997: 36). However, they remain still, in the memories of some, as powerful statements of what Europe was and should be now; acting as a counterfactual statement of EU otherness. Their place as historic background to the EU–neighbourhood nexus is examined below.

The historical construction of Europe

What is now in the past was once in the future. (attributed to F. W. Maitland)

While EU-isation has a relatively short history, the notion of Europeanisation is not new. The Enlightenment has already been mentioned as a key period in the emergence of the contemporary paradigmatic notion of Europeanism. The following presents notional periods of pre- and post-Enlightenment Europeanisations. Thus, we can observe that Europeanisation is an ongoing process across time and space and that it is a continuously reconstructed phenomenon 'where Europeanisation is seen as a process of ideational diffusion and identity construction based on ideas of different origins.' (Flockhart, 2010: 793). EU-isation is a 'present reality' of Europeanisation; a construct of previous Europeanisations and, as Maitland's statement implies, where 'the past' emerges as the 'future'. It is evidently, however, not necessarily accepted as present reality for all present Europeans.

It is important to reiterate that the construction of a European narrative is primarily an elite-based phenomenon whose actors have been selective in their treatment of the past, which is made to fit 'the reality of the present' (Flockhart, 2010). Incorporated within these narratives is a changing interpretation of what it means to be European. 'We' is always accompanied by a definable 'other', thus establishing geographical and cultural boundaries to any current reality of Europe at any one time. Thus, the idea of Europe (as current reality) is established within an identity that changes over time, according to changing notions of the European 'we' and 'other'. Inevitably, one further problem for the pervasiveness of 'being European' is the dichotomy that is periodically evident in elite and mass perceptions of what Europe is and who makes up its 'other', a situation more than apparent in the contemporary challenges faced by the EU (see Chapter 2).

The last element of this historical constructivism that is relevant to our objectives is the direction of the flow of European norms 'across time and space' (Flockhart, 2010). Each historic period identified here may be perceived as a net internal *recipient* or external *projector* of norms and values. Thus, periods from the fall of the Roman Empire to the 1500s and from 1919 to the 1950s reflect a net inflow of ideas from, respectively, Muslim, Tartar, and returning Crusaders and traders; and in the latter period from US-originating internationalism and democratic idealism. Dominant periods for the external projection of European values are evident in the Enlightenment/ modernisation period and now the contemporary EU project itself. Any unidirectional recognition of these complex ideational flows undervalues and simplifies notions of Europeanisation in its historical context, 'thereby preventing a thorough and cumulative understanding of the origins and its shifting sociological, normative and ideational contents across time and space.' (Flockhart, 2010: 790).

What follows is an extended version of the author's categorisation of historic Europeanisations (Bretherton and Mannin, 2013; also Davies, 1997; Flockhart, 2010; Hobson, 2004). There are, in this iteration, six stages of development. The significance of the first three of these periods in the centuries prior to the Enlightenment should not be discounted for our analysis of Europeanisation in the new neighbourhood and are outlined below.

Pre-Europe to Enlightenment and modernisation

Pre-Europe (to AD 700), though primarily a Mediterranean phenomenon, left a Greek cultural heritage of democracy, scientific method, philosophical argument and architectural sophistication. Roman Empire and Republic gave the example of civic organisation within diversity, codified law, a transport network and the notion of universal citizenship. Roman law, 'one of the pillars of European civilisation' (Davies, 1997), survived to compete with customary and canon law from the Middle Ages to Napoleonic Europe. The *Pax Romana* provided the security for emergent European Christianity to emerge and to survive. Later – with the Empire moving from Rome to Constantinople – came a persistent religious division that has remained to this day (Catholicism versus Orthodoxy). These and other bequests to subsequent versions of Europe emerged over time as interpretations/myths of the past to fit the imperialism of Napoleonic Europe, nineteenth- and twentieth-century European democratic idealisms, and Mussolini's justification for a twentieth-century *Mare nostrum*.

Europe as Christendom (700–1450) presents a more coherent notion of a cultural/geographic Europeanisation (Davies, 1997; Flockhart, 2010; Hobson, 2004). An established and expanding Roman Church provided a cultural 'we' that emerged to match the contours of Southern and West-Central Europe. The emergence of Islam and the Crusades against Islam and later Orthodoxy provided a cultural known 'other' for European-wide Catholicism. A parallel political entity, the Habsburg Holy Roman Empire, was less pervasive but provided the secular arm of defence against the threat of the Islamic 'other'. Also of lasting note is the division between Catholic and Orthodox views of religion and politics. Orthodox regions were to escape many of the challenges that the Reformation and Enlightenment periods presented to Catholicism. The hierarchical and transnational structure of Catholicism can be contrasted with Orthodox autocephaly that gave relative authority to Diocesian bishoprics and their close association with national and state entities. The result is that today, 'The various Orthodox churches support a more exclusionary than traditional Europe [*sic*], that is less open to foreigners' (Risse, 2010: 211).

Unlike Catholicism, which has perceived Europeanisation in several historic forms as a vehicle for extending its moral outreach, Orthodoxy confronts modernising/liberal and secular values with an anti-liberal and exclusive version of Christianity. Both Christian forms proved to be influential forces in subsequent periods of Europeanisation and can be seen as significant players in the extension of EU values to Central and Eastern Europe and now its new neighbours (Risse, 2010; Schimmelfennig and Scholtz, 2008).

The period *c*.1500–1700 (referred to here as The Europeanisation of New Worlds) embraced the influences of both Renaissance and Reformation and led to the diffusion of ideas and discovery of diverse European views to other worlds (Headley, 2008). Notions of Europeanisation as 'the West' were increasingly evident as a means to note a cultural worldview of Europeanisation. Universal views of humanity/rights, technological superiority, diverse Christian views and moral rights/duties spread to the Americas and Asia via European control of trade, military invasion and eventually political submission through empires (Headley, 2008; Flockhart, 2010). A civilisational missive to a heathen 'other' was paralleled by a now more secular threat from a Middle Eastern political 'other' in the shape of the Ottoman Empire after the fall of Constantinople in 1453. The emergence of a pan Euro-Russia also presented both a secular and religious challenge to the dominance of European Catholicism. In this period Western/ European civilisation became associated with progress as a superior value to the state of nature purported to categorise the New World and parts of Asia (Judt, 2004). Today, unsettled EU/Russian relations, the dilemma of Turkish membership made more complicated by Islamic overtones, and insistence by the EU on prescribed political, economic and social transformation as 'progress' for aspirant member states, present a contemporary iteration of this period (Delanty, 2002).

Enlightenment and modernisation, 1700–1919

We have previously acknowledged the debt that a paradigmatic notion of Europeanism owes to Enlightenment values as well as some contradictions in their application that 'enlarged the margins of intellectual tolerance' (Davies, 1997: 596), nineteenth-century imperialisms, patriotic nationalisms, and the emergence of discrete national identities as diverging responses to the late eighteenth-century French and American revolutions. Technological, social and economic revolution claimed as the mark of cultural superiority, was exported through competing imperial networks. A disrupted European population sought opportunity and refuge in internal (local) and external (world) migration. The effect of this 'modernisation' became a focal point of a Europeanised worldwide economic system and established the distinction between developed and developing countries (Davies, 1997: 764).

Social and economic change brought with it challenges to the existing political order manifested in a new critique of conservative and religious values in the secular interpretations of morality. From this emerged new political structures and associated ideological frameworks that took root in the emerging and varied intellectual environment of the time. Both liberalism and, later, socialism, presented not only different routes to modernisation but their interpretation and permeation within the nineteenth-century European geopolitical scene also varied between states. British, Italian and French liberalism, Russian authoritarianism and German conservatism offered markedly different soil for ideological pathways to take root. There was, in effect, no single coherent vision of European progress and modernisation (Davies, 1997; Delanty, 1995).

Furthermore, since the nineteenth century, being European has been enmeshed with the evolution of nations, nation states and their agendas (Hutchinson, 2003). While nationalism flowered in the light of a new European liberalism and shared revolutionary zeal, emerging nation states were, in essence, independent entities. A willingness to pool sovereignty did exist – as in the development of German and Italian unity – but it varied within the external historical and contemporary constraints of emergent statehood. Also, since ethnic nationalisms sometimes predated the nation state, the legitimacy of often contrived administrative borders was challenged from the outset. Thus, the establishment of loyal citizenship was problematic. A modernist notion of civic nationality, a legitimating concept for economic progress in France, can be contrasted with the less integrated emergence of an Italian nation state, whose civic pretensions to nationhood were complicated by historically derived, regional dissensus. Nineteenth century liberal nationalism continued to be challenged by resistant imperial entities and their reaction to the nationalist consciousness. Russia sought to contain Polish, Ukrainian, Byelorussian and Finnish nationalisms in different ways – by the total rejection of a nation's separate identity (Ukraine and Byelorussia) or by offering relative autonomy (Finland). Polish nationalism, itself containing the seeds of its own imperial historic past, had 'the longest pedigree, the best credentials, the greatest determination ... and the least success' (Davies, 1997: 826).

There are two points worth noting here. Deep-seated historical memories both assisted and challenged nineteenth-century liberal nation statehood and persisted to the twentieth and twenty-first centuries, shaping perceptions of what 'being European' should be. Second, a more obvious point is that nineteenth-century European nations were not only challenged and shaped by their prior historic experiences but were themselves subsequently shaken by periods of military, ideological and economic shock during the first half of the twentieth century. European wars and their aftermath evidenced dormant and new nationalist aspirations, irredentist pressures and, thus, challenges to the nineteenth- and twentieth-century boundaries of states, particularly in Central-Eastern and South-Eastern Europe.

Europeanisation and disputed visions 1919–89

The Great European War of 1914–18 did not result in the demise of Russian, German and Austrian imperialisms alone; both new ('Wilsonian') notions of democratic, self-determined politics and ideologically driven authoritarian systems competed to replace these *ancien* regimes. The subsequent struggles between fascist, communist and liberal-democratic visions of Europe illustrate very different interpretations of European history values and thus Europeanisation.

For Nazi Europe, the excluded other was racist – a Slavic East and the Jewish enemy within were, in effect, a cultural European boundary founded on historic myth and enmity. Anglo-Saxon and Nordic peoples were only reluctantly perceived as enemies (Davies, 1997: 38). Communism embraced a different view of Europe's past and future. It was both enemy to fascism and liberal democracy and was based on the Marxist notion of scientific rationalism with its own principles of historic stage development, democratic centralism and economic determinism. Progress was to be achieved through a developmental process that excluded capitalism and liberal democracy but was still based (as was fascism) on economic growth through modernisation and industrialisation. Extreme nationalism was a rallying force for both and provided 'an ideological framework for a new universal vision of Europe ... both attempts failed' (Davies, 1997: 36). The depth and breadth of this ideological zeal was in part reliant on previous historical experiences and mythologies associated with past national and imperial European visions. Totalitarian ideologies provided different and partial interpretations of European history and remain significant today as statements of 'otherness' in the formation of a contemporary liberal democratic European identity.

The Treaty of Versailles (1919), however, provided not only a symbolic but also an institutional basis for both national democratic self-determination and international organisation. The League of Nations (1919) and the Briand Plan for European Unity (1930), though both ill-fated, were forerunners of a post-Second World War international settlement for conflict resolution and social and economic stability. For Western Europe at least, the defeat of fascism in 1945 and the desperate post-war conditions, plus the uncertainties of a peaceful coexistence with an erstwhile ally, the Soviet Union, produced a domestic and international idealism conducive to Europe-wide post-war political solutions and future. The US-led Marshall Plan and North Atlantic Treaty Organization (NATO) provided the economic and defence security blanket around the notion of an Atlantic community whose 'other' was an emerging Eastern European Soviet-dominated bloc. Although the Europe-led notion of a continent-wide federation was also available in the shape of the Council of Europe (1949), this was to gain much less political traction in the perilous situation of emerging Cold War than the idea of security through the West European–North American alliance. Euro-Atlanticism, with the accepted leadership of the USA, as a counter to this threat of communism, defined both the geopolitical and ideological limits of Western Europe and indeed the notion of 'the West' for the next two generations (Bretherton and Mannin, 2013).

The period after 1948, however, presented a rather different version of Europeanisation for Central and Eastern Europe. The Cold War that divided Europe into two dangerously armed camps created conditions that produced a bipolar post-war European integration reflecting the interests of its two major protagonists; the USSR and the USA. These conditions were an ideological, economic and military stand-off resulting in an antagonistic and (largely) multilateral dialogue between Western regional organisations (the EEC and NATO) and their Eastern counterparts (the CMEA and the Warsaw Pact), referred to by one commentator as 'a debate between deaf mutes' (Senior Nello, 1991) and limited bilateral relations between Eastern and Western states, often driven by economic self-interest. The vestiges of cultural, historical and political connections cut sporadically across this limited dialogue. These divisions were marginally reduced by the existence of pan-European organisations, the Council of Europe and the Conference (then Organisation) on Security and Co-operation in Europe (OSCE) that eventually offered some opportunity for East–West dialogue in the later period of the Cold War (Mannin, 1999: 5–6). The legacies of Central and Eastern Sovietised Europeanisation, from 1947 to 1989, and their subsequent relationship with Russia, remains a significant determinant of EU-near neighbour relations, evident in Part II of this volume.

The EU-isation of Europe? 1989–present

It is only in this relatively short contemporary period that the EU (EEC) and its gradual enlargement to the south and east has emerged as a dominant regional and global economic player. Notions of functional integration prevalent during the war years (Mistrany, 1966) were adapted to fit a European stage with particular notions of the role of the state, external policy, military intervention, environmentalism and social welfare that emerged as either nuanced or markedly different from US liberal market internationalism. Thus, the USA has emerged as both a significant 'we' and 'other' in the shaping of an EU identity. The end of the Cold War and the resultant expansion of the European Union from its neo-functional origins as a coal and steel community (ECSC) to a proto-EU federation during the late 1990s, represented a gradual EU-isation of continental Europe and thus a more indigenous vision of Europe's future, less reliant on the Euro-Atlantic model of the mid-twentieth century (Bretherton and Mannin, 2013).

It was towards the EU that the USA looked in addressing the ensuing political and economic problems after 1989 (Mannin, 1999). Notwithstanding the significant role that the EU plays in its own Eastern and Southern backyard, Euro-Atlanticism (or what Davies identifies as the 'Allied view of history' (1997: 40)) continues to exist as a parallel, sometimes competing vision for Europe's future. Through NATO, bilateral 'special' relations (not only with the UK), and in US–EU projects, Wilsonian principles of self-determination, democracy, and free markets continue to sustain the values of the post-Second-World War Euro-Atlantic community.

These values and their promotion are, however, occasionally embarrassed by US-led world ventures where 'coalitions of the willing' are not universally supported by all EU member states and their citizens. The latest iteration of this dichotomous Europeanisation is evident in the dilemmas experienced by negotiators over the establishment of a transatlantic free-trade area.

Other perspectives have emerged to confront both the EU project and Euro-Atlanticism since the 1990s. In part as a response to the security threat of US-led NATO expansionism and also to the challenge of economic and diplomatic expansion of the EU to its borders, Russia has responded with a series of counter models. Initially, complementary ideas for a 'greater' or 'wider' Europe emerged during the Gorbachev years in ventures such as the Common European Home. This notion of a 'wider Europe' model was revived later by then President Medvedev (2008) in the shape of a European Security Treaty. In a similar vein to one of his predecessors (Charles de Gaulle), French President Sarkozy also presented a similar notion of a common economic security area – or a 'common European space' – that stretched from the Atlantic to the Pacific. In 2010, President Putin called for a strategic partnership within a greater Europe and as recently as 2014 was raising the now tenuous possibility of a free trade zone from the Atlantic to the Pacific (Sakwa, 2015: 31–2).

The reluctance of Euro-Atlanticists (especially the USA) to perceive such initiatives as anything less than a disguised bid for Russian superpower revival, together with the growing suspicion of NATO and EU expansion as one and the same thing by Russian elites, seem to have buried such idealism. As Sakwa suggests; 'the Atlantic security partnership began in ideological terms to merge with the EU's Wider Europe' (2015: 48).

The turn, therefore, to a counter model of Russo-Europeanisation by Putin and the creation of a Eurasian Economic Union (EEU) in 2014 as an extension of the Eurasian Customs Union (2010), presents both an alternative architecture and a challenge to the notion of a Western-directed wider Europe. In effect, post-Cold War Euro-Atlanticist, EU expansionist and Euro-Asian models of Europeanisation stand in potential cooperation and competition with each other. The crucible of this dynamic and unstable phenomenon is played out in the geopolitics of Europe's new neighbourhood (see Chapters 3 and 4).

The past and present reality: the EU and its Eastern neighbours

We have argued that notions of Europeanisation and EU-isation are shaped by historical and social constructions through selective past perceptions of Europeanisation. EU-isation therefore has a genesis in its reconstructed pasts and its reception by its new neighbours is itself subject to interpretation based on their own historic/mythic interpretation of what Europeanisation is (Börzel and Risse, 2012b). In effect, beneath what Schimmelfennig terms a 'thin' form of EU-isation – that is, acquiescence to the politics and constitutive rules of the EU – exists a 'thick' Europeanisation that involves a cultural assimilation of the shared values of an EU community (Europeanism). This is the stuff of that elusive concept, European identity (analysed in Chapter 2) (Schimmelfennig, 2001; Flockhart, 2010: 791). The point here is that 'thick' Europeanisation, as a contrived element of prior experiences, may, for some, sit uncomfortably alongside the desired 'present reality' of EU-isation. Selective memories of Roman grandeur, Christian-Catholic hegemony, Orthodox traditionalism, imperial authoritarianism, past national unity/state sovereignty, colonial hubris and fascist/Nazi and post-war Communist experiences of modernisation and other historic cultural memories are all aspects of complex social/historical construction by elites and peoples of contemporary 'European reality'.

Among existing member states, the EU-isation process is influenced by past national and European constructions of the 'present reality' that is more than evident in the EU's current ongoing economic malaise (Mair and Zielonka, 2002; Zielonka, 2001). German and French, British and Greek, Finnish and Polish elite and mass perspectives towards the EU can only be understood in the light of these experiences (Bretherton and Mannin, 2013). Even Brexit must – at least in part – be explained by Britain's historical experiences/myths as much as the 'current realities' of immigration levels or an alternative global trading future. For other member states, the net advantage offered by membership would still seem to be a powerful binding factor in maintaining a somewhat battered EU integration. However, without any tangible opportunity for membership in the foreseeable future, countries, nations and regions of the Eastern neighbourhood can be forgiven for considering their own futures in the light of there being only limited advantage in accepting either thin or thick notions of EU-isation.

Economic austerity, migration flows, and most recently Brexit, must inevitably lead to the questioning of McCormack's (2010) conclusion that the distinction between the EU and 'Europe' can be assumed to be 'increasingly meaningless'. This being the case, an appreciation of the historic cultural frame (the Enlightenment values of Europeanism) would seem to be a key element in understanding the complexity of twenty-first century EU–near neighbour relations given the competing 'current realities' of EU-isation, Euro-Atlanticism and Euro-Asianism. Table 1.2 lists some contrasting interpretations of norms and values that may have had an enlightenment genesis but now compete for the essence of what it means to be European in each perceived 'reality'. These cannot be rigidly aligned to specific countries or areas: for example, that Russia can recognise the significance of soft power; the EU has adopted neoliberal values alongside notions of social solidarity; and recourse to independent military solutions by the US is (at

Table 1.2 Europeanisation and its contemporary manifestations (adapted from McCormick, 2010)

EU-isation	Euro-Atlanticism	Euro-Asianism
Cosmopolitanism	Exceptionalism	Exceptionalism
Multiple identities	Single identity	Dominant identity
Communitarianism	Individualism	Community
Collective state	Minimal state	State dirigisme
Welfarism	Materialism	Growing materialism
Civil/industrial complex	Military/industrial complex	State/business complex
Sustainable development	Consumerism	Consumerism
Redefining the family	Redefining the family	Maintaining the family
Life-work balance	Work-life balance	Work-life balance
Criminal rights/ rehabilitation	Societal protection/ retribution	Societal protection/ retribution
Secularism	Pluralist religiosity	Secularism/religious limits
Oppose capital punishment	Capital punishment	Oppose capital punishment
Perpetual peace	War as a solution	War as a solution
Soft power	Hard power	Hard power
Multilateralism	Unilateralism	Multilateralism mixed with unilateralism
Social liberalism	Social conservatism	Social conservatism
Liberal world view	Realist world view	Realist world view

least now) more considered. But Table 1.2 does indicate a promotion of competing tendencies of norms and values by political actors that, in turn, become reflected in internal policy making and external action. In effect they are competing notions of a European 'present reality' that is played out in the theatre of EU-Eastern neighbourhood politics.

Prior experience contrives to shape contemporary issues. Thus, irredentism challenged national identities, Cold War ideological hangovers, porous border security, and poor economic performance – not helped by EU conditionalities – disincentivise near neighbour elites and social groups to find value in what it would be like to be a contemporary EU player. These national and regional perceptions are explored in Parts II and III of this book. The extent to which the past constructs 'present reality' and so impacts on the formation of European and other identities is also considered in Chapter 2.

2 Nora Siklodi

Defining contemporary
European identity/ies

European identity is, perhaps, the most studied and, at the same time, most contested aspect of contemporary European integration, politics and policymaking. A range of approaches and (as a result) contradictory conclusions have been reached about its actual meaning and significance (for a comprehensive overview see Kaina and Karolewski, 2013). Some investigate European identity from a bottom-up perspective, exploring citizens' sense of civic, political (European Union) and cultural (continental or national) identities (see, for example, Bruter, 2005; Fligstein, 2008). Others consider the top-down significance of European identity, exploring its role in the creation of common values and symbols (Risse, 2003), positive self-images of the EU (Habermas, 2003) and the transfer of identities through EU policies – such as the European Neighbourhood Policy (ENP), for example (Karolewski, 2011). The range of approaches to European identity is, to a large extent, fuelled by ambiguity of the concept of identity for the purposes of social and political research (Brubaker and Cooper, 2000: 2).

Scholars draw attention to the multiple and multi-layered character of identity (Citrin and Sides, 2004) and the influence of intersecting social factors, including gender, race, class, social standing and so on (Yuval-Davis, 2007: 562–563). Even when they recognise that identity is likely to be multiple in practice, some argue that such identities do not (necessarily) clash. Instead, it has been proposed that *some* layers of identity are prone to comprise others (Taylor, 1989: 25). This is expected to be the case for emerging senses of (cosmopolitan) political identities in particular. European identity may be viewed as one such example, promoting the endorsement of pre-existing and often clashing political and cultural aspects of national identities (see, for example Beck and Grande, 2007; European Commission, 1973). Furthermore, certain elements of national identities – such as a sense of belonging to the nation state and to Europe – are expected to be sustained, while others are disputed, especially the perception of the non-national European 'other' (Siklodi, 2015a).

Uncertainties about what European identity signifies are distorted further by the European Commission's (hereafter the Commission) ever-changing discourse on this issue. Using discursive evidence (following the guidelines provided by Fairclough, 2013),[1] this chapter reveals that while the Commission (1973) has recognised the legitimising role European identity has for the EU as an emerging political community, it has failed to adopt a consistent approach to this issue. Instead, the Commission tends to propose significantly different processes – shifting between top-down and bottom-up processes – and focuses on different aspects of European identity – for example, the 'other'. So, rather than crystallising what European identity refers to, the Commission's discourse activates a context in which various European identities can be framed by political elites and then realised by citizens regardless of whether these operate within or outside the EU's borders.

Therefore, rather than working on an empty ideal of a single European identity that cannot be realised in practice, this chapter proposes that we understand European identity as closely as possible to reality – as a combination of various elements. More to the point, it proposes focusing on three elements of European identity, including a sense of belonging to political communities in Europe, a sense of 'we' among the members of the EU's (emerging) political community, and a common recognition of the 'other' – of those persons, cultures and issues that are not part of the EU and Europe. The chapter argues that considering these three elements together can account for the variety in European identity – whether in theory or practice – and can also draw out the key differences between what these European identities are expected to look like, and what they actually entail within *and* beyond the EU's borders.

Initially, the chapter considers some of the conceptual challenges linked to the concept of identity and, more to the point, to defining a single European identity. Subsequently, the chapter sheds light on the ideals of European identity as set out by the European Commission, using discursive evidence. The final part of the chapter attempts to bring together the different theoretical and elite-led approaches to European identity/ies and draws attention to the aforementioned elements of European identity.

Towards a definition of (European) identity

Perhaps the reason for most of the disagreement over what European identity signifies can be attributed to the different forms and roles identity has adopted across community building processes. For instance, renowned as the most common form of political community (Greenfeld, 1992), the nation state and national identity especially has become infused with exclusionary and cultural ideals, nourishing group struggles for recognition

(Brubaker, 1998). However, other communities have also experienced con-
testations linked to identity (see Karolewski, 2009: 20–22). In fact, identity
was a critical component in the very first formation of a political community
that we know of – the Greek *polis*. The latter was upheld by Greek citizens'
understanding of 'one another's characters' (Aristotle, 1946: 292). Even in
the Roman Empire – often championed as the source of liberal ideals (Isin
and Turner, 2002) – there were question marks over belonging and the main
characteristics of individual Roman citizens (Magnette, 2005: 19).

The Middle Ages and Renaissance then highlighted the impact social
groups, in particular professional (Weber, 1998: 44) and religious groups
(Riesenberg, 1992: 88), can have on identity. In light of the extensive role
identity has played in these historical processes of community building, it
is then not at all surprising that European identity has been identified as
an important component of European integration (Risse, 2010: 39–46).
Ongoing debates about the nation state and the EU (Medrano, 2010), the
fluid nature of territorial borders (Bruter, 2005), the tension stemming from
current migration and mobility flows (Boswell and Geddes, 2011), and
the dual, albeit contested, citizenship statuses of most European citizens
(Preuss, 1996) suggest that the issue of European identity is as important
today as ever. It mirrors the debate introduced in Chapter 1 on the complex
historical and cultural nature of Europeanisation.

Owing to the widespread recognition of the significance identity can
have, there remains much disagreement among scholars about the genuine
meaning of, and the most appropriate methods for, addressing this issue.
For instance, scholars disagree about the importance and implications of
different levels of identity; the individual and the collective (for two contradictory approaches see, for instance, Bellamy, 2008: 10–15; Smith, 1992).
While, in most cases, empirical research on European identity has been concerned with the individual level of identity, studying individual perceptions
of and attitudes towards the EU (Bruter, 2005; Kuhn, 2015, for exception
see, for example, Duchesne et al., 2013), normative studies have promoted
collective ideals where members are expected to recognise and identify with
key features of their fellows *collectively* (Habermas, 2003). By mixing the
level of analysis, it has become 'increasingly difficult to navigate through
the "state of the art" on European identity' (Kaina, 2013: 186).

The widespread use of the concept of identity has posed challenges of
its own (for an excellent overview see Brubaker and Cooper, 2000, especially pp. 2–14). For example, the multi-disciplinary application of this
concept among, for example, political scientists, sociologists and psycholo-
gists, has been deemed unfortunate, stimulating an ambiguity in the use of
the term (Kanter, 2006: 502). Different approaches have also prevailed in
attempts to *measure* identity (for an overview see Abdelal et al., 2009:
27–31). Some studies examine individual awareness of legal status (at the
cognitive level), others evaluate the key feelings associated with such status

(affective level), and others again are interested in the collective motivations of identity (behavioral level). While looking at significantly different issues, there is a general agreement among these scholars that identity is strongest when it has collective behavioral implications and can shape the contours of the political community (Bellamy, 2008).

Yet, the multiplicity of approaches to the concept of identity led some scholars to conclude that it is meaningless for the purposes of social research (Brubaker and Cooper, 2000: 2). Accordingly, introducing the ideal of European identity may have only added further challenges to an already disputed process of community building in Europe (Kaina and Karolewski, 2013). In response to such criticisms, more and more attention has been paid to the concept of 'identification' – 'a process that accounts for the way individuals develop a feeling of belonging to a group' (Duchesne, 2008: 403). This has been the case among more recent studies about identity in the EU and European (national) contexts especially (Duchesne et al., 2013; van Ingelgom, 2014; White, 2011).

In order to provide a more systematic framework to understanding identity, scholars have become interested in disaggregating this concept. From historical examples we already know that identity usually includes a combination of elements (see, for example, Brubaker, 1998; Smith, 1996), including attitudes towards a sovereign political community (a sense of belonging), association among those who belong to an 'imagined' community (a shared identity), and the categorisation of those people, cultures and practices that are different from the community (a recognition of the 'other'). Furthermore, it has been demonstrated that the strength and prevalence of these elements have shaped community building processes (Heater, 2004). This volume is interested in elucidating the role of identity or, rather, identities within the EU and its neighbourhood, *and* across various arenas of policy making, from citizens' identification with national and European communities, to national and European level policy making on issues of foreign, energy and security policy, and so on. To really understand what European identity/ies signify in these contexts however, we must also be aware of what it has been expected to signify to start with. To this end, the next section of the chapter provides an overview of how the EU's executive, the European Commission, tends to approach European identity.

The EU and its declarations on European identity/ies

European identity has been an integral part of European integration and EU policy making ever since discussions about a possible EU-level democracy emerged (Stråth, 2002). Owing to the very definition of democracy – government by the people – a common sense of identity among these people has been observed as a prerequisite for the (effective) functioning of any political community (Isin and Turner, 2002). Against this backdrop, the EU can be viewed as an emerging political community whose identity has been – to some extent at least – shaped by various policy actors, the most important of which is the EU's very own executive, the European Commission. However, a closer inspection of the Commission's relevant discourse in the framework of a larger project on EU citizenship (Siklodi, 2015a) has revealed that important dissimilarities exist on what a European identity has been expected to look like, not to mention how these expectations fare compared to the *actual* shape of European identity.

In fact, two different approaches have dominated the Commission's discourse on European identity. One concentrates on citizens' sense of European identity via a people-led, bottom-up process. The other promotes the identity of the EU as a whole via an elite-led, top-down process. As part of the first approach, the Commission (1993; 1997) has assumed that the introduction of EU citizenship in the Maastricht Treaty would, ultimately, enhance citizens' sense of European identity. In fact, this assumption has dominated the workings of various Commissioners in the past twenty-five years, most notably Wallström (2007) and Reding (2013) and the specific Directorate Generals (DG) – including DG Justice (European Commission 2013a) and DG Communication (European Commission, 2014a) – tasked with promoting and defending EU citizenship. But sectoral DGs have also incorporated the ideals of EU citizenship and built their policies on the expectations that (future) citizens will have a sense of European identity. For example, sectoral DGs such as DG Development and Cooperation (2016b) have, among others, promoted cross-border cooperation at the individual level to assist in developing a sense of solidarity among people and across national borders.

As the DG responsible for EU citizenship, DG Justice has been particularly outspoken about the fact that EU citizenship was originally established 'with the aim of fostering [citizens'] sense of identity with the Union' (European Commission, 1993: 2). To this end, particular emphasis has been placed on promoting intra-EU mobility among citizens, resulting in a fairly dynamic approach to European identity and one that reflects the broader economic, social and political context. For example, the website of DG Justice now includes profiles of EU mobile citizens and underlines the significance of EU citizenship for their everyday lives. These profiles are used as evidence that mobility leads to a sense of European identity among citizens (see, for example, European Commission, 2010). Moreover, DG Justice (European Commission, 2008a, 2013b: 53) has proposed, time and again, that the political participation of citizens in novel (volunteering or protesting) and traditional forms of engagement (voting in European Parliament (EP) and local elections) are fruitful for their emerging sense of European identity (Wallström, 2007: 5). These communications reveal that, through bottom-up processes, the Commission has adopted a similar approach to

developing citizens' sense of European identity that has historically prevailed at the national level (Heater, 2004). Accordingly, emphasis has been
placed on involving citizens in the economic, social and political life of an
emerging political community (see, for example, Painter, 1998, 2008).

There is, however, mounting empirical evidence about the differences
between citizens' sense of European identity across the EU (Duchesne et al.,
2013; Medrano, 2010). Even more, disparities in the identity of different
categories of citizens – especially mobile and non-mobile EU citizens (citizens of EU member states) – have also been detected (Siklodi, 2014, 2015a
and 2015b). Despite its dynamic approach to European identity and EU
citizenship, the Commission has, so far, failed to recognise these differences
in its communications. Ironically, its references to EU-wide surveys (autho-
rised by DG Communication) provide ample evidence of citizens' multiple,
cross-cutting, hierarchical or nested senses of identities (see, for instance,
TNS Social and Political, 2013). This data reveals that approximately 45
per cent of EU citizens have a sense of attachment to the EU and 91 per
cent feel the same for their country of origin. Thus, there is likely to be
much overlap between citizens' senses of European *and* national identities.
The way in which these two identities overlap is also multiplied by the different 'frames' applied by member states (and non-member states) to the
European integration process (Medrano, 2010). Currently, twenty-eight
member states as well as the Commission frame European identity, allowing
for twenty-nine different 'frames' to emerge when we just consider European identity from *within* the EU alone. We also know that these 'frames'
are likely to be multiplied further if we adopt a more inclusive approach to
European identity and include parts of the European continent not currently
in the EU. Therefore, it is most likely that the majority of EU and, more
broadly, European citizens hold both national and European identities
simultaneously. Yet, the Commission has failed to acknowledge such multiplicity in its discourse and has spoken of European identity as a one-
dimensional issue driven from and by the EU and, specifically, by EU
citizenship. In light of the empirical evidence, the Commission's expectations of a causal relationship between the exercising of (formal) EU citizenship rights and citizens' sense of European identity seem too idealistic.

This is not to say that the Commission has not adopted other means to
promote European identity. In fact, extensive and elite-led campaigns focusing on the ideal of a *common* European identity had begun much sooner
than when the ideal of EU citizenship was first brought to the negotiating
table (Stråth, 2002). These campaigns have focused on a range of commonalities across the EU and quite often across the European continent as
a whole (European Commission, 1973, 2013b), including similarities in the
values, history, religion and culture of nation states (often compared to
the rest of the world), a shared commitment to democratic principles, and
the role of symbols (such as the flag, the common currency and the hymn)

as key to appreciating what European identity signifies today (for a comprehensive academic overview see Kaina and Karolewski, 2013: 33–38).
Such an elite-led campaign currently shapes the 'Europe for Citizens'
(2014–20) programme that is run by DG Communication (European Commission, 2016c). This programme aims to facilitate an interaction among
an emerging EU-level civil society and non-governmental organisations that
have an interest in realising a Europe-wide public sphere that reaches
beyond the EU's shifting borders (European Commission, 2014b).

While such elite-led campaigns have been on the scene for well over fifty
years (though initial discussions took place within the framework of European integration), they have been, and remain, framed by rather broad
ideals. For instance, in the very first document declaring the very existence
of European identity – suggestively entitled 'Declaration on European identity' (European Commission, 1973: 2) – the then nine member states'
'attachment to common values and principles, the increasing convergence
of attitudes to life, the awareness of having specific interests in common
and the determination to take part in the construction of a United Europe'
are set out early on. However, the document fails to pin down the way in
which these issues may materialise in practice. In fact, we never learn about
these common values and principles nor do we ever get to find out what a
'United Europe' may look like.

In its more recent discourse, the Commission appears to have become
slightly more realistic, recognising that a 'United Europe' is still only 'on
the horizon' (Reding, 2013). As a result, it does not attempt to bring to the
fore the commonalities across (and possibly beyond) the EU's member
states. Instead, the Commission accentuates the diversity that persists across
Europe. One example for this is the overuse of the 'Unity in Diversity' motto
– a go-to phrase accentuating the challenges the EU faces in its attempt to
realise a political and democratic community (see, for example, European
Commission, 2007). 'Unity in Diversity' is also an integral part of current
considerations about further enlargement rounds as well as decisions about
the most appropriate neighbourhood policies (European Commission,
2016d) (as was predicted by some academics, notably Moravcsik, 2010).

In light of its inconsistent discourse on European identity, perhaps it is
not surprising then that empirical evidence also finds that EU symbols and
policies have had varying success (see, for example, Kuhn, 2015; Risse,
2003, 2010). Even when we can observe some positive effects of the more
'tangible' top-down processes at the individual level – most notably the
Euro (Risse, 2003) or the EU flag (Laffan, 2006) – considerable differences
in their impact is apparent at the aggregate level, between and across
member states (Siklodi, 2014). What these results suggest is that more often
than not the Commission pronounces what it *would like to see* when it
comes to European identity, rather than reflecting on what European identity actually signifies. In the midst of the EU's manifold economic and

political crises, calling for further information about the *actual* commonalities that are supposed to feed European identity may seem simplistic at first. Nonetheless, as more and more questions are raised about the very rationale for the EU and EU membership (Webber, 2014), providing such information in an accessible manner should become a priority. It could also, potentially, assist in making the effects of elite-led campaigns on this issue more consistent over time.

The elements of European identity/ies

The first element of identity is a sense of belonging to a sovereign political community. The emphasis is on a three-fold process; how individuals identify with the community, whether the community accepts these individuals as one of its members (Smith, 1992: 59f), and recognition of the community's collective self-image from within and from outside – by members and non-members alike (Díez Medrano and Gutiérrez, 2001: 754). Top-down processes, such as the establishment of definite geographical borders, common symbols (e.g. a hymn, a flag or a common currency), shared values (e.g. democracy and peace) and the projection of a positive self-image – internally and externally (e.g. democracy promotion beyond borders) – have been used by the elite to promote a sense of belonging among the actual and would-be members of the community. It is important to note that individuals can belong to a number of political communities and, at the same time, a number of cultural, economic and social groups (Risse, 2010). As a result of the diversity in their sense of belonging, we can trace separate, nested, cross-cutting or multi-layered identities (Herrmann and Brewer, 2004: 8–10). The presence of separate multiple identities may indicate that there is no overlap between the different identities individuals hold (Risse, 2010). In comparison, nested multiple identities suggest that a hierarchy exists between these identities – perhaps based on the size of the social, cultural and economic groups, and the political communities individuals belong to (see also Díez Medrano and Gutiérrez, 2001). This assumption is often used in surveys that seek to research and measure *collective* identities (e.g. Eurobarometer). Cross-cutting, multiple identities reflect that multiple memberships in groups and communities may exist, but do not necessarily overlap. In such cases, identities can clash – for example on the basis of ethnicity and citizenship (Carey, 2002).

Multiple identities have also been observed from a multi-layered (or 'marble cake') perspective (Risse, 2010), where identities are blended together (rather than separated), making the individual's dominant identity context specific. Recent empirical studies have underscored that the context specific feature of identity corresponds to reality most closely (Ross, 2014; Siklodi, 2015b). Finally, as an increasing share of the population belongs to national (traditionally ethnic) and transnational (civic) political communities but may also identify with broader cultural cohesions (within a continent, for example) we can distinguish between different aspects of identity along ethnic, civic and cultural lines (Brubaker, 1998; Bruter, 2005).

In the EU and European contexts, an inclusive approach to promoting a sense of belonging – such as geographically, culturally, socially or politically – are present in the ideal of a 'normative power Europe' (Manners, 2006). While EU actors welcome such ideals (European Commission, 2016e), they have also put these ideals to the test through the EU's neighbourhood policies and especially during various enlargement rounds (Eder and Spohn, 2005). For example, much of the criticism about the 2004 and 2007 Eastern enlargement round was due to the failure of the then chiefly Western member states to convey to new countries (and often their own citizens and politicians) what it really means to belong to a transnational political community (for an evaluation from an economic and cultural perspective see, for example, Kahanec and Zimmermann, 2010). The subsequent diversity in the EU's membership has only made such attempts more challenging (Epstein and Jacoby, 2014).

By comparison, EU states seem to agree that, after more than twenty years of accession period, the necessary cultural and political convergence in the case of Turkey is insufficient. In a largely Christian EU, religion has also been found to be an important detrimental factor for Turkish accession (Hurd, 2006; Macmillan, 2016). Moreover, the prospect of Turkish membership of the EU is likely to be hampered by the continuing threat of a Cypriot veto (Kambas, 2015).

Yet, accepting its differences and intensifying cooperation with Turkey – and other, culturally diverse candidate countries in the Balkans, for example – could pave the way for a better-coordinated and potentially more successful programme of democracy promotion (Thiel, 2012). The recent re-admission agreement should be considered in this light (European Commission, 2016e). Since the objective of this agreement is highly ambitious and contested – not least due to a requirement for Turkey to help resolve the EU's migration crisis – (Bal, 2016), we need more time to pass before we can evaluate the genuine impact of this agreement for the accession process and for a generalised sense of belonging to the EU. For now, however, Chapter 9 in this volume provides a good indication of the direction this accession process is likely to take. Other chapters shed further light on the extent to which subsequent Eastern enlargement rounds may shape current understanding of a sense of belonging to the EU as well as to Europe more broadly.

The second element of identity is that a shared identity can have an important effect on the ability of individuals to exercise their rights and to live on an equal basis with one another as 'legitimate members' of a political community (Bellamy, 2008: 12–13). Even though the importance of shared identity has been disputed by some scholars, it is expected to produce social trust, which has in turn been recognised as a necessary precondition for participation in, and acceptance of, democratic decision-making processes (Bellamy, 2008: 12–13). Shared identity requires a *collective* recognition of features and attributes among members of the community, including a common purpose, history, language and culture (Risse, 2010: 25–26),[2] all of which reinforce the cognitive and emotional levels of identity (Citrin and Sides, 2004: 165). Shared identity can also be enhanced by social interactions among the members of the community, leading to mutual recognition of a common fate and purpose (Citrin and Sides, 2004: 165). It should be noted however, that shared identity is expected to be 'both inherently limited *and* sovereign' (Anderson, 1983: 6, emphasis added). This is because not every member of a community can know each other. Hence their shared identity is built on a mutual understanding – rather than a proven fact – that their fellows have the same identity. This is why some scholars have proposed that a shared identity defines an 'imagined community' (Anderson, 1983; Risse, 2010): a 'we' feeling among the members of a community.

While often cited by political actors and scholars (see, for example, European Commission, 1993 and Risse, 2010), there is very little evidence that a community of EU citizens and, more broadly, a community of Europeans exists. The Lisbon Treaty has made an important alteration to the previous legal framework, allowing for member states to seriously consider and take up the option to leave the EU. This option has been considered by some states already – most notably in the context of 'Grexit' and 'Brexit'. In the first case, issues linked to an EU economic community have dictated the debate (Hodson, 2015), in the second, political, social and cultural matters have been drawn upon successfully (as apparent in the June 2016 EU referendum result) (Dagnis Jensen and Snaith, 2016). However, it is not only the emergence of an imagined community from within the EU that is under pressure today. Actually, the emergence of *any* transnational community in Europe is doubtful in light of some of the EU's very own policies. For instance, the EU's discourse that guides the ENP and EaP promotes a differentiated approach to Eastern partners. A recent study has concluded that policies towards Armenia, Azerbaijan, Belarus, Georgia, Moldova and Ukraine clearly categorise these countries into separate geopolitical camps (Hett, Kikić and Meuser, 2015; see also Chapter 3). Such practices challenge the basis on which a 'community of Europeans' exists beyond the EU's borders and sheds a dubious light on the likelihood of such a community emerging in the future. These characteristics of a fragmented community of EU citizens and Europeans are touched on in later chapters.

The third element of identity to be considered is that the ability to distinguish an imagined community means that we can also identify 'they' or 'the other' – those cultures, practices and people that are not members of our community. In fact, the level of identity is anticipated to be enhanced by both the recognition of the commonalities community members share with one another *and* the capacity to distinguish this community from 'the other' (Castano et al., 2002: 319). Actually, for collective identities to emerge, clear definitions of both 'the community' and 'the others' are required. Since these definitions must be recognised by the majority of the members in the community, the 'other' is only meaningful if it is also defined collectively. The difference between the community and the 'other' can be enhanced by certain 'codes of distinctions', including definite geographical, political, economic and cultural self-images (Herrmann and Brewer, 2004: 6). These codes reinforce the boundaries of the political community and make an initially 'imagined community' *real* in the minds of its members (Risse, 2010: 23). This element of identity turns political communities into a form of 'categorisation'. While 'categorisation' is often regarded as one of the most significant components of *collective* identity (Citrin and Sears, 2009: 146; Risse, 2010: 26), it also underscores the controversial and exclusive character of political communities (Bellamy, 2008: 52–54). This is because 'categorisation' is often the source of negative attitudes (and even feelings) towards the 'other'. As collective identities become more conventional and accepted by the members of the community, their rejection of the 'other' is also enhanced (Neumann, 1996: 150–154).

Varying definitions of the 'other' are used as a force of categorisation in the EU's neighbourhood policies – as apparent in the EaP for instance – and are often relied on or, for that matter, contested by the elite and the people who operate along the EU's borders. It has already been mentioned that some of the EaP's policies distinguish between neighbouring states based on their geopolitical positions (Hett, Kikić and Meuser, 2015). An even more striking feature of categorisation in the EU's foreign policy is the approach which has prevailed towards Turkey and Russia. While there has been gradual acceptance of opening up the Single Market and promoting ideals of democracy and human rights to Turkey – despite its much cited religious and cultural differences – a similar approach towards Russia is lacking (Smith, 2005). In fact, following the crisis in Ukraine, Russia is now seen as the de facto example of what is *not* 'EU'-ropean (Vieira, 2015).

Russia's role as the EU's 'other' has strong historical roots. Its predecessor, the Soviet Union, was *the* alternative to the EU's predecessor, the European Coal and Steel Community during the Cold War. For the Eastern neighbours, Russia continues to offer an alternative to 'EU'-led European integration and competes with the EU across different policy areas, including economic policy, for example, establishing and coordinating its very own Eurasian Customs Union (Dragneva and Wolczuk, 2012; see also Chapters 3 and 4 in this volume). Furthermore, Russia has built bilateral relationships not only with the EU but with some member states. Some of these states enjoy a 'special' relationship with Russia – most notably Hungary – going as far as to undermine common EU policies. For example, setting up a sustainable energy policy is one of the most important – if not *the* most important – areas in which Russia has become a real 'threat' to EU interests (Fernandes, 2016).

By continuing with the accession process in the case of Turkey and by offering an alternative to the EU for non-member and member states alike in the case of Russia, these countries clearly question the significance of the Commission-defined EU political community and European identity. While both countries may consider themselves 'European', it is clear that they do not wish to 'belong' to the EU community to the same extent. While Turkish accession to the EU is ongoing, suggesting that there is an underlying support for EU ideals, an important aspect of Russia's self-determination in recent years has been to openly reject the way in which EU actors, especially the Commission, has taken ownership of defining what European identity means (Headley, 2012; see also Chapter 4 in this volume). These issues then put particular pressure on the ideal of a single European identity, highlighting the requirement to adopt a more inclusive approach and recognising European identities, which do exist today.

Conclusion

This chapter has provided a definition of European identity that is drawn on in the latter chapters of this volume. Owing to the inconsistency among academics and policy makers about what this concept entails, this chapter has proposed understanding European identity as a combination of elements. It has been suggested that the elements of European identity – a sense of belonging to the EU, Europe and the nation state; a shared identity among 'Europeans' and a recognition of non-European cultures, values, practices and persons – may appear in various configurations, depending on social and political contexts. As a result, the chapter has recommended considering European identity not as a single ideal but as a blend of identities, leading to a potential multiplicity in European identity/ies. It has been argued that by observing the concept of European identity/ies as a combination of elements, we can provide a more accurate and comprehensive portrait of what European identity signifies. Based on the ensuing discussion, the elements of European identity/ies can be summarised as in Table 2.1. While it is not necessary for all elements shown in Table 2.1 to be present when empirically addressing the issue of European identity/ies, since there is much overlap between these elements, it is useful to break down the concept of European identity/ies in this way for the purpose of coherence and to reflect reality.

The observation that European identity/ies are a collection of elements is taken up in other chapters of this volume. The chapters illustrate the presence and strengths of European identity/ies across various policy and

Table 2.1 Defining European identity/ies: A conceptual framework

The elements of European identity/ies		
Empirical indicators	A sense of belonging to Europe and the nation state (cultural aspect) and to the EU (political aspect)	Shared identity among 'Europeans' (a sense of 'we')	Recognition of the 'other' (non-European cultures, values, practices and persons)

academic perspectives today. Chapters 8 on the Balkans, 9 on Turkey and 13 on Language are particularly illustrative of these perspectives. This will provide a much-needed contribution to building consistency in European identity research.

Notes

1   In order to provide a conceptual framework of European identity, this chapter draws on evidence from critical discourse analysis that was carried out as part of a larger research project, exploring the Commission's ideals on EU citizenship (Siklodi, 2015a). Discourse is understood as a 'form of social practice' that is 'socially shaped and … constitutive', and which sustains and reproduces the status quo (Fairclough, 2013: 92). For the purposes of illustrating the presences of European identity/ies, the chapter includes an in-depth analysis of legislative proposals, evaluations, reports and media statements that were first and foremost written by the Commission or by Commission representatives on European identity specifically.

2   These criteria have been identified as the content of identity, without which collective identities cannot exist (Abdelal et al., 2009: 27–31). They are usually 'the outcome of a process of social contestation within a group' (Abdelal et al., 2009: 27). For the purpose of this edited volume, the content of identity is understood to be continuously shaped and revised by citizens and the political elite alike (similar points are made by Karolewski, 2009).

3 Paul Flenley

The limitations of the EU's strategies for Europeanisation of the neighbours

As an explicit part of its security strategy, the European Union sought to ensure that the 'countries on our borders are well-governed' (Council of the European Union, 2003a). In pursuit of this, the EU adopted a range of strategies and instruments which have aimed to promote stability, good governance and democratic values in the neighbourhood as well as promoting the economic and security interests of the EU. Building a 'ring of friends' was to be good for the EU and also for the neighbours. This approach reflects the interplay between interests (security) and values (good governance), which is a key theme of this book. However, continuing authoritarianism in Belarus, war in Ukraine, tensions with Russia, internal political developments in Turkey and the migration crisis would suggest that these strategies are failing. This chapter considers the strategies adopted by the EU in relation to its Eastern neighbours and identifies common problems and obstacles to the EU's approach and how these limit EU-isation.

External governance approach

A key feature of the EU's approach to its neighbours has been the attempt to extend its norms and values. This 'EU-isation' was to be achieved through 'conditionality'. This meant the offer of a closer relationship with the EU and possibly even membership in return for domestic reform (Schimmelfennig and Sedelmeier, 2004). The approach was derived from the EU's perceived success in transforming the countries of Central and Eastern Europe to meet the EU's Copenhagen Criteria (1993). Conditionality worked in these cases in spreading norms because there was the credible offer of membership of the EU at the end (Grabbe, 2006). The domestic costs of rule adoption were outweighed by the concrete offer of EU membership in the negotiations (Schimmelfennig and Sedelmeier, 2004). In principle, this offer of membership is open to any 'European' state which, according to the Treaty of Amsterdam (Article 6), respects principles of freedom, democracy, human rights and the rule of law. For many of the EU's neighbouring states in our study – such as Moldova, Ukraine, Georgia and Turkey – the desire for EU membership is still part of the national agenda. However, after the 2004 enlargement, many have questioned the ability of the EU to include more members (Silander and Nilsson, 2013: 444).

A key dilemma for the EU has been how to promote EU-isation in those countries where membership is not likely in the near future or, indeed, ever. The fear has been that saying 'no' to eventual membership may undercut domestic democratic forces and put an end to any EU influence. The success of the 'external incentives model of governance' (i.e. conditionality) in the initial enlargement process to Central and Eastern Europe was such that it was envisaged it could be applied in the EU's relations with its new neighbours (Lavenex, 2004; Sasse, 2008). In 2004, the European Neighbourhood Policy (ENP) was launched to include the former Soviet bloc states of Eastern Europe (excluding Russia) which had been left out of the enlargement process. Following lobbying from certain EU member states, it also included the EU's Southern neighbours such as Egypt.[1] The policy offered maximum integration with the EU without actual membership, sharing 'everything but the institutions' (Prodi, 2002). The idea was to offer 'more for more' – the more the reform the more the integration with the EU, or so-called 'positive conditionality' (Börzel and Risse, 2012a). There would be no penalties for failure to reform, only rewards of greater engagement with the EU that was reflective of the degree of reform. The reforms spanned areas such as democracy, the rule of law, human rights, economic liberalisation and the adoption of EU standards (European Commission, 2004).

Action Plans were worked out with each country of the ENP to identify the priority areas of reform. These were then to be incorporated into domestic reform programmes. The ENP had two major weaknesses. First, often painful domestic reforms were expected in return for little in the way of concrete integration. Second, the end goals were very vague in view of the fact that the ENP included states in the South – for which there was no prospect of EU membership – alongside those in the East – which still harboured such hopes. As a consequence, the EaP was launched in 2009 to provide greater focus and to speed up the integration of the six post-Soviet states. It meant effectively two ENPs with the East having a clear 'Europeanisation' dimension.

The Russo-Georgia War of 2008 had made clearer policy towards the Eastern partners more imperative (Tolstrup, 2014: 195). The EU would work with partners across four platforms: democracy and good governance; economic integration; energy security; and contacts with people. A range of specific incentives was offered, in particular visa liberalisation and closer trade and financial assistance in return for reform. If there was a 'sufficient level of progress in terms of democracy, the rule of law and human rights' then the EU was prepared to move to signing an Association Agreement (AA) including a Deep and Comprehensive Free Trade Area (DCFTA). The latter were comprehensive treaties with the EU in which the 'European choice' of a neighbour would be deepened and even greater regulatory convergence and trade with the EU would be promoted (Emerson and Movchan 2016: 2). It was hoped that the prospect of signing the latter would give real substance to the EaP (European Commission and High Representative, 2013). In 2014, Georgia, Moldova and Ukraine (after Yanukovych's initial rejection in 2013) signed AAs, including DCFTAs, with the EU. These entered fully into force in 2016 (see Emerson and Cenusa, 2016; Emerson and Kovziridze, 2016; Emerson and Movchan, 2016 for detailed analyses of the agreements).

However, even these AAs do not hold out the promise of EU membership. The same inhibition to effective reform remained – substantial domestic costs were expected in return for no concrete end (Wilson, 2014: 4). A further disincentive was the time delay in terms of benefits. While the costs of adjusting to EU regulations under the AA/DCFTAs come early, the benefits only come later. The EU is ready to help in the adjustment process but this is not commensurate with the initial costs of reform.

Turkey has been in this situation of ambiguity over its membership perspective the longest. It signed an AA in 1963 with a view to accession to the then European Economic Community. In 2016, as part of an EU–Turkey agreement in the face of the EU's need for Turkey's cooperation in the migration crisis, there was a vague commitment to revisit the process of Turkey's accession. The fundamental problem of the EU's relations with such partners has therefore been apparent for a long time in its vagueness and lack of commitment on end goals and neither taking a 'no' nor a 'yes' position to membership. The policy creates a hope which is followed by disappointment. In the case of Ukraine, both in the Orange Revolution and the Euromaidan, this can have destabilising consequences as the hopes of the mobilised crowds to join Europe are not fulfilled. The countries of the neighbourhood are left in a state of tension between belonging and being the 'other'.

In response to some of the problems of its policy towards its neighbours, the EU announced the results of a review of the ENP in November 2015 (European Commission, 2015b). The one-size-fits-all policy was to be abandoned. It was clear that not all the EaP countries were seeking the same kind of relationship with the EU. The EaP's 'more for more' approach had assumed that they were all on the same path. It had applied the same broad external governance approach of conditionality – essentially, 'more integration in return for more reform'. However, Belarus, Armenia and Azerbaijan have no desire for full integration with the EU, while Ukraine, Georgia and Moldova aspire to membership. The EU needed to respect those differences in strategic choices rather than punishing or downgrading the former group.

In practical terms, this means more pragmatic and flexible relations with partners.

Recent structural changes in Brussels have tried to reflect this reality. Previously, the division dealing with the Eastern Neighbourhood within the European External Action Service (EEAS) had one unit dealing with Belarus, Ukraine and Moldova and another unit dealing with the South Caucasus. Now, one unit deals with those partners pursing AAs (i.e. Ukraine, Georgia and Moldova) and another unit deals with Belarus, Armenia and Azerbajan (Kostanyan, 2015a: 24). For the latter countries, where a DCFTA is not sought, lighter trade agreements will be offered, such as Agreements on Conformity Assessment and Acceptance (ACAAs). Neither Armenia nor Azerbaijan seeks an AA with the EU. In the case of Armenia, an 'Enhanced Partnership Agreement' is likely to be signed, similar to the one with Kazakhstan. Azerbaijan has sought a 'Strategic Dialogue' with the EU, free from the conditionality constraints of the EaP. Although still maintaining broad commitments to promoting human rights, the rule of law and good governance, the ENP review indicates that there will be more focus on specific areas, especially economic development, migration and security (Kostanyan, 2015b) Whether this means abandoning the normative agenda of 'Europeanisation' in the case of some countries (such as Belarus) or being more realistic in terms of what can be achieved in such cases is a matter of debate.

Such a variation in the EU's application of conditionality in practice comes as nothing new. Within the ENP, more authoritarian regimes in the Southern neighbourhood have been treated differently from the East in the name of stability and security. Similarly, the EU's energy interests in the Caspian Sea could be said to influence why authoritarian Azerbaijan is treated differently from Belarus (Börzel and Pamuk, 2012). Clearly, at times, the EU's interests are taking precedence over 'norms' (Casier, 2013: 1383). However, it would be very surprising indeed if states pursued norms which damaged their own state interests. A more charitable view of EU behaviour would be that the EU has been prepared to accept 'more-for-less' in some cases because it realises the limitations of what the neighbour can offer in terms of reform. To insist would risk losing influence over the neighbour altogether. Engagement with Ukraine under Yanukovych before 2014 continued and expectations were reduced even though democratic reforms were going into reverse. The priority was to support democratic forces and not 'to lose' Ukraine (Kubicek, 2016).

For some neighbours, however, it is the rhetoric of the EU's normative agenda which has been the fundamental problem. The EU presents itself as a normative power (Manners, 2002) and seeks to project such norms as democracy and human rights in its relations with its neighbours (Haukkala, 2008; Horky-Hluchan and Kratchovil, 2014: 264). This is at the core of the EU project and its legitimacy (Kaina and Karolewski, 2013; see also

Chapter 1). For some neighbours, especially Russia, the EU is asserting a moral superiority (Casier, 2013). The process of EU-isation is a one-way process of civilisation of the neighbours by the EU (Zielonka, 2013: 35). The EU is therefore not engaging with others as equals. The Eastern neighbours have to accept their 'otherness' and inferiority (Horky-Hluchan and Kratchovil, 2014: 255; Sakwa, 2015: 557). The very name 'European Neighbourhood Policy' implies that countries such as Ukraine are on the edge of Europe rather than part of it. This EU-centric discourse is reinforced by the EU's practical processes of policymaking towards the neighbourhood. For example, reports from the neighbourhood written by EU delegations are often rewritten to fit in with EU priorities and language. There is a lack of an 'outside-in' perspective whereby the EU's policy is understood from the perspective of the neighbour and fed back to the EU (Keukeleire, 2014: 237).

The EU's sense of 'superiority' emerged out of the dominant Western interpretation that the West 'won' the Cold War. In this triumphalism the West became the font of superior values (Sakwa, 2015: 555) and the EU saw itself as defining European values (see Chapter 1). Not surprisingly this lies at the root of the problems of the EU-Russia relationship (see Chapter 4). Putin's speech to the Russian State Duma after the annexation of Crimea articulates the resentment at this approach since 1991 (Putin, 2014). In view of this, Russia under Putin rejected the conditionality of the EU's approach and the normative underpinning of the Partnership and Cooperation Agreement with the EU signed in 1994 (Flenley, 2008: 199; Lavrov, 2007). Rather late in the day, the EU attempted to address this issue in its relations with Russia. The 'Partnership for Modernisation' of 2010 was supposed to mean a resetting of relations based on mutual interests rather than conditionality (Flenley, 2015).

Asymmetry and partnerships

One problem with the EU's external governance approach is that it contradicts the rhetoric of the 'partnerships' which the EU has with its neighbours – Partner and Cooperation Agreements, Strategic Partnerships, Eastern Partnership (Gawrich et al., 2010; Korosteleva, 2011). These are not real partnerships of equals. The power is generally perceived to be one way. There is an asymmetry between the priorities and interests of the EU and those of the partner. While the EU insists on neighbours meeting EU regulatory standards for access to EU markets and greater openness of the neighbours markets to EU business, common demands from neighbours – such as visa-free travel to the EU – have been blocked (Gawrich et al., 2010: 1126; see also Chapter 12). In August 2016, the Turkish Foreign Minister was threatening to withdraw help to the EU on the migration crisis if the promise of visa-free travel continued to be delayed (Stratfor, 2016). In some cases, the priorities for the neighbours involve existential threats to the integrity of the state, whether it is the threat from Russia for Ukraine, the existence of frozen conflicts and rogue states in Moldova, Azerbaijan, Armenia and Georgia, or mass migration, terrorism and military coup in the case of Turkey. In these contexts, EU priorities such as human rights and democracy may take second place. There are also differences in economic priorities. In the case of the differences between Russia and the EU over the Energy Charter Treaty of 1994, the EU as a consumer of Russian energy demands liberalisation of markets, while for Russia, its national interests as a producer logically mean maintaining the strength and position of its energy companies such as Gazprom (Casier, 2011: 548). Asymmetries are reinforced by a fundamental flaw in the EU's 'more-for-more' approach. The promise that greater reform will be rewarded by greater integration with the EU and access to EU markets is limited by the fact that, ultimately, individual EU member states will want to defend their own domestic interests.

The geopolitics of the neighbours

The geopolitical position of the neighbours is a key factor limiting EU-isation. For the EaP countries the relationship with Russia colours their relations with the EU. For these 'in-betweeners' (see Chapters 5, 6 and 7) the 'either or' choice of integration with the EU or close relationship with Russia can be an impossible one. As indicated in the Ukraine crisis of 2014, it can create instability in the neighbourhood. Under Yanukovych, an economically weak Ukraine found it difficult to resist Russia's offer of discounts in the price of natural gas, preferential loans and trade concessions as opposed to the prospect of signing the EU's Association Agreement which involved substantial and painful domestic reforms (Wilson, 2014). Moreover, while the EU was not even offering membership at the end, Russia was offering full membership of the new Eurasian Economic Union (EEU) which started in January 2015. The relationship with Russia can work in different ways for the neighbours. For Armenia, the 'either or' choice has meant joining the EEU rather than signing an AA with the EU in view of the greater priority of the security and economic relationship with Russia. In the case of Georgia, the Russia factor has worked in the opposite direction. The EU is seen as a way of escaping Russian dominance and interference in its internal affairs (e.g. over the enclaves such as South Ossetia). An AA with the EU was therefore signed in 2014.

Originally, Putin perceived that Eurasian integration in the form of the EEU would not be in opposition to the EU: 'Eurasian union will be built on universal integrationist principles as an inalienable part of greater

Europe, united by common values of freedom, democracy and the law of the market' (Putin, 2011). He envisaged the EU and the Eurasian Union as parts of a polycentric continent cooperating in a common economic space from Lisbon to Vladivostok. However, in practice, so far, the EEU has been presented as part of the 'either or' choice for the neighbours. It is not possible to both integrate with the EU through an AA and be a member of the EEU. There has been reluctance so far to try to align regulations between the two (see Romanova in Chapter 4 of this volume). As yet, analysts are sceptical as to whether the new EEU will develop into an equivalent to the EU (Roberts and Moshes, 2015). The non-Russian members are keen to limit the degree of integration and maintain relations at the level of economic cooperation rather than pursue a political transformative project along the lines of the EU. Especially after Russian intervention in Ukraine, they are keen to protect their own sovereignty (see Chapter 5 on Belarus). While they depend on Russia they fear its potential to dominate such a union (Roberts and Moshes, 2015).

In contrast to integration with the EU, however, the EEU is attractive to some neighbours as it does not challenge existing networks and practices or ask questions about democracy and human rights. While not requiring adoption of EU norms, it is doubtful whether the EEU will become the focus for the promotion of an alternative vision of Europeanisation or 'Eurasianism' (see Chapter 1) in spite of its name. Eurasianism remains a theme in Russian political thought. However, the latter variant's association with Russian nationalism and Russia's position as a great power makes the development of a common interpretation of Eurasianism shared by Kazakhstan, Russia and other members of the EEU unlikely. While Russia itself under Putin may seek to present itself as an alternative normative pole of values to the EU, the EEU is unlikely to be the focus of this as well.

Irrespective of the existence of Russia or the EEU as an alternative pole of attraction for neighbours, Russia does see itself as having vital interests in the area, which cannot be ignored. Referring to the Ukraine crisis, Russian Foreign Minister, Sergei Lavrov, said: 'Everyone knows the root cause of the crisis: we were not listened to. Kiev was forced into signing arrangements with the European Union which had been drafted behind the scene and, as it eventually turned out, were undermining Ukraine's obligations on the CIS free trade area' (Lavrov, 2014). Moreover, an aspect of Russia's self-image as a 'great power' is to be able to exert influence in its own neighbourhood (Brzezinski, 1997). NATO enlargement combined with EU programmes such as the EaP are seen as ways of excluding Russia from its rightful area of influence (Flenley, 2008: 200; see also Chapter 4 in this volume). The Euromaidan revolution in Ukraine of 2014 merely confirmed this view. The EU has claimed that it has been mindful of Russia's interests and pursued a 'Russia aware' policy in the neighbourhood (Mandelson, 2007).

The dilemma for the EU is how far a third party, Russia, should have a say in the foreign policy of a sovereign state such as Ukraine (Blockmans, 2014). Why should Russia have a say in the EU's relations with Ukraine or indeed Moldova? To some extent the war in Ukraine has already partly answered that question. There was a trialogue between the EU, Russia and Ukraine to resolve the gas pricing dispute between Ukraine and Russia in 2014. Russia was able to delay the implementation of the DCFTA with Ukraine until 1 January 2016 and insist on 'systemic adjustments'. At the time of writing, the Russian presence in South Ossetia in Georgia, the Russian-backed separatist enclaves in Donetsk and Luhansk in Ukraine, and Russian influence in Transnistria in Moldova de facto give Russia a say in the internal affairs of key neighbours and their relations with the EU.

The answer may be to end the zero-sum game of the neighbours. This would mean the EU recognising the reality of the neighbours' relationship with Russia. It would involve assuaging Russia's security fears by unlocking the link between the spread of EU influence and NATO enlargement and taking the latter off the agenda. An ultimate solution would involve reducing the differences between the AA/DCFTAs and EEU regulations. Building a 'common space' between Russia and the EU to include those 'in-between' would help to avoid the alternative of continuing instability in the EU's neighbourhood (Flenley, 2015).

Legitimacy, resonance and domestic narratives

The success of EU strategies very much depends on how far they coincide with the interests of domestic elites. If reform involves restructuring which damages the economic interests of incumbent elites with the promise of little in return it will be resisted, as has been the case in Eastern Ukraine (Riabchuk 2007; Vachudova, 2005). This resonance extends particularly to existing practices, power structures and networks. In many of the neighbours, governance is largely conducted through personal networks rather than formal open structures. Personal loyalties are crucial – a form of neo-patrimonialism (Robinson, 2011). The EU has to work through these networks. If reforms such as anti-corruption, democratisation and rule of law challenge these networks, and hence the power of the domestic elites, they are unlikely to be successful. It is the paradox of EU-isation in the neighbourhood that in order to be implemented, many of the reforms require the cooperation of the very elites whose power and resources will be undermined (Flenley, 2015). The more authoritarian the system, then the more the incumbent elites have to lose by reform. However, experience of the revolutions in Ukraine and Georgia has shown the capacity of mass mobilisation to challenge the blocking power of reluctant elites (Welzel and Ingelhart, 2008). In 2014, in Ukraine, the

EU was used by the crowd as a reference point to attack the elite and demand reform.

There are cases where Europeanisation in the form of policy convergence (EU-isation) can be successful in spite of there being no clear EU member-ship perspective, high domestic costs of reform, and a lack of resonance between the policy practices and institutional arrangements of the EU and those of the neighbour (Langbein and Börzel, 2013: 572). EU-isation can be used as a pathway to greater access to global markets (Langbein, 2014: 161–162). In such cases a particular aspect of diffusion theory is operat-ing: normative emulation. A state wishes to become a legitimate member of the wider international community. The EU provides a ready-made set of institutional solutions which can be emulated (Börzel and Risse, 2012a: 10). Sometimes EU-isation can also be successful due to the alignment of domestic political forces within a neighbour. The EU can be used as a form of leverage in the arguments between domestic elites, strengthening the hand of reformers (Vachudova, 2005). In the Ukrainian telecommuni-cations sector, a pro-reform alliance was built up between operators and legislators using links within the ruling elite to push forward regulatory convergence (Langbein, 2014: 164). This politicisation of the success of EU-isation is perhaps most apparent when considering anti-corruption poli-cies. These can be used to remove political opponents and promote political agendas. In Georgia, anti-corruption campaigns were used by Saakashvili to break up the former president Shevardnadze's networks (Börzel and Pamuk, 2012).

Studies have also suggested that measuring the degree of successful EU-isation in terms of policy convergence needs to be more complex in its approach than just categorizing one country – such as Georgia – against another – such as Azerbaijan. We can measure variations in convergence between policy sectors in the same country and also measure differences in the type of compliance. In some cases there will be 'outcome compliance' (i.e. real behavioural changes) while in other cases there will be just 'output compliance' (i.e. a formal adoption of a policy to satisfy EU requirements) (Ademmer and Börzel, 2013) or, what some refer to as 'Europragmatism'. The key determining factors in the degree of compliance is how far the adoption of EU regulations benefits the relevant domestic elite in that sector, or at least a significant section of them. In Ukraine, the costs of the adop-tion of EU technical regulations for industrial products were high. Russia did not demand such regulations. Consequently, the heavy industry sector, which traded most with Russia, blocked change in this area, overriding the interests of the smaller machinery producers.

In the case of shareholder rights, however, there has been full compliance with EU regulations. The difference here was the need to attract international investment. Hence, the EU was used to help reach international standards. In Armenia, an anti-corruption policy has been applied superficially (output compliance), largely to attract foreign and especially diaspora investment but, unlike Georgia, without really attacking the interests of any section of the elite (Ademmer and Börzel, 2013). The more instrumentalist approach to Europeanisation or 'Europragmatism' outlined above is said to be prevalent over much of the EU's neighbourhood (for Russia, see Chapter 4 in this volume; and for Ukraine see Stegniy, 2011). Rules are superficially adopted to gain wider benefits but lack deep socialisation. For some theorists this is not a problem as the very process of engaging with formal procedures will gradually change behaviour (Finnemore and Sikkink, 1998).

Deeper or 'thick' Europeanisation is more likely to occur if integration with the EU can become part of the dominant domestic narrative of the future of the country. Successful integration of the Central and East European countries and the Baltic States was ultimately possible because, after the collapse of state socialism, there was no equally powerful narrative about the countries' future other than a 'return to Europe'. For many in Ukraine, the anger of the Euromaidan was not about economics. Yanukovych not signing the AA 2013 signalled a denial of the country's future. The EU symbolised modernisation, good governance and an end to corruption. The alternative narrative was one of continuing to be dominated by Russia and ruled by a corrupt oligarchy.

In the East of Ukraine of course, the narratives were rather different – not just fear of job losses but threats to identity and the resurgence of old narratives about Ukrainian nationalism and even fascism. In the Balkans, we also see different EU narratives being played out between Croatia and Serbia, often informed by historical memory (see Chapter 8). In the case of EU–Russia relations, the dominant narratives have been at variance since 2012, if not before. For many in the EU, especially among the new member states, Russia is the defining 'other' of Europe. In Russia, the narrative is one of the EU seeking to weaken Russia and exclude it from its 'own neighbourhood'. This speaks to an older narrative about Western intentions, going back to the nineteenth century (Flenley, 2008). Russia sees itself as European and promoting European values without any need for recognition by the EU (see Chapter 4). Russia has latterly recognised the need to promote its narrative in the neighbourhood through the media – in particular through Russian television and organisations such as 'russkii mir (Russian world). Similarly, EU-isation needs the effective use of soft power tools of promotion, the cultivation of local norm entrepreneurs and advocacy networks (Börzel and Risse, 2012a: 7).

Elites, civil society and Europeanisation

A key problem with the EU's conditionality is that, in practice, it involves a top-down approach to Europeanisation (Ladrech, 1994). This has several consequences. First, it essentially involves an EU elite talking down to a domestic elite. This can provoke resentment. The clearest examples of this are in the Balkans. In Bosnia and Herzegovina and Kosovo, Europeanisation is seen as being more or less imposed by the EU (Noutcheva, 2009). In Serbia, such conditionality as cooperating with the International Criminal Court has been seen as an external imposition. In addition, such a top-down approach to the elite process of Europeanisation can also actually undermine domestic democratisation processes. Changes are imposed locally by domestic elites following conditions laid down by the EU elite. There is little room for involvement by the domestic public in the decision-making process (Tema, 2011). The relationship is between elites, often in the face of domestic opinion (Raik, 2006). This complaint is also articulated by many within the EU itself. Populist parties of both left and right argue that EU directives are imposed, thus undermining the sovereign rights of parliaments. In the Greek financial crisis, for example, the EU 'troika' was seen as imposing its economic conditions in the face of the democratic decision of the Greek people in electing an anti-austerity government.

Deeper Europeanisation needs to go beyond elites talking to each other, and involve wider civil society, creating a much denser range of relationships (Checkel, 2005). One of the main reasons for the success of the earlier enlargement process was the extent to which a range of transnational networks – such as political parties, civil society organisations and twinning arrangements – were built between the candidate countries and existing member states thus facilitating socialisation (Risse-Kappen, 1996: 57–58). A range of organisations beyond the EU – for example, NGOs and foundations such as the Soros Foundation – were also involved in funding, training and development. Exchange programmes such as Socrates/Erasmus helped in mobility and training.

The problem for the new neighbours is that the density of contact (and especially citizen-to-citizen) in both directions is limited. In this context the widespread demand of neighbours such as Ukraine and Turkey for visa-free travel is particularly apt. Nevertheless, there have also been a wide range of groups assisting in areas such as democracy promotion, civil society development and capacity building (McFaul, 2007). Civil society organisations in the neighbourhood are able to access funds through a variety of instruments, such as the European Instrument for Democracy and Human Rights (EIDHR), the EU's European Endowment for Democracy (EED) and the Development Cooperation Instrument (DCI). The European Neighbourhood Instrument for 2014–20 has dedicated 15 per cent of its budget for general capacity building and 5 per cent for direct support to civil society (EEAS, European Neighbourhood Instrument, 2014). A key feature of the Eastern Partnership in 2009 was to place much more specific emphasis on civil society than had previously been the case with the ENP. Civil society was one of the areas where multi-lateral projects were to be encouraged across the region (European External Action Service, n.d.) This meant funding the Civil Society Forum, which aims to provide financial, technical and political assistance to civil society, and promote regional networking between local organisations.

However, direct access to civil society organisations can be difficult and relies on the acquiescence of central government (Raik, 2006). The EU still tends to channel funding to civil society organisation via governments rather than directly to NGOs. This practice is reinforced by the ENP's essentially 'output-centred' approach. It aims at targets such as anti-corruption, democratic reform, and good governance rather than (the less measurable) broader 'socialisation' (Börzel and Pamuk, 2012). Achievement of targets in these output areas requires the cooperation and support of government officials, especially in countries such as Armenia and Azerbaijan – empowering independent civil society too much risks alienating these officials and hence losing the chance for impact at all. In addition, those civil society organisations which the EU does engage with tend to be the large, well-established and professional organisations. Smaller, highly local and especially rural NGOs tend to miss out. Much of this is a consequence of the complexity of the EU bidding and accounting process which means that only large, well-experienced NGOs have the capacity to access EU funding (Aliyev, 2016). Aware of the problem, the EU has in some cases allowed 'sub-granting' to bring smaller groups in.

Funding and capacity building in the neighbourhood policy

In its engagement with domestic actors, the EU seeks to promote changes through capacity building and empowering local actors. This was an important part of the process of preparation for membership (Schimmelfennig et al., 2003) and is now applied to the neighbours. In March 2014, in response to the crisis in Ukraine, the EU pledged up to €11 billion from 2014 to 2020 to support recovery and democratic transition (European Commission, 2015a: 22). Overall, in 2014 the EU committed €730 million to new programmes in the EaP and spent almost €550 million on continuing programmes (European Commission, 2015a: 5). However, in the case of the neighbourhood, the size of the funds available is very limited in comparison to funds available for the development of existing members and those preparing for membership and not enough to make much of a difference to stabilisation (Soros, 2015). An additional constraint on capacity building is the limited staff and time available to EU diplomats and civil servants to actually engage with actors in the neighbourhood, especially if one includes outreach to civil society and political parties. The capacity to build relationships is also limited by the lack of language acquisition and area-specific knowledge of EU staff. This is further inhibited by the rotation of staff between posts (Keukeleire, 2014: 236).

Divisions within the EU

One complaint about EU policy towards the Eastern neighbours is that it lacks coordination. This is in many ways a practical reflection of the contradiction at the heart of the EU: is it an intergovernmental or a supranational institution? Member states wish to promote a more coherent foreign and security policy but they also wish to protect their own interests (Furness, 2013) and want to pursue their own bilateral relations with neighbours (see Chapter 10). Trying to arrive at a common EU policy can result in delay and adopting the lowest common denominator. This was seen in the response to the crisis in the Balkans in the 1990s. Much of the lack of commitment towards neighbours such as Turkey and Ukraine over membership arises from divisions between member states over whether membership should be offered.

In the case of EU–Russia relations, the differences between member states have often inhibited the development of a consensus on policy towards Russia (Schmidt-Felzmann, 2008: 182). Russia has complained that one of the consequences of enlargement was that the new member states such as Poland and Lithuania brought an anti-Russian agenda to the fore. In practice, Russia has benefited from this as it prefers to deal with individual states – such as Germany and Italy – on a bilateral basis. Nevertheless, where necessary the EU has managed to reach consensus and respond to crises. In spite of disquiet by some member states, unity was achieved on the imposition of sanctions against Russia after the annexation of Crimea, at least up to the time of writing.

The neighbours are also presented with a range of confusing signals from the EU as to priorities. Different institutions in Brussels, such as the Parliament or Commission, will emphasise different issues – for example, human rights or trade. This is compounded by the different priorities of the member states. Member states tend to upload value issues – such as human rights and democracy – in dealing with the neighbourhood to the EU level institutions while they pursue interests – such as security and commerce – on a bilateral basis.

The main attempt to develop greater coordination of policy came with the Lisbon Treaty (2009). This led to the establishment of the EEAS in support of a High Representative (HR) for Foreign Affairs and Security Policy to be responsible for the coordination of all external policies. The EEAS staff were drawn from the Commission, the Council Secretariat and seconded from the diplomatic staff of member states. The EEAS is separate from the European Commission and while some Commission competencies were moved to the EEAS, others, such as trade, development and the Neigh-bourhood Policy, remain within the Commission (Vanhoonacker and Pomorska, 2013). Consequently, in the case of relations with neighbours, the EEAS has to work closely with the Directorate General (DG) for Neigh-bourhood and Enlargement Negotiations, created in January 2015, as well as other DGs such as trade.

In negotiating Association Agreements, the EEAS has led on the political aspects. However, in the case of technical sectoral chapters, the EEAS refers to the relevant DG. In the case of the DCFTAs, however, DG Trade actually leads the negotiations. The relationship between the EEAS and DGs can therefore be problematic and a source of tension, especially over priorities in relations with a neighbour. This leads to mixed signals for the neighbour. For example, while the EEAS backed by most member states saw faster integration with Moldova as a political priority, DG Trade regarded Moldova as insignificant from a trade point of view and was initially reluc-tant to commit its scarce resources (Kostanyan, 2014). Relations between the EEAS and member states can also be problematic. The former is actually responsible to the latter. They set the priorities and in negotiations the EEAS has to regularly report back to a committee of member states – for example the Council of the European Union's Working Party on Eastern Europe and Central Asia (COEST) (Kostanyan, 2015a: 23). The EEAS's negotiations over the AAs are therefore constrained by the fact that the member states are divided about whether a neighbour should be given a clear membership perspective or not. Moreover, member states have the final right of approval of any AA with a neighbour, hence the Netherlands referendum on the Ukraine AA in April 2016.

When analysts criticise the EU for lack of clarity or vision in the ENP and vagueness over membership, it is largely because the EU institutions such as the EEAS are not free agents. They have to reconcile these differ-ences between member states when negotiating with a neighbour. However, some analysts suggest that, in time, the EEAS could develop a clearer EU policy to neighbours which is not hostage to specific member states. This could come via the Union (formerly Commission) delegations which are now directly responsible to the HR/EEAS and do not necessarily share their information with the diplomatic missions of member states (Blom and Vanhoonacker, 2015: 217–219).

Europeanisation and securitisation

To return to the introduction to this chapter, EU strategies for EU-isation are expected to promote stability in the neighbourhood and thereby add to the EU's security. EU mechanisms such as the ENP and EaP take a long-term perspective of trying to promote stability in areas of conflict such as the South Caucasus through help for institution building, humanitarian assistance and confidence building, to bring parties together (Whitman and Wolff, 2010; also see Chapter 14 for the link between democratisation and security in the neighbourhood). However, the EU is less effective in conflict management. Neighbours have felt that the EaP lacked a clear commitment to resolving regional conflicts and that they are left to deal with conflicts on their own (Nitou, 2011: 472). As former commissioner for External Relations, Ferrero-Waldner, has said, 'the European Neighbourhood Policy is not in itself a conflict prevention or settlement mechanism' (Blockmans, 2014: 3). In this area, the EU is subject to many of the problems identified here – the lack of agreement between member states over how far to engage with conflicts in the neighbourhood, given the relationship with Russia. Mechanisms such as the EU Special Representative (EUSR) for the South Caucasus and the rule of law mission (EUJUST Themis) have been established (Whitman and Wolff, 2010: 4). However, they lack the staff and the political will to be that effective. Even with the apparent greater coordination under the EEAS, the first HR, Catherine Ashton, saw a limited role for the EU as a crisis manager (Vanhoonacker and Pomorska, 2013).

The EU's greatest impact in security crises has been through ad hoc shuttle diplomacy by high-profile EU leaders operating in a mediation capacity (such as Sarkozy's intervention in the Russo–Georgia War of 2008 under the French presidency of the EU and Merkel's and Hollande's mediation with Putin in the 2014 Ukraine crisis). Paradoxically then, while NATO and the EU were seen as vehicles for preventing conflict between states in Europe in the Cold War, since then, their neighbourhood policies have actually not been that successful – from the Balkans conflict in the 1990s to Ukraine 2014 and tensions with Russia to date. Apart from the Organization for Security and Co-operation in Europe (OSCE), there is still a lack of a pan-European security architecture. In this fundamental area of ensuring security in the neighbourhood there is still no effective vehicle for EU-isation.

Conclusion

As we have seen, there are many ways in which the strategies adopted by the EU for Europeanisation in the neighbourhood are thwarted or distorted in practice. Fundamentally, the EU confronts the often immutable interests of the neighbours both in terms of their geopolitical position and their own domestic power structures and priorities. The EU language of conditionality and the external governance approach can also conflict with the self-identity of the neighbours. This does not mean that the EU's approach has no effect. However, it does mean that the effect may not be what the EU intends. In extreme cases, EU strategy can actually be counterproductive and contribute to destabilising the neighbourhood. EU-isation can also be taken up by the neighbour but for their own interests and priorities and interpreted in their own way. The complexities of EU external policymaking itself have also had an effect on the coherence and effectiveness of EU-isation. These themes are taken up in more detail in the area and sector-specific chapters which follow.

Note

1 Russia decided to stay outside the ENP largely due to the conditionality element (see later in this chapter) and has had its own strategic bilateral relationship with the EU involving the building of 'Common Spaces'. The Western Balkans, also covered in this volume, participate in the EU's Regional Cooperation Council which superseded the Stability Pact for South-Eastern Europe in 2008. Turkey has its own bilateral relationship with the EU and has had an AA since 1963. For reasons of space we have not looked at the operation of these in detail in this chapter but many of the problems of the external governance approach of the ENP also apply to these relationships.

PART II

Country/Area studies

4 Tatiana Romanova

Europeanisation and Russia

The process of Europeanisation is a familiar theme in Russia. It has long been a substantial component of Russian political and economic life. However, current Europeanisation – or rather EU-isation (Wallace, 2000) – is drastically different from past experience and, therefore, presents a challenge for Russia.

This chapter first summarises Russian literature on Europeanisation/EU-isation. It then turns to the past Europeanisation of Russia and contrasts it to the present processes of EU-isation. A distinction is drawn between normative and instrumental EU-isation. The following sections examine Russian policy towards EU-isation through these distinctions between Russia's past Europeanisation and present EU-isation, between instrumental and normative EU-isation. The chapter argues that Russia rejects normative EU-isation but pursues instrumental EU-isation, in line with Moscow's historical experience of Europeanisation. The final section demonstrates that in the shared neighbourhood.[1] Moscow challenges any independent EU-isation. Instead, it promotes Eurasian integration while encouraging instrumental EU-isation of the Eurasian Economic Union (EEU) and its members.

Europeanisation and EU-isation in the studies of Russia and Russia–EU relations

The term 'Europeanisation' has been in use in Russia for centuries. Most frequently, the term is associated with the reforms of Peter the Great at the beginning of the eighteenth century, intended to bring Russia closer to Europe through the top-down imposition of European practices. However, some studies indicate that Russian Europeanisation started in the fifteenth century (with the fall of Constantinople and Moscow acquiring the title of the 'third Rome') or even with the Christianisation of Russia in the ninth century (Chernikova, 2014; Morozov, 2009; Talina, 2014). Historians define this Europeanisation as 'the process of constant and targeted mastering and use of various Western European practices in Russia, which was gradually becoming a part of its internal life and was reflected in its international position' (Chernikova, 2014: 11). The term 'Europeanisation' is also ubiquitous in studies of Russian education reforms, resulting from the Bologna process and exchange programmes (Kostrigin, 2015; Lomakina, 2012; Molokova, 2013, 2014; Tregubova and Sitdikova, 2015). These studies, however, do not look at the role of the EU and frequently make use of the term 'Europeanisation' without defining it.

Chapter 1 examines in depth the literature on EU-isation which is defined here as 'the process of ideational, institutional and policy transformation within EU members and other European states whose major force emanates from the EU as a centre of political discourse ... directed towards the achievement of EU core values and political objectives' (Bretherton and Mannin, 2013: 15). Literature on Russia's EU-isation, however, is scarce. Most frequently, it is concluded that Russia is not a part of this process because EU-isation conflicts with the discourse of the Russian elite about their country, challenges sovereignty, and is viewed in Moscow as the EU's neo-imperialism (Kratochvíl, 2008; Medvedev, 2008; Schimmelfennig, 2015; Torbakov, 2013).

Russian studies of EU-isation are mostly limited to reviewing existing Western writings (Fadeeva, 2009; Gromoglasova, 2010; Latkina, 2013). Russian experts have no problem applying EU-isation to the EU's internal processes or its relations with the wider Mediterranean region (Betmakaev, 2014; Kornienko, 2013; Latkina, 2014; Polyvyannyi, 2015; Tischenko-Steblinskaya, 2013; Vinogradov, 2010). EU-isation has also been used to analyse the EU's policy in the shared neighbourhood (Bolgova, 2014; Devyatkov, 2006, 2011, 2012; Klimovich and Shirokanova, 2011; Strelkov, 2010, 2011). However, EU-isation is rarely applied to the study of EU–Russian relations. Partly it is the result of the poor attention to theory in Russian International Relations and European Studies, which remain mostly empirical and practice-oriented rather than theory-interested (Avdonin, 2006; Romanova, 2015a). The application of EU-isation to the regions above results from borrowing concepts and methods in the West. However, the lack of studies of Russia's EU-isation reflects a misfit between the processes of EU-isation and how Russians (irrespective of who is in the Kremlin) see themselves and their country in the world.

Some studies discuss a certain legal approximation between the EU and Russia. Novikov (2004), when discussing what parts of EU legislation Russia should copy, de facto develops a concept of limited EU-isation of Russia (without applying this term, however). Meloni (2008a, 2008b), who suggests a transformation of the concept of Europeanisation to incorporate Russia, concentrates on specific examples of successful EU-isation (competition policy, company law or consumer protection). Romanova (2012, 2014) describes convergence in various parts of energy legislation. Analysing changes in Russian law, Kalinichenko (2013: 5) talks about 'Europeanisation', which manifests itself in changes in overall Russian legal culture but also and particularly in modifications of various acts (see also Petrov and Kalinichenko, 2011). Studies of the Russian regions, which have aligned some practices with those of the EU, make use of the concept of Europeanisation (Gänzle and Müntel, 2011; Obydenkova, 2006; Yarovoy, 2010). Finally, both Bordachev (2007) and Vieira (2013) agree that selective EU-isation of Russia is still possible.

Is there a contradiction between overall denial of Russia's EU-isation and examples of its success? Studies of political ideas suggest identifying 'policy solutions, problem definitions, and public philosophies or zeitgeist' (Mehta, 2011: 1), moving from technicalities and instruments to a concept or paradigm. Vivien Schmidt (2008) similarly discussed policy solutions and programmatic ideas 'that define problems to be solved' and worldviews. Finally, studies of political convergence talk about three 'variables': 'the overarching goals that guide policy in a particular field, the techniques or policy instruments used to attain those goals, and the precise settings of these instruments' (Hall, 1993: 279). In other words, various levels of abstraction and aggregation can be discerned in the ideas.

These works help explain what seems to be a contradiction in the Russian attitude towards EU-isation. While the EU, through the processes of EU-isation, promotes its philosophy/worldview/paradigms, Russia at best is ready to agree with problem definitions/programmatic ideas/policy instruments, to use the terminology of three approaches above. In other words, Russia insists on picking and choosing instruments, which fit its own philosophy/worldview/policy paradigm and refers to its policy as pragmatic and interest-oriented. This process should be called 'instrumental EU-isation' in contrast to a deeper, normative EU-isation, which the EU insists upon.

Frank Schimmelfennig (2001) famously drew a distinction between 'thin' (rational) Europeanisation and 'thick' Europeanisation where affected parties naturally follow the solutions preferred by the EU. The distinction between instrumental and normative EU-isation overlaps with the distinction between thin and thick Europeanisation but is not identical to it. Thin Europeanisation does not mean that the EU's system of values is challenged or the EU's authority is rejected. Instead, behaviour is interest rather than identity driven. This can change over time towards a 'thicker' version. Instrumental EU-isation means picking and choosing aspects of EU-isation, some instruments and policy solutions, while belittling its paradigm and worldviews as flawed and not appropriate.

In what follows it is demonstrated that instrumental EU-isation is natural for Russia because it is akin to Russia's historical Europeanisation experience. It will then be explained how Russia belittles normative EU-isation and promotes instrumental EU-isation (in line with its historical past). As will be seen, the difference between instrumental and normative EU-isation is also crucial for the Russian attitude to the EU-isation of the shared neighbourhood.

Europeanisation vs. EU-isation

Russian historical Europeanisation differs from current EU-isation in at least four aspects. First, Europeanisation was historically a voluntary Russian exercise since Russia chose to import some features. There was no single external actor to promote it coherently as a system of views; rather it was a chaotic mix of borrowing from various countries, based on what various Russian representatives (primarily its Tsars but also elites) came across. Second, no authority questioned Russian European credentials, or made them conditional on fulfilling any requirements. Already in the eighteenth century, Russia was asserting that it belonged to Europe. Catherine the Great was the first to state that 'Russia is a European power' in her guidelines to a state commission in 1767–68 (see also Chernikova, 2014: 16). These statements, however, were addressed inside, not outside the country. They were to provide an orientation in internal debates where parts of the Russian elite challenged the need to adopt anything from Europe and argued for the preservation of Russian originality (Chernikova, 2014; Morozov, 2009). Third, although Europeanisation presupposed some borrowing of values, the attention was focused on techniques and ways of doing things. Hence, historians refer to it as 'surface Europeanisation' (Chernikova, 2014). Finally, Europeanisation was elite-driven and controlled from the top and did not lead to any fundamental change in the perspectives of society as a whole.

Current EU-isation is different. First, in contrast to the voluntary character of Europeanisation, EU-isation is driven by one political actor, the EU, which gives a subjectivity to this process. In other words, the EU presents itself as the key instigator of EU-isation and as a key controlling body for this process (including for countries which are not in the EU). The EU has integrated a set of political objectives in its basic treaties (Article 21 of TEU), inserted a reference to these values to its external agreements and checks whether they are being respected whenever it deepens relations. This is particularly the case with visa liberalisation, economic assistance and market access. Second, the EU has monopolised the notion of 'Europe', preventing Russia 'from taking part in Europe's most important affairs' (Lavrov, 2015). The EU reserves for itself the right to speak on behalf of Europe and to assess whether a country has achieved the necessary level of respect for human rights, democracy and the rule of law to be European. In undertaking this assessment and reserving for itself the role of the judge, the EU challenges not only Russia's European credentials but also its equality with major powers. Russia, for its part, opposes the EU's monopolising of the notion of Europe (see President of Russia, 2008). Third, EU-isation is conceived as a fundamental transformation in values and paradigms, not as a surface experience. It is for this reason that the EU insists on political changes as the foundation of any deep economic reforms. This was well manifested in EU-Russian debates on modernisation (Romanova and Pavlova, 2014). Finally, normative EU-isation presupposes wider civil society involvement. This is in contrast to instrumental EU-isation, which is elitist in that it requires the exposure only of people involved in the making and implementation of decisions. Russia, for its part, is sensitive to any external promotion of democracy and the rule of law on its territory which might undermine stability and is seen as intervention in internal affairs.

Throughout the 1990s Russia was mostly open to cooperation with the EU/the West on their terms (on the distinction between Europe and the West for Russia see Morozov, 2009). Being a true European was fashionable in the political elite which believed that the end of the Cold War was a shared victory for the East and the West. In this context, Russia and the EU signed a Partnership and Cooperation Agreement (PCA) in 1994, which inter alia presupposes Russian political and economic transformation with the assistance of the EU. It includes references to human rights, democracy and the rule of law – which Russia has to establish (with the help of the EU) – and provisions on copying EU rules (shown most clearly in Article 55 of the PCA).

However, while recognising the EU's experience in various fields of regulation, Russia has never agreed with the position of a weaker partner, unequal to the West. Multipolarity (and the denial of any unilateral prescribing of the world order) quickly returned to major speeches and documents (for example, President of the Russian Federation, 1998). The Russian Ministry of Foreign Affairs (MID) never liked the role of being a recipient of the processes of EU-isation. Diplomats started returning to Russian traditions after the change in Minister of Foreign Affairs in 1996. The Russian political elite also gradually became disillusioned with their position in the global arena. Moreover, NATO and the EU continued to enlarge, confirming Russia's fear of exclusion. The arrival of Vladimir Putin in the Kremlin in 2000 and Russia's economic revival, fed by oil market dynamics, finally facilitated a change of the rhetoric to a more critical attitude to EU-isation.

In sum, in the course of the 1990s Russia evolved from an initially optimistic attitude to EU-isation to a more critical one. This latter attitude is in line with Russia's historical experience of Europeanisation. Russia cannot deny the existence of the EU, which gives subjectivity to the concept of EU-isation. However, the present Russian position is predetermined by the four differences between Europeanisation and EU-isation described above. These are, first, the subjectivity that the EU gives to Europeanisation;

secondly, the EU's monopolisation of the notion of Europe; thirdly, Russia's insistence on an instrumental, surface approach in contrast to the EU's normative vision and, finally, Russia's elitist approach as opposed to the EU's wider civil society outreach. Therefore, the term 'instrumental EU-isation' is more adequate to describe the attitude of today's Russia. Its five pillars are examined in the next section.

Russia and EU-isation today: in defence of instrumental EU-isation

Russia's present policy towards EU-isation rests on five pillars which originate from the difference between historical Europeanisation and present day EU-isation. The first is a belittling of the EU. This is a result of the EU giving subjectivity to EU-isation and profiling itself as the ultimate authority. This belittling was institutionalised in 2011 when Russia published its first report on human rights in the EU. However, traces can also be identified previously in the critique of EU policy in the former Yugoslavia and Iraq, of secret prisons in Europe and of the rights of the Russian-speaking population in the Baltic countries. Thus, Russia first and foremost criticises the EU for not living up to its own norms and values (Ministry of Foreign Affairs [MID], 2011, 2012, 2013). This critique of the EU ranges from accusations of restrictions on the freedom of the press to the violation of economic rights and the rights of asylum seekers and prisoners (Romanova, 2016b).

A further way of Russia belittling the EU can be found in the prolific 'regrets' about the EU's numerous crises. Low growth, instability of the Eurozone and the decrease in social protection are the economic problems of the EU which are most often discussed. Russia criticises the EU for the inflow of migrants, which it provoked by interference in the internal affairs of several countries, and for the inability to curb terrorist activities within member states. The EU is lambasted for the betrayal of its values when making a deal on migrants with Turkey or not helping asylum seekers. Various apocalyptic scenarios linked to the collapse of the Schengen zone or 'Brexit' are elaborated in the mass media. Finally, the EU is accused of not being independent of the United States in its external relations, sacrificing its economic interests to promote the political interests of Washington. This strategy of belittling sends a message that the EU does not have any right to be the ultimate judge in deciding what is right or wrong. The message is that the EU is just one actor among many and that it should not promote its own solutions in a one-way direction (for example, Putin, 2013).

The second pillar of Russian policy towards EU-isation is the assertion that Russia is a part of Europe. This assertion was absent from the first foreign policy concept (MID, 1993) but made its way to key documents on foreign policy at the turn of the millennium. Citing Russian history and culture, the foreign policy concepts (President of Russia, 2008, 2013; President of the Russian Federation, 2000) assert that Russia is a part of Europe, one of the branches of this civilisation and on a par with Western Europe or the United States. Most recently, Sergei Lavrov, enumerating various events from 988 (the date of Russia's Christianisation), stressed 'Russia's special role in European and global history' rather than camping 'in Europe's backyard' or being 'Europe's political outsider' (Lavrov, 2016). It flows logically that Russia does not need any external recognition of its Europeanness and hence defies any normative EU-isation. Both the equality of Russia vis-à-vis the EU and its sovereignty, basic features of its foreign policy-thinking (President of Russia, 2008, 2013; President of the Russian Federation, 2000), are also guaranteed as a result.

The EU's and Russia's definition of Europeanness are different in temporal terms. The Russian view hinges on history and culture. Hence, the current leadership does not have to prove its credentials or to ensure that certain values are respected. The EU's definition, in contrast, places the responsibility of being European on the current leadership and civil society. They are expected to ensure that the values of democracy, rule of law and human rights are respected. To put it simply, as discussed in Chapter 1, Russia's historical definition defies the EU's more contemporary, values-based definition.

If the EU is not the ultimate authority and Russia is a European power and enjoys equality with the EU and other major powers, Moscow can advance its own set of norms and values and provide its own interpretations of good and bad. Thus, the third pillar of Russian policy on EU-isation is about demonstrating that Russia has its own worldview, public philosophy or policy paradigm. It is also yet another way to claim equality with the EU. Russian official discourse emphasises social and economic rights rather than individual political and civil human rights. The EU is criticised for cutting social benefits to stabilise the Euro. Russia also promotes group rights above those of the individual. This is illustrated in particular by the *Pussy Riot* case and by the prioritising of the interests of national security over the rights of the individual to confidentiality in their private life. The EU is criticised for its inability to deliver internal security. In Russia, democracy is viewed from the perspective of international rather than domestic politics. Thus, the West is criticised for promoting an undemocratic unipolar international system. The rule of law is interpreted as non-intervention in the domestic affairs of states. In providing these interpretations, Russia is neo-revisionist rather than revisionist (Sakwa, 2011). It does not challenge values as such, rather it undermines the authority of the EU to judge others and to unilaterally decide what is right and normal.

Russia also promotes some specific values. One is acting as a mediator in inter-civilisational dialogue – between Christianity, Islam and other religions and between various ethnic groups. Its experience springs from its geographical position as well as the multitude of different cultures on its territory. Another one is a set of conservative values, of which stability, and traditional family values are key. These are opposed to the EU's liberalism. Finally, Russia insists on the 'correct' interpretation of history which does not distort Russia's role, in particular the role of the Soviet Union in the Second World War. These values and the ability to promote them are essential not only for Russia's global position and for shielding it from normative EU-isation but also for internal identity-building. Not everybody in Russia shares this vision, however. Polls in 2016 revealed surprising consistency: support for the President was over 80 per cent with around 60 per cent of the Russian population having a negative attitude to the EU (Levada, 2016a, 2016b).

This challenge to the EU's normative authority is complemented, however, by an interest in certain achievements of the EU in the technical and regulatory field – referred to as 'modernisation', 'technical alignment' or 'new industrialisation'. In essence, it is instrumental EU-isation, a voluntary borrowing of various EU policy solutions, which fits the Russian policy paradigm, public philosophy or world view of today and at the same time helps solve specific problems. This is the fourth pillar of current Russian policy on EU-isation.

The launch of the 2005 roadmaps for the four EU–Russian common spaces (in particular, the economic one) intensified this instrumental borrowing. The 2010 Partnership for Modernisation further bolstered these activities. The work mostly took place in some twenty sectoral dialogues, bringing together EU and Russian officials but sometimes also business representatives. Dialogues were set up in various domains (energy, trade and investment, regulation of various products, environment, agriculture and many others) and varied a lot in their agenda, depth and intensity of work as well as their results. In particular, Russia and the EU achieved significant progress in aligning their legislation and technical regulations on energy efficiency and gas transit (Romanova, 2014), on competition policy, consumer protection, and company law (Meloni, 2008a, 2008b). Intensive cooperation also characterised dialogues on space and on telecommunication. There is also cooperation on standardisation, certification and accreditation between Russian Rosstandart (The Federal Agency for Technical Regulation and Metrology), the European Commission and CEN (European Committee for Standardisation).Various EU technical assistance programmes have supported this. Finally, various EEU bodies carefully study the EU's integration experience to detect successes and failures. In particular, the Eurasian Commission has been interested in establishing cooperation on statistics and various standardisation activities.

The process nearly came to a halt with reciprocal sanctions introduced in 2014 (Romanova, 2016b). Meetings of the various dialogues were suspended in early 2014. Where they did take place (in medicine, aerospace, energy, telecommunication), they were of an ad hoc nature and only dealt with issues that required immediate settlement (such as space-related activities, division of telecommunication frequencies, or certification of some medicines). Standardisation, certification and accreditation activities, on the other hand, have been maintained. It seems that they were kept afloat because they were financed through EU technical assistance programmes, which had a tight time schedule and could not be postponed. It reflected the practice of the late 1990s when the PCA and technical assistance were kept separate so that if there were a need to suspend the PCA, then additional lines of communication were kept open. Finally, the EU and the EEU also maintain contacts, although they are limited because the EU still does not officially recognise the EEU.

The final pillar of the Russian attitude to EU-isation concerns its limitation to the level of elites. It is a logical result of the surface, instrumental approach and denial of the need for normative convergence. It also follows the pattern, established by Russia's historical Europeanisation. Thus, Moscow supports contacts between officials at various transgovernmental levels. The Russian Permanent Mission to the EU is one of the biggest in Brussels. It is composed of representatives of various ministries, which allows the latter to maintain contacts with respective services of the Commission and other bodies. Numerous dialogues were set up to provide a venue for the interaction of officials from different ministries and bodies at different levels. However, officials involved in this interaction have limited competences due to the centralised Russian state system. Their room for manoeuvre is limited. Moreover, the MID is fully in control of the agenda and limits any concessions which might make Russia look unequal. Therefore, MID interventions frequently exclude sector-specific results. The MID also insists on the approximation of standards not on the basis of the EU's rules and norms but rather in the context of various international organisations like the UN Economic Commission for Europe or the International Maritime Organisation. This better ensures equality of status between the EU and Russia. Otherwise it is feared that instrumental EU-isation would lead to normative EU-isation of Russia, therefore constraining instrumental EU-isation and damaging Russian equality.

Moreover, Russia insists on the alignment of technical standards within a dialogue between the EU and the EEU, rather than between the EU and Russia. For many years Russia was envious of the EU's interplay between national and supranational levels. It believed that the EU 'plays' with various levels of governance for the purpose of extracting the best possible outcome of the negotiations (Sokolov, 2007). Currently, with the help of the EEU, Russia can replicate EU tactics thus ensuring equality. Furthermore, it is difficult to profess values and norms to the technocratic Eurasian Commission. Besides, the EEU remains a rather elitist project, little known in Russia or its other member states. Therefore, insistence on dialogue between the EU and the EEU can also be viewed as a way to limit EU-isation to the elite and to its instrumental version.

Similarly, in its transnational contacts Russia mostly favours business links being pragmatic, technical and interest-based. Russian interest in business contacts have intensified since sanctions were introduced in 2014. Moscow does not miss a chance to stress the losses that European business is incurring as a result of sanctions. The St Petersburg Economic Forum was turned into a Russian foreign policy event. However, the room for manoeuvre for business is limited due to the specificity of Russian capitalism with its significant role for the state and its oligarchic nature. Hence, the development of business links promotes instrumental EU-isation and sustains its elitist character.

At the same time, Russia is sensitive to any attempt by the EU to engage with Russian civil society. When the EU–Russian Civil Society Dialogue was set up, Russia reacted coldly. As EU–Russian relations grew tense, so did Russian policy regarding its own relations with non-governmental organisations (NGOs). Russian NGOs were subject to systematic inspections. All bodies that receive foreign finance were obliged to acquire the status of 'foreign agents' while the mass media started labelling them as 'the fifth column'. Most recently, Russia reacted forcefully to one of the five points of the new EU policy to Russia (European Union, 2016) which called for intensified cooperation at the level of civil society. The MID (2016) stressed that Russia had a mature civil society which fully supported Moscow's official 'independent' policy line, whereas the EU's efforts to engage civil society was characterised as 'a mere propaganda trick and doubletalk'.

Both the EU and Russia, in fact, stick to their logics in transnational contacts. Russia is interested in instrumental EU-isation. It promotes pragmatic contacts between officials and business representatives that limit EU-isation to elites. Freedom of manoeuvre of both civil servants and business is limited so their contacts are unlikely to provoke much normative EU-isation. However, this strategy certainly underestimates the potential for socialisation. The EU, for its part, is looking for systemic transformation, for normative EU-isation, and, therefore, targets civil society at large. However, the EU's sanctions limit the socialisation of officials and business. They lead to a rallying around the flag in Russia and to ostracising liberal NGOs. They also postpone visa liberalisation, thus constraining the interaction of civil societies. Sanctions present a challenge to both instrumental and normative EU-isation but the damage to normative EU-isation seems to be more substantial.

In sum, Russia's present policy towards EU-isation can be defined as instrumental EU-isation. It recognises the existence of the EU and its major influence on the process yet, in line with Russian historical Europeanisation experience, it is based on five pillars. These are: belittling the EU; the assertion that Russia is a European power; the promotion of an alternative policy paradigm, worldview or public philosophy through an alternative interpretation of key values; an interest in EU technical and instrumental solutions, which fit Russia's policy paradigm; and restriction of EU-isation to the elite, shielding wider civil society from it. This approach is certainly reflected in Russia's policy in the shared neighbourhood.

What does the Russian approach to EU-isation mean for the neighbours?

Although Russia engages in instrumental EU-isation, it remains critical of the same EU policy initiatives in the shared neighbourhood countries and counters them in various ways. Russian policy in the shared neighbourhood is conventionally observed as impeding EU-isation through either presenting alternatives (Casier, 2013; Hagemann, 2013) or making EU-isation changes costly (Ademmer and Börzel, 2013; Hagemann, 2013). Indeed, Moscow criticises any attempt by countries in the region to deepen their relations with the EU. It also uses various ways to discourage countries in the neighbourhood. For example, it increases prices for energy goods which were previously supplied at preferential, low prices. Supplies of energy goods can also be interrupted for the sake of the maintenance of pipelines or other technical reasons. Moscow can create various problems at the border or customs control. Various phyto-sanitary deficiencies have previously been found in the products of neighbourhood countries in question (wine, vegetables and fruit, milk or meat products). Therefore, in a similar vein to the EU, Moscow uses trade instruments to put its message across, although Brussels rarely uses coercion.

The strategy of moving to the sharing of the same standards (i.e. a technocratic solution) has never been given a chance. For example, trilateral discussions on the EU–Ukrainian Association Agreement and Russia's alignment with the EU's technical standards have been kept separate. While Russia accepts approximation to the EU's rules and standards for itself, the alignment of Ukrainian rules and standards to those of the EU present a problem for Moscow. It has even demanded a veto over the latter. The Russian Ministry of Economic Development raised concerns over the end of cooperation in production with Ukraine in some areas and also Russia facing the dumping of Ukrainian goods which could not meet EU standards and could not therefore be sold in Ukraine or the EU. Some Russian studies (see, for example, Vinokurov et al., 2015) have also demonstrated potential losses to the Ukrainian economy if the Association Agreement were applied. Moreover, participants in trilateral EU–Ukraine–Russian negotiations reveal that, on some occasions, working groups developed technical solutions to reconcile the positions of the EU, Ukraine and Russia but MID representatives promptly disavowed these provisional solutions. Clearly, the current Russian ruling political elite does not believe that EU-isation of the shared neighbourhood will be purely instrumental and is wary of the geopolitical consequences of any EU-isation. It also feels that even instrumental EU-isation broadens the options available to the shared neighbourhood countries, making them less predictable partners. However, Russia is not a unitary actor. Some of its business representatives support limited EU-isation in the neighbourhood (Langbein, 2013).

At the same time, Russia has been consistent in the distinction between instrumental and normative EU-isation in Eurasian integration. The EEU members have a shared history and culture. Experts have also speculated about the values' foundation in Eurasian integration. For example, 'the three Ds' – *dukhovnost* (spirituality), *derzhavnost* (strong statehood) and *demokratiya* (democracy) were suggested as the basis of this integration (Panarin, 2011). Yet, this integration has always been presented as non-ideological, technical and pragmatic. For example, Putin – in his key conceptual paper on Eurasian integration – argued for 'primarily trade and production links ... for transforming of integration into an understandable and attractive for citizens and business, sustainable and long-term project' (Putin, 2011). He then developed ideas of how attractive this project will be for business because of dynamic markets, based 'on single standards and requirements for goods and services, mostly unified with the European ones' (Putin, 2011).

Furthermore, Putin seems to accept that standards in both Russia and the shared neighbourhood countries will be unified with those of the EU in the process of the construction of a 'common European economic space' or a free trade area from Lisbon to Vladivostok. However, this alignment should take place between the EU and the Eurasian structures rather than between the EU and individual states directly. That would prevent integration from being modelled solely on the EU. Putin also justifies this approach by the necessity of maintaining 'the identity of nations in the historical Eurasian space in a new century and in a new world', to create 'an independent centre for global development, rather than remaining on the outskirts of Europe and Asia' (Putin, 2013). Thus, the EEU was set up as compatible with the EU but yet also as an independent entity, which should engage in instrumental EU-isation with Brussels for all its members but preserving its own overall normative paradigmatic uniqueness. Russian officials try to guide the process by referring their EU counterparts to the EEU institutions, although at present this is also a useful tactic for evading sanctions. It is also curious that, recently, some experts argued that the EEU should slow down contact with the EU because the EEU is not strong enough and ready for a balanced interaction with the EU. This only confirms Moscow's orientation towards instrumental compatibility but yet independence at the level of norms interaction with the EU.

In sum, in the shared neighbourhood Russia adopts a three-fold reaction to EU-isation. First, it counters any form of independent EU-isation of neighbourhood countries. Second, it promotes Eurasian integration in a technical, pragmatic and instrumental form. Third, instrumental EU-isation is a long-term goal for relations between the EU and the EEU. Its restriction to policy instruments is meant to guarantee that the EEU remains an independent centre in today's world, thus preserving its normative specificity.

Conclusion

This chapter has addressed two subtopics of this book: varying levels of Europeanisation and the geopolitical pull of interests, identity and values. It first looked at Russia's historical experience with Europeanisation and contrasted it with present EU-isation, identifying four differences between the two. These are: subjectivity, that is the EU-driven process of today vs the voluntary Europeanisation of the past; the challenge to Russia's European credentials today; Russia's preference for surface Europeanisation vs normative EU-isation; and elite-oriented Europeanisation vs wider civil society involvement in EU-isation. Furthermore, the chapter differentiated between normative and instrumental EU-isation, arguing that Russia challenges the former while adhering to the latter, because it is in line with Russia's historical experience.

The chapter then demonstrated that present Russian policy on EU-isation is based on the Russian historical experience of Europeanisation. First, Russia belittles the EU as a promoter of EU-isation. Second, Moscow reasserts its own European credentials, and, therefore, its equality. Third, Russia strives to provide alternative definitions to key European values, thus demonstrating that it has a different worldview, public philosophy and policy paradigm. Fourth, Russia insists on instrumental EU-isation and has successfully incorporated EU policy instruments in certain narrow fields. Although progress has been limited as a result of the 2014 sanctions, some cooperation on instrumental EU-isation has continued since then. Finally, institutionally Russia does its best to keep EU-isation elitist and limited, thus challenging all-embracing EU-isation, which emanates from Brussels and targets wider civil society.

This Russian strategy of selective, instrumental EU-isation, however, seems short-sighted. It ignores the fact that current Western forms of production require a particular societal ambience and legal environment based on the rule of law and democracy. Moreover, an entrepreneurial spirit presupposes respect for human rights and the rule of law. In sum, it seems highly unlikely that instrumental EU-isation can be sustainable and successful without eventual normative EU-isation. However, if Russia evolves in that direction it will do so in a bottom-up manner, from an instrumental approach to eventual normative EU-isation through gradual socialisation. This path will be difficult because of the patterns of historical Europeanisation. However, there is little alternative and, in policy terms, instrumental EU-isation should be promoted on both sides, even if initially it is limited to business and civil servants.

Finally, the distinction between instrumental and normative EU-isation has consequences for the shared neighbourhood. Here Russia has tried to limit any independent EU-isation of the countries in the region, promotes technical and pragmatic alignment in the EEU and argues for the eventual instrumental EU-isation of the EEU and its members. The strategy will remain in place in the medium term, but its long-term sustainability will depend on the EEU's ability to cope with the normative influence of the EU. However, the EU's present internal weaknesses, indeterminate future and economic and security risks, limit EU attractiveness and create a favourable short- to medium-term context for Russia's strategy in the region.

Note

1   This territory initially covered three European countries (Ukraine, Moldova and Belarus) and three Caucasian states (Georgia, Armenia and Azerbaijan). However, recent EU communication on new policy towards Russia (EU, 2016) makes clear that the EU intends to broaden its Neighbourhood/Eastern Partnership policy to include Central Asian states, which broadens the area of shared and contested neighbourhood to all post-Soviet states.

5 Nadiia Bureiko and Teodor Lucian Moga

'Bounded Europeanisation': the case of Ukraine

Since the proclamation of its independence, Ukraine has vacillated between the two competing centres of power gravitating around post-Soviet Eastern Europe: the Euro-Atlantic community and Russia. Both regional actors have developed political initiatives and cooperation frameworks meant to attract countries from their shared neighbourhood, perhaps the most contested of which was Ukraine. Since 2004, which saw the launch of the European Neighbourhood Policy (ENP), the European Union (EU) has envisaged a platform of deeper engagement with its Eastern neighbours. The multilateral policy instruments subsequently added – Eastern Partnership (EaP) and Black Sea Synergy (BSS) – have reiterated the EU's interest in the post-Soviet area and provided additional premises for closer cooperation. However, European actions have not kept Russia idle; the emergence of the Customs Union (2010), the Common Economic Space (2012) and, most recently, the Eurasian Economic Union (2015), have raised additional challenges for the EU's transformative power and complicated the internal and external political options for the states in-between. On top of that, the current conflict in Ukraine which sparked the most serious crisis between Russia and the West since the end of the Cold War has considerably impacted the sensitive positioning of Ukraine in the current *in-betweener* environment. Particularly after the annexation of Crimea, the rivalry between the two blocs has reached a critical state, as Russia lent its support to the pro-Russia rebellion in the Donbas region, and the Euro-Atlantic community backed up the newly elected pro-Western government in Kiev.

This chapter inquires whether the Europeanisation process in the case of Ukraine has been 'bounded' by a key factor, which we conceptualise under the term *in-between-ness*. By using a double analytical perspective – foreign and domestic – we argue that the country's *in-betweener* environment between the two poles of power – the EU and Russia – has been a decisive stumbling block to the Europeanisation process. As such, the external balancing act between West and East has not only been a primary cause of the country's inability to fully embrace the European path, but has also generated divergent political and societal views domestically.

The analytical design is based on mixed method research (Johnson and Christensen, 2014) which combines qualitative and quantitative instruments. As far as the qualitative approach is concerned, causal process tracing (Blatter and Haverland, 2012) is arguably the method which best allows us to study the mechanisms which have determined Ukraine's *in-between-ness*. From a quantitative perspective, this study explores and centralises the findings of the most recent three surveys conducted in Ukraine by the Razumkov Centre, the Ilko Kucheriv Democratic Initiatives Foundation and by the University of St Gallen.[1] These data are aimed at offering a clearer picture of the distribution of Ukrainians' perceptions and preferences which could further explain the complexities within the country. Our study also looks at the impact the 'idea of Europe' has had in Ukraine following the question-based approach developed by Olsen (2002: 922–923). Thus, we look at *what* has been changing with regard to people's perceptions over the past years, *how* the 'idea of Europe' has been received across the country and *why* (i.e. under which specific circumstances). Apart from these inquiries, we raise another question (*who*), which adds to the puzzle and offers us a broader view on the population groups and their representation across Ukraine's regions.

The first section of this chapter discusses how Europeanisation is being limited in the case of Ukraine by a constant perception of *in-between-ness*. The second section further explains the concept of *in-between-ness* and looks at how it has affected the political choices and societal preferences in Ukraine. The third section presents an overview of the current attitudes towards Europe and also shows how the current crisis in Ukraine has brought about a growing support for the EU across the country[2] that, in turn, could potentially contribute to a stronger Europeanisation pace. The final section summarises the findings and presents conclusions.

Europeanisation versus *in-between-ness*

Recent contributions to the European integration literature have increasingly paid attention to the spill-over effects the Europeanisation process carries beyond the EU's boundaries. By and large, Europeanisation outside the EU's current borders has limited impact on the neighbouring countries, as opposed to member states and candidates for EU membership. The lack of the EU's top incentive – the membership promise – is particularly detrimental to the EU's efforts to push for the development of democratic and market-oriented institutions. In the case of Ukraine, the EU's 'transformative power' has been seriously constrained by the lack of a membership perspective (Barbe et al., 2009; Bauer et al., 2007; Gawrich et al., 2010;

Melnykovska, 2008). For instance, significant parts of the elites resist reforms, which could threaten their vested interests, particularly when EU membership is not on offer (Kapitonenko, 2015: 2).

In the absence of the membership promise, the term 'neighbourhood Europeanisation' is employed to describe the relatively modest impact EU norms and rules have on the neighbouring states which usually takes place through a process of 'socialisation from the outside' (Schimmelfennig, 2003: 74). Schimmelfennig believes that 'socialisation comprises all EU efforts to "teach" EU policies – as well as the ideas and norms behind them – to outsiders, to persuade outsiders that these policies are appropriate and, as a consequence, to motivate them to adopt EU policies' (Schimmelfennig, 2012: 8). Likewise, socialisation implies a process of 'cultural hybridiza-tion', whereby close and continued contact between the EU and the neigh-bouring state sparks changes in the latter's preferences and identities (Dumka, 2013: 4). In the case of Ukraine, ENP Action Plans bilaterally agreed between Kiev and Brussels and based on 'joint ownership' – 'a core principle of the socialization mechanism of Europeanization' (Schimmelfen-nig, 2012: 19) – have incentivised the Ukrainian political establishment to open up the economy, to undertake internal reforms, and to take steps towards enhancing their democratic standards.

However, the effectiveness of the 'socialisation' mechanisms cannot be taken for granted (see Figure 5.1). Ukraine's *in-betweener* environment has meant that a wide range of complex external and internal factors and causes – the involvement of external powers, the Soviet legacy, the distribution of power among the elites and, more recently, the ongoing crisis in the Donbas region – have constantly precluded the process of embedding the EU's con-stitutive norms and practices into domestic institutions and discourses. Moreover, Ukraine's polarisation existing at the regional level has proved to be a strong impediment to reform.[3]

In-between-ness patterns in Ukraine – foreign and domestic

Ukraine has always been referred to as a country 'between Europe and Russia' not only in ordinary public discourse and media, but also by top officials and diplomats in both the European Union and Russia, as well as in Ukraine itself (Pulišová, 2012). Pachlovska (2009: 48) sees Ukraine as 'the centre of the global encounter between the West and the East, a place

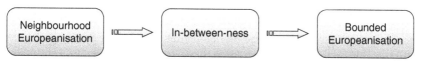

Figure 5.1 'Bounded' Europeanisation.

of conflicting, unfinished discourse between them, which continues to the present'. In the same vein, Wilson considers that

> Ukraine is neither as incontrovertibly 'other' nor as 'non-European' as many have seen it as being in the past; nor is it incontrovertibly 'European' as Ukrainian nationalists would have it in the present. Ukraine has always stood at a crossroads of cultural influences – at times a key part of a Europe that has itself been constantly redefined, at others not. (Wilson, 2009: xiii)

This acute status of *in-between-ness* carries, apart from geopolitical connotations, a pattern of cross-cultural blending and mixed-identity feelings. Such a characteristic reveals Ukraine as a country situated at the crossroads – a bridge between East and West (Zubrytska, 2009: 160), or simply *in-between*. According to Petersen (2008) the notion of *in-between-ness* refers to a geographical, political, cultural or economic area that has alternately served as a barrier or corridor, 'no-man's land' or vital buffer between empires, states and spheres of influence. 'Regions in-between serve both as economic gateways and borderlands, shifting from the dominance of one established power to another. They serve as "cultural bazaars" in which distinct traditions coexist and/or clash' (Petersen, 2008: 60). For this reason, countries placed in-between are constantly constrained by their geophysical location to adjust their internal and external political decisions according to the poles of power gravitating around them (Browning and Christou, 2010; Parker, 2008).

The hasty collapse of the Soviet Union and the swift move to independence meant for the newly established Ukrainian state a certain degree of 'self-searching'. Unlike the Central and Eastern European countries (CEECs of the former communist bloc which managed to embrace the European path, Ukraine has remained stuck between the two centres of power – the Euro-Atlantic world and Russia. Ukraine's geographic *in-between-ness* has also been translated into a political, societal and cultural one. For instance, a multi-faceted judgement employed at the decision-making level by the Ukrainian leadership has often fuelled an ambiguous foreign policy and a contrasting domestic behaviour. Internal societal cleavages, language concerns, different attitudes towards historical events and personalities, dissimilar distribution of votes during elections and the lack of clear consensus among elite vis-à-vis Ukraine's future political orientation have all been a constant source of anxiety.

However, the *in-between-ness* factor cannot be fully understood without taking into account the complex influences to which Ukraine has been subjected. Causal explanations for Ukraine's multi-vector thinking at the level of foreign policy trace back to Ukraine's early years of independence, just after the dissolution of the Soviet Union. According to Krushelnycky (2013), Ukrainian politics has often been a 'high-wire act with varying degrees of political acumen and cynicism, playing off the European Union's desire for a closer relationship against Moscow's efforts to bind the country into some form of Russian-led bloc'. After Ukraine proclaimed its independence in 1991, its official political line evolved into an active policy of engagement with the Euro-Atlantic structures. The 1993 Decree 'On the Main Directions of Ukraine's Foreign Policy' ranked the country's 'Western' political orientation among its top national priorities. The decree stated that 'in order to maintain stable relations with the EU, Ukraine shall conclude a Partnership and Cooperation Agreement, the implementation of which shall become the first step towards its association and, later, full membership in this organisation' (Verkhovna Rada, 1993). Concurrently, the strong political and economic ties with Russia meant also that the development of harmonious relations with its Eastern neighbour had to be considered. This laid bare that any engagement with 'Europe' would always have to be balanced by a concern for a healthy relationship with Russia and vice versa. Hence, from the early beginnings of its statehood, Ukraine has self-assigned itself a 'bridge' role:

> Opposing any territorial claims or attempts of interfering into its domestic affairs, Ukraine will undertake all measures to translate relations with Russia into good neighbourhood, mutual respect and partnership. Ukraine will direct its foreign policy efforts as such in order to become a reliable bridge between Russia and the Central Eastern European countries. (Verkhovna Rada, 1993)

Another causal process observation for the multi-faceted character of Ukraine's external policy corresponds to the year 1997 when both the Treaty on Friendship, Cooperation and Partnership (the 'Big Treaty') with Russia and the Charter on a Distinctive Relationship with NATO were signed, in the same year the first Ukraine–EU summit took place in Kiev. Such moves aimed at maintaining good relations with both regional centres of power but did not manage to alleviate the 'pendulum' pattern of the country's foreign policy strategy. On the contrary, by gravitating between West and East the country sought to maximise its geographic advantage in a pragmatic fashion by increasing its bargaining position. Accordingly, 'local leaders used the game of balance both to extract resources from Russia and the West alike, and to excuse their lack of reform. De facto, such policies meant that such countries preferred their room for manoeuvre and did not really want to join up with either Russia or the EU' (Wilson, 2014: 15).

Compelling evidence is further adduced to illustrate the country's permanent oscillation. For instance, in 2002, President Kuchma's address to Verkhovna Rada defined European integration as Ukraine's core project for the next decade. The rapid implementation of reforms in line with the EU's standards was ranked among the top strategic national priorities (President of Ukraine, 2002). In the same year, Ukraine also expressed its will to join NATO (Verkhovna Rada, 2002), whereas during the 2002 NATO summit in Prague the first Ukraine–NATO Action Plan was adopted. However, in 2004, the ratification by the Ukrainian Parliament of the Host Nation Support Agreement with NATO became a 'bone of contention' with Russia. Strong pressure from Moscow ultimately pushed Ukraine to accept participation in the Single Economic Space, a Russian-led economic framework.

An additional causal conjuncture traces back to 2004, in the aftermath of the Orange Revolution, when the ambiguous foreign policy approach took its first toll. Despite electing a pro-European leadership, Ukraine continuously experienced political crises. The then president Viktor Yushchenko was a staunch supporter of Ukraine's EU and NATO memberships and pushed for an intense dialogue with the Euro-Atlantic community. However, despite clear commitments, Ukraine's endeavours have been strewn with difficulties. NATO membership aspirations were abandoned when Yushchenko's successor, Viktor Yanukovych, announced in 2010 Ukraine's new non-bloc status.[4] The non-aligned role was determined by 'the external competition between Eurasianism and Euro-Atlanticism' and was meant to adjust Ukraine to increasing regional competition (Demenko, 2010: 310; Zlenko, 2012). As far as European integration prospects were concerned, reforms have been partially carried out, while references to Europe have been only selectively introduced in the domestic policy field (Melnykovska, 2008). According to Langbein and Wolczuk (2012: 870), the Ukrainian leadership engaged in a merely 'declarative Europeanisation' without ensuring the whole 'implementation chain'. Only in some cases, depending on circumstances – pro-reform trends, often in line with the EU demands – Europeanisation managed to spread unevenly across different segments of population and sections of the state apparatus, generating so-called 'enclaves of Europeanisation' (Wolczuk, 2007: 5).

The pressing question about the country's participation in a future regional alliance has never been fully clarified, arising again on eve of the November 2013 Eastern Partnership Summit in Vilnius. Signing the Association Agreement (AA) would have strongly anchored Ukraine to the EU putting an end to the country's multi-faceted approach. However, until the very last moment, the Ukrainian leadership sought to use the same strategy: despite edging closer to the EU, Viktor Yanukovych changed sides and refused to sign the AA, instead seeking financial assistance and closer ties with Russia. The unexpected withdrawal from the AA negotiations sparked off a wave of protests across the country. Everything culminated with the Euromaidan movement which led to the toppling of Yanukovych's regime and to the outburst of a set of sudden events, such as the annexation of Crimea and the war in the Donbas region.

Finally, in June 2014, in the midst of its internal crisis, Ukraine eventually signed the AA agreement pledging to launch a new set of political, economic and juridical reforms. Current president Petro Poroshenko announced that 'economic integration and political association with the EU is our [Ukrainian] understanding of successful development' (President of Ukraine, 2014a), whereas the AA represents the 'first yet very decisive step' towards Ukraine's membership of the EU (President of Ukraine, 2014b).

The constant process of 'eschewing choice' and maintaining a difficult balancing act between East and West has been equally transferred on the ground, from the foreign to the domestic level. Hence, the distribution of preferences for the country's foreign policy orientation mirrors a similar West–East clash. In February 2005, just after the Orange Revolution, preferences towards Ukraine's place in the existing regional configurations varied considerably: 67.3 per cent of the population in the West and only 18 per cent in the East manifested their support for enhanced cooperation with the EU. Concurrently, increased links with Russia were supported by 57.6 per cent of the population in the East and 9.7 per cent in the West. The distribution of preferences would not alter significantly until 2015. The conflict in Donbas meant increasing support for the EU both in the Western and the Eastern parts of Ukraine in 2015 and strongly declining support for cooperation with Russia (see Table 5.1).[5]

Generally, Ukrainian society still finds itself at odds with the future orientation of the country, whereby the divergent tendencies – pro-European West versus pro-Russian East – in terms of foreign policy preferences among the population remains invariable. For instance, Figure 5.2 points out a negative correlation between the preferences for deeper cooperation with the EU and the one with Russia: the higher the support for establishing stronger ties with the EU, the lower the support for increased cooperation with Russia becomes. The peak in this trend was reached in 2014 according to the latest survey undertaken by the Razumkov Centre.

Apart from divergent foreign policy options, other West–East polarising patterns exist at the domestic level. First, language is a strong indicator of West–East differences (see Table 5.2). The west of the country, geographically situated in the EU's proximity, is mainly Ukrainian-speaking and traditionally much more attached to 'Europe'. In the Eastern regions which

Table 5.1 Preferences for foreign policy direction of Ukraine. Regional parameters (%)

	West				East			
	2005	2008	2012	2015	2005	2008	2012	2015
Cooperation with the EU	67.3	65.5	70.1	82.6	18	21.5	11.9	35.8
Cooperation with Russia	9.7	93.1	7	0.5	57.6	58.1	60	25.9

Source: Authors' own representation according to data provided by sociological polls conducted by the Razumkov Centre (2005: 48; 2008; 2012; 2015a: 5).

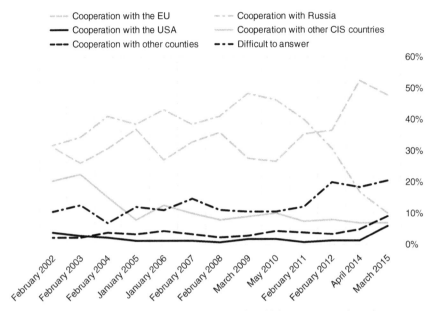

Figure 5.2 Which foreign policy direction should be a priority for Ukraine? (2002–15).

Table 5.2 Native language in Ukraine (%)

		Native Ukrainian	Native Russian	Both
		2013	2013	2013
Western regions	Ivano-Frankivs'k	98.9	0.6	0
	L'viv	96.1	1.8	1.5
	Ternopil'	97.9	0.7	0.7
Eastern regions	Donetsk	10.9	47.4	37.6
	Luhansk	4	53.6	34.8

Source: Authors' own representation according to data provided by the project 'Region, Nation and Beyond: An Interdisciplinary and Transcultural Reconceptualization of Ukraine' (University of St Gallen, 2013).

share the border with Russia, more people define Russian as their native language and are considerably more pro-Russian. Moreover, data from Tables 5.1 and 5.2 unveil an obvious correlation between the spoken languages across the territory of Ukraine and the foreign policy options favoured by the population. By and large, Ukrainian-speaking respondents manifest a strong attachment to the EU, whereas Russian-speakers favour increased cooperation with Russia and, generally, feel closer to their Eastern neighbour.

Second, another indicator of the internal *in-between-ness* revolves around divergent perceptions and interpretations of historical personalities and historical events.[6] In this case, the West–East divide is largely contingent on the historical past of different regions which make up the current territory of Ukraine. Such antagonistic views are obvious when analysing, for instance, the perception *vis-à-vis* two of the most controversial and often politicised historical figures – Vladimir Lenin and Stepan Bandera. While the first personifies the Soviet era, the latter is often associated with the Ukrainian movement for independence. The location and existence of monuments honouring the two are a strong indicator of societal dichotomies. In Western Ukraine, the majority of the population have managed to dissociate the country's past from Lenin's image whereas in the East these monuments still enjoy solid support. A similar split, this time reversed, is observed in the case of the monuments dedicated to Stepan Bandera (see Table 5.3).

West–East cleavages have also been fuelled by the authorities who have often sought to score political gains at the expense of the country's internal coherence. For instance, according to Wilson (2014: 49), one of Viktor Yushchenko's final acts – to make Stepan Bandera a Hero of Ukraine – 'was so provocative to voters in Eastern Ukraine, and so proactively timed in between the two rounds of voting [at Ukraine's 2010 presidential elections]'.

By the same token, regional gaps are also visible when observing the attitude towards important historical events. Thus, there is a clear distinction between Eastern and Western regions when assessing the attitudes *vis-à-vis* the main historical events since the country's independence: the collapse of the Soviet Union, Orange Revolution, Euromaidan and the signing of the AA (see Table 5.4). The aforementioned findings show how the West of the country is becoming almost entirely disconnected from its Soviet past,

Table 5.3 Positive attitude towards the monuments (%)

	Region (Oblast)	Monument to Stepan Bandera	Monument to Vladimir Lenin
Western regions	Ivano-Frankivs'k	85.6	0.6
	L'viv	87.7	2.2
	Ternopil'	75.8	0
Eastern regions	Donetsk	1.9	38
	Luhansk	1.4	45.7

Source: Authors' own representation according to data provided by the project 'Region, Nation and Beyond: An Interdisciplinary and Transcultural Reconceptualization of Ukraine' (University of St. Gallen, 2013).

Table 5.4 Positive attitude towards the historical events in the history of independent Ukraine (%)

Region (Oblast)	Collapse of the Soviet Union	Orange Revolution	Euromaidan	Association Agreement
Ivano-Frankivs'k, L'viv, Ternopil'	88	81.7	94.3	94.5
Donetsk	12.3	7.5	12.3	18
Kharkiv	31.3	29.6	36.3	33.6

Source: Authors' own representation according to data provided by Ilko Kucheriv Foundation (2015).

whereas Soviet times continue to appeal to Ukraine's East. For instance, the Ukrainian population from the East has not rated favourably the so-called 'national movements' during the Orange Revolution and Euromaidan.

Third, Ukraine's internal West–East dichotomies have also been reflected in the distribution of votes during elections. For instance, during the 2004 presidential elections, Eastern regions supported the pro-Russian candidate Viktor Yanukovych (93.5 per cent in Donetsk region, 91.2 per cent in Luhansk region), while Western regions gave their votes to the pro-European president Viktor Yushchenko (96 per cent in Ternopil' region, 95.7 per cent in Ivano-Fankivs'k region, 93.7 per cent in Lviv region) (Central Election Commission of Ukraine, 2004).

The internal societal cleavages were again exacerbated before and during national elections when the two camps of 'Westernizers' and 'Slavophiles' engaged in an ideological battle. According to Zhurzhenko (2002: 13), 'it is not language differences that create tensions and conflicts, but rather various political forces articulate these differences and formulate the positions of the language groups'. For instance, Viktor Yanukovych's rule relied heavily on a divisive internal identity narrative, constantly inflaming domestic divisions to win elections (Wilson, 2014: 60). The language controversies were

> first used by Yanukovych's people about Viktor Yushchenko in 2004, when both Russian and pro-Russian media branded the seemingly pro-Western Yushchenko a virtual Nazi. Nor was the 2004 campaign a one-off. It [Party of Regions] based its 2010 and 2012 campaigns on mythical threats to the Russian language. So the rhetoric about west Ukrainian 'fascists' came easily in 2014. (Wilson, 2014: 60)

Despite the West–East dichotomies inside Ukraine at the level of foreign policy preferences, spoken languages, historical past and distribution of votes, in 2013 self-identification as Ukrainian was present across all the country (albeit not entirely evenly distributed), both in the Western and Eastern regions (see Table 5.5) and was asserted by a plurality of citizens.

Table 5.5 Self-identification (%)

	Region (Oblast)	Ukrainian	Russian	European
Western regions	Ivano-Frankivs'k	95.3	0.5	51.6
	L'viv	94.6	2.3	59.4
	Ternopil'	96.4	1.2	60.2
Eastern regions	Donetsk	69.2	32.4	15.2
	Luhansk	77.8	15.5	20

Source: Authors' own representation according to data obtained from the project 'Region, Nation and Beyond: An Interdisciplinary and Transcultural Reconceptualization of Ukraine' (University of St Gallen, 2013).

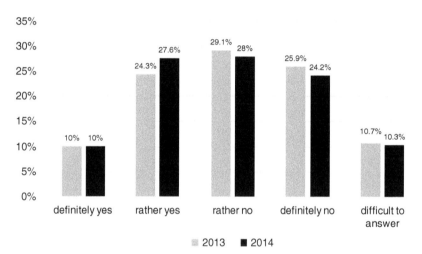

Figure 5.3 Do you consider yourself European?

European perceptions in times of crisis

As argued, Ukraine's persistent *in-between-ness* has generated mixed attitudes among the population towards 'Europe'. More than half of Ukraine does not perceive itself 'European', whereby 'European identity' is still a nascent notion across the country. In 2014, only 37.6 per cent of population manifested a clear attachment to European values, traditionally more in the West (59 per cent) than in the East (28.5 per cent) (Ilko Kucheriv Foundation, 2014a; Ilko Kucheriv Foundation, 2014b; Razumkov Centre, 2014). However, the percentage is constantly growing, according to the latest surveys. Since 2008 the dynamic has been positive and constantly rising from 25 per cent in 2008 to 38 per cent in 2014 (Ilko Kucheriv Foundation, 2014a; Ilko Kucheriv Foundation, 2014b) (see Figure 5.3).

Particularly when perceived as a driver for enhanced democracy, improved transparency, human rights and reforms, the 'idea of Europe' acquires strong legitimacy in the eyes of Ukrainians. Thus, apart from the level of financial welfare (58.8 per cent), a 'European feeling' among Ukrainians is primarily being stirred by the level of law protection (40.5 per cent), the respect for democratic values and human rights (32.4 per cent), the possibility of travel to Europe without a visa (24.5 per cent), the level of liberties (15.2 per cent) and by the existence of free and democratic elections (14.6 per cent) (Razumkov Centre, 2013a).

In general, the AA between Ukraine and the EU has been positively rated by Ukrainians as a compulsory tool for fostering improved transparency, human rights and reforms. Besides bringing about economic development (52.5 per cent), Ukrainians consider the AA an effective framework for democracy improvement (51.9 per cent), enhanced education services, science and technologies (51.4 per cent) (Razumkov Centre, 2013b).

The younger generation (aged 18–29) is by far the most pro-European group followed closely by the 30–39 and 40–49 age groups (Ilko Kucheriv Foundation 2014b). These groups actively support the country's European integration efforts. The older generation (aged 60 and over) exhibit a lower attachment to a 'European' identity (see Figure 5.4). Collected data also

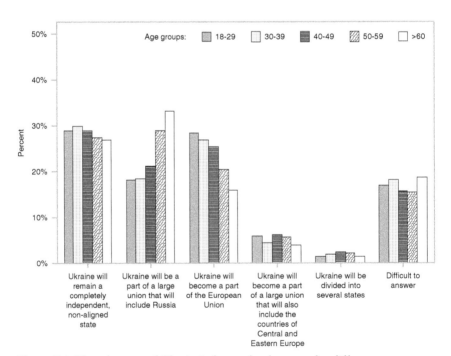

Figure 5.4 The relevance of Ukraine's future development for different age groups.

shows that a strong sense of 'European belonging' is particularly manifested by those who have previously studied abroad at least for a short period of time. Well-educated people, eager to travel more often and to practise more than one language, also belong to the pro-European group (see Figure 5.5). The inserted data points to the fact that the idea of shared European values, principles and norms is becoming increasingly more appealing to Ukrainians. This growing pro-European stance has been even further amplified by the country's current turmoil from the Donbas region which made Ukraine even more resolute in seeking to strengthen its relationship with the EU.[7]

Conclusion

This chapter has inquired whether Ukraine's *in-between-ness* has been one of the salient factors hindering the diffusion of the Europeanisation process.

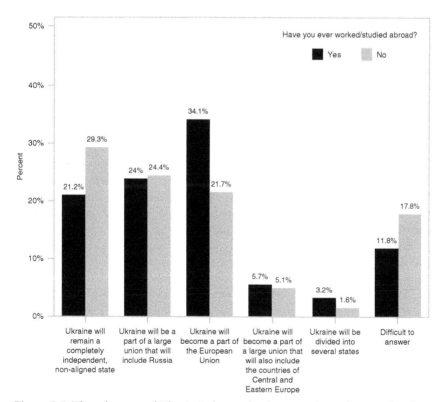

Figure 5.5 The relevance of Ukraine's future development depending on the place of study/work.

Thus, we have argued that, despite being amenable towards the EU, the country's *in-betweener* environment coupled with its multiple intrinsic contradictions have all been primary causes for Ukraine's inability to fully embrace the European path. Caught between two poles of power –the EU and Russia – Ukraine has since early 1990s experienced a permanent West–East vacillation reflected both externally and internally.

First, in terms of foreign policy, the difficult strategic balancing between East and West continuously undertaken by the Ukrainian leadership has hampered the country's European integration perspective. The main trend in the Ukrainian political system has always presupposed a multi-faceted judgement which led to internal quarrels among key political figures, numerous confrontations between political elites and the population and diplomatic rows between the Ukrainian leadership and outside powers. Naturally, the relationship between the EU and Ukraine has undergone a series of ebbs and flows which made Ukraine's European future look uncertain.

Second, Ukraine's fragmented and complex realities existing in the domestic realm have complicated the path towards European integration. According to our findings, in Ukraine there are clear regional cleavages in public attitudes towards language preferences, historical events, ideological stereotypes, voting habits and, ultimately, European integration. Moreover, the lack of public consensus has made the manipulation of public opinion possible and allowed certain political forces to question the 'idea of Europe' with huge social implications: the Euromaidan movement can be seen as a culmination of a wave of dissatisfaction with the then Ukrainian leadership which finally ousted Yanukovych's regime.

The overall conclusion is that Ukraine has not yet managed to reconcile all its internal views to undertake a fully fledged Europeanisation endeavour. Still, the EU's approach towards Ukraine also has not proved to be fully fitted to the specific particularities of its Eastern neighbour which ultimately questions the efficacy of the EU's transformative power. Several other questions thus remain *vis-à-vis* the consistency, resilience and effectiveness of the Europeanisation strategy not only towards the specific case of Ukraine, but also towards other *in-betweeners* (Moldova, Belarus and South Caucasus states). Even if such strategy exists, it remains disputed whether the neighbourhood Europeanisation process can be considered a driving force to overcome the countries' *in-between-ness* in the absence of a fully fledged EU membership promise. As shown in the latest polls, pro-European feeling has been on the rise in Ukraine and it is likely to remain so, bearing in mind that the ongoing conflict with Russia has not only created a stronger sense of nationhood but also committed Ukrainians to taking the country forward on the European path. Hence, future debates on the kind of institutional set-up between the EU and Ukraine capable of tackling the internal divides and ensuring the country's stability are to be welcomed.

Notes

1 Razumkov Centre is a non-governmental think tank founded in 1994 which carries out independent research of public policy in the following spheres: domestic policy; state administration; economic policy; energy; land relations; foreign policy; social policy; international and regional security; national security and defence. The Ilko Kucheriv Democratic Initiatives Foundation is a non-governmental think tank founded in 1992 which focuses its activities on developing reasonable recommendations in the sphere of democratic transformations and Ukraine's European integration for decision makers and civil society representatives. The surveys undertaken in 2013 and 2015 are part of the international project entitled 'Region, Nation and Beyond: An Interdisciplinary and Transcultural Reconceptualization of Ukraine' coordinated by the University of St Gallen, Switzerland.

2 With the notable exception of the Donbas region.

3 The regional differences between East and West are usually depicted by using a demarcation line which cuts across the country, alongside the Dnieper River. This dichotomy West–East (pro-European versus pro-Russian) has been constructed upon language and historical arguments. However, the authors do not share Riabchuk's opinion about the existence of 'two Ukraines' (Riabchuk, 2003). The West–East demarcation line recognises only the diversity within the Ukrainian nation and claims the need to study the peculiarities of each region individually (Hrytsak, 2002).

4 The political controversy over NATO membership ended in 2010 during the first year of Viktor Yanukovych's presidency when the newly adopted Law of Ukraine 'On the Foundations of Internal and Foreign Policy' confirmed Ukraine's non-bloc status. NATO membership was excluded from Ukraine's foreign policy agenda (Verkhovna Rada, 2010). The issue had hardly been a matter for political and academic discussion before the annexation of Crimea and the war in Donbas.

5 The results for Donbas region do not vary significantly from those obtained in the other Eastern regions (35 per cent of respondents support cooperation with the EU as a foreign policy priority for Ukraine while 21.1 per cent support cooperation with Russia).

6 Different territories of today's Ukraine have been under Austro-Hungarian, Ottoman and Russian/Soviet rule which logically generated different interpretations of the past.

7 However, the attachment to 'Europe' in Donetsk and Luhansk regions remains rather low as well as self-identification as Europeans (see Table 5.5).

6 Kiryl Kascian

Belarus: does Europeanisation require a geopolitical choice?

In October 2015 a predictable presidential election took place in Belarus. Following the results of this election, the European Union suspended and subsequently lifted sanctions against high-ranking Belarusian officials despite the lack of substantial domestic changes in the country. Moreover, Belarus remains the only country of the EU's Eastern Neighbourhood free from any kind of ethnic or territorial conflict. In view of this, the study of the nature of Belarus–EU relations is of particular significance. Belarus and the EU have differing perspectives on the relationship. In the case of Belarus, its authorities stress economic factors at the expense of the political dimension. In the case of the EU, despite recent concessions to the Belarusian authorities, the Union has not renounced its critical engagement policy towards the country. Thus, this chapter aims to understand the positions of both Minsk and Brussels in their search for an effective framework of bilateral cooperation which would also take into account the geopolitical configurations in the region. To understand the current situation of bilateral Belarus–EU relations, the chapter addresses the history and framework of these relations, the geopolitical situation in the region, as well as views on these relations from Minsk and Brussels. Equally significant are the perspectives of the Eastern Partnership (EaP; see Chapter 3) region's development within a wider geopolitical context. Thus, the chapter addresses the role of Russia and the 'Russian world' concept promoted by its authorities, as well as the impact of the Ukrainian conflict on the situation in Belarus. The conclusion focuses on the mechanisms which could contribute to mutual Belarus–EU engagement within existing windows of opportunity.

Belarus's geopolitical background

Contemporary Belarus is often perceived through its geographical location between the European Union and Russia, being treated merely as an object for geopolitical competition between these two 'centers of gravity in Europe'

(Ioffe, 2012a). There are two core elements which are claimed to explain Belarus' alliances. The first is the nation's Soviet legacy, which includes an alleged 'backward[ness] in terms of national and civic identity' and wide distribution of the Russian language among Belarusians (Potocki 2002: 145–146). Following this logic, some analysts conclude that Belarus is a bi-national Belarusian-Russian state (Kuzio, 1998), while others argue that 'after more than twenty years of statehood, Belarusians have not developed a distinctive national identity' (Ioffe, 2012a). The second element is the nation's domestic political system, firmly linked with the personality of the President Aliaksandr Lukashenka and encapsulated in the formula 'Belarus, Europe's last dictatorship' (Wilson, 2011). Out of six Eastern Partnership countries, Belarus is characterised by the lowest degree of engagement with the EU. At the same time, it has the highest level of participation in Russian-led integration projects, including the Treaty on Eurasian Economic Union and the Common Security Treaty Organization. However, this engagement in Russian-driven integration projects reflects Belarus's rational economic interests rather than the alleged 'cultural preconditions' emphasised by some commentators (Kascian 2014: 3). Furthermore, after the seizure of Ukraine's Crimean peninsula by Russia in March 2014, Belarus became the only Eastern Partnership country not involved in any inter-ethnic or territorial conflict.

The present state of bilateral Belarus–EU relations is closely connected with the policies of President Lukashenka and with the EU's reactions to these policies. Political relations between Belarus and the EU were frozen in 1997, while their possible resumption was conditional upon the Belarusian authorities' willingness to eliminate the existing deficit of the rule of law and democracy (European External Action Service, n.d.). This has contributed to the current deadlock in Belarus–EU relations, which can be best described as short term and ad hoc (Kascian, 2014).

The essence of this deadlock is seen in the difference between the *Realpolik*-dominated attitude of the Belarus authorities and the values-based EU approach towards the political regime in Minsk. The logic behind the Belarusian authorities' position is aimed at eliminating the issues of democracy and human rights from bilateral relations and replacing them with 'an open, sincere and equal dialogue with the European Union', although without seeking EU membership (Belarusian Telegraph Agency, 2014; Official website of the Republic of Belarus, 2014).

Two elements should be taken into account with regard to the framework of Belarus–EU relations. The first is related to the formal configuration of this framework, that is, the platforms for and rules of these relations. The second includes the political dimension of bilateral relations and largely displays the dynamic developments occurring in the international arena. These two elements are interconnected. However, the political dimension is subordinate to the formal one.

From the formal point of view, Belarus–EU relations are related to the country's participation in the EaP track of the European Neighbourhood Policy. Therefore, a number of default country-specific aspects in the existing formal framework of Belarus–EU relations should be taken into account. First, Belarus participates only in the multilateral track of the EaP (European External Action Service, n.d.). Second, the country's perspectives within the EaP formal framework can be assessed through the international alliances of Belarus, primarily the country's observer status at the World Trade Organization and its fully fledged membership in the Russian-driven Eurasian Economic Union. Neither of these alliances meets the formal threshold required for starting Association Agreement negotiations with the EU in general, and its Deep and Comprehensive Free Trade Area part in particular (European Commission, 2014b; see Chapter 3). Consequently, from the formal EU perspective Belarus can be regarded as an outsider of the EaP. This formal outsider status within the EaP is inseparable from the political context of Belarus–EU bilateral relations, particularly the character of the country's political regime. Since relations are bilateral, it is necessary to address the logic behind both Brussels' and Minsk's points of view.

The view from Brussels: formalised critical engagement

The first peculiarity in the case of Belarus is that it is the only EaP country which lacks its own Partnership and Cooperation Agreement (PCA) with the EU (European Commission, 2014b). Unlike the other five EaP countries which signed their PCAs in the second half of the 1990s, '[r]atification of an EU–Belarus Partnership and Cooperation Agreement (negotiated in 1995) has been frozen since 1997 in response to the political situation in the country' (European External Action Service, n.d.). Consequently, the problems with democracy and the rule of law, restrictions on political opposition, civil society and the media, violations of human rights and electoral standards, as well as the existence of political prisoners in Belarus have become concerns which the EU has regularly been addressing in its relations with Belarus (European External Action Service, n.d.). This approach is designated by the EU as a policy of critical engagement and determines the contents of the Conclusions of the Foreign Affairs Council adopted on 15 October 2012, which delineates the current stance of the relations between Belarus and the EU. Hence, the full reactivation of bilateral Belarus-EU – relations has been conditional on the readiness of the Belarus authorities to rectify the political shortcomings mentioned above. The EU has therefore maintained its values-based threshold, which determines the conditions which Lukashenka's regime should meet to resume the bilateral dimension of Belarus-EU relations.

The Czech EU Presidency Programme (2009) clearly stated that Belarus's participation in the EaP and the attendance at the EaP opening summit in Prague by the Belarusian officials was conditional on the steps taken by the government in Minsk. As a result of these measures by the Belarusian authorities, the EU expected step-by-step improvements in bilateral relations through the enhancement of mutual rapprochement in political and social matters. In the political dimension, Brussels counted on establishing a momentum for a more assertive dialogue with Belarus. The social dimension focused on the support of Belarus's civil society (Czech EU Presidency, 2009). In all circumstances, 'the inclusion of Belarus into the EaP framework can be seen as a breakthrough, as it opened the way for the institutionalisation of relations, at least at multilateral level' (Vasilevich, 2014).

This reference to the Czech EU Presidency Programme serves to illustrate the development of the EaP in general and Belarus–EU relations in particular. Contextual analysis of the EU Presidency Programmes and the 18-month programmes of the Council of the European Union provides a picture of the consistency of EU policies toward all six EaP members at both bilateral and multilateral levels.

For example, the 18-month Programme of the French, Czech and Swedish Presidencies applies the above-mentioned principle of political conditionality towards Belarus and confirms the possibility of re-launching fully fledged relations with Belarus within the EaP framework if 'the political situation in Belarus significantly improves' (Council of the European Union, 2008). Thus, while the political dimension of Belarus–EU bilateral relations does affect their intensity it has no impact on their format.

The three subsequent 18-month Trio programmes underline the significance of EU–EaP cooperation with regard to customs and list all the partner countries, including Belarus (Council of the European Union, 2009; Council of the European Union, 2011; Council of the European Union, 2012). At the same time, however, the 18-month Programme of the Italian, Latvian and Luxembourg presidencies does not contain any reference to Belarus, so remains the only EaP country not specifically mentioned in the document. The only other reference to Belarus can be found in the 18-month Programme of the Irish, Lithuanian and Greek Trio. It stipulates that the EU's High Representative (HR) and the European External Action Service 'will closely monitor domestic developments in … Belarus, in the wake of the parliamentary elections in th[is] countr[y]' (Council of the European Union, 2012). This formulation largely corroborates the principles of EU critical engagement policies towards Belarus. Moreover, it is therefore consistent with the idea that the EU; 'stands ready to improve and deepen its relations with Belarus', and 'remains prepared to assist Belarus in democratisation and modernisation' upon significant improvement of the political situation in the country (EU delegation to Belarus, n.d.).

In addition to the inaugural Czech EU Presidency Programme, the only two individual EU programmes that specifically list Belarus are those of Sweden and Poland, the initiators of the EaP. In the case of the Swedish EU Presidency, Belarus is mentioned within the context of EU foreign relations aimed at increasing the level of EU–EaP relations and supporting 'these countries' integration with the EU in important areas such as trade, migration and legislation' (Swedish EU Presidency, 2009). The Polish EU Presidency Programme (2011) affirms that it would seek to encourage Belarus to cooperate with the West, provided that the country observes principles of human rights and democracy. The latter wording includes two elements. First, it confirms the significance of EU rapprochement with Belarus. Second, it establishes its own framework for this rapprochement which, in essence, is based on EU values. This framework therefore creates a threshold which Belarusian officials should reach if they strive to activate the bilateral dimension of the country's relations with the EU.

Furthermore, the EU acknowledges that Belarus is 'an integral part of the European heritage and the European community of nations' (EU delegation to Belarus, n.d.). However, membership of the Union – even in the very long-term perspective, has never been a subject of discussion. In a situation where political cooperation is still limited, mutual Belarus–EU engagement can still focus on the social and economic dimensions, including regional and sectoral cooperation. Although politics may negatively affect the *intensity* of mutual social and economic cooperation, these two dimensions of Belarus–EU relations function rather independently from politics.

The EU is Belarus's 'principal partner in trade and [an] important partner in sectoral and regional development' (EU delegation to Belarus, n.d.). For instance, since the mid-2000s over 150 EU projects have been successfully accomplished in Belarus. Following the European Commission's assessment, many of them continued. As of 2014, fifty-nine projects were under way. Local and regional-focused endeavours proved to be the most successful. These initiatives fell inter alia within the scope of the Comprehensive Institution Building (CIB) initiative, the Cross-Border Cooperation (CBC), BELMED (International accreditation of testing laboratories for medical products and support to healthcare in Belarus), and RELOAD-2 (Support to regional and local development in Belarus) programmes (Korosteleva, 2014). At the same time, the current Multi-annual Indicative Programme for EU support to Belarus (2014–17) determines three primary sectors of EU intervention which include social inclusion, environment, as well as local/regional economic development.

Taking into account the vision of Belarus–EU bilateral relations in Minsk, the economic, and subsequently social, spheres could maintain a common ground for mutual rapprochement and simultaneously serve as a channel for implementing EU standards and values in the country. As a result, this practice-oriented, more inclusive, sector-driven and targeted democracy promotion embodied in numerous small and mid-scale projects may seem a more effective tool for democracy promotion feasibly bringing new norms and practices into the daily life of Belarusian society (Korosteleva, 2014).

The view from Minsk: the appeal to a wider Europe

The authorities in Minsk see bilateral relations with the EU from a somewhat different perspective. The Belarusian Foreign Ministry sees the European Union and Russia as the country's two big neighbours. Belarus is presented as the EU's 'reliable partner' in the spheres of crime control, energy safety, human trafficking and security. Moreover, the Belarusian Foreign Ministry underlines the need for extended cooperation with the EU in the economic sphere, environmental issues and contacts between people. In this regard, the EaP is viewed as one of the platforms for the maintenance of Belarus–EU 'equitable dialogue and comprehensive cooperation' (Belarusian Ministry of Foreign Affairs, n.d.).

Emphasis on the equitable character of the partnership with the EU is the keynote aspect stressed by Belarusian officials since the first years of the Eastern Partnership. For instance, Siarhei Martynau, the then Belarus Foreign Minister, in his article for *Baltic Rim Economies* (2010) stressed the need to ensure freedom of choice between equitable partnership with the EU and integration into it, so that each partner country should enjoy 'equal access to all Partnership benefits' regardless of their choice. Thus, Minsk perceives the Eastern Partnership platform as 'a result-oriented cooperation framework, based on common democratic values' which 'should serve pragmatic interests of all partner states and the wider Europe in general by fostering sustainable development, economic and social modernisation in this part of the continent' (Martynau, 2010).

Uladzimir Makei, who currently holds the post of Belarus's Foreign Minister, has repeated the argument of his predecessor and emphasises that Belarus seeks 'an open, sincere and equal dialogue with the European Union' (Belarusian Telegraph Agency, 2014). Additionally, he urges 'a dialogue whenever it is possible and beneficial for Belarus and the European Union' so that Belarus will not seek EU membership and both parties could maintain 'a long-term cooperation strategy' (Belarusian Telegraph Agency, 2014; Official website of the Republic of Belarus, 2014).

The Belarusian authorities are 'attempting to "de-politicize" Belarus's bilateral relations with the EU [...] thus ignoring the EU's conditioning of normalisation of relations to the prior release and rehabilitation of political prisoners' (Vasilevich, 2014). Additionally, the official Minsk position uses the notion of a 'Wider Europe' which rather demonstrates its intention to 'secure a balanced and mutually beneficial cooperation with both Russia and the European Union' (Belarusian Ministry of Foreign Affairs, n.d.) and includes Russia within Belarus–EU relations. The reference to the Russian factor and the appeal to the equitable partnership with the EU mean that the Belarusian authorities do not favour making a geopolitical choice between the EU and Russia as designated by the EaP formal framework. Thus, to Belarus the engagement with the EU is largely an attempt to recast the existing cooperation framework by detaching from EU political conditionality and exploiting the economic and social dimensions of these relations. This focus could be explained as an attempt to diversify the country's economy and to some extent lessen Belarus's dependence on Russian markets and resources.

Belarus and the EU: clash of multiple approaches?

Although both Brussels and Minsk acknowledge the importance of Belarus–EU relations and the potential scenarios for their improvement and further development, the views of each party are based on different foundations which results in a clash of approaches. The formalised EU approach is embodied in the EaP framework and appeals to EU values which determine the EU's critical engagement policies towards Minsk. To put it succinctly, in order to become a fully fledged beneficiary of the EU-designed EaP framework, Belarus must show considerable progress in implementing human rights and democracy standards in the country. This process is about applying EU-designed values, standards and frameworks in determining the nature of bilateral Belarus–EU relations. It is already being pursued in the form of numerous practice-oriented and sector-driven EU projects in the country. Therefore, the settings of Belarus's "Europeanisation à la Brussels" represent a kind of EU-isation process, but without a membership perspective, even in the long term.

In their relations with the EU, the authorities in Minsk largely strive 'to force the EU to swap a values-based approach for a more pragmatic *Realpolitik*-based one' (Vasilevich, 2014). The core element of this approach is the removal of the political aspect of bilateral relations. Moreover, the freedom to choose the type of engagement with the EU combined with the possibility of using all EaP benefits regardless of the option chosen, means that the Belarusian authorities reject the 'more-for-more' principle which is central to the ENP approach (see Chapter 3).

Within these two aforementioned approaches towards Belarus–EU relations, the Russian factor should be considered. On the one hand, Brussels underlines that '[i]t is the sole right of the EU and its partners to decide how they want to proceed in their relations' (European Commission, 2015). On the other hand, Belarus is a party to multiple Russian-led post-Soviet alliances. Thus, the perspective of the Belarusian authorities could be characterised as twofold. First, Minsk strives to abstain from making the 'either/

or' choice between integration with the European Union or Russia. Second, while the partnership with Russia is prioritised, Belarus seeks to keep in-depth, mutually beneficial and pragmatic relations with the EU.

For the EU, the depth of bilateral relations is conditional on the political situation in Belarus, which requires the Union's ability to react efficiently, exactly and promptly in case of potential changes in Belarus. At the same time, the contents of the individual EU Presidency Programmes and 18-month Trio Programmes reveal three tendencies. First, Belarus has never been a prioritised central member of the EaP initiative. Second, the EU's critical engagement strategy towards Belarus essentially cannot serve as a long-term approach. Third, the European Dialogue on Modernisation cannot take this role either. Its focus is an 'understanding on the vision of what a modern and democratic Belarus could look like and about what would be needed to take us there'[1] (EU delegation to Belarus, 2012). At the same time, this multi-stakeholder Belarus-related platform cannot predict the development and intensity of the possible changes in the country. Additionally, despite the importance of the involvement of Belarus's political opposition and civil society, state actors are largely unwilling to take part in this process (National Platform of the Eastern Partnership Civil Society Forum, 2013).

References to the individual EU Presidency Programmes and 18-month Trio Programmes confirm the peripheral nature of the current status of Belarus in the EaP. Moreover, the contents of these documents reveal the ineffectiveness of the critical engagement policy instrument in mid- and long-term perspectives. For instance, the 2013 Vilnius EaP Summit was viewed by its participants as 'a defining moment in the EU's relationship with Eastern European partners' (Joint Declaration of the Eastern Partnership Summit, 2013). Nevertheless, Belarus was the only EaP country which was not mentioned in the Lithuanian Presidency of the Council of the European Union. The same 'exceptional status' of Belarus can be observed in the cases of the 18-month Programme of the Italian, Latvian and Luxembourg presidencies and particularly the Latvian EU Presidency which hosted the 2015 Riga EaP Summit. This situation demonstrates that the EU had neither developed a strategy toward Belarus, nor expected anything significant from its authorities.

There are three outcomes to this situation. First, both Belarus and the EU seemingly got used to the present balance in the bilateral relations. Second, the EU deems not to have a well-grounded and comprehensive long-term strategy towards Belarus. Third, the EaP is viewed as a platform 'based on shared values such as democracy, the rule of law, respect for human rights and basic freedoms' (EU delegation to Azerbaijan, n.d.). However, if the EU renounces its critical engagement approach towards Belarus, it would mean its moral defeat regardless of the current domestic and international Belarus-related political configurations. As a result, the

EU's capacity to manoeuvre as a regional player could be considerably reduced. The Ukrainian crisis and its projection to the Belarusian case could serve as an illustration of this limited EU impact.

Windows of opportunity vs ultimate choice

Ukraine's association with the EU is often interpreted as the country's geopolitical and civilisational choice in favour of Europe. This framework of choice has three important consequences. First, this interpretation largely echoes Huntington's (1996) concept of civilisations' clash in which Ukrainian elites 'gravitate toward civilizational magnets in other societies'. Second, all Ukraine-related settings are largely applicable towards Belarus, as its potential vulnerability is also determined by the country's borderland position. Third, this geopolitical choice or civilisational clash involves the Russian factor.

Thus, Belarus is often portrayed as an 'in-betweener' country situated between two major 'centers of gravity' which has to make a choice and ally with either the EU or Russia. Scholars and commentators have utilised the periodic opinion poll on the geopolitical preferences of Belarusians conducted by the Lithuania-based Independent Institute of Socio-Economic and Political Studies. The question of this poll foresees three alternative answers: joining the EU, integration with Russia and don't know/no answer (IISEPS, 2015). Thus, the answers rather reflect the vision of Belarus as a country located between two global 'centers of gravity' and do not include any other option, be it neutrality or multi-dimensional cooperation with different global players. However, the setting of this opinion poll, and consequently all analyses which refer to it, lead to two main observations. First, the poll essentially compares a virtual world of EU integration with the real world multi-level participation of Belarus in the Russian-led post-Soviet alliances. In other words, within the current formalised framework and politically conditioned status quo of bilateral Belarus–EU relations, the scenario of Belarus joining the EU per se remains virtual even in a long-term perspective. Second, within this setting the opinion poll treats Belarus largely as an object of international relations but not its subject. This approach limits Belarus's freedom of political action to side either with Russia or with the EU. However, an ultimate choice of either option at the expense of the other is costly. Neither does not fit the interests declared by the Belarusian authorities, whose tactics can be described as engaging all main political actors, though with diverse priorities and intensity of bilateral relations.

The Ukrainian crisis which resulted in the Russian annexation of the Crimean peninsula and war in the Donbas region was linked to Ukraine's rapprochement with the EU. Despite potential threats of a similar scenario in Belarus, the crisis opened a window of opportunity for Belarus's foreign policy. First, the very fact of holding the negotiations on Ukraine in Minsk can be seen as the biggest achievement of the diplomacy of independent Belarus, at least since 1994 when Lukashenka became the country's president. Second, a summit in Minsk was hosted by Lukashenka, a person whose name was at that time on the EU sanctions list. Third, the negotiation process brought to Minsk leaders of the two core EU countries – German Chancellor Angela Merkel and French President François Hollande. Although Lukashenka was not a party to the negotiations on Ukraine, the choice of the venue had significant outcomes both for the Belarusian President and the country. On the one hand, the negotiated package of measures is colloquially known as the Minsk Agreement. Therefore, the very name of the document emphasises its link with Belarus and reminds the world about this country. On the other hand, the choice of venue and the composition of the negotiation parties were of purely foreign origin. In other words, the choice of Belarus as the most convenient location for the negotiations was a purely technical matter, by no means linked to domestic developments in the country or the contents of Belarus–EU relations. However, it is the Ukrainian crisis which provided Belarusian authorities with additional capacity for manoeuvre in their relations with the EU. On the one hand, this capacity is linked to a more positive perception of the country and its political regime in the international arena. On the other hand, it could be perceived as an indirect attempt by Minsk to address the vulnerability of Belarusian independence and the need for support by major global actors in the light of the ongoing war in Ukraine and Russia's role in it.

All these achievements of Belarusian diplomacy have not been linked with domestic developments in the country which was confirmed by the presidential election held on 11 October 2015. First, the alternative candidates were not perceived as serious alternatives and consequently contributed to a Lukashenka re-election (Belsat, 2015). Second, the release of political prisoners in August 2015 was a pragmatic and targeted move by the Belarusian authorities on the eve of the election in order to achieve a positive image of the campaign in the West. In other words, it was not the result of the EU's critical engagement policy. Third, the tactic of the Belarusian authorities was quite effective. Though, according to observers, the electoral process did not meet international standards, some positive developments such as the peaceful nature of the elections and its aftermath were acknowledged (OSCE/ODIHR, 2016). As a result, in October 2015 the EU suspended and in February 2016 lifted its sanctions against Belarusian high-ranking officials.

Thus, the Ukrainian crisis has provided some additional capacities to intensify Belarus–EU relations through the prism of Belarus's potential vulnerability. However, it has neither affected the existing status quo based on the EU's critical engagement policy, nor caused noticeable domestic developments in Belarus. At the same time, the logic behind Belarus's choice as a venue for the talks on the Ukrainian crisis required that the issue of Belarus' self-perception on the geopolitical map of Europe be addressed.

EU-isation, the 'Russian World' and self-centric Europeanness

As described above, the idea of European integration within the scope of the EaP (i.e. EU-isation) cannot be viewed as being on the political agenda with regard to today's Belarus for two reasons. First, the EaP framework does not offer a full membership perspective. Second, integration with the EU is not a political goal of the current regime in Minsk. Instead, it calls for equitable Belarus–EU partnership in numerous areas and refers to a 'wider Europe' concept which per se includes the factor of Russia. More-over, the implementation of various EU projects in Belarus is twofold. First, it addresses nearly all groups of the country's society and thus 'enabl[es EU] norms' codification and their inculcation into the daily practices of Belaru-sian people' (Korosteleva, 2014). Second, it implies cooperation with the Belarusian authorities and complies with the vision of Belarus–EU relations as 'serv[ing Belarus'] pragmatic interests' and 'fostering sustainable develop-ment, economic and social modernization'.

As Löwenhardt (2005) observes: 'Belarusians proudly claim (as do many Poles and Lithuanians) that they are in the *heart* of Europe because their country hosts its geographical centre.' The same approach is promoted by the Belarusian authorities who claim that the country is located in the 'center of Europe' (President of the Republic of Belarus, n.d.). In geographi-cal terms this implies the perception of Europe as a space extending from the Atlantic to the Urals and coincides with the notion of a 'Wider Europe' used by Belarus's officials. Such an approach treats Europe and the Euro-pean Union as two different political and spatial concepts, not equivalent to each other. In other words, to be European within this view does not necessarily mean being an EU Member State, a candidate or an associated country.

Within this approach, 'Europeanness' plays the role of a certain marker of Belarusian identity, as it emphasises a Belarus-centric self-perception and the perception of their neighbours. This self-perception has a clearly defined cultural and social dimension and thus Belarusian authorities further under-line that 'the peculiarity of the Belarusian culture is in its Europeanness, and Europeanness underlines its Belarusianness' (Belarusian Ministry of Culture, 2011). This exemplifies the divergence between the cultural and political perception of 'Europeanness' in Belarus. The cultural form has 'domestic' origins of self-perception unaffiliated with the EU. The political dimension is limited to EU-isation. Additionally, in terms of EU-isation Belarus is per se a peripheral state, as the EU sees the EaP countries as a part of its *Neighbourhood*.

Similarly, Belarus remains peripheral within the doctrine of the so-called 'Russian World', actively promoted by the Russian state and the Russian Orthodox Church. Within this doctrine, 'world' is referred to as 'a trans-state and transcontinental community united by its adherence to a specific state and the loyalty to its culture' (Tishkov, 2008) while 'Russian' implies connection with the Russian language as well as a 'Russian spiritual and cultural tradition which forms the foundations of the national identity or its significant part' (Moscow Patriarchate, 2009). Such an approach complies with the vision of 'homeland' described by Anthony D. Smith (1991) as 'a repository of historic memories and associations'. Thus, the peripheral status of Belarus within the 'Russian World' doctrine is twofold. First, the concept is essentially Russo-centric, as it views Belarusian (and Ukrainian, Moldovan, etc.) culture as subordinated or complimentary to the Russian one. Second, Belarus substantially lacks any elements crucial for the doctrine's mythology or symbolic sites comparable to Kyiv or Sevastopol. In addition, the view of the country's history in Belarus's constitutional acts is incompatible with the milestones of the 'Russian world' (Kascian, 2016).

The vision of the country as a centre of Europe actively promoted by the Belarusian authorities can ultimately be seen as an attempt to avoid choosing between the EU and Russia (i.e. the West and the East). As President Lukashenka stressed,

> It is our fate that we are situated between East and West. [...] We cannot get rid of it, but it does not mean that we try to sit on two chairs. This is what we do not accept, it is not the core of our foreign policy and economic doctrines. (Naviny TUT.by, 2014)

This approach can be interpreted in two ways. First, it is as an attempt to play a bridging role between the EU and Russia within a wider Europe concept. Second, it is an option which allows Belarus to seek a balance of relations with *both* the EU and Russia, without making an ultimately costly geopolitical choice. This implies that in its foreign policies the Belarusian authorities are trying to exploit the 'engaging all' option, though with different intensity and depending on the actual political and economic configurations in the region.

Conclusion

Belarus is a nation that sees itself as a part of Europe in terms of geography and history. However, the authorities in Minsk have their own vision and understanding of what should be the foundations of Belarus–EU relations. This vision essentially dismisses the critical engagement policy based on EU values. At the same time, Belarus and the EU are engaged in diverse, targeted and sector-driven technical cooperation as embodied in various projects.

In view of the clash of approaches between Brussels and Minsk, the actual format of Belarus–EU relations within the EaP track does not seem relevant for the context of these relations. However, it does serve the pragmatic needs of both parties. While Minsk has room for at least formal cooperation with the EU, Brussels includes Belarus as a part of its multilateral cooperation track. Ultimately, the EaP was designed without considering the peculiarities of the political alliances of all its participants. It incorporates the clash between the pragmatic *Realpolitik*-based approach pursued by Minsk and a values-based policy of critical engagement designed by Brussels. As a result, Belarus is an outsider in the Eastern Partnership.

In other words, this incompatibility of the EaP format with Belarus's membership in the Russian-led integration projects raises three important aspects. First, the measurement of the EU policies towards Belarus should be pursued not through the existing framework of high politics which has largely remained frozen for more than a decade and is determined by the EU value-based approach, but through the people-focused impact of practical policies (Chandler, 2014) to form the first pillar for mutual cooperation within the existing window of opportunity. Second, the EU-led Eastern Partnership and the Russian-driven Eurasian Economic Union are generally regarded in terms of mutual competition and thus Belarus's pro-Russian political alliances are interpreted as a Russian success in 'the tug of war for Belarus due to its businesslike Belarus policy' (Ioffe, 2012b). However, the attitude of the Belarusian authorities towards these two 'centers of gravity' can be described as an attempt not to make the 'either/or' choice between the integration vectors, while prioritising its partnership with Russia and keeping mutually beneficial, in-depth and pragmatic relations with the EU. Moreover, the Belarusian leadership often appeals to a 'Wider Europe' and repeatedly emphasises the European character of the nation's culture which can become another pillar of Belarus-EU relations in the current political situation.

Note

1   The European Dialogue on Modernisation with Belarus was launched on 29 March 2012 by the then Commissioner for Enlargement and European Neighbourhood Policy, Stefan Fule. It aimed at promoting democratic and economic reform in Belarus by the EU engaging with stakeholders in Belarus especially experts and civil society. The EU was to provide support in this process.

7 Kamil Całus and Marcin Kosienkowski

Relations between Moldova and the European Union

The idea of cooperation with the European Union has been, in principle, promoted by Moldovan governments since achieving independence from the Soviet Union in 1991, while its integration aspirations were announced in the second half of the 1990s. Interestingly, European aspirations were expressed by the communists who ruled Moldova for most of the 2000s and the political elites who came to power in 2009 have made integration with the EU their top priority.

However, despite its European inclinations, Moldova can be defined as a country that is torn between West and East, in effect, an 'in-betweener' as already indicated in this volume. On the one hand, it is a country with Latin roots, namely its Romanian language, Romanian culture, and historical ties with Romania,[1] which has been a member of the EU since 2007. On the other hand, Moldova is a country with strong links to its Soviet past and Russia, which perceives the whole post-Soviet area as its sphere of influence. Key elements of this are: an evident Soviet mentality and nostalgia, economic dependency on Russia, Russian-speaking minorities constituting 20–30 per cent of Moldova's ('right-bank') population, and the existence of the Russian-oriented breakaway region of Transnistria where Russian troops are stationed. All these affect and complicate the process of Moldova's Europeanisation that is understood here as the development of cooperation with the European Union including, eventually, meeting the criteria for greater integration as outlined by the EU (EU-isation).

This chapter seeks to analyse the development of Moldova–European Union relations since the beginning of the 1990s. It analyses motivations and obstacles to cooperation between Moldova's governments and the EU, as well as the attitudes of the Moldovan population toward Europeanisation. The chapter is divided into three sections concerning consecutive decades – the 1990s, the 2000s and the 2010s – marked by changes of Moldovan governments with their own agendas towards European integration and by growing involvement of the EU in Moldova.

The 1990s: the strangers

Following the disintegration of the Soviet Union, the EU decided to establish and define relations with the newly independent states. However, the EU turned out to be reluctant to work out an appropriate agreement with Moldova. This pushed the Moldovan authorities into launching diplomatic efforts in 1993/94 to start negotiations. A Partnership and Cooperation Agreement (PCA) was signed by the parties in November 1994 (Chirila, 2002: 37–42). It was seen by Moldova as a first step toward joining the EU, which was identified, for the first time, as one of its main external policy aims in the 1995 Moldovan Foreign Policy Concept (Concepţia politicii externe a Republicii Moldova, 1995). Additionally, the EU and Moldova decided that provisions on trade would be applied even before ratification of the PCA.

The idea of European integration appeared more frequently in Moldova's official political discourse in the late 1990s. Its integration aspirations were expressed for the first time to European officials by President-elect Petru Lucinschi in December 1996. His government initially pursued the idea of becoming an associate member of the EU, but this met with a cold reaction from the EU which put primary emphasis on implementation of the PCA that had only just entered into force in 1998 (Chirila, 2002: 53–55). From 1998, Moldovan governments continued to pay attention to European integration in their programmes, maintaining it as a strategic objective (Klipii, 2002: 9–26). Moreover, since the launch of the Stability Pact for South Eastern Europe in 1999, the Moldovan authorities made efforts to join this new EU initiative. They hoped that joining the Balkan group of potential EU candidates would provide Moldova with a clear perspective of EU membership (Ungureanu, 2002: 68–79). However, an Eastern orientation of Moldovan foreign policy was not abandoned.

Moldova developed its relations with the EU as part of its policy of achieving broad recognition of its newly established independence and strengthening its statehood. Furthermore, it wanted, to some extent, to balance Russia's dominance in the region. Certainly, its Latinity favoured the idea of cooperation with the West. An important stimulus to Moldova's orientation to the EU came from the former Soviet satellites of Central and Eastern Europe, which had commenced the path towards full integration with the EU. This was especially true of neighbouring Romania. Unlike Russia at the time, the EU attracted Moldova, the poorest state in Europe, with its economic wealth. Moldovan political elites counted on reviving their shaky economy with immediate European development assistance which accounted for €147.7 million in the 1990s and rapid development of trade relations (Löwenhardt et al., 2001: 617–620). The latter turned out to be an urgent priority when Moldova's Commonwealth of Independent States (CIS) oriented economy was badly hit by the 1998 Russian financial crisis.

Crucially, there were favourable domestic conditions to promote a European orientation. According to a survey conducted in the first half of 2000, 60 per cent of the Moldovan population had a very, or fairly, positive attitude towards the EU as opposed to 6 per cent against. However, only one-third thought of themselves as 'Europeans'. The vast majority underlined the importance of good relations with Russia. Finally, respondents mentioned economic development and political stability as dominant benefits of Moldova's EU membership (White et al., 2001: 293–296). Most political parties wanted Moldova to integrate, or at least develop relations, with the EU but pro-European slogans were not initially evident during election campaigns. A cross-party pro-European declaration was published in June 2000 (Klipii, 2002: 27–30). Although the signature of the biggest parliamentary party – the Communists (PCRM) – was missing, it did not oppose this EU direction (Löwenhardt et al., 2001: 618).

Despite considerable support for Moldova's integration with the EU, elites and society had little understanding of all the implications of such an orientation. Supporting Moldovan elites seemed to perceive it as a foreign policy choice and membership of an international club rather than as a task to include taking far-reaching domestic reforms. As a result, the pro-European narrative was rarely followed up by actions (Shapovalova and Boonstra, 2012: 54–55).

The EU, in its turn, was initially reluctant to enhance relations with Moldova because it was perceived as a politically and economically unstable country, affected by the Transnistrian conflict and dominated by Russia. A further discouraging factor was initially Moldova's seemingly inconsistent foreign and domestic policies. Moreover, the EU was preoccupied with other problems such as conflicts in the Western Balkans, enlargement to Central and Eastern Europe and, during the 1990s, establishing itself as a foreign policy actor (Shapovalova and Boonstra, 2012: 51–55).

The 2000s: the new neighbours

The 2000s brought important changes to relations between Moldova and the EU. First, ahead of the 2004 Eastern enlargement, the EU decided to develop a comprehensive policy toward its southern and new Eastern neighbours. This included Moldova, directly bordering the EU since 2007 when Romania became a member. While Moldova had little economic importance, it became a potential source of security threats and a challenge for EU border integrity. As a weak state with a frozen conflict on its soil, Moldova could be seen, with reference to the 2003 European Security Strategy, as a troubled place located on the EU's borders. In order to enhance its security, Brussels set itself the task of promoting a ring of stability, consisting of democratic and prosperous countries in the neighbourhood. Crucially, however, membership was not on offer (Ratzmann, 2012).

During this period, Moldova experienced significant change. The PCRM achieved a supermajority in the legislature after the February 2001 elections and in a parliamentary vote its leader – Vladimir Voronin – was chosen as the Moldovan President, taking all power in the country. Despite election slogans about joining the Russia–Belarus Union, anti-European rhetoric, some democratic reversals, and enhancing relations with Russia after taking power, the Communist government did not turn their back on the EU. In June 2001 Moldova joined – as the only post-Soviet country – the Stability Pact for South Eastern Europe. The 2002 draft of the foreign policy platform declared European integration as a strategic objective of Moldova (Infotag, 2002), while in 2003 the Concept for the Integration of the Republic of Moldova in the EU was further elaborated. In addition, during this period some domestic institutions to support Moldovan-EU interaction were set up.

In 2003, the European Commission adopted a communication entitled 'Wider Europe Neighbourhood: A New Framework for Relations with our Eastern and Southern Neighbours', the foundations of the 2004 European Neighbourhood Policy (ENP). In these circumstances Moldova's relationship with Russia became more problematic. Initially, the Moldovan authorities were disappointed with this initiative because it did not offer the prospect of membership and linked countries with disparate backgrounds and objectives towards the EU. In the end, Moldova finally decided to join the ENP.

The Communists held on to power in the 2005 elections but in the midst of what came to be called 'an orange evolution' (March and Herd, 2006). The PCRM government declared their full commitment to further European integration and the newly elected parliament adopted a declaration of political partnership to achieve the objectives of greater European integration. All parties signed the ENP Action Plan. Moreover, the EU appointed a Special Representative for Moldova dealing mainly with the Transnistrian problem and, together with the United States, joined negotiations on resolution of the conflict as an observer. Finally, the European Commission opened its delegation in Chişinău and deployed the EU Border Assistance Mission to Moldova and Ukraine (EUBAM) to the Ukrainian-Moldovan border, including its Transnistrian section.

The PCRM showed an increasing inclination towards authoritarianism, being classified by the Freedom House (2010) as a semi-consolidated authoritarian regime in 2005 and also in 2008–10 (with their most critical concerns regarding media freedom and electoral fraud). However, further integration with the EU was still among Moldova's priorities. The EU granted Moldova trade preferences: GSP+ (Generalised System of Preferences) in 2006 and then ATPs (Autonomous Trade Preferences) in 2008.

An EU Common Visa Application Centre was established in Chişinău in 2007, while the following year the parties signed visa facilitation and read-mission agreements and a Mobility Partnership facilitating legal migration of Moldovans.

In 2006, together with the Western Balkans group, Moldova joined the South East European Cooperation Process (SEECP). The PCRM was, however, critical of the Eastern Partnership (EaP) initiative which became an official EU programme in 2009. It was aimed at assisting new neighbour-hood states from Eastern Europe and the Caucasus in the hope of binding them closer to the EU. Moldova sought a deeper Association Agreement which stipulated EU membership. The EU indicated its readiness to consider a new and deeper agreement including free trade and visa liberalisation but with the PCRM under strict conditionality of conducting transparent and fair elections in 2009 (Shapovalova and Boonstra, 2012: 55–62).

Several factors explain the Communist government's pursuit of a pro-European orientation. The first was related to geopolitics. Owing to Mol-dova's location in a contested neighbourhood, the PCRM could oscillate between the EU and Russia and played on the differences between them for their own benefits (Korosteleva, 2010; Weiner, 2004). It was anticipated that the EU was afraid to be too critical of communist policies, for fear of driving Moldova towards the Russian sphere. Furthermore, more commit-ted engagement by the EU in its Eastern neighbourhood allowed Moldova to potentially balance the excessive influence of Russia much more effec-tively than in the 1990s (Cantir and Kennedy, 2015). The result of this somewhat delicate balancing act was a gradual worsening relationship with Russia in 2003–6. However, the EU did not want to provoke a geopolitical confrontation with Russia and it withheld fulsome support for Moldova. As a result, the PCRM moved to re-enhance its relations with Russia in 2006.

The second motive behind the pro-European course taken by the PCRM was internal: they wished to secure electoral popularity and remain in power. As in the 2001 parliamentary election, foreign policy formed a sig-nificant part of the Second Plan, receiving much more attention in following elections. The popularity of EU membership oscillated between 57 and 76 per cent in the 2000s (Institutul de Politici Publice, 2015: 97). But at the same time, many Moldovan voters appreciated keeping good relations with Russia (Korosteleva, 2010: 1281–1282). A positive EU outlook was elector-ally vital when examining voter motivation: economic prosperity (57 per cent), freedom of movement (38 per cent), democracy (32 per cent) and stability (30 per cent), as a 2008 survey showed. Additionally, a majority of respondents believed they had much in common with Europeans (Korosteleva, 2010: 1281).

The pro-EU platform of the Communist Party adopted in the February 2005 parliamentary election undermined the opposition campaign which was not able to use European slogans exclusively for its own benefit. In the aftermath of the election it also assisted in achieving the necessary parliamentary support – including from their arch-rival, the Christian-Democratic People's Party – to elect Voronin for a second term as President (Kennedy, 2010). The benefits of the pro-EU platform were also evident in 2009. Before, during and after the April 2009 crisis – triggered by alleged fraud in the April 2009 parliamentary elections and street protests in Chişinău violently suppressed by the police – the ruling communists generally got support from the EU in the name of retaining political stability in Moldova and keeping Moldova on its Europeanisation course. For example, the EU tried to convince the opposition to provide the communists with one more vote in the parliament needed to elect a president (Raik and Dinesen, 2015; Tudoroiu, 2011: 301–304). However, the opposition did not accept this and following the dissolution of Parliament, the communists lost power in the snap parliamentary elections of July 2009.

A third motivation for the promotion of an EU orientation concerned boosting the Moldovan economy and the general modernisation of the country. Put simply, the PCRM could not ignore the fact of the increasing share of EU–Moldova external trade and increasing amount of transfers from Moldovans working in the EU. A major effort was made to diversify Moldova's traditionally CIS-oriented exports into new EU markets. This became especially important when Russia – in punishing Moldova for tightening relations with the West – imposed sanctions on the import of the main Moldovan export products (wine, fruits, vegetables, and meat) between 2005 and 2006, a serious hit to the already shaky Moldovan economy. Moldovan exports to the EU increased from 32.3 per cent in 2001 to 52.0 per cent in 2009, while exports to the CIS decreased from 60.9 per cent to 38.2 per cent (National Bureau of Statistics of the Republic of Moldova, 2014).

Furthermore, European sources of assistance grew considerably. The EU granted Moldova €173.0 million between 2000 and 2006, mainly under the Technical Assistance for the Commonwealth of Independent States (TACIS) and the Food Security Program. In 2007, the European Neighbourhood and Partnership Instrument (ENPI) became the main source of European aid to Moldova. It envisaged €209.7 million for Moldova till 2010. Through budgetary support and technical assistance, the ENPI aimed to support: democracy development and good governance, regulatory reform and administrative capacity building, and poverty reduction and economic growth (Boian, 2010). Importantly, Moldova became the second greatest recipient of EU assistance per capita after the Palestinian territories. On the other hand, Russian sanctions on Moldova could not be completely discounted and needed a response to mitigate their impact.

The final factor behind the choice of an EU pathway by the Communist government was the resolution of the Transnistrian conflict. Initially, it was believed that Russia would be a major player in its resolution. Indeed, Russia presented its own plan, the Kozak Memorandum secretly negotiated with Moldova and Transnistria independently of other international actors. However, it was dismissed by President Voronin shortly before the signing ceremony in November 2003 under Western and domestic pressure and because of the inclusion in the text of a regulation allowing Russian troops to stay in Moldova until 2020 on which there had allegedly been no consultation. As a result, relations with Russia worsened and Moldova turned westward for a diplomatic solution. The conflict in Moldova had already developed an EU dimension. Apart from its formal role in ongoing negotiations for conflict resolution, the EU engaged in low-profile confidence building between conflicting parties, supporting border management, curbing the scale of cross-border smuggling, facilitating Transnistria's legal trade within Moldova's economic space, and in general fostering people-to-people contacts. However, the EU's involvement was in the background and piecemeal to avoid antagonising Russia (Popescu, 2010: 38–65). This approach was inevitably disappointing for the Moldovan government.

For the most part Europeanisation was mainly perceived by the communist government in geopolitical terms. They did not associate the necessary corollary of a deep EU relationship with considerable internal reform. Some progress was made in the establishment of institutional frameworks and the approximation of domestic legislation to EU standards but the implementation of reforms was poor, especially with regard to judicial reform, fighting corruption and media freedom. If these reforms had been progressed, the implication for the PCRM would have been a commensurate loss of its power base that remained dependent on patronage and partiality. Additionally, lack of clear EU membership prospects and Russia's punitive sanctions policy were conflicting and discouraging factors. However, in the case of issues of pressing importance to the PCRM, namely trade and freedom of movement with the EU, they were ready to implement reforms. Crucially, the EU found this beneficial too and was ready to assist Moldova with a policy of 'credible conditionality', that is to offer tangible benefits (such as wider access to European markets) in return for limited but real reforms. Similarly, on some other issues such as development assistance and the Transnistrian conflict, where the preferences of both parties converged there existed a mutual incentive to cooperate successfully (Bosse, 2010: 1306–1307; Hagemann, 2013).

The 2010s: the partners?

With the failure of the PCRM in Moldova's parliamentary elections of 29 July 2009, a new chapter in relations between Moldova and the European Union opened. On 8 August 2009, the openly pro-European election winners – the Liberal Democratic Party of Moldova (PLDM), the Democratic Party of Moldova (PDM), the Liberal Party (PL) and the 'Our Moldova' Alliance – agreed to create a ruling coalition. According to the coalition agreement, the key priorities for foreign policy were to integrate with the EU and, in particular, to sign an Association Agreement (*Declaraţie privind constituirea*, 2009). On 25 September, the Alliance voted in a pro-European government led by Vlad Filat, which on 1 December adopted a new, four-year activity programme European Integration: Freedom, Democracy, Welfare (Programul de activitate al Guvernului Republicii Moldova, 2009). The programme clearly stated that the new government saw Moldova's integration with the EU as a 'fundamental priority of the domestic and foreign policies of the Republic of Moldova'. The document also stressed that Europeanisation was 'the most efficient way to achieve political, economic and social modernization of the country'. The programme underlined Moldova's willingness to sign an Association Agreement with the EU and its wish to join the Union in the foreseeable future. Although subsequently, as a result of political crises and elections, the name of the coalition, its members and leadership has changed, since 2009 the country has been ruled by the same political elite.

Moldovan governments and the EU holy grail

There were four reasons behind the choice of European integration as an ideological base and political leitmotif of the pro-European parties in Moldova. No doubt, one of the most important was that the pro-European agenda could secure the support of the pro-European voters, a significant part of Moldovan society. Presenting itself as pro-European was important to the coalition parties for subsequent parliamentary elections in November 2010 and, especially, November 2014. In the latter election, despite a number of corruption scandals, pro-European parties could still attract a large section of voters who welcomed pro-European slogans even though coalition credibility had declined. This was possible because leaders of pro-European parties managed to convince the majority of Moldovan people that even with a parallel minority upsurge of pro-Russian political sympathy for an Eastern integration with the (then) Eurasian Customs Union (ECU), a vote for the government coalition was in fact a sounder geopolitical choice and the only way to keep Moldova on a modernising track (Socor, 2014). Even now when support for EU integration in Moldova is falling, authorities maintain a pro-European rhetoric because it allows them to sustain this core pro-European electorate. To change this geopolitical orientation would indicate unreliability and indecision from the perspective of many voters and could risk a catastrophic drop in core electoral support.

The second political driver towards an EU future was a desire to curb Russian influences in Moldova and ultimately to separate from the Russian sphere of influence. Gaining independence from Moscow was perceived by Chisinau as a chance to obtain more presence on the international stage. It was also a straightforward and popular stance – a cultural and historical 'return to Europe' at least among Romanian and pro-European electorates.

Third, cooperation with the EU promised faster development of the country by drawing in new investment; creating employment and new production technologies and thus modernising the existing industrial base. Better access to European aid programmes and loans, and getting wider access to the European markets which traditionally accounts for about half of Moldovan external trade, were part of a logic of modernity.

In 2011, the coalition partners started preliminary talks with EU officials on the Association Agreement, including (what was to be the most important aspect in the short term) a Deep and Comprehensive Free Trade Area (DCFTA) (*Second Joint Progress Report*, 2011). This would shrink their Russian dependence and minimise future political pressures from the Kremlin (in the shape of embargos or the cancellation of investments). Another important step by Moldovan authorities was to join the Energy Community in 2010. The contracting parties are committed to ownership unbundling in the field of energy which means splitting the generation of electricity from its transmission to a distribution system operator or to the consumer.

Fourth, it was hoped that a firm rapprochement with the EU would help towards a settlement of the Transnistrian separatism issue. The anticipated outcome of integration (i.e. improved economic conditions and evident modernisation) was meant to also become a tempting perspective for Transnistrian society and elites. The coalition hoped it could lead to stronger political and economic cooperation.

The European Union and its members: perspectives

The EU greeted the new, 2009, pro-European Moldovan government with clear satisfaction. Within the next few months, the EU's engagement in the country increased significantly. It was also boosted by the launch of the Eastern Partnership in May 2009. In January 2010, the EU agreed to negotiations for an Association Agreement and in June 2010 Moldova and the EU began talks on granting Moldovan citizens visa-free access to the Schengen area for 90 days. The EU also offered Moldova concrete and increasing financial support to implement necessary key reforms. Between 2010 and 2013, Moldova gained €550 million in assistance. In 2014, the EU supported Moldova with more than €130 million (Delegation of the European

Union to Moldova, 2015; European Commission, 2014a). Since 2010, EU
political advisers have also been assigned to help Moldovan state reform
and observe the work of Moldovan public institutions (Delegation of the
European Union to Moldova, 2010).

From the perspective of Brussels, involvement in Moldova was mostly
aimed at providing stability beyond the new EU borders, especially in the
context of Transnistria (Dias, 2013a). Pro-European Moldova was expected
to become a more transparent and predictable partner. For example, by
granting Moldova a visa-free regime to the Schengen zone, the EU forced
the Moldovan government to seal its borders, reform the state border guard
service, bolster control of the Transnistrian border and introduce biometric
passports and an automated passport control system. The aspiration of the
EU was to turn Moldova into a model state within the Eastern Partnership
which could be a positive example to other EaP countries like Ukraine.
However, as with other EaP members, the EU was not interested in offering
Moldova any clear prospect of future membership. This was reflected in
the content of the Association Agreement, eventually signed by Moldova
in June 2014.

Moldova's integration with the EU was particularly important to two
EU member states: Romania and Germany. From Romania's perspective,
Moldova's rapprochement with the EU was a chance to repair mutual relations which had suffered during the Soviet era, by extending economic and
cultural cooperation, securing its eastern border and pulling Moldova away
from a Russian sphere of influence (thus moving Russia further away from
Romania's borders). Romanian–Moldovan relations intensified as soon as
the pro-European coalition was formed in Chisinau. Romania tried to
exploit the European aspirations of the new Moldovan government by
becoming Moldova's main advocate in the EU. By creating a platform of
cooperation to allow EU states to build friendly bilateral relations, Romania
sought to enhance its position within the EU. A good example of such
activity is the creation of the Friends of Moldova Group in cooperation
with France.

From Germany's perspective, European integration of Moldova was seen
as a helpful tool in the implementation of crucial elements of German
foreign policy: improvement of EU border security, control of migration
and the resolution of the Transnistrian conflict. Moldova was also the
litmus test for Russia's reaction to further EU enlargement to the east.
Germany's interest in Moldovan affairs has been increasing since 2009
when a German was appointed the head of the EU delegation in Chisinau
and head of the EUBAM to Moldova and Ukraine.

The EU offered the pro-European coalition in Chisinau almost uncondi-
tional support, refraining from open criticism of the Moldovan authorities
despite evident examples of corrupt, unlawful or undemocratic practice.
The EU was concerned not to contribute to any decline in internal support

for the government that might result in the return of more pro-Russian parties to power.

Only a few months after the pro-European coalition was established, the EU had already labelled Moldova as a 'success story' of the Eastern Partnership. Negotiations on the content of agreements such as the DCFTA were making rapid progress, especially in contrast to Ukraine. Moldovan citizens were the first citizens of a post-Soviet state (except the Baltic states) to enter a visa-free regime for the Schengen zone.

This positive evaluation of Moldova by Brussels lasted until the beginning of 2013 when the Filat government collapsed as a result of a political crisis (Całus, 2013). This revealed the extremely high levels of corruption among the Moldovan ruling elite. For a substantial part of Moldovan society, in the last few years Moldova has become the 'captured state' in which public institutions are subordinated to local politicians and oligarchs (Całus, 2014; Tudoroiu, 2014). It became clear that Moldovan politicians were interested in securing their own private businesses, rather than focusing on the modernisation of the country. In spite of the EU's growing disappointment with Moldova, the country managed to initial and eventually sign the Association Agreement (in November 2013 and in June 2014, respectively). EU officials noted, however, that in spite of the narrative of Moldovan government officials and the formal enactment of several laws, key reforms (especially judicial reform, decentralisation and financial sector reform) were either not implemented or their progress was very slow. The EU did not criticise Moldova openly prior to the elections in November 2014. However, the EU changed its attitude at the end of 2014. It was concerned not only with the moderate success of pro-European forces in Moldova but also with the scandalous behaviour of two main coalition partners – PLDM and PDM – during elections. Abuses in the election process and inability to form a government during the following three months opened the way for a highly critical Commission Progress Report on Moldova (European Commission, 2015c).

Moldovan popular opinion and the EU

Popular attitudes towards European integration have clearly evolved in recent years of rule by the pro-European coalition. To Moldovans, rapprochement with the EU still predominantly means the opportunity to improve living conditions, legal permission to work abroad and increasing stability. These expectations are the result of a somewhat idealised picture of the EU created by pro-European political parties, and by nearly 300,000 Moldovan migrants working in the EU. The message that has been sent to people is that the EU is a remedy for all the country's problems. However, paradoxically, the establishment of overtly pro-European governments coincided with a deterioration in the level of support for the European idea and European integration among Moldovans As a result, in March 2015 support for European integration declined to 40 per cent (Institutul de Politici Publice, 2015: 97). This has been a consequence of two factors.

The first – and most important – factor was the establishment of the ECU by Russia in January 2010, seen as a tangible alternative to the EU. The idea of rapprochement with the then ECU (and later, from 1 January 2015, Eurasian Economic Union – EEU) has canalised pro-Russian sentiments for some parts of Moldovan society. It was additionally fuelled by active promotion of this organisation in Moldova by Russia and pro-Russian political forces (including the PCRM which has promoted integration with the ECU/EEU since 2011). The ECU/EEU was presented as an organisation similar to the EU, based on the European integration model but, at the same time, more modern and more resistant to economic disruptions (the economic crisis that hit Europe seemed to have bypassed Russia). The Russian-led economic integration project was also pictured as an organisation more adjusted to Moldova in terms of religion and culture. Eastern Orthodoxy – unlike in the EU – is the dominant religion in the EEU: more than 80 per cent of Moldovans are members of the Moldovan Orthodox Church which is subordinated to the Russian Orthodox Church. Member states of this organisation are also presented as more conservative in terms of values (e.g. negative attitudes toward sexual minorities), fitting the traditional conservatism of Moldovan society (Barbarosie, 2015).

Propaganda promoting the ECU/EEU intensively exploited sentiment toward the Soviet past still present among a large number of Moldovan citizens. It also highlighted cultural affinities between the member states and Moldova which derive from the long-term experience of common statehood (from 1812 until 1918 within the Russian Empire and from 1944 until 1991 within the Soviet Union). A pro-ECU/EEU narrative strongly focused on the prospect of immediate economic benefits: guaranteed access to the Russian market, migration opportunities (as of 2014, between 300,000 and 350,000 Moldovans work in Russia), and a long-term contract for cheap gas deliveries, and so on (Cepoi, 2014). The establishment of the ECU was thus a factor in the significant public decline in EU support with sections of Moldovan society increasingly perceiving the EU as an organisation promoting abstract ideas and values, unlike the Russian-led project which was seen as a pragmatic, international organisation oriented towards economic opportunity.

Transformation of the ECU into the EEU remained virtually unnoticed by the overwhelming majority of the Moldovan public, which perceives it as practically the same organisation. Therefore, it did not influence the level of support for the Russian integration project among Moldovans. It is interesting that even the outbreak of the Russian–Ukrainian conflict in February 2014 did not really change their attitude toward the ECU. In

March 2015, the idea of Eurasian integration was supported by 58 per cent of Moldovans (Institutul de Politici Publice, 2015: 97).

A second reason for this decline in support for the EU has been the negative stereotyping of the EU that has spread as part of a campaign promoting the ECU/EEU, and which is particularly visible in the Russian media popular in Moldova. Pro-Russian parties (such as the PCRM and the Party of Socialists) also launched a campaign aimed at discrediting the EU with certain myths and false rumours. Since knowledge of the EU by Moldovans is low, many accept negative stereotypes as the truth. The EU did little to counter this: the Delegation of the European Union to Moldova has not provided a consistent or broad-based information campaign which could counter Russian propaganda. The result is that many Moldovans concluded that Moldova's accession in the EU will mean the loss of a new independence; by others it is perceived as part of the government's hidden agenda to reunite with Romania. Such a perception is particularly popular among national minorities, for example Gagauzians (Totul, 2014).

Another further disappointment with the ruling pro-EU elite is that despite its European reformism it has failed to reduce levels of corruption. Neither has there been tangible economic improvement which is evidently visible to Moldovan citizens. Massive corruption scandals involving pro-European elites have played their part in undermining the legitimacy of government and thus its manifesto for an EU future. Moreover, the attitudes of EU politicians and officials seen supporting the Moldovan government, no matter what it was doing in the country, did not meet with warm reactions in Moldova. Some Moldovan opposition politicians and experts have also criticised the EU; that by refraining from criticism, the EU has slowed down reforms and encouraged corruption (Noi, 2015). Although the Moldovan electorate has been regularly informed about the stream of European financial aid coming to Moldova – the highest rate per capita among all the Eastern Partnership states (Central European Policy Institute, 2013) – this has hardly been visible in public opinion. Since there seems to be no tangible public impact, with a considerable amount of EU aid being spent on institution building, a critical public has accused politicians of stealing European money.

A balance of cooperation

Six years of rule by a pro-European coalition has certainly brought Moldova closer to the EU. The country's greatest successes in this period were ultimately the signing of an Association Agreement (including the DCFTA) and the liberalisation of the visa regime. Successive governments have kept Moldova on a pro-EU course despite strong political and economic pressure from Moscow (including trade embargoes and energy blackmail). The EU has provided substantial financial and technical assistance to Moldova, whose governments have attempted to process some of these EU condition-alities. However, many reforms have not been implemented, even though they have been legally adopted. Those most likely to be implemented are reforms that offer no threat to the large political-business interests of the ruling elite or likely to be immediately popular and therefore vote catching. This is why Moldova has moved so quickly to obtain the visa-free regime status and sign the symbolically significant Association Agreement. But reforms of the judicial system (overseen by Vlad Plahotniuc, a sponsor and de facto leader of PDM) and the financial sector (policed by Vlad Filat) have failed. It could be claimed that the EU, having weighed up the political disadvantages of negative consequences from the possible overthrow of pro-European coalitions, has ducked away from any serious attempt at Moldovan EU-isation in the near future.

Conclusion

Despite the steady intensification of relations between Moldova and the EU, in the twenty-first century they have been plagued by significant problems. One is that the priorities of Moldovan governments and population, and the EU, do not coincide. The Moldovan government has a principal aim of EU accession, while the EU is not ready to offer them any clear perspective for membership. Furthermore, the priority for Moldovan political elites has been to maintain power. This has encouraged successive governments to use pro-European rhetoric and implement some EU originating reforms for electoral purposes. However, a desire to stay in power has simultaneously prevented the introduction of many other EU required reforms, especially with regard to the judiciary and curbing corruption.

   With regard to the external pressures from the EU, these have been shaped to sustain internal regime stability. On the one hand, it has offered financial support for Moldova's development and assistance to reforms. On the other hand, it has sought to avoid political confrontation with Russia, which opposes Moldova's integration with the EU, and offered relatively uncritical support for the Moldovan authorities, regardless of the real merits in progressing towards EU-isation.

   Finally, the Moldovan population, which for some time was strongly Euro-enthusiastic, initially associated European integration with improve-ment in its socio-economic future. Failures by the present government to curb corruption and provide tangible economic change along with the appearance of an alternative – the Russian-led integration project – have led more recently to a considerable decrease in public support for Moldova's accession to the EU.

However, the fact that ruling 'pro-EU' parties have lost so much of the trust and support of their electorates does not mean that the idea of European integration is no longer tempting for Moldovan society. A European ideal – when preached by popular political forces – can still attract the interest of the electorate, and sustain noticeable support. At the same time, while the Russian–Ukrainian conflict has not impacted visibly on the EU policy toward Moldova, the unpopular actions of the Moldovan political elite did. The EU has finally acknowledged that Moldova can hardly be considered a 'success story' of the Eastern Partnership. From the end of 2014 and through to 2015, the perception of Moldovan authorities by the EU and trust in their desire to truly reform the country deteriorated dramatically. It became clear that the pro-European ruling elite is corrupt and is mostly focused on an internal battle for control over state institutions and financial flows. In consequence, the EU has ceased its ostensibly open support for the Moldovan government and instead has started to promote the pro-EU idea rather than specific pro-EU parties. This step – if connected with an effective EU information policy on the benefits of European integration directed to Moldovan society – may gradually restore dwindling public trust in a Moldovan future within the EU.

Note

1   Until the nineteenth century the territory of present-day Moldova, located on the right bank of the Dniester River (Bessarabia), constituted the eastern part of the Principality of Moldavia which, together with the Principality of Wallachia made up Romania in the second half of that century. Moldova was a part of Romania during 1918–40 and 1941–44.

Value-oriented aspects of EU-isation: the case of the Balkans

The Balkans is an area noted for complex ideas of entrenched nationalism operating in an environment lacking traditional identity-based boundaries. Moreover, it is characterised by conflict, political instability and arrested economic development. This often isolated and least understood region is returning to the agenda of European politics in the context of the EU's enlargement initiatives. These efforts also serve as an opportunity to examine whether the EU, as well as providing myriad benefits associated with EU membership, is also able to instil a collective European identity as a residual effect. The concept of EU-isation has traditionally been associated with the impact of the EU on domestic policy coalescing political, social and economic factors. This phenomenon, however, is much more encompassing and often quite elusive in its definition as well as in its origins. It represents a certain reality, but it also embodies a symbolic and even mythical ideological notion. Is it therefore truly possible to weave the concept of EU-isation into the fabric of the Balkan cultural domain and will there ever be a European identity in the Balkans?

In an attempt to further this ongoing debate, this chapter focuses primarily on the value-oriented aspect of EU-isation, placing a particular emphasis on identity formation. The process of EU-isation has been traditionally associated with an economic and political transformation, often undermining the value-based aspects of the process, such as a country's or a nation's acquiescence in taking on a European identity. This dual nature of EU-isation is particularly important in the Balkans where a highly established sense of 'self' is deeply embedded in the fibre of its people. The goal of a unified Europe and the Balkan ability or even willingness to become *European* is central to the subsequent discourse. A key facet of EU-isation is to create, promote and more importantly sustain a sense of a pan-European identity. However, within a multi-ethnic and conflicting environment, the idea of a national identity is often unresolved as is most vividly illustrated in the Balkans, particularly in the case of Bosnia-Herzegovina and Kosovo. An attempt is made, above all, to conceptualise the notion of EU-isation within a firmly identity-based framework, discrediting the essentialist approach to identity formation in favour of a more constructivist model. The thesis which this chapter puts forward suggests that the notion of a European identity is in fact a shared social value, rather than a tangible idea easily applicable to every situation. The Balkans provides a particularly difficult case study because no generic Balkan identity exists. In essence, the underlying question developed hereon after is: what does the process of EU-isation really mean and how viable is it in the context of a complex environment such as the Balkans?

When discussing the notion of EU-isation it is difficult to reject the role of material and political interdependence. However, identity is a crucial element that exerts considerable influence in the Balkans. Moreover, identity is undoubtedly an aspect that cannot be underestimated as part of the discourse on nationhood or regionalisation in this complex environment. Before analysing the role exerted by the EU-isation process, identity – as a unique, independent entity of any given society – needs to be explained more fully.

Conceptualisation of identity

As Chapter 2 shows, the concept of identity has been dissected and explained in a multitude of ways depending on the applied theoretical foundations. For example, one of the most common theoretical approaches often included in the debate on identity is that of the 'primordialists'. This school of thought clearly sees identity – especially within a regional context as in the case of the Balkans – reflecting a set of shared cohesions. These shared cohesions – or common traits – in a given group, tribe or society represent all the fundamental elements that bind individuals into a unique unit. These include a common language, traditions and customs, dominant social and familial structures and world views. Furthermore, these shared cohesions can transcend social and cultural characteristics to include architectural style, commonality of dress and a uniform way of 'doing things'. This is particularly relevant when discussing the Balkans for this particular region is undeniably a unique cultural space with a unique set of shared cohesions. Jovan Cvijić, a nineteenth-century Serbian anthropogeographer, further elaborates the notion of *homo balcanicus*, attributing these identity-based traits as being a part of a distinctive Balkan *mentalité* (Ancel, 1929; Cvijić, 1918). To conceptualise such a notion would essentially mean that 'being' Balkan is an identity that is *sui generis*.

There is, however, an undeniably conflictual aspect to analysing the Balkans through a strictly primordialist lens. Although this region retains some characteristics that deem it uniquely 'Balkan' rather than 'European', and despite shared traits of cohesion, it is nonetheless at the same time an area with a long tradition of ethnic, religious, linguistic, political and cultural heterogeneity. Therefore, the primordialist analysis of identity in the Balkans is not entirely accurate. This region certainly fulfils the necessary prerequisites of what in the field of international relations is often referred to as a regional subsystem, an area that possesses interrelatedness, geographic proximity and shared characteristics (Thomson, 1973). However, its heterogeneity directly challenges the monolithic notion of *homo balcanicus*.

Identity can also be debated from an essentialist viewpoint. This approach implies a resistance to change, a permanence. The belief is that an individual or a group, such as belonging to the Balkans, is innately constructed with a set of characteristics and traits that are almost inherent and therefore unmodifiable. If such logic is followed, one could go as far as attributing the explosion of 'ancient hatreds' in Bosnia in the early 1990s as essentially stemming from Balkan propensity to violence and not as a consequence of political changes directly resulting from Yugoslavia's dissolution.[1] Moreover, if an individual or group already in possession of a Balkan identity is one whose identity cannot be altered and or replaced then the process of EU-isation of the region is virtually impossible for one must be Europeanised from 'birth'. The argument can be reinforced even further through a current presumption that Balkan identity is in fact generic and if someone comes from Albania and is Muslim, he or she is virtually indistinguishable from an individual who speaks Serbian and calls Republika Srpska his or her home. Fundamentally, this theoretical and categorical approach, at least in the context of the Balkans, is deeply flawed.

Fortunately, the essentialist approach to identity formation is counteracted by the constructivist school of thought. The shortcomings of an essentialist argument are thwarted by constructivists who see identities, for instance, as outcomes of social, historical and ideological construction. In other words, constructivists see the creation, erosion or alteration of identities as being influenced by ever-changing processes and are consequently created by social interaction (Adams, 2010: 742). Constructivists deny the essentialist assertion that an individual or a group is born with a set of characteristics that ultimately shapes a corresponding identity. A regional identity is contingent on social interaction and processes that include – but are not limited to – the synergy among various actors as well as the exchange of shared knowledge and values. Moreover, in acknowledging that identity is never static but rather dynamic in its nature, constructivists theorise how identity can actually serve a dual purpose: to promote a sense of cohesion with respect to Self all the while maintaining a sense of variance with regard to the Other. In doing so, a construction of the concept of Other versus Self actually has a unifying and solidifying effect on a group.[2]

According to these conceptualisations, regional identity is acquiescent and not permanent, affording EU-isation as a concept considerable leverage in its endeavours. The discursive boundaries so often created when dealing with deeply rooted identities as well as cultural and historical representations of Self can in fact be eliminated, or at least lessened with time and increased social interaction. That also might mean that, if a constructivist approach is adopted, EU-isation can in fact infiltrate to the core of a group so as to effectively reshape and 'reprogramme' its values, perceptions and ultimately its identity, even in the Balkans where nationalism is exceptionally embedded. Certainly this remains to be seen.

Conceptualising Balkan identity

The term 'identity' is as nebulous as it is prosaic, especially in the framework of the Balkans. We can conceptualise it as being, for the most part, a condition with a set of characteristics that define an individual, a group, or a nation state. In most cases the connotations are positive, invoking a sense of pride, intercultural respect and recognition. However, what makes the study of identity in the Balkans even more interesting is the fact that the notion of a Balkan identity has, for the most part, been conceptualised in rather pejorative terms. As mentioned, the concept of 'being' Balkan is most often equated with terms such as backwardness, subservience, stagnation, or arrested development. Moreover, the Western world quite often evokes nationalism as an omnipotent driving force behind identity formation in this part of the world, especially in the wake of the wars of the 1990s. This is erroneous on many counts, although denying altogether the nation-centric characteristic of identity politics in the Balkans is, at the same time, not entirely accurate. The prevalence of nationalist narratives in the quest to conceptualise and, more significantly, formulate identity in this region is important, but it is equally significant to illustrate that there are other key variables at play. Consequently, this can obfuscate the study of identity.

The discourse on identity in the Balkans is even more complicated because of the occurrence of ethnic mimicry among minority groups, especially among Roma. This phenomenon essentially means that a group, usually disadvantaged, proceeds to camouflage its identity by taking on the identity of another – often more prestigious – group in an attempt to advance socially. This also results from economic, political or social pressures (Duijzings, 2000: 147). The irony, however (as pointed out by Duijzings (2000)), is that in doing so these groups never fully assimilate or integrate into the group whose identity they assume. One such example is that of the Balkan Egyptians. This ethnic group is considered by some to be a variation of the Roma but they themselves have undergone this process of ethnic mimicry. At various points in history they have identified themselves as, for example, Albanian or Serbian. According to

Barjaktarović (1970: 748), in former Yugoslavia at any given moment in time there was an opportunity 'to meet Rumanian, Albanians, Turks, Slovenes, Serbs, Macedonians and others, but who nonetheless have an outstanding Gypsy physiognomy'. This voluntary, affirmative taking-on of an identity is the subject of much scholarly debate, citing that in fact it has nothing to go with a group's willingness to assume an identity, but is a result of pressures generated by their instinct for survival. Popov (1992) refers to this voluntary identification as possessing a 'preferential ethnic conscience'.

The notion of a Balkan identity can also be discussed from a construc-tivist viewpoint. In doing so, however, we acknowledge that there are a plethora of other equally important and challenging elements within Balkan societies, often accompanied by limited understanding on behalf of their outsider 'European' counterparts. Identity, however, is undeniably a part of it. The difficulty associated with this attempt stems partly from the fact that, despite earnest efforts, there is still a need for greater conceptual clarity because a precise and coherent definition of what it means to be Balkan has yet to be established. Scholars such as Todorova (2004), for example, go as far as arguing that not only is there no single uniform identity, but there is not even one single Balkan culture. Furthermore, when pondering about the concept of a Balkan identity it is equally important to address its duality, first, by conceptualising the way it is perceived, discussed and studied from an outsider point of view as well as how it is regarded and assimilated by the people of the Balkans themselves. This distinction is necessary because it allows a clearer understanding of this complex issue to emerge. Namely, the bloody Yugoslav wars of the 1990s greatly contributed to a pejorative and incomplete portrayal of all things Balkan, even further solidifying the already vastly prejudiced and stereotypical impressions of the West. This unique land along with its culture and history was essentially reduced to 'a virgin frontier land to civilize ... a ghetto to contain unwanted populations from emigrating to the West' (Ditchev, 2002: 1). Ditchev goes on to say that this imagery was thusly appropriated into the then emerging 'identitarian' debate, prompting the questioning of whether being Balkan is something that should be embraced or rejected.

In spite of the limited scope of acquiescence among scholars with regards to what constitutes a Balkan identity and how it is formed, its role in shaping the historical and political destiny of the region is undeniable. Assessing the events of just the last one hundred years, one cannot deny the enormous impact identity – whether ethnic, national, religious, or linguistic – has exerted over the course of inter-state relations (Bechev, 2004). Identity, as just a single element, has indeed been a powerful factor in the many irredentist movements. Identity politics in the Balkans led to fragmentation, bloodshed, ethnic cleansing, economic stagnation and inter-ethnic division. When the Yugoslav model of unity and brotherhood failed in the wake of the wars that followed, a proceeding remedy was drawn up in an effort to alleviate this emphasis on identity and an ethno-national agenda by shifting the focus onto cooperation and coexistence, based upon mutual welfare and economic interests. This notion of identity politics coalescing with democratisation, as epitomised by the EU, for example, in itself seems antithetical. The former has a tradition and history of discord and conflict, while democratisation is associated with functional cooperation and stability. This method of analysis illustrates not only how important a role identity plays in the Balkans, but more importantly for our argument, shows the scope of difficulty which may be encountered when attempts are made to alter or modify identity.

To better illustrate the trajectory of this identitarian debate, let us briefly consider a case study of two Balkan states: Croatia and Serbia. The two nation states have exerted an enormous role in shaping the Balkan socio-political and historical landscape. By most accounts, from a Western perspective both states are emblematic of 'Balkan identity' in their sphere of influence over the course of history, but also their Slavic, religious and linguistic ties. Hence, a closer examination of these two states augments our discussion of the nature of a generic Balkan identity and, more importantly, how plausible is the idea that EU-isation can be successful, or even deemed as appropriate bearing in mind that, as argued in this chapter, a unitary Balkan identity does not exist.

Croatia and Serbia illustrate two very contrasting conceptualisations of identity. One is a paradigmatic Balkan state, while the other goes to great lengths to shed its Balkan affiliation. Croatia serves as an example of the latter in its quest for political independence and its desire to accentuate a unique Croatian identity. More importantly, the country, under the leadership of its then President Franjo Tudjman, made considerable strides to dissolve any ties to its Balkan brethren, especially with Serbia. This is what Subotic (2011: 315) calls a 'paradigmatic Balkans state', in lieu of undergoing a process of 'Croatisation', or 'Europeanisation' of identity (Croatian Ministry of Education and Sports, 1999). Tudjman's ideology, referred to as 'Franjonism', focused on a unified and independent Croatia (see Kearns, 1997). His political rhetoric – epitomised in his policies of uniting cleavages and all Croats under one national identity – was to be the fulfilment of a 'century-old dream' (Bellamy, 2003: 67). Bellamy writes that Croatians' identity under Tudjman was characterised by an attempt to unify the nation by situating them alongside an 'other', the Serbs, by contesting cultural, historical and geographical differences between these two nations, while noting Croatian superiority on all counts (Bellamy 2003: 68). His ideology and subsequent political direction even further solidified the belief that Croats do not belong in the same category as other (lesser) Balkan nations. His 1992 interview poignantly illustrates this point, where he states that

> Croats belong to a different culture – a different civilisation from the Serbs. Croats are part of Western Europe, part of the Mediterranean tradition. Long before Shakespeare and Moliere, our writers were translated into European languages. The Serbs belong to the East. They are Eastern peoples like the Turks and Albanians. They belong to the Byzantine culture … despite similarities in language we cannot be together. (Cohen, 1995: 211).

Furthermore, he argued that not only was Croatia historically and culturally similar to Europe rather than to its Serbian neighbour, but geographically there was a considerable difference. Croatia was, at its core, in Central Europe while Serbia was inherently Balkan which means that there was, as Bellamy (2003: 69) puts it, 'a difference of civilisations'. Even beyond 'Franjonistic' ideology, among intellectuals and Croatian nationalists an endeavour was further initiated, aimed at distinguishing and thus disassociating the Croatian language from its very similar Serbian counterpart (Greenberg, 2004). Moreover, as Lindstrom (2003: 317) notes, the prevailing discourse in Croatia since the early 1990s portrayed Croatians as 'more progressive, prosperous, hard-working, tolerant, democratic or, in a word, European, in contrast to their primitive, lazy, intolerant, or Balkan, neighbours'. Ever since Croatia became a sovereign and independent state, its identity construction had a dual purpose: it should absolutely retain its Croatian uniqueness while at the same time work to be thoroughly Europeanised (Subotic, 2011: 315).

Let us now consider the dichotomy of the identitarian debate by briefly illustrating the case of Serbia. For Serbia, the 1990s, like Croatia, was a period of many changes and significant socio-political transformations. The collapse of Yugoslavia had a profound effect on Serbian political influence in the region, its society and, undeniably, on its process of identity (re) construction. Unlike its Croatian neighbour, however, the country embraced a very ethno-nationalist agenda with its stance firmly pro-Serbian, rather than pro-Western. The reasons for this are numerous but an important causal factor worth mentioning stems from the fact that Serbia played a dominant role in its desperate attempts to retain regional control and exert its superiority over its neighbours, consequently seriously damaging its relationships with the West. Its campaign of ethnic cleansing and persecution of Bosnian Muslims and later Kosovo Albanians, only solidified its perception of its uniqueness, which simultaneously reaffirmed the sense of pride in its Serbian history and roots, cutting across the European and Western influences aimed at undermining this belief. Certainly in light of the Western-imposed NATO bombing during the Kosovo war, Serbia adopted its anti-European attitude even more sternly. Furthermore, Serbian rhetoric was that of self-victimisation and self-defence against an outsider adversary (MacDonald, 2002) in a continued effort of self-preservation and protection of 'Serbian interests' (Popov, 2000), which of course included its identity. Moreover, the nationalist narrative was also deeply reinforced by the Serbian Orthodox Church, which plays a vital role in socio-political affairs. Over the course of history, it has also been a noteworthy transmitter of Serbian identity.

The nationalist and anti-Europe rhetoric continued to influence Serbian politics long after Milosević's rule was over. A pivotal example of this sentiment is the assassination of Zoran Đinđić in 2003. His brief tenure on Serbia's political stage, if allowed to flourish, could have been the turning point the country desperately needed. Đinđić was known for his pro-Western policies, his cooperation with the International Criminal Tribunal at The Hague and his firm belief that Serbia's future was in fact with the EU. Instead, Serbia's course turned away from Europe when Koštunica seized power with his defiant position on EU accession and cooperation with The Hague. Interestingly enough, however, despite its well-documented ethno-nationalist stance and fervent identity, Serbia has paradoxically attempted to 'have its cake and eat it too'. This has meant that the country has begun to soften its previously harsh anti-EU attitudes, exemplified by its bid for membership in October 2010.

Despite this, both the European Commission and the Council reaffirmed their belief that the future of Serbia does in fact lie within Europe. Although the country's decision to put forth an application for EU membership came as a result of a consensus among political parties, Serbia, nonetheless, remains a country whose political elites have been divided between those who firmly believe Serbia's future is within the EU, and those who strongly oppose it. Serbia, as a country deeply rooted in its legacy of nationalism, has undergone a considerable socio-political metamorphosis which, in part, characterises its current approach towards EU integration as the coalescing of Europhobia *and* Europhilia. Some scholars would argue that acquisition of membership automatically entails an eventual acquisition of a European identity. Perhaps this is so, but does it mean as an auxiliary or entirely altered identity? The Serbian scholar, Slobodan Antonic accurately sums up this reluctance to undergo EU-isation: 'as much as it seems improbable, there is life beyond the EU. And as much as it seems improbable, such life may not be that bad' (Subotic 2011: 322). This of course remains to be seen.

What can be deduced from our brief analysis of two nations occupying the same Balkan lands for centuries, possessing a nexus of historical, cultural ties and yet with two very opposing identitarian attitudes? Croatian distinctiveness is very much interlinked with the notion of 'Europeanness', unlike its Serbian neighbour whose identity is based on ethno-nationalist sentiments. Thus, with regards to any attempts at EU-isation in the Balkans, it is safe to deduct from this example that a multidimensional approach is absolutely necessary. This is simply because a generic Balkan identity simply does not exist and its variations are as numerous as the many sundry tribes and ethnic groups that have inhabited the region for centuries. It is therefore worthwhile spending some time pondering the notion of identity as it is uniquely constructed in the Balkans; only then can we attempt to discover if it is in any way malleable. These two cases support these claims, thus making the process of EU-isation very challenging and questionable. Moreover, dissecting the process into a hub of potential advantages associated with becoming more 'European' does not necessarily produce uniform and desired effects across all Balkan societies. In fact, as the Croatian case clearly shows, considerably fewer resources and efforts are needed to entice this nation to fully become a part of 'Central Europe' and be no longer a part of the Balkans.

Serbia, on the other hand, has proved much more resilient to any changes that might alter its deep regard for its roots and identity. The EU's power of attraction has not infiltrated Serbian politics and society with the same tenacity as in other Western Balkan states who embraced their newfound status or their willingness to become less 'Balkan'. Serbia is once again at a historical crossroads, either becoming a modern, liberal democracy grounded in the values of the EU or resorting back to being a traditionalist, xenophobic and an isolated entity. The country's historical legacy serves as an ideological rubberstamp of some of the present-day challenges it faces on its path towards democratisation and European integration. The most obvious political after effect of its complicated and often bloody past is the issue of Kosovo, which is also a significant part of its identity formation, both historically and in the present day.

Conceptualising EU-isation in the Balkans

Having discussed identity as a concept within a Balkan framework, let us now fuse our identitarian discussion with the concept of EU-isation. The notion of 'Europeanising' states, groups and even individuals is most often discussed in the framework of political and economic processes aimed at states ultimately 'adapt[ing] EU rules' (Schimmelfennig and Sedelmeier, 2005: 7). The concept of EU-isation is not limited to a uniform definition with a broad applicability. In the framework of generally understood definitions of EU-isation, the primary method of EU's influence in the Balkans can be understood in terms of creating programmes such as the South East European Cooperation Initiatives, which promoted cooperating in the field of transport and border control, or through the Multinational Peace Force for South East Europe. Such regional EU-sponsored projects aim to bridge the EU–Balkan divide within the political and socio-economic spheres. A value-oriented aspect of EU-isation in this case is the amendment of the term 'Balkan' to South East Europe. This serves a dual purpose: it emphasises the European connection but more importantly, it has a de-Balkanising effect. However, our discussion thus far takes into consideration a more extensive definition, one that accounts for EU-isation as a process that, according to Katzenstein (2006: 20), not only constructs and disperses certain formal and informal rules but, in our opinion, also transmits, promotes and even imposes certain shared values that are deemed 'European'.

Efforts aimed at transforming an identity can be conceptualised within the EU's normative power. Often the EU's role within international relations is measured by its political influence and military capability. However, the concept of EU-isation illustrates a definite shift where the exertion of European authority now includes a value-oriented approach. It could even be argued that the EU's fulfilment of 'ever closer union' may be, at least in certain respects, far more successful through its 'ideological power' (Galtung, 1973) rather than the traditional 'carrot and stick' approach favoured thus far. This conviction is best illustrated by an American economist and political scientist, Richard Rosecrance (1998: 22), who said that 'Europe's attainment is normative rather than empirical ... It is perhaps a paradox to note that the continent which once ruled the world through the physical impositions of imperialism is now coming to set world standards in normative terms.'

Europe's greatest asset in securing regional cooperation in spite of the plethora of cultural, social, economic and linguistic differences among nation states is in fact an active promotion of a common European identity. This undertaking requires a conscious effort to refocus the existing emphasis from political, economic and military power in favour of a value-oriented approach. People are always more likely to empathise and associate with one another when a sense of commonality, equality, mutual understanding and trust is established rather than through – although at times effective – impermanent means (i.e. economic or political policies). The ideational impact of EU-isation (of identity) is related to the EU's role as a normative power (Manners, 2002). Furthermore, an attempt to (re)construct identity in the Balkans through a process of EU-isation is certainly a measure of what Galtung (1973: 33) calls 'ideological power' in an attempt to 'Europeanise', 'civilise', stabilise and transform this region. But can it be done? He claims that ideological power is 'powerful because the power-sender's ideas penetrate and shape the power-recipient'.

How effective, and more importantly, how well-received is this transmission of ideas on behalf of the West by the Balkan recipients? Ian Manners (2002: 242) outlines the EU's normative basis into four 'core norms' – peace, democracy, rule of law and human rights, enshrined in the abundance of treaties and declarations that go as far back as the 1950s. These principals were first elaborated upon in 1973 within the Copenhagen Declaration on European Identity. Furthermore, Manners continues his discourse of the normative power of the European Union by outlining four more elements which he categorises as 'minor norms' – anti-discrimination, sustainable development, good governance and social solidarity (Manners, 2002: 243); but it is the latter that applies most to our discussion on identity.

Certainly, the initial stages of forming a new collective identity for the Balkans in an effort to bring the region closer to Europe have begun to crystallise, but the road is arduous nonetheless. EU-isation in the Balkan context, especially with regards to identity formation, should certainly be viewed as a process over the *longue durée*. Furthermore, even if all Balkan states eventually join the EU, this in itself does not necessarily minimise the potency of each respective national identity, nor does it guarantee their potential dissolution or transformation into an exclusively European one. The blueprint for successful integration of the Balkans in the EU, as well as the simultaneous promotion of a universal European identity, is contingent upon cultivating a political climate that shifts away from the repetitive practice of analysing the Balkans through a Western perspective. Furthermore, the existent 'Us versus Them' paradigm so often applied to the discourse on the region, whether from a political or cultural standpoint, only exacerbates the already fragile and often misunderstood relationship between Europe and its Balkan periphery. The EU-isation process in all of its aspects cannot be fully realised if the approach undertaken promotes the pejorative elements of what it means to be Balkan while simultaneously underlining the superiority of retaining a European identity and world view.

As mentioned, the concept of a (European) identity is embedded within the basis of the EU's normative power and more specifically within the notion of social solidarity. This even further supports the EU's commitment to universal principles which are at the heart of its relations with member states as well as aspiring states. Considering the hybrid nature of the EU, and certainly the diverse landscape of the Balkan nations characterised by cultural, historical, linguistic, political and economic differences, a common European identity is the one crucial constitutive factor that drives the EU-isation process forward. If only the Balkan societies, which historically have been treated as non-European, could undergo a transformation of sorts. This idea then begs the question whether such a metamorphosis can be genuine or rather a consequence of 'ethnic mimicry'. Although it can be argued that this is voluntary, it does not necessarily mean it is welcomed, but perhaps forced upon as a result of political and economic pressures. If the reality is equated to the latter scenario, then complete assimilation is virtually impossible, thus making the EU-isation process of identity illusory.

Conclusion

This chapter has aimed to extend the discourse on value-oriented aspects of EU-isation on Balkan identity formation, adhering to a constructivist analytical framework. In doing so, it has illustrated that Balkan identity is far from stagnant and has undergone a series of transformations in response to historical circumstances and ever-changing political reconfigurations. More importantly, this transformative facet has also been a process of externalisation as well as internalisation of this identity (Eriksen, 2015). EU-isation of the region can in some cases be associated with deliberate *de*-Balkanisation. Perceptions of what it meant to be Balkan by the outsiders looking in during the Yugoslav hegemony under President Tito were considerably different and perhaps even less disparaging than the periods following the Federation's dissolution.

Europe, although never entirely abandoning its cautious approach towards its South-Eastern periphery, certainly credited the region with more esteem than its communist counterparts in Eastern Europe under Moscow's iron grip. Furthermore, it is important to underline the fact that EU-isation in the Balkans should be undertaken with care using a multidimensional approach. It should be recognised that the process of transformation, especially of value-oriented components such as identity, will require considerable time and – more importantly – the level of success will vary from country to country, as evidenced by the examples of Serbia and Croatia. Anastasakis (2005: 86) sums up this point best by stating that 'EU-ization in different states may be based on the same exogenous principles and the use of the same instruments, but it is a distinctly national exercise of change and adaptability'. The economic and political benefits of joining the EU appear to far outweigh the potential disadvantages, but the concluding assessment rests on the belief that replacing or even diluting a Balkan identity in favour of a pan-European identity cannot be automatically assumed nor expected. On the contrary, a deeply embedded sense of self, based on ethnicity, religious and cultural norms and traditions, and history, particularly in the Balkans, cannot be transformed so easily. Lastly, it is probable that EU-isation in any case can only go so far; perhaps it can contribute to bringing about political and economic changes while leaving the value-oriented elements, such as identity and respective affiliations, unaffected. It is perhaps worth considering that a complete identitarian transformation of *any* society is simply an impossible project.

Notes

1 For further discussion on the concept of 'ancient hatreds', see Rebecca West (1937), *Black Lamb and Grey Falcon: The Record of a Journey through Yugoslavia*.
2 This solidifying component has its origins in a study of ethnic identity formation by Frederik Barth (1969) in *Ethnic Groups and Boundaries*.

9 Dimitris Tsarouhas

Turkey: identity politics and reticent Europeanisation

Turkey constitutes a particularly challenging case with regard to Europeanisation studies as well as the importance of identity politics in its relations to the European Union (EU). While Turkey can certainly count itself among Europe's neighbours, it is also much more than that. A candidate country with EU aspirations, an emerging economy comprising a mostly young and increasingly better educated population, Turkey's cultural diversity and regional importance make it a particularly worthy case study.

Starting from the 1960s and the signing of the Turkey–EU (then the European Economic Community (EEC)) Association Agreement, the relationship between the two sides has been, and remains, tumultuous, subject to calculations and tactical manoeuvring resulting from a changing political and economic landscape. While EU accession has long been at the core of Turkey's Westernisation and modernisation strategy, which would cement its role within the Western security and political economy nexus, this approach has been subject to change in recent years. Interestingly, this development has occurred precisely at the time when relations with the EU have strengthened, negotiations to join the EU have been launched and partnership with the Union has extended to more policy fields. To explain this rather paradoxical development, one needs to approach the issue from another perspective too, namely that of the EU.

Enlargement to Central and Eastern Europe (CEE) proved controversial among the EU-15 public and the notion of 'enlargement fatigue' swiftly entered the European elites' vocabulary. Hesitation and (in some quarters) outright hostility to the prospect of Turkish EU accession have led to a serious backlash in Turkey. Domestic political elites have signalled, in turn, their unwillingness to 'bow' to EU pressure, leading to an escalating war of words that has – perhaps fatally – undermined the prospects of Turkish accession in the future.

Nevertheless, Turkey's key geographic location, ample economic potential and assertive policies in the region render the EU–Turkey relationship subject to contingent factors with long-term repercussions and do not afford the elites of either the opportunity to draw a concluding line to this relationship. Instead, the politics of pragmatism and the need for mutual cooperation have resurfaced in recent times, not least due to the spill-over effects of the Syrian civil war and the huge migration and refugee crisis (European Commission, 2015d). The latter has placed a premium on EU–Turkey relations and both sides, however unwillingly, are conscious of their mutual dependence in such turbulent times.

In line with one of the key themes of this book, this chapter considers the tensions between values and interests in the Turkey–EU relationship, using a longitudinal method. It engages with the Europeanisation literature in exploring the values and interests nexus, not least because of the frequent application of the Europeanisation research agenda to Turkey. In bringing values and interests into the debate and by engaging with the extent to which Turkey has been subject to the dynamics of Europeanisation, the chapter also sheds light on the role of domestic political and economic elites as well as public opinion. Finally, the chapter addresses recent developments in Turkey–EU relations that go beyond bilateralism, underscoring the salience of factors such as migration and instability in the Middle East as added variables to this relationship.

The chapter argues that Turkey's Europeanisation trajectory is far from straightforward. While the country's intensified relationship with EU institutions since the late 1990s has led to important political and economic reforms, pointing to a sort of Europeanisation effect, this process has been neither steady – given recent reversals – nor linear. Therefore, it is crucial to make a distinction between different periods. While the early phase (roughly from the late 1990s to 2007) was characterised by an enthusiastic adoption of EU conditionality to achieve the aim of launching accession talks, subsequent phases have led to a slowdown and partial reversion of this adoption. More importantly, the early phase was driven by top-down conditionality. Considerable legislative changes were introduced to pursue the accession objective without serious consideration of the possible repercussions of these changes and the need for proper implementation. A form of 'thin' Europeanisation had emerged by the mid-2000s and the deteriorating relations with the EU then led to a freezing of relations. Though the country maintains an accession perspective (albeit blurry and uncertain), its adaptation of EU values and norms, the identity-driven element of Europeanisation, is far from present. In addition, domestic political considerations now interact heavily with the country's foreign policy orientation – majoritarian politics and heavy societal and party political polarisation have undermined Turkey's EU prospects. Just when Europeanisation was supposed to kick in and 'lock in' progressive political reforms, these have been undermined – and the EU has been little more than an observer to the process.

This chapter continues with a theoretical discussion on Europeanisation and applies this framework to accession countries through the prism of conditionality and the specific role of candidate countries. The next section introduces EU–Turkey relations by analysing some of the main patterns of Turkey's identity politics that have contributed to its domestic as well as international political outlook since the foundation of the Republic. The following two sections discuss both the 'opening' of Turkey since it acquired EU candidate country status in 1999, as well as subsequent developments that have undermined its EU aspirations. The final section, prior to the conclusion, accounts for these reversals and underlines how the 'thick' domestic-foreign policy nexus of the present time has led to policy choices and priorities incompatible with the country's membership desire.

Europeanisation: member states and candidate countries

Europeanisation studies have traditionally concentrated on the ways in which the Union has been able (or unable) to affect domestic political structures within member states (Börzel and Risse, 2003). In order to examine the precise conditions in which this works, the relative 'distance' between domestic and EU legislative and institutional practices often becomes the focus point ('goodness of fit'). It is at this conjuncture that institutionalist theory could enter the realm of EU studies by offering the opportunity to use sociological, historical or rationally grounded approaches to observe the degree to which Europeanisation can actually work (Tsar-ouhas, 2012).

There is, however, an alternative, 'bottom-up', approach less focused on elite interactions and more concerned with the absorption of EU norms and practices at a societal as well as political level. Here the EU becomes an intermediate variable while the search for causal explanations begins and ends at the national level, that is, with the member state concerned (Vink and Graziano, 2008: 9). The biggest obstacle in searching for convincing evidence of the Europeanisation effect is to identify the precise mechanisms through which the process occurs and in that way move beyond anecdotal evidence. One important contributor in that direction is Knill (2001), who has offered: a) changing domestic opportunity structures; b) framing beliefs and expectations; and c) institutional compliance. In line with Chapter 1 of this volume, it is crucial to underline that Europeanisation cannot and should not be seen as an a priori fixed and static process. It is subject to ideational diffusion travelling across space and time and subject to a variety of influences (Flockhart, 2010). The Turkish case study reveals the potency of such a depiction of Europeanisation.

The following analysis discusses the high relevance of such a typology to Turkey. As the mechanism on domestic opportunity structures suggests, the EU accession process did indeed offer the opportunity for a rebalancing of political forces within Turkey as a result of EU conditionality and the introduction of important institutional changes. Although institutional compliance is more applicable to member states bound by EU law, this third mechanism on framing is also relevant to Turkey. The expectation of accession mobilised dormant forces and led to the active participation of civil society in Turkey by way of reforming policies and institutions. This mechanism is important in that it underlines the agency role of the EU, which seeks to mould beliefs and expectations along an EU trajectory and operates cognitively rather than through 'hard' mechanisms. It also does so through particular political discourse that legitimises certain types of policy behaviour as more 'appropriate' than others (Radaelli and Schmidt, 2004).

Europeanisation and the politics of conditionality

The Europeanisation literature has developed a framework to examine EU influence on candidate countries as well. This framework is by necessity different from the one directly applicable to member states by use of hard law. Instead, candidate countries have to be enticed through a carrot-and-stick strategy to adjust their policy paradigms to those prevalent among member states (Schimmelfennig and Sedelmeier, 2005). This is a less formal, but not necessarily less powerful, set of incentives to arrive at desired policy outcomes (Bulmer and Radaelli, 2004).

The credibility of conditionality is central to this literature. For reform to be implemented in candidate states, the EU should guarantee to offer membership to them upon fulfilment of the specific criteria (political, economic and administrative) set out in the 1993 Copenhagen Summit (Avery, 2004). The chapter discusses this at length, pointing to the lack of credible commitment on the part of the EU towards Turkey, which eventually led to the deterioration of bilateral relations. A second key factor is the salience placed by the EU on specific policy areas. The literature assumes that conformity to EU norms and policies is much greater in those policy areas on which the EU places a premium, and that there is less pressure in those the EU regards as less important.

Turkey's multiple identities and relations with Europe: 1923–1980s

Relations between Turkey and the then EEC stretch back to the early 1960s and the signing of the 1963 Association Agreement. The Agreement envisaged a step-by-step approximation of the two sides on economic matters, which would then lead to the signing of a Customs Union, and then examine the possibility of Turkey's participation in the Community (European Economic Community, 1963). In this important respect Turkey has always enjoyed a privileged relationship with the Community, prior to receiving a date to start accession negotiations. The Association Agreement, also known as 'the Ankara Agreement', is significant for two further reasons. First, it was indicative of Turkey's early recognition that the EEC would come to play a leading role in terms of economic cooperation in Europe and that Turkey ought to engage with this new entity to obtain maximum benefits from its existence. The fact that Greece had signed an Association Agreement a few years earlier was a further motivation for policy makers in Ankara. Second, and as important as the economic potential of the EEC was, its significance for Turkey was larger still. The EEC, just like other institutions and organisations in the Western world (the Council of Europe and NATO, for instance) was a goal to strive for in terms of confirming the country's Western and secular identity.

The Republic established by Mustafa Kemal Atatürk in 1923 attempted a clean break with the Ottoman past, and Turkey's full incorporation into Western structures and organisations became synonymous with Atatürk's vision of a nation fully in tune with modernity, technological prowess and enlightened thinking (Landau, 1983). The West was viewed as representing those ideals and the consolidation of a staunchly secular regime in Turkey went hand in hand with the country's conscious efforts to emulate Western practice in all spheres of political, economic and cultural life. Atatürk's revolution and Turkey's Western identity were two sides of the same coin. Finally, domestic political consensus on the desirability of Turkey's membership of the Community was widespread (Eralp, 2009).

During the1960s and 1970s, EEC integration stalled and the dynamic of integration was halted. A staunch intergovernmentalism acquired powerful dimensions during the de Gaulle era in France as the General successfully stalled Britain's EEC membership prospects twice within the space of seven years. Yet even after de Gaulle's departure from office, the Community faced serious obstacles on the way towards further integration: the 'golden era' of welfare capitalism came to an end in the 1970s while regional instability in the Middle East and the surge in oil prices contributed to stagnation. Rising unemployment and the stagflation phenomenon eventually acted as an impetus towards further integration in the 1980s, not least through the adoption of the Single Market project. However, the road was full of obstacles and Europe's inability to break the cycle of economic crisis and political discord became apparent (Gilbert, 2012).

On the surface, this period does not herald important changes regarding Turkey's approach to the EEC. The dynamics of the Cold War and Turkey's role in it led to no change in calculations regarding the usefulness of Turkey as a Western ally in the region and relations with the EEC were characterised by stability. Nevertheless, and through the prism of identity politics, this period is of utmost importance. The introduction of multi-party democracy in Turkey in 1950 and the successful challenge of the 'periphery' in the form of the Democratic Party under Prime Minister Menderes demonstrate the existence of multiple identities within Turkey's domestic socio-economic and political landscape. The 'core', which comprised all major state institutions as well as the party created by Atatürk, the Republican Peoples' Party (CHP), was faced with the first set of objections to its dominant role in identifying the character of the Turkish Republic, as well as its desire to singlehandedly determine the country's future trajectory, based on a 'raw' interpretation of secularism and the ascribing of a particular political and cultural stance in the public as well as private sphere. It is no coincidence that the country's armed forces emerged in this period as the guardians of the Republican regime and intervened in political life to 'safeguard' the Republic's achievements from forces inside or outside the country suspected of seeking to undermine them.

In the same period and especially after the 1970s, political Islam emerged as an explicit party political force and set out a narrative about the country and its 'soul' in sharp contradiction to the state ideology (Ayata, 1996; Gülalp, 2001). In the context of the Cold War, its ability to determine the country's future direction was limited, but it helped contribute to an increase in dissenting voices that sought to pull Turkey away from the EEC. It succeeded, however, in creating a precedent in the country's approach towards the West in general and the EU in particular, which came sharply into focus after Turkey became an official candidate country and when negotiations for EU membership were launched.

Following the adoption of the '24 January' economic programme in 1980, Turkey sidestepped its import substitution model of development and liberalised its economy. The process continued in leaps and bounds for most of the following four decades, although the country was plagued by serious political instability. The military coup of 1980 put a hold on the nascent process of political pluralism that the radical 1960s had helped initiate, and appeared to confirm that a 'strong state' was necessary to guarantee tranquillity at home and the country's continued alliance with the Western world at the international level. The country's Prime Minister and later President, the late Turgut Özal, epitomised the 1980s and 1990s and his political and cultural legacy resonated heavily with the majority of Turkey's pious, conservative and centre-right voters.

During Özal's period of office, Turkey's complex dynamics and conflicting identities found their expression domestically as well as in foreign policy terms. Domestically, Özal represented the periphery in its modernised version: conservative and observant in social and cultural terms yet welcoming of a US-style capitalism that aimed to catapult Turkey into the frontrunners of neoliberal restructuring (Önis, 2004). Reminiscent of Thatcherism in Britain, Turkey's Özal favoured an ever-expanding role for the private sector in economic affairs and did not hesitate to set up state structures – parallel to the existing ones – to bypass administrative hurdles towards a free(r) market economy. On the international front, Özal recognised the salience of the EEC following the adoption of the Single Market and the economic opportunities that it entailed for the nascent export-driven sectors of the Turkish economy. Yet he also inaugurated a careful but determined shift in foreign policy that came to embrace the newly independent Turkic Republics of Central Asia as constituting Turkey's 'near abroad' and stressed the need to cultivate much stronger cultural, economic and political ties with Turkey's 'cousin states', whose liberation from the 'communist yoke' offered ample opportunities for Turkey in the region (Aral, 2001).

This process is very significant because it resonates with one of Turkey's many identities, namely the idea of Pan-Turkism. This asserts a singular definition of Turkic identity which is inexorably linked with the idea of fraternal unity among all of its subjects and which prioritises the cultivation of unity among the Turkic peoples. This is not a de facto negation of Turkey's Western aspirations or its membership of institutions like the EU. It only becomes one to the (very real) extent that the EU presupposes the existence and implementation of a set of liberally minded values and practices (such as respect for minorities and cultural pluralism within member states) (Hintz, 2013). Since such values and practices cannot but impede the desired unity of the Turkic people, they stand in the way of realising the potential that such unity holds for its members. Further, this reading of Turkish identity finds little difficulty in articulating an opposition to 'Western imposed' practices and values that are deemed unworthy of Turkey and which can then be portrayed as reflecting the Western world's (or Europe's) 'hypocrisy' or 'double standards' against Turkey, whose cultural difference from 'Europe' can then be taken for granted (Kushner, 1997).

If the Republican and Pan-Turkic identities offer important clues about the complexity of Turkey, a third and vitally important one is that of a synthesis between religion and nationalism, sometimes described as 'Turkish-Islamic synthesis'. Nationalism and religion (the latter interpreted and understood strictly along the lines of the majority Sunni sect) are hereby combined and thus stand in sharp opposition to Europe's liberal premises. On both national and religious grounds, this line of reasoning identifies multiple incompatibilities between the European vocation and Turkey's role in international affairs. Sharing similarities and differences with both the Republican and pan-Turkic visions, this sub-identity has grown steadily over time. Its flexible nature has turned it into a potent sociological force in Turkey, and elements from its core premise of combining nationalism with religiosity are widespread within and across political parties.

Before turning to a more explicitly political analysis of EU–Turkey relations since the 1990s, it is important to clarify that the sub-identities are not exhaustive of Turkey's complexity. Moreover, they are adaptive and their political utilisation or expression can take place in ways that break down the analytical barriers between them. Such is the case with the ruling Justice and Development Party (AKP), whose long period in office has clearly revealed the coexistence of alternative versions of identity politics and the domination of one identity over another expressed in concrete political action. The interesting question (which this chapter attempts to answer) then becomes: which factors contribute to the rise of a particular interpretation of identity politics? The answer has vital repercussions with regard to Turkey's EU vocation and the extent to which it desires, and is able, to join the Union.

EU–Turkey relations post-Helsinki: Europeanisation or not?

The Helsinki EU Summit of 1999 is a milestone in Turkey's relations with the EU since it decided to grant Turkey the status of a candidate country. It was followed by a period of intense political reform (Yesilada, 2002). Both the 1999–2002 coalition government headed by the veteran Bülent Ecevit as well as the single-party AKP government were determined to capitalise on the momentum created by the Helsinki summit. For all the changes that Turkey and Europe had undergone since the original application was launched by Özal in 1987, EU membership remained a key point of majority convergence for the country's elites as well as vast swathes of the population. Pre-accession conditionality worked remarkably well in addressing some of the core issues of concern for Europe, especially with regard to civil–military relations (Duman and Tsarouhas, 2006; Sarigil, 2007), the abolition of the death penalty and the liberalisation of political discourse (Heper, 2005; Müftüler Bac, 2005). The start of accession negotiations in 2005 was seen in Turkey as the decisive step towards membership and the realisation of a foreign policy goal that had long symbolised the country's suitability in a Western community of values and principles derived from a liberal world view. In the post-9/11 world plagued by the rise of a culturalist reading of international affairs and rising Islamophobia fed by ignorance and/or prejudice, Turkey was now assuming a new position away from a Cold War-oriented calculus.

Turkey was being modelled, and sought to model itself, as the primary example of a Muslim majority country at ease with a liberal democratic set of principles governing its domestic and international political behaviour. Traces of this approach were evident long after relations with the EU deteriorated. The 'zero problems with neighbours' approach at the international level and successive 'openings' towards discriminated minorities or groups within Turkey (primarily Kurds and Alevis) sought to underline the break with Turkey's past and usher in an era of expanded pluralism for all citizens of Turkey. Importantly, this modelling of Turkey along the lines of a fully Europeanised identity was not limited to Turkey itself. For the United States, Turkey could now play a new model role that would display the rightness of Washington's attempts to coerce democratic reforms in the Middle East in the aftermath of the 2003 Iraq invasion.

Given Turkey's embrace of this role and its conscious cultivation of a 'soft power' image in the region by use of TV series, free trade deals and visa waiving agreements, the strategy bore fruit. For many in the Middle East, Turkey's EU vocation became an experiment of intense interest to gauge both Europe's readiness for such an embrace and Turkey's own handling of its membership bid. The apparent success of conditionality appeared not only to back the theoretical exposé on Europeanisation and its (desirable) effects discussed here; it also seemed to confirm the empirical reality of 'normative power Europe' (Manners, 2002), which can entice positive reform in candidate countries and confirm the centrality of a liberal approach to international affairs (Aydin and Açikmeşe, 2007; Oğuzlu, 2013). Turkey's privileged relations with the EU through the 1995 Customs Union could now take a more serious turn and expand to the political sphere in a way unimaginable just a decade earlier. The EU was happy to credit itself with Turkey's transformation and both sides appeared content, with self-congratulatory descriptions of change.

Relations between Turkey and the EU deteriorated rapidly soon after the accession negotiations were launched and the pro-reform momentum stalled. The Arab Spring events of 2010–11 have also led to the resurfacing of an old debate: Western commentators argued over 'who lost Turkey' (Pipes, 2014) and the country's depiction as part of the Middle East problem instead of a European solution soon gathered pace. In 2016, and despite the hesitant revival of EU–Turkey relations on the back of mutual needs and dependencies, Turkey was as far from membership of the EU as it ever was in recent memory.

What has gone wrong? Why has Europeanisation not worked in this case? Is Turkey a *sui generis* case whose analysis cannot, and should not, follow standard Europeanisation tools? What sorts of calculations and policy preferences have led to the current divergence, and under what conditions may Turkey be able to return to the sphere of EU influence? The next section argues that identity politics is of central importance to understand the deterioration of relations, both with regard to the EU and Turkey. Nevertheless, identity politics in itself says little about contemporary EU–Turkey relations if it is not combined with a careful tracing of domestic political developments since 2007–8 and the rise of majoritarian politics in Turkey which then combined with foreign policy developments and the EU's own ambivalence towards it to produce the current outcome.

The EU debate on Turkey since the 2000s

Europeanisation theory rightly argues that the credibility of conditionality is a decisive variable in gauging a candidate country's commitment to, and implementation of, EU-conforming reform. Turkey's EU accession story is remarkable in that this credibility appeared to evaporate rapidly precisely at the time when the country's efforts towards membership started acquiring structural characteristics.

The period in question is the early 2000s. Owing to the multiple electoral cycles in EU member states, a centre-left Council majority was replaced by a conservative majority whose appreciation of Europe as a cultural, as much as a political, entity complicated Turkey's membership bid. The rise of identity politics in Europe had already started some years earlier, as mass immigration undermined traditional party political cleavages and starkly demonstrated the increasing divide between the 'winners' and 'losers' of globalisation in Europe as well as the rest of the world. In addition, enlargement to Central and Eastern Europe had by that time become a fait accompli, even if it would not include all candidate countries at the same time (Szolucha, 2010). Popular resentment towards enlargement, though often motivated by genuine concerns regarding the absence of socio-economic convergence between Western and Eastern Europe, revealed a growing discontent with the pace and direction of European integration. It was also symbolic of a rising wave of EU rejectionism whose most profound expression has been seen in the xenophobic and hard Eurosceptic parties that nowadays flourish across Europe and beyond.

These processes had direct consequences for Turkey and often in unpredictable ways. Regardless of the merits or not of treating Turkey as a special case compared to Eastern European candidates, many EU leaders made a conscious, well-calculated and deeply populist attempt to portray Turkey as a country culturally alien to 'Europe' and the values that go with it, instead of a candidate country whose future fulfilment of the Copenhagen criteria would lead, if and when achieved, to full EU membership (Müftüler Bac, 2000). President Sarkozy of France was explicit in that regard, arguing that Turkey is an 'Asia Minor' state and therefore not eligible for EU membership (Mahony and Spongenberg, 2007). Words were then matched with deeds as France unilaterally blocked five of the thirty-three *acquis* chapters, erroneously stressing that such chapters would lead to full membership and thus had to be placed off the table. Sarkozy's successor, François Hollande, lifted France's veto on one of those chapters, yet the other four remain blocked. Combined with blockages imposed by the Council and Cyprus, Turkey is the only candidate country which, after a decade of (nominal) negotiations, has only been able to provisionally close one chapter.

The divisions between a primarily political approach to Turkey *vis-à-vis* a culturalist/identity-driven one was not simply down to individual leaders or enlargement fatigue. It was also directly related to the crisis that European integration went through in that same period, namely the failure of the Constitutional Treaty and the strong backlash that Europe's leaders experienced at the time (Startin and Krouwel, 2013). The long institutional crisis, resolved through the adoption of the Lisbon Treaty in 2009, left a bitter legacy and enlarged the (fictitious or real) divide between Europe's peoples and its leadership. Instead of being a sought-after prize for geopolitical influence, larger markets and a more assertive foreign policy, Turkey's EU membership bid now appeared as an unpredictable gamble in a crisis context and as grist in the mill of inward-looking populism.

Turkey's policy change and EU membership

Yet if identity politics matters regarding the Union's stance towards Turkey, it matters as much regarding Turkey's waning enthusiasm for membership. The earlier discussion on Turkey's multiple and conflicting identities demonstrates not only the pluralism inherent in Turkey, but also the extent to which such identities are subject to appropriation by policy entrepreneurs. After assuming office in 2002, the single-party AKP government made it immediately clear that its understanding of Turkey's role in regional and global affairs was very different from the exclusively Western-oriented rationale that had dominated, with some exceptions, the state bureaucracy and mainstream political parties until then. According to former Prime Minister and earlier adviser to Presidents Gül and Erdoğan, Ahmet Davutoğlu, Turkey has the unique potential to punch above its weight due to its geographical location, rich cultural resources and 'soft power' potential in regions such as the Balkans, the Middle East and the Caucasus region (Aras, 2009; Davutoğlu, 2001, 2008).

This was not (and is not) to deny the importance of EU membership for Turkey and the prestige and resources that would accompany it. After all, EU membership is still characterised by senior political figures in Turkey as the country's 'strategic goal'. It is, however, indicative of a mindset that acknowledges Turkey's special role and status *vis-à-vis* 'conventional' European powers and which sought to diversify Turkey's foreign policy as a sign of its increasing assertiveness. Multiple free trade deals and visa waiver agreements in the regions as well as mediation efforts in the Arab–Israeli conflict (Altunişik and Cuhadar, 2010) and elsewhere were used to imply that the Ottoman Empire may be no longer, but that the 'new' Turkey that emerged after the rise of AKP to power would do everything possible to reclaim a large part of the Ottoman past with regard to Turkey's central role in former Ottoman lands.

Until its re-election in 2007, the AKP government complied with EU requirements and appeared to freshen up Turkey's approach to regional disputes, not least with regard to its proactive policies for a settlement in the decades-old Cyprus dispute (Çelenk, 2007). The attempt to close down the AKP as a 'focal point' of 'religious extremism' reminded many in the party and outside it that old political habits die hard and that consolidating its ability to govern rather than administer the country still hang in the balance. Able to count on stringent EU support, the AKP not only survived the crisis through a favourable Constitutional Court ruling but also returned to office with an increased majority and proceeded, over time, with the initiation of a careful set of tactical moves to transform the state apparatus in its favour (Saatçioğlu, 2014). Given the shortcomings of the opposition and the overwhelmingly positive view, by most Turkish citizens, of former Prime Minister and today's President Erdoğan, the party succeeded in monopolising the ability to dictate the political discourse and to transform the party system towards a dominant model (Ayan Musil, 2014). The process has been successful, but not without cost. Turkey's ability to act as a pole of attraction, at least for Middle Eastern countries, has by now been replaced by frozen conflicts and open animosity with most neighbours, including states with which relations flourished precisely due to AKP policy prescriptions in the early 2000s.

The Arab Spring has played a decisive role, albeit in an indirect way, in the deterioration of EU–Turkey relations. Previously, Turkish policy makers were able to match solid Western alliances with a bold rhetoric on 'regional power Turkey' and its ability to attract others due to its cultural resources, economic might and political stability (Davutoğlu, 2008). The Arab Spring changed all that. Turkey chose to follow a 'principled' foreign policy opposing authoritarian regimes, albeit in an inconsistent manner. Soon afterwards, Turkey became embroiled in conflicts in Libya, Egypt and, most of all, Syria. Though this is hardly inconsistent with the new leadership's self-image, it became increasingly problematic as Turkey's priorities and concrete policies started to openly contradict those of allies such as the United States and the EU. More importantly, foreign policy became part of a domestic political discourse and the portrayal of political adversaries as 'national traitors' in the case of foreign policy disagreements marked a new low in the history of the Turkish Republic. Upping the stakes and committing to the support of particular groups in countries such as Syria led to a largely unsustainable set of policy contradictions from which only a quick end to the Syrian civil war may provide an exit. Even then, the reversal of previous bold domestic reforms in a number of policy areas guarantees that Turkey's EU accession path will be fraught with near insurmountable obstacles for some years to come.

Conclusion

Among all the countries examined in this volume, Turkey has had the longest and most intense relationship with the EU. Mutual relations remain intense and active and the migration and refugee crisis is the best illustration of the fact that the two sides need each other more than they often care to admit. However, the analysis in this chapter has made it pretty clear that the extent to which Turkey has been Europeanised is ambiguous at best. It has not hesitated to follow a set of policies that are at odds with EU priorities. It has occasionally doubted the wisdom of EU membership and has openly accused EU states of hypocrisy, double standards and more. More worryingly, 'reform fatigue' (Patton, 2007) has recently been replaced by regressive reforms in vital areas, such as the judicial system.

How can one begin to explain this emotional and, at least to many, irrational stance? In the preceding analysis we have discussed the existence of multiple identities that have historically coloured Turkey's approach towards the West in general and Europe in particular. The staunchly pro-Western stance of the early Cold War period reflected the dominant political consensus and brought the set of social forces espousing that goal to the fore. During the 1970s and 1980s, and as part of the rise in identity politics throughout the world, a more exclusive type of nationalism was coupled with the rise of political Islam to complicate Turkey's domestic dynamics. This had little bearing on Turkey's foreign policy priorities and outlook for as long as Cold War 'stability', relative economic backwardness, and the domestic political equilibrium could be taken for granted.

By the 2000s, Turkey had changed to an extent that would have been hard to foresee a few decades earlier. It had created a deregulated economy at ease with neoliberal globalisation and was actively pursuing a multi-dimensional foreign policy premised on a combination of soft power and geopolitical realities (Murinson, 2006). Domestic political developments, however, are by now intensely intertwined with its foreign policy goals and the separation line between the two has largely disappeared. Since the onslaught of the Arab Spring, Turkey's sense of foreign policy direction has been disturbed and its long-standing alliances are now shakier than ever in the post-Cold War period. More perilously still, relations with Russia have entered a dangerous downward spiral and averting the worst on multiple crisis fronts constitutes the only credible political alternative. Turkey's Europeanisation prospects are now very dim indeed, and a recovery in its relations with the EU does not merely hinge on a reversal of current trends within Turkey. As stressed earlier, Europeanisation is neither linear nor given. Finally, a genuine revival in EU–Turkey relations that goes beyond immediate, interest-based calculations also presupposes the ability of the EU to emerge successful from long-term, strategic challenges such as Brexit and economic stagnation. It is a tall order and hard to fathom the best ways to bring it about.

PART III

Issues and sectors

New member states' economic relations with Russia: 'Europeanisation' or bilateral preferences?

This chapter examines connections between economic issues and the various challenges to, and conundrums of, Europeanisation associated with the EU's relations with Eastern neighbours. It focuses on trade between EU member states and Russia, which until recently had been growing steadily, with particularly rapid expansion after the EU's eastward enlargement in 2004. The significance of the Russian market means that disruptions to trade caused by sanctions are both costly and contentious. Their effects upon individual EU states obviously vary depending on the extent and type of trade with Russia, other important indicators of interdependence (such as energy sector integration) and the degree of overall damage to import demand in Russia. Though no EU state has vetoed sanctions, the Ukrainian crisis has undoubtedly tested the resilience of an EU multilateral approach to Russia. It has also highlighted the relevance of bilateral instruments for trade and economic cooperation with Russia, the role they play and extent to which they complement or maybe even circumvent multilateral strategies. Furthermore, certain new member states' attitudes to sanctions have been interpreted not only in terms of economic and business rationale but also, for some elite segments at least, as a product of excessively close political relations with Russia. Relations with the Eastern neighbourhood have even been linked to questions about a core dimension of the Europeanisation process that new EU member states were until recently assumed to have undergone. Notions of 'disappearing democracy' and 'democratic backsliding' in new EU member states have gained traction (Inotai, 2015; Meuller, 2014; Sedelmeier, 2014) with some narratives highlighting the influence of Russia, or at least its model of democracy, as a factor.[1]

This particular study concentrates on the experiences of the three 'small' 'Visegrad states' – the Czech Republic, Hungary and Slovakia – all of which have been at the forefront of the EU export boom to Russia. They are also in the group of EU countries that have harboured most reservations about sanctions against Russia with the leaders of Hungary and Slovakia among the most vocal critics (Dangerfield, 2015) and have fought hard to protect their interests in the sanctions process. When the second round of sanctions on Russia were being formulated in July 2014, Laca and Tomek (2014) reported that, whereas security concerns overrode economic ones for Poland and the Baltic states, 'economic concerns take precedence for the governments in Budapest, Prague and Bratislava ... [t]hey're trying to change the definition of what the sanctions might look like in to avoid their economies being hurt'. The three are therefore clearly very appropriate case studies, not only due to their interventions on the sanctions issue and significance of current levels of trade but also because they have, for historical reasons, dense and intensive relationships with Russia.

This chapter begins with a brief analysis of trade patterns during the period between 1993 and 2003, essentially a long period of transition. The second part outlines the main developments in trade between the Czech Republic, Hungary, Slovakia and Russia after EU accession. The third part focuses on bilateral instruments for trade and economic cooperation with Russia. The fourth section discusses the possible relevance of new 'strategic' visions for economic development that emerged after the Eurozone crisis and the final section draws attention to the important influence of alternative internal perspectives on economic and business relations on Russia. The conclusions sum up what the fine detail examination of economic relations tell us about the interplay of national/bilateral and European/multilateral approaches towards this key Eastern neighbour and also whether the more sensational narratives, in particular the idea that criticisms of sanctions are the result of sudden recent 'lurches' to Russia or even 'Putinisation', bear close scrutiny.

Czech, Hungarian and Slovak trade with Russia during EU pre-accession: the 'long' period of transition

The end of communism heralded a dramatic reduction of all former communist countries' mutual trade and especially trade between the USSR and Central and East European (CEE) members of the former Council for Mutual Economic Assistance (CMEA). After 1991, direct economic relations with Russia became a reality. Trade with Russia followed the same broad pattern for the Czech Republic, Hungary and Slovakia and remained more or less stable during 1993–2003. The key feature of this period was a structural trade deficit on the part of all three countries caused by a combination of energy dependence on Russia and stagnant or deteriorating export performance. With some modest fluctuations along the way, the 1993 and 2003 US$ values of Czech and Slovak exports to Russia were virtually unchanged, meaning a substantial fall in real terms. Hungary's situation was even less favourable with a fall of around 30 per cent in even the nominal value of exports over the same period. Steadily increasing import bills exacerbated trade deficits, with (between 1993 and 2003) a 255 per cent increase for the Czech Republic, 218 per cent for Slovakia, and 152 for Hungary (Dangerfield, 2015).

Numerous factors, well documented at the time, accounted for these post-CMEA trade patterns between Russia and these three countries (see Dangerfield, 2000). These included loss of competitiveness, general chaos and weak demand in the Russian economy and Russia's own economic opening to the West. On the part of the three and CEE as a whole, there was of course their own and far more profound strategic reorientation of trade to the West, encouraged by Europe Agreements and a rapid move to free trade with the EU. They also took steps to revive their own mutual trade in the framework of the Central European Free Trade Agreement (CEFTA), which was a regional integration initiative founded exclusively by and for CEE and, as such, was the closest thing to a revival of the CMEA grouping. By 1997, the level of intra-CEFTA trade was standing in stark contrast to the Soviet domination of intra-CMEA trade and marginal role of trade among the 'six': Czech exports to CEFTA were eight times greater than exports to Russia, Hungary's three times greater and Slovakia's sixteen times greater (Dangerfield, 2000). Finally, it is worth noting that the case of Slovakia, where revival of CMEA-era levels of trade with Russia was the core economic (and foreign policy) strategy during the 1994–98 period, showed that differences in official attitudes to Russia had no discernible impact on export levels.

Trade with Russia after EU accession – new trends

Exports to Russia moved into a phase of strong growth after EU accession. Between 2004 and 2013, Czech exports increased by 581 per cent, Hungarian exports by 344 per cent and Slovak exports by 906 per cent. In 2012, Czech exports to Russia accounted for 20.4 per cent of total extra-EU exports, compared to 10.8 per cent in 2004. For Hungary, it was 13.1 per cent in 2012 compared to 9.8 per cent in 2004, and 25.6 per cent and 9.1 per cent for Slovakia respectively (Dangerfield, 2015). Despite these increases the trade deficit with Russia widened both for Slovakia and Hungary due to higher values of imports from Russia over this period, mainly caused by increased energy prices. Nevertheless, as exports grew faster than imports the deterioration in trade balance was moderated. Czech export growth easily outpaced that of imports and, thanks to some diversification of energy supplies, the trade deficit narrowed over this period. As for commodity structure, the most important Czech exports to Russia are in a wide range of manufactured industrial goods including machinery and transport equipment (especially cars), chemicals, food products and construction materials. Slovakia's exports to Russia are concentrated in machinery and transport equipment (especially cars), chemical and allied products, other industrial goods and fabrics. For Hungary, the most important product categories are machinery and transport equipment, mobile phones, pharmaceuticals, chemical and allied products and foodstuffs. Imports from Russia in all three countries are dominated by raw materials and oil and gas, which account for around 85 per cent, 90 per cent and 90 per cent of the imports of the Czech Republic, Slovakia and Hungary respectively.

Though the surge in exports to Russia became apparent after 2003, there is no strong evidence that EU entry per se was the key cause, although there was a significant statistical impact which in fact further emphasises that the key influences had already occurred by the time EU accession took place:

> [b]efore EU accession exports of TNCs [Transnational corporations] from Central European subsidiaries were mostly counted in EU export as a result of firm level agreements between subsidiaries and their headquarters in the EU. After accession to the EU, this practice changed, and these exports were counted into the export of Central European countries. This statistical change also explains the sudden and radical modification of export structures in favour of manufacturing industries, since most of the FDI [Foreign Direct Investment] firms exporting to Russia were operating in this category. (Novak, 2014a: 11)

This underscores certain economic consequences of EU pre-accession that played a major role. In particular, large inflows of foreign direct investment built up export capacity in sectors that have been of special importance in overall EU exports to Russia and which have experienced rapid growth in recent years: for example, passenger cars/road vehicles and medicinal and pharmaceutical products which accounted for 11 per cent and 7 per cent respectively of total EU exports to Russia in 2010 (Eurostat, 2011). The changing capacity of the three enabled them to ultimately join many other EU states in benefiting from the 'boom' in Russian imports that took off after 2000. This in turn was on the back of high levels of economic growth and the Russian state's use of buoyant oil revenues to significantly raise household incomes and fuel consumer spending. Between 2005 and 2010, the value of Russia's imports more than doubled from US$79,712 million to US$197,472 million, having reached a pre-crisis peak of US$230,494 million in 2008.[2] As well as the three, most EU states experienced strong growth in their exports to Russia, demonstrating that the growth of the three's exports was mainly part of a wider trend.

Finally, some comments about more recent trade patterns. In 2013, Czech exports for the year declined by 6 per cent compared to 2012, Hungary's by 1 per cent and Slovakia's by 7 per cent. Thus, some levelling off and even slight decline of exports to Russia was evident even before the onset of the Ukraine crisis. As would be expected, the downward trend for exports continued in 2014 with falls of 8.25 per cent for the Czech Republic and 6.2 per cent and 18.5 per cent for Slovakia and Hungary respectively.[3] This was of course part of an overall trend of significantly reduced import demand in Russia caused by a combination of the broader effects of sanctions on the Russian economy, the plummeting oil price (which more than halved in the second half of 2014 and has stayed in the doldrums since) and the resultant effect on state revenues, and the drastic collapse of the Rouble, which lost around half of its value against the US$ during the last six months of 2014. Otherwise, the EU sanctions and the Russian response have so far not focused on the key exports sectors of the three. As noted, when the second round of sanctions were negotiated by EU leaders in July 2014, the three lobbied hard to avoid sanctions that would hurt their economic interests with Russia. Robert Fico, for example, said at the time that if 'more sanctions are proposed, I reserve the right in the name of the Slovak government to reject certain sanctions that would hurt national interests' while Czech Prime Minister Bohuslav Sobotka said that '[w]e would like to achieve a change in the conditions of the currently prepared sanctions so that they affect Czech machinery exports as little as possible' (Laca and Tomek, 2014).

Lobbying occurred at other levels of EU governance too. On 10 March 2016, Czech MEP Jiří Maštálka was awarded Russia's highest honour for a foreigner, the Order of Friendship. *Prague Post* (2016) noted that as well as serving the cause of Czech-Russia friendship for over twenty years, at 'the European Parliament he has pushed for a softening of European sanctions against Russia over the annexation of Crimea and war in Eastern Ukraine'. These lobbying efforts were clearly successful to an extent. For example, an important exemption on nuclear fuels imports from Russia was secured, despite pressure from some EU member states (and Westinghouse lobbying) to include it. Even though EU agricultural exports have been affected, the direct effects of the Russian measures have had only a 'negligible effect' and exclude many of the products that Hungary exports to Russia in significant quantities (*Diplomacy & Trade*, 2014).

Bilateral intergovernmental cooperation on trade and economic relations

As well as the export boom discussed above, bilateral cooperation around trade and economic cooperation between Russia and the governments of the three has clearly strengthened since EU accession. In 2004, the Czechs and Russians established the Czech–Russian Intergovernmental Commission for Economic, Industrial and Scientific Cooperation (C-RICEISC). A year later, the Hungarian–Russian Intergovernmental Committee for Economic Cooperation (H-RICEC) was created and the Slovak–Russian Intergovernmental Commission on Cooperation in the Economy, Science and Technology (S-RICCEST) was revived, having been abolished by the Dzurinda government in 2002. These bilateral commissions bring together leading politicians, civil servants, regional actors, industrialists and other business/commerce representatives from both sets of countries for ongoing contact and extended meetings that mainly map out medium and long-term economic cooperation but can also lead to specific contracts.

The structure, activities and actors involved in the bilateral commissions are broadly the same for all three countries. To give the Hungarian case as an example, H-RICEC (Hungarian-Russian Intergovernmental Commission on Cooperation in the Economy, Science and Technology) consists of Hungarian and Russian parts, headed by co-chairmen both of whom are senior government figures. In 2015 they were State Secretary of the Prime Minister's office (currently Péter Szijjártó) for Hungary and Minister of Agriculture (currently Nikolai Fyodorov) for Russia. The H-RICEC contains eight working groups that reflect the main areas of cooperation. In the H-RICEC case these are: agriculture, construction, energy, ICTS and innovation, military technology, medicine and pharmacology, regional cooperation and tourism. Each H-RICEC is headed by top-ranking officials of the relevant ministries or state agencies and representatives of the business community are also important members. The chairmen and working group staff are in regular contact and meet on a number of occasions. The main H-RICEC annual event is a two-day plenary meeting attended by not only all the state representatives of Hungary and Russia, including Szijjártó and Fyodorov, but also by representatives of those Russian and Hungarian companies that are heavily involved in mutual economic relations. The plenary sessions alternate between Hungary and Russia and involve detailed discussions in the working groups (first day) and working groups' reports on the year's achievements, relevant issues and problems (second day). The H-RICEC chairmen have active roles in the working groups' discussions, especially where solutions to any acute problems are needed. Another important outcome of the plenaries is the 'Protocol of the Plenary Session', signed by both sides. This document summarises progress to date in all the main areas of cooperation and contains a jointly agreed action plan for the coming year, covering all the working groups.

The bilateral commissions now appear to be firmly entrusted with the task of promoting trade and various aspects of economic cooperation between Russia and each of the three. While they have primarily been viewed as bodies 'responsible for "oiling" economic ties, and taking strategic decisions' (Wikileaks, 2012) and have not been ascribed with generating a vast amount of export opportunities for firms that would be new to the Russian market, they have nevertheless been credited (in the case of the C-RICEISC at least) with 'some success in removing trade barriers' (Wikileaks, 2008). In early 2014, the Russian News Agency TASS remarked that there 'is a successfully operating Hungarian–Russian Intergovernmental Commission for Economic Cooperation (IGC), whose framework is suitable to solve any controversies that may arise in bilateral economic relations' (TASS, 2014). Other official statements over the years seem to affirm that these bilateral bodies are regarded positively and can be good vehicles for trade development and other forms of economic cooperation (see Dangerfield, 2015). The commissions have also been regarded as useful channels for intergovernmental communication and dialogue across a range of themes and issues, thus serving a direct political function as well. To give an example, in March 2013, the S-RICCEST plenary included a bilateral meeting between the Slovak and Foreign co-chairmen (Foreign Ministers Miroslav Lajčák and Sergei Lavrov) who 'exchanged views on further development of relations and cooperation vis-à-vis the European agenda as well as views on a range of current key international issues from the wider global context' (Slovak Ministry of Foreign Affairs, 2013).

Until the onset of EU sanctions on Russia at least, the bilateral instruments did not contradict the EU-level multilateral trade framework that regulates member states' trade with Russia. Rather, they had become increasingly recognised as supplementary processes which illustrate – contrary perhaps to CEE states' initial expectations – that EU entry did not in fact mean that all competences on economic and trade relations with Russia were now gone (to the Brussels level) and many possible avenues for productive bilateral cooperation on trade and economic relations were actually still open. The relationship between bilateral and multilateral instruments has become somewhat ambiguous in the context of the Ukraine crisis, however. While there is no evidence that bilateral arrangements can be used to circumvent sanctions, they have certainly helped to ameliorate the impact on the overall economic partnerships. Even though plenary meetings were not held during 2014, much of the regular work carried on in a low-profile way and included bilateral meetings of the chairmen and continuation of the activities of the working groups. For example, Péter Szijjártó made a working visit to Moscow on 19 November at the invitation of Russian Foreign Minister Sergei Lavrov and also met with his counterpart in H-RICEC Nikolai Fyodorov as part of the schedule. Earlier in the year, on 19 May, Slovak Foreign Minister Mirolslav Lajčák met the Russian Foreign Minister in Moscow and

> after meeting Lavrov, Lajčák also unofficially met with Russian Vice-premier Dmitry Rogozin, who co-chairs the Slovak-Russian Intergovernmental Commission for Economic and Scientific Cooperation. Both agreed to postpone the meeting of the commission, which was previously scheduled to take place in Slovakia next month. (*Slovak Spectator*, 2014)

This meeting took place around the time that the S-RICCEST plenary meeting would have occurred. More telling, in 2015 it became increasingly

clear that business-as-usual in bilateral arrangements had only been suspended temporarily. In February 2015, the Hungarian government declared
that Putin's visit to Budapest had resulted in strengthened cooperation
with Russia with five new bilateral agreements being signed (Hungarian
Government, 2015). Annual meetings of H-RICEC were also resumed and
the 2015 meeting took place in Kazan, Tatarstan on 9–10 April. Slovakia also took the same step and the seventeenth meeting of S-RICCEST
was held in May 2015 in Bratislava (*Spief16 News*, 2015). In the Czech
Republic, differences over the C-RICEISC split the government in 2015.
In January 2015, the Czech Ministry for Industry and Trade declared that
it wanted 'a meeting of the Czech Russian Intergovernmental Commission for Economic, Industrial and Scientific Cooperation to take place in
March' (*Prague Post*, 2015a) but the Czech Prime Minister sided with the
Ministry of Foreign Affairs and Ministry of Defence and postponed the
meeting until further notice. Nevertheless, 'meetings of working groups
representing the Czech Ministry for Industry and Trade and the Russian
regions have been held on a regular basis. For example, the ministry's representatives are to meet with the government of Sverdlovsk Oblast this May'
(Groszkowski, 2015).

New 'strategic visions' after the Eurozone crisis?

For the bulk of the post-communist period, all of the new EU member states
have had an economic strategy focused on the EU as the main 'development
centre'.[4] In the light of the Eurozone crisis and stagnating growth in the
EU, Novak (2014b: 30) raised the question: 'will [the EU] remain the development centre for the whole region despite the problems with its economic
development and the widening division between countries?' Novak suggests
that the weaker, export-dependent new member states that fall into the
category of 'South' in the post-Eurozone crisis notions of a North–South
divide within the EU are more prone to seeking extra-EU development
centre possibilities.

   Hungary seems to fit this pattern since its attempts to cultivate economic
links with Russia, and the 'East' more broadly, have been formalised into
a wider strategic vision known as the 'Eastern Winds Doctrine'. This has
emphasised dialogue with Asian and former Soviet states to generate new
sources of investment and business relationships. Since first aired by Orbán
in 2009 and operationalised into a cornerstone of foreign policy after 2010,
it has involved high-level missions to Azerbaijan, Kazakhstan, Malaysia,
Philippines, Saudi Arabia, Thailand, Turkey and many others. There have
also been multiple trips to China and Russia (Kalan, 2014). In May 2013,
Szijjártó's spokeswoman said that 'economic cooperation with the former
Soviet member states are the foundation pillars of that government' strategy

of the Eastern Opening' (*Hungarian Spectrum*, 2013). At the same time, the Eastern Winds Doctrine also seems to involve avoiding any antagonisms with significant 'Eastern Winds' partners such as Russia. Kalan has noted this tendency as especially visible in Hungary's policy to Ukraine, which has involved development of 'trade relations with Russia but political dialogue has been limited to the issue of the Hungarian minority in Transcarpathia'. Novak (2014b: 29) also notes that engaging with different potential development centres causes complications because not all centres operate 'according to the same rules' and contradictions with the rules and regulations of the EU are possible. Hungary's 2014 nuclear deal with Russia/Rosatom, which has been under serious challenge from the European Commission, is a clear illustration of this.

While the Czech Republic and Slovakia have no such formal strategies, like most EU states, the three have now reached the stage where they are less fixated with the EU market alone. In January 2016, the Czech Minister of Industry and Trade told a meeting of Czech export leaders that Czech export dependence on the EU had actually increased to 88.4 per cent in 2015 'despite the government's efforts to diversify' (Radio Prague, 2016a). This diversification strategy has included endeavours to expand and consolidate existing extra-EU partnerships, especially with Asia. The Czechs are clearly seeking to achieve a burgeoning economic relationship with China. An economic forum held at the Žofin palace in Prague on 28 and 29 March 2016, attended by President Xi Jinping (along with a large delegation of accompanying businessmen) in the first ever visit to the Czech Republic by a Chinese head of state, resulted in the signing of over '30 trade agreements covering various areas' (Radio Prague, 2016b). After the summit Czech President Zeman announced that the value of those agreements would amount to 95 billion crowns (Radio Prague, 2016c).[5] This Czech–Asia focus also includes other important investors such as South Korea which is 'the third largest foreign investor in the Czech Republic and companies such as the Hyundai Motor, Hyundai Mobis and Nexen Tire have poured close to 76 billion crowns into investment projects in the country, helping to create around 12,000 new jobs' (*Prague Post*, 2015b). State agencies are also involved in nurturing new export and investment possibilities. The Slovak Investment and Trade Development Agency (SARIO), for example, organises major trade and investment events in Slovakia and its staff join official visits overseas as part of SARIO's 'mission to attract foreign investors and to strengthen trade relations' (SARIO, 2015). Strategies to enhance trade and economic cooperation with Russia through additional economic diplomacy and placing more emphasis on the role of the bilateral intergovernmental commissions are clearly part of a broader pattern for all three countries, and reflect, if not a search for a new development centre, a definite strategy of seeking to access new, dynamic export markets and extra-EU inward investment.

Alternative political party perspectives on Russia

There can be no doubt that alternative political party perspectives have been an important determinant of incumbent Czech, Hungarian and Slovak governments' inclination to cultivate economic links with Russia. In all three countries, official attitudes to Russia have varied over the post-1990 period (for detailed analyses see Duleba, 2003; Póti, 2003; and Votápek, 2003). Changes in government have tended to mark turning points in the official tone of relations with Russia in a willingness to engage in closer political contacts and in attitudes to the importance of further developing economic and business relations. As Dangerfield (2013: 181) wrote, over the post-1990 period, as a whole, divergent attitudes to Russia have tended to broadly correspond with the political spectrum:

> (p)arties in the anti-Russia or Russia-cautious camp tend to be centre-right and more committed to Atlanticism while the parties of the left/centre-left are willing to give Russia a higher priority in foreign policy and less reserved about cultivating closer relations with Russia (usually emphasising the importance of Russia as an economic partner). Parties that belong to the anti-Russia/Russia-cautious camp include Fidesz in Hungary, the Civic Democratic Party (ODS) in the Czech Republic and the Slovak Democratic and Christian Union-Democratic Party (SDKÚ-DS) in Slovakia. Those that fall more into the pro-Russia camp include the Czech Social Democratic Party (ČSSD), the Hungarian Socialist Party (MSZP) and Direction-Social Democracy (SMER-SD).[6]

While the above categorisations were fairly reliable in the EU pre-accession period, the situation has, however, become rather more complex and nuanced since EU membership and Russia's growing importance as a trade partner. This has mainly involved the traditionally Russia-cautious or Russia-hostile parties changing position or successfully managing to separate political and economic dimensions of relations with Russia.[7] To give an example of the latter, in the case of the Czech Republic, the political tensions of recent years – including the ramifications of the proposal to locate part of the US Ballistic Missile Defence system in the Czech Republic and Poland and various criticisms of the Russia state (over its democracy and human rights records, actions in Georgia etc.) that came from the Ministry of Foreign Affairs – did not prevent a largely 'business as usual' approach in the economic and business sphere. An important role in this was played by the Czech Ministry of Industry and Trade, whose influence on Czech relations with Russia grew, as Kratochvíl and Kuchyňková (2010: 206) inform us, 'in direct proportion with the increasing importance of Czech–Russian trade relations. Contrasting with the problematic political relations (especially during 2007 and 2008) the representatives of the Ministry of Industry and Trade strived to separate the political and economic dimension of the mutual relations'. The Czech Ministry of Industry and

Trade, of course, have responsibility for the C-RICEISC. A notable part was also played by another branch of the Czech administration. The 'Russia-friendly' president of the time, Václav Klaus, led various Czech trade and economic cooperation delegations to Russia that were organised in the framework of the C-RICEISC. Klaus's 'role was prominent especially in 2007, in connection with his visit to Moscow accompanied by a delegation of Czech businessmen, and in 2009, when he assumed the position of representative of the presidency country at the EU-Russia summit in Khabarovsk' (Kratochvíl and Kuchyňková, 2010: 206).[8]

Open divisions within the political administrations have also been evident. Recent differences within the Czech government over whether or not to approve a 2015 meeting of the C-RICCEST have already been mentioned and the interventions of presidents have sometimes been at odds with the government of the time. For example, in 2008 the *Topolánek*-led ODS government and the President gave different assessments of the Russia–Georgia crisis, with Klaus taking Russia's side (Dangerfield, 2013). Around the same time, Duleba (2009: 21) noticed similar discrepancies in the positions of the Slovak Prime Minister, Robert Fico and the then Slovak Minister of Foreign Affairs, Ján Kubiš, on the deployment of the BMD (Ballistic Missile Defence) system and the causes of the Russia–Georgia conflict. As for U-turns on policy towards Russia, the Fidesz government in Hungary over the last few years has been particularly spectacular in this respect. Viktor Orbán was

> outright antagonistic during his first four years in office. And, while in opposition, he fiercely attacked both Péter Medgyessy and especially Ferenc Gyurcsány for trying to mend fences with Russia. He was especially critical of Gyurcsány's efforts to make a deal with Russia on the Southern Stream. He managed to blacken Ferenc Gyurcsány's name in Washington where the Bush administration was certain that Gyurcsány was not only interested in obtaining natural gas but that somehow he was ideologically attracted to the semi-dictatorial Vladimir Putin. (*Hungarian Spectrum*, 2013)

After the election in April 2010, various meetings of important bilateral economic cooperation committees were cancelled by the Russian side. Orbán's first meeting with Putin in November 2010 was reported as unproductive with 'the Kremlin's mistrust and Hungary's lack of interesting assets having had a very negative impact on the talks' (Ugrosdy, 2011). Thereafter, the Hungarian government clearly jettisoned its anti-Russia credentials and has evolved into one of Putin's strongest allies within the EU. Rácz (2012) noted an early indication of this when the Orbán government refrained from any criticism of the 2011 Russian parliamentary elections. Trade relations with Russia have become a key part of the 'Eastern Winds Doctrine' and in 2013 Orbán moved his deputy (Szijjártó) to what he saw as the key post of Chairman of the H-RICEC. A metamorphosis of energy strategy has occurred also, including support for the (now cancelled) South Stream gas pipeline and, as noted earlier, the January 2014 deal with Russia for the Paks nuclear site. Together with Robert Fico, Orbán has also been one of the strongest critics of the EU sanctions on Russia during the Ukraine crisis.

It seems rather clear that internal party divisions over Russia have become more blurred since the EU pre-accession period not so much because of EU entry itself but because the post-2004 period has coincided with the export boom to Russia. Laca and Tomek (2014) remarked that the 'economic calculus' is side-lining memories of Soviet tanks that crushed uprisings in 1956 and 1968 in Hungary and the two former members of Czechoslovakia'. Different perspectives on relations with Russia may play out in some internal debates and rhetoric on the dangers of close relations with Russia may (in the case of Hungary and Orban) be used for electoral purposes, but the 'economic calculus' also seems to have played a key role in rendering the traditional inter-party divisions increasingly less relevant when it comes to governments' policies towards commerce with Russia. As noted, the order of the day for all parties is an increasingly pragmatic approach to relations with Russia, including the strategy of separating politics and trade/business during periods of centre-right rule in the Czech Republic and a blatant U-turn in the case of the Orban government.

Conclusion

The EU's success so far in maintaining a united front on economic sanctions against Russia does not mean that there is a common perspective on trade and economic relations with Russia. Divergent attitudes towards the sanctions policy and the use of bilateral instruments for trade and economic cooperation during the Ukraine crisis simply affirm the well-known fact that EU member states' policies towards and priorities in relations with Russia are at best only partially Europeanised in that bilateral relationships and arrangements sit alongside EU multilateral ones. Since divisions between and within parties and governments over relations with Russia have been evident ever since the end of communism, anti-sanction statements of the Hungarian and Slovak government and pro-Russia interventions of certain politicians in the Czech Republic (e.g. President Miloš Zeman) clearly do not represent a sudden surge in loyalty/closeness to Russia. Czech, Hungarian and Slovak hesitant and/or critical responses to sanctions, along with the rather minimal impact on bilateral trade and economic cooperation instruments, are actually a rather natural and predictable outcome given that more intense trade and economic cooperation with Russia has been a key feature of the post-accession period.

In the case of Hungary, the nature and impact of relations with Russia obviously raises questions about the Europeanisation of not only policy but also of politics. There seems no dispute that the narrative of a lurch to the Russian illiberal model of democracy and even charges of 'Putinisation' in Hungary has merits. Yet when it comes to reasons for opposition to sanctions, statements in favour of close economic ties with Russia, and bilateral economic cooperation activities, the sheer importance of economic links with Russia clearly suggests a pragmatic reflex. In addition, close political ties usually follow in the footsteps of close economic and trade ties. It should be mentioned that the government of Orbán's predecessor, under Ferenc Gyurcsány, was if anything even closer to Russia and Putin. Moreover, in the Czech Republic, where there is certainly no 'Putinisation' process, there is however an equally stubborn refusal to disengage from close economic relations with Russia. As Groszkowski (2015) observed, 'the Czech government, regardless of the political option, have been making efforts to conquer the Russian market for years. Furthermore, Czech business and political circles are convinced that even if Czechs withdraw from the east, they will be replaced for example by Germans or the French anyway.' Finally, if the current drift to illiberalism in Poland is indeed emulating Hungary, the attitude towards Russia could not be more different: 'As for Mr Putin, if Mr Orbán cannot conceal his infatuation, Mr Kaczynski sees Moscow as a serious threat. He is pressing NATO to set up permanent bases in Poland to deter Mr Putin's revanchism' (Stephens, 2016).

All this suggests that any drifts towards a model of democracy that resembles the Russian Federation, should not be necessarily attributed to the development of more intensive relations with Russia itself. Novak (2014a: 16) has written that – for Hungary especially – the attraction of Russia-inspired illiberalism is 'its authoritarian style that makes the stabilisation of the power of the same interest groups possible'. This certainly affirms that illiberalism ought to be treated as a phenomenon in its own right with a specific and complex set of causes and implies that its roots may be more connected to the communist past and some transitional experiences that Hungary and others share with Russia.

Notes

1 As Inotai (2015: 168) has written, 'the most important factors attracting international interest to Hungary after 2010 are non-economic issues, such as the rapid deterioration of democratic values, the limitations to media freedom, and the abolition of a checks-and-balances system of key official institutions, from the Constitutional Court through the judiciary system to civil organisations'.
2 Data on Russian growth, consumer spending and imports from the *Federal State Statistics Service of the Russian Federation*.
3 Data from Czech Statistical Office, Hungarian Central Statistical Office, Statistical Office of the Slovak Republic for 2014.

4 Defined as a state or region that underwrites economic development in smaller and less developed 'peripheral' states or regions by simultaneously acting as a strategic market for expansion of exports and as a key source of external financing for economy development, usually in the form of FDI.

5 Though one year after there were doubts about this Chinese investment wave would actually occur or would turn out to be 'unfulfilled promises'. See *Prague Daily Monitor* (2017).

6 The relationship between centre-left orientation and disposition to Russia is in some measure connected to the significance of CMEA/socialist era networks of government officials, with the leaders of left-leaning parties usually ex- 'reform socialists' who were USSR-educated, comfortable in Moscow and able to enjoy close and friendly relations with their Russian counterparts. It should also be mentioned, however, that Slovakia has been labelled 'a 'quasi-Russophile' country and party variations are somewhat milder in that no major party could be classed as anti-Russia. Both major parties, for example, support close economic ties with Russia, but the centre-left tends to be somewhat more accommodating and supportive of Russia's security and foreign policy concerns. Hence in October 2009, 'Slovak prime minister Fico pinpointed that as long as he acts in the capacity of prime minister, the United States will not be allowed to deploy the anti-missile system in Slovakia' (Dangerfield, 2013: 181).

7 In line with a phenomenon increasingly observable in many of the new EU member states, the party systems have also tended to become increasingly unstable and new parties have burst onto the scene. In Hungary, Jobbik is cast as a far right party but supports close relations with Russia.

8 Milos Zeman has carried on this pro-Russia tradition since becoming Czech President, though his perspective has long been evident. When the Czech Social Democratic Party formed the government in 1998 with Zeman as Prime Minister it marked a switch towards a more conciliatory foreign policy approach to Russia.

EU energy security policy in the eastern neighbourhood: towards Europeanisation?

While energy security crises facing Europe (such as the oil crises of the 1970s) are not new, the assumption that the European Union should be acting to mitigate them is a relatively novel phenomenon. Indeed, the EU has historically had a limited role in energy policy, a fact often considered a paradox given the role of coal in the EU's founding treaties (Belyi, 2009: 203). Nevertheless, after a few decades of benign and relatively stable energy markets throughout the 1980s and 1990s, by around 2005 energy security had rapidly moved up the policy agenda of European countries. This growing politicisation of energy (Wilson, 1987) and attendant growing calls for the Europeanisation of energy policy were driven primarily by two twin energy security pressures: rising prices and the threat of supply restrictions from Russia.

The period from approximately 2005 to 2014 saw a very substantial increase in the rise of oil prices with a barrel of crude increasing from around $50 a barrel in 2005 to around $110 a barrel by 2014 (and a high of $150 in 2008) (Dempsey et al., 2016: 3). With gas prices often linked to oil prices, high energy prices are damaging to the economies of energy dependent countries given their impact on inflation and spending. The EU as a whole is very dependent on external oil and gas imports, although dependence levels vary considerably between member states. While many Western European countries have a fairly diversified base of supply for their external supplies, some member states such as Poland, the Baltic states and Bulgaria are heavily reliant on one supplier: Russia (Baran, 2007).

Indeed, it was the consequences of dependence on Russia – and the Russia–Ukrainian gas crisis in 2006 in particular (and subsequent crises with Belarus in 2007 and Ukraine again in 2009) – that really increased the salience of energy security matters in the EU. In January 2006, Russia (or Gazprom to be precise) cut gas supplies to Ukraine following a long-running dispute with Kiev over prices (Hafner, 2015). This precipitated a major gas shortage in Europe, with a number of countries (such as Bulgaria) almost entirely cut off from supplies. This event, more than any other, led to growing calls for an integrated EU approach to energy policy and external energy policy in particular.

As European actors looked around for additional supplies to reduce dependence on Russia, a number of neighbourhood countries presented a viable, but often geopolitically challenging, alternative to Russian imports. While dwindling European reserves mean that the EU is increasingly energy-poor (at least in terms of conventional oil and gas), the 'wider EU neigh-bourhood' and the broader Eastern neighbourhood (including the Caspian region) is rich in hydrocarbon deposits. Given Europe's dependence on foreign energy (and its dependence on Russian gas in particular) and the fact that energy prices increase in proportion to the distance they have to travel to market, accessing the energy resources of the European periphery became an important stated objective of the EU (European Commission, 2011: 5).

In practice, however, the EU's wider energy security policy and, by extension, the application of that policy to the EU neighbourhood has been difficult and characterised by limited successes. This chapter examines the EU's energy policy towards its Eastern neighbourhood seeking to identify areas of an integrated EU strategy (Europeanisation) in external energy policy and evaluate areas of success and ongoing challenges. By the term 'Europeanisation', this chapter is referring to the establishment of an inte-grated EU energy policy based on the projection of EU norms and rules pertaining to energy. When necessary, the term 'EU-isation' is also employed for clarification.

The chapter is structured as follows. The first section presents an over-view of the broader challenges facing EU energy security policy in terms of divergence over European energy goals and the challenge of 'speaking with one voice' towards Russia. The second section outlines the EU's interaction with energy-rich producer countries and geo-strategically situated transit countries in the (wider) Eastern neighbourhood and the Caspian in particu-lar. The final two sections then offer a respective examination of the EU's efforts to achieve two key policy goals: the promotion of 'European' energy governance towards (non-Russian) energy producers in the wider Eastern neighbourhood and the establishment of (non-Russian) pipeline routes as a means of supply diversification. In both cases, Europeanisation is mixed and the EU as a whole has had limited success.[1]

External energy (and Russia): A challenging policy area

The development of a common external EU energy policy – including an EU security of supply policy towards states in the Eastern neighbourhood – has been fraught with difficulty. Much of the scholarly analysis of European energy politics highlights the sense of discord and incoherence that is often thought to characterise the EU's attempts to establish a common energy policy (Braghiroli and Carta, 2009; Kovačovská, 2007; Schmidt-Felzmann,

2008, 2011; Youngs, 2009). The EU has faced successive difficulties in reaching agreement on external energy policy in a number of areas. The questions of divergence over *mid-stream* energy supply diversification plans are tackled in the following sections. This section focuses on the challenges inherent to the formulation of a common position towards core energy suppliers, notably (but not only) Russia (Baran, 2007; Götz, 2008; Leonard and Popescu, 2007; Schmidt-Felzmann, 2008).

One of the major themes of the literature on EU foreign energy policy (and a backdrop to many of the debates about other areas of energy policy, such as internal energy policy or pipeline diversification) is the historic incoherence between member states and EU institutions when it comes to foreign energy policy and the consequent failure to 'speak with one voice' on energy matters, particularly towards Russia (Buchan, 2009; Schmidt-Felzmann, 2011; Youngs, 2009). Discussions of EU–Russia energy relations are animated by a familiar paradox in EU foreign policy studies: why, when the EU faces so many external energy challenges (most notably relating to energy dependence on Russia), have member states not managed to formulate a cooperative response? Indeed, the challenge of overcoming European disunity in energy policy often seems to mirror the well-documented difficulties that the EU has experienced in formulating a wider Common Foreign and Security Policy (CFSP) despite the apparent rational benefits of doing so (Hill, 1993; Toje, 2008). Braghiroli and Carta (2009: 2) describe EU–Russia energy relations as an 'emblematic case that puts into question the EU's foreign policy coherence and normative distinctiveness'. Likewise, Claes (2009: 58) exemplifies the EU's predicament when he stresses that the EU would be in 'a stronger and better position if the member states subsume to a unified strategy. This is so far not the case towards its most important external energy supplier at the moment – Russia.' Schmidt-Felzmann (2008: 170) cites former EU Trade Commissioner Peter Mandelson as noting 'the incoherence of European policy towards Russia over much of the past decade has been frankly alarming'.

EU member states, it is argued, have switched 'between neo-institutionalist and neorealist temptations in their relations with Russia' with national capitals simultaneously seeking to engage Russia in regional, rules-based institutions while attempting to pursue their national interests bilaterally (Braghiroli and Carta, 2009: 2). While the EU had less difficulty formulating a common position towards Russia in the 1990s, coalescing around a strategy of democratisation and Westernisation in a weakened Russia, this plan is no longer viable – and all the more so since the Ukraine Crisis (Barysch, 2007: 4; Leonard and Popescu, 2007: 1). Schmidt-Felzmann (2008: 172) suggests that European countries attempt to 'upload' their own strategic policy preferences and bilateral disputes with Russia to the European level when it is in their interests to do so, while at the same time those that can (predominantly the larger member states) also pursue their relations with Russia bilaterally, outside of EU forums. While 'uploads' are often couched in the language of the European interest, Schmidt-Felzmann (2008: 172) argues there has been 'no real indication that a concern for the "common EU good" is driving their national foreign policies'.

Scholars have similarly highlighted divisions between 'new' and 'old' member states with regards to Russia (Braghiroli and Carta, 2009; Leonard and Popescu, 2007). Old (read Western European) member states have tended to perceive of their energy dependence on Russia in relative terms, seeing energy trade dependence on Russia as a positive part of mutual inter-dependence (Braghiroli and Carta, 2009: 6). By contrast, Braghiroli and Carta argue that 'new [member states] still perceive the absolute dependence on the exchanges with Russia as a form of 'dominance' (further complicated by the claim that Moscow pursues a form of unilateral coercive politics)' (Braghiroli and Carta, 2009: 6).

Similarly, Youngs (2009: 40) draws attention to tensions inside EU institutions. He notes that the European Council and Commission have regularly been in conflict over the contours of the EU's foreign energy policy. Youngs (2009: 40) suggests that the former High Representative for Foreign and Security Policy Javier Solana's public rhetoric on energy policy was far more political than his Commission colleagues and highlights the fact that senior figures in the Council Secretariat had misgivings about the Commission's liberalisation agenda in energy. Youngs (2009: 41) also highlights how some argue that the European Commission *instrumentally* promotes a liberal approach to energy because doing so fits with policy areas where the Commission already has competences (for example, competition, internal market, trade). Youngs further notes that, while some policy makers across the EU felt that energy policy making had dangerously slipped into the hands of 'national security strategists', others opined that the Commission (and Directorate General Transport and Energy in particular – now DG Energy) was an '"energy technocracy"', whose market-based recipes were blind to geo-political realities' (Youngs, 2009: 41). It seems that similar arguments over whether foreign affairs ministries or energy/economic ministries should control energy policy were also held within member states (Youngs, 2009: 39).

Looking East: the Caspian and EU energy policy

While the EU has had a number of difficulties in developing a common position towards Russia, it has been, slowly but surely, developing a regional energy security policy towards the broader Caspian region – a site of considerable oil and gas riches within the wider neighbourhood. Some might argue that developing relations with other energy-rich regions is actually more important than developing a more cohesive position towards Russia. The key to a less dependent relationship with Russia is arguably diversification and accessing energy resources in other parts of the neighbourhood is intrinsic to a more diversified supply base. The energy riches of the Caspian loom large in these considerations (Baran, 2007; Roberts, 2010).

The EU focus on Caspian energy policy was primarily driven by factors exogenous to the region. The Russia–Ukraine gas crisis of 2006 (and subsequent crises with Belarus in 2007 and Ukraine again in 2009) added to the already tense atmosphere of heightened global demand and rapidly increasing energy prices (Lussac, 2010: 619; Schmidt-Felzmann, 2011: 575). The 2006 and 2009 gas crises fundamentally challenged core European assumptions about the security of external energy supplies and, in particular, significantly damaged EU member states' perception of Russia and Ukraine as reliable energy suppliers (Umbach, 2010: 1230). The more or less simultaneous timing of the EU's increased attention to energy security concerns and its increasing focus on the Caspian region is of course no coincidence. Unsurprisingly, given its natural resource wealth, proximity to the EU and potential source of diversification for both oil and gas, the Caspian region loomed into focus for EU foreign and energy policy makers as a potential source of additional energy supplies (Youngs, 2009: 101).

The EU is not alone in this endeavour, however. Indeed, the energy resources of the Caspian region have been the focus of much strategic attention since the end of the Cold War (Barylski, 1995; Kalicki, 2001). The Caspian is frequently presented as the epicentre of a 'new great game' where today's protagonists (Russia, the United States, China and the EU) are thought to vie for influence and power in Eurasia, just as Britain and Russia did in the nineteenth century (Zabortseva, 2012). From an EU perspective, the post-Soviet states of the Caspian Sea region (Kazakhstan, Turkmenistan and Azerbaijan) are seen to possess the energy resources needed for the prospective pipeline routes of the 'Southern Corridor' that would, in transporting energy to Europe via the Caucasus and Turkey, reduce reliance on Russian energy supplies and infrastructures (European Commission, 2011: 5).

The following sections discuss two key dimensions of the EU's external energy policy in the Caspian region: the EU's promotion of 'European' energy governance (i.e. EU-isation) and the attempted development of new pipeline infrastructures along the so called 'Southern Corridor'. Both of these areas are essential if Europe's overall dependence on Russia is to be reduced through growing engagement in the Caspian. Both objectives – and the extent to which they have been Europeanised – are now examined in turn.

Europeanising energy governance in the Caspian?

The European Union has been active in the Caspian region since the early 1990s. Following the fall of the Iron Curtain, EU regional reconstruction packages such as Technical Assistance to the CIS (TACIS) that targeted the natural resources sector were quickly adopted by European member states in an effort to help support the weak economies of the Newly Independent States, including those in the Caspian (Hadfield, 2008: 325). In particular, the INOGATE energy programme (Interstate Oil and Gas Transport to Europe), itself part of TACIS, sought to provide technical assistance to ageing Soviet infrastructures, increase regional energy integration between the EU and markets in Eurasia and, ultimately, to secure the flow of energy resources to the European Union (Hadfield, 2008: 325).

It was in the mid-2000s (and in 2006–8 after the first gas crisis in particular) that the EU stepped up its focus on the Caspian region. In 2004, the EU included the countries of the South Caucasus and Central Asia in the Baku Initiative, a regional energy programme designed to facilitate energy cooperation between Black Sea and Caspian Sea littoral countries and the EU (European Union, 2006). In 2006, at the second Ministerial Conference of the Baku Initiative, the programme was scaled up with the signing of a detailed energy cooperation 'road map' (the so-called Astana Road Map). Likewise, in 2006 the EU signed memoranda of understanding (MOU) on energy with Azerbaijan and another, later in the same year, with Kazakhstan. In 2007, the EU launched its flagship Central Asia Strategy with energy and transport as one of the seven core areas of cooperation and with other areas of the strategy, such as trade and investment and the rule of law, overlapping with energy policy concerns (European Union, 2009: 21–23). In 2008, a MOU was signed with Turkmenistan as part of the closer, but still tentative, cooperation between Brussels and Ashgabat. On the European side of the Caspian, Azerbaijan was included in both the European Neighbourhood Policy (ENP) in 2004 and the Eastern Partnership (EaP), announced in 2008 – both seeking, inter alia, to facilitate cooperation on energy policy.

However, while there has been a concerted (and broadly cohesive) EU effort to promote energy governance in the Caspian region, the extent of Europeanisation is mixed. This is, first, because the EU's governance efforts have had limited traction in a set of states with fundamentally different political and economic systems, and a fundamentally different relationship between political power and the energy sector. Second, those elements of European-promoted governance that have had traction in the Caspian are a mix of both 'EU' and 'international' governance in their origins.

The governance matrix promoted by the EU in the Caspian

The EU's governance promotion in the wider Eastern neighbourhood is promoted through a matrix of macro and meso governance structures. *Macro structures* are the strategic institutions (such the Central Asia

Strategy or European Neighbourhood Policy) that 'lay down the overall goals and instruments' of EU–periphery relations (Lavenex et al., 2009: 3). These delimit strategic areas of cooperation, outline levels of approximation (goals) and set out the rules (EU or international) on which this approximation occurs (means). Such institutions are 'EU' structures in that they are established and administered by EU institutions (in conjunction with partners) and they exclude other third parties (such as Russia) (Lavenex et al., 2009: 3).

The EU's energy governance matrix in the Caspian comprises four macro structures: Central Asia Strategy, European Neighbourhood Policy, the Eastern Partnership and Partnership and Cooperation Agreements (PCAs). These documents appear to reflect a degree of Europeanisation in the EU's efforts. However, it should be noted that these macro structures are essentially strategic documents that set out aspirations for EU governance transfer, rather than concrete measures or commitments by Caspian states to adopt EU rules. The actual content of EU governance promotion is conducted through meso structures. Here, the picture of a Europeanisation process is more mixed.

Meso structures relate to 'sectoral modes of interaction' that represent the externalisation of EU (or other) rules and are motivated by 'functionally-driven answers to situations of interdependence and the externalities produced within individual sectors' (Lavenex et al., 2009: 3). Of the five meso structures employed by the EU to transfer governance in the Caspian, two are strictly speaking 'European' (EU-ised) in that they are established by the EU, exclude any third parties and aim to promote EU rules: PCAs and the Baku Initiative.

Bilaterally, the EU's relationships with Caspian states are governed by PCAs. Unlike the Central Asia Strategy, which is essentially a political-strategic document, the PCA is a comprehensive bilateral legal agreement that forms the basis of EU–Caspian state relations. It has a number of energy-related provisions. The EU has recently negotiated an 'enhanced PCA agreement' with Kazakhstan that will, according to the European Commission, 'bring about better conditions for the trade and investment relations between the two parties' (European Commission, 2012). Full details have not yet been released at time of writing, however.

The Baku Initiative (also known as the enhanced INOGATE programme), established by the EU in 2004 and expanded at a meeting of foreign ministers in Astana in 2006, aims to further cooperation in energy between the states of the Black and Caspian seas through a harmonisation of standards based around EU internal market rules (European Union, 2006: 1). However, the Baku Initiative is not legally binding and while it represents an ambitious framework for ongoing cooperation in the area of energy in the Black/Caspian Sea regions, aspirations for most Caspian states are watered down. For example, while the Initiative encourages 'open and non-discriminatory

Table 11.1 The macro and meso structures of the EU's energy governance matrix in the Caspian

NP	AP	Central Asia Strategy	PCAs (B)	Baku initiative	ECT (I)	WTO (I)	ITI (I)
Azer	Azer	Kaz, Tur	Kaz, Tur, Azer	Kaz, Tur, Azer	Kaz, Tur, Azer	Azer (candidate), Kaz	Zer, kaz

Key: Azer – Azerbaijan, Kaz – Kazakhstan, Tur – Turkmenistan, (I) international institution, (B) – bilateral.
Source: Author's own elaboration.

access to investment in energy resources and networks', the 'approved actions' for the Central Asia region (those parts that Central Asian governments have agreed to) do not reiterate this objective, focusing instead on less sensitive issues such as the rehabilitation and building of new infrastructures (European Union, 2006: 7).

As mentioned, the EU also promotes sectoral energy governance through institutional structures that are not European, but rather international (i.e. are not directly established by the EU) that include third parties and that promote internationally accepted norms. These are the Energy Charter Treaty (ECT), The World Trade Organization (WTO) and the Extractive Industry Transparency Initiative (EITI) (see Table 11.1).

While the ECT is an international treaty designed to manage trade and investment in hydrocarbons, provisions in the areas described above are strongly influenced by both international and European law. First, a wealth of Bilateral Investment Treaties (roughly 500 at the time of the ECT negotiations) and the investment chapter of the North American Free Trade Area provide the substantial basis in law for the investment aspects of the ECT (Konoplyanik and Wälde, 2006: 528). Second, EU law on the licensing of upstream resources, transit, utility procurement and non-discriminatory access form an integral part of the ECT (although states still retain the right to control access). Third, the trade chapter provisions of the ECT are essentially those of the General Agreement on Tariffs and Trade (GATT – now WTO) in 1994 (Konoplyanik and Wälde, 2006: 528). It was assumed that all ECT members would join the GATT/WTO and thus the ECT was seen as a first step towards WTO (then GATT) membership and full trade liberalisation (Konoplyanik and Wälde, 2006: 542).

The WTO, for its part, is also seen by EU officials as an important part of the governance of energy in the Caspian.[2] While energy did not feature specifically in the negotiations of the GATT and while no agreement on natural resources was reached at the Uruguay round of trade negotiations that established the WTO in 1995, *generally applicable* trade provisions of the WTO do relate to trade in energy products (Selivanova, 2007: 11, 37). As such, EU officials place a lot of stress on the potential role of the WTO in Caspian energy governance.

Finally, in the Caspian region, the EU promotes transparency through the Extractive Industry Transparency Initiative (European Union, 2009: 24). The EITI (again an international energy governance regime) seeks to improve transparency by requiring natural resource companies to publish their payments to host governments and for governments to publish receipt of these payments. These processes are audited by independent accountants and validated by an EITI multi-stakeholder group composed of governmental, civil society and energy company officials (EITI Secretariat, 2013: 1). The European Commission participates in the board of the EITI and in the EITI Multi-Donor Trust Fund administered by the World Bank (EITI Secretariat, 2010). Twelve EU member states are also donors and supporters of the initiative (EITI Secretariat, n.d.). EU officials stress the importance of encouraging transparency in upstream markets to improve both the governance and the investment climate.[3]

Pipelines: The limits of Europeanised diversification plans

While the EU has been broadly cohesive in terms of the energy governance it has promoted in the Caspian, divisions between member states have also been more evident over the various pipeline routes (actual and potential) that bring energy supplies to Europe (Braghiroli and Carta, 2009; Feklyunina, 2008; Schmidt-Felzmann, 2011). Three major pipeline projects have triggered most of the controversy. Nord Stream and South Stream (both supported by Russia with partnership from a number of EU member states) and Nabucco (supported by the EU institutions and, at least rhetorically, by member states) have served to highlight EU energy policy divisions at perhaps their most strident (Schmidt-Felzmann, 2011: 585). At the time of writing, only one of these – Nord Stream – has been built. Nevertheless, the debates surrounding Nabucco, the South Stream and the 'Southern Corridor' highlight the difficulties inherent in developing big Europeanised pipeline projects.

Nord Stream

The Nord Stream pipeline, backed by Russia and Germany (but also with the participation of France and Denmark), brings gas from Russia via the Baltic Sea to Germany (and on to France, Denmark and the UK, among others). Nord Stream is viewed by some Central and Eastern European states (particularly Poland and Estonia) as a means for Russia to be able to increase pressure on them without damaging its main consumer base in

Europe (Schmidt-Felzmann, 2011: 585). Götz (2008: 94) argues that Nord Stream (and South Stream) follows an emerging Russian strategic logic (supported by France and Germany) of avoiding difficult transit states, most notably Ukraine. While some Eastern member states argue that Russian pipeline routes are designed to circumvent their territory, Moscow in turn accuses the EU of trying to build pipelines – such as Nabucco – that avoid Russia (Götz, 2008: 93). Part of the problem lies in the fact that dependency on Russia is higher in Eastern than Western Europe. Indeed, in Western and Southern EU states, such as Italy and France, dependence on Russia is not a major preoccupation as levels are low. For them, increasing reliance on Russia in fact reduces dependence on other (perhaps riskier) suppliers such as Algeria or Libya. At the time of writing, Berlin and Moscow are in the process of developing a new Nord Stream 2 that would bring additional Russian supplies to Germany. Like Nord Stream 1 this project is controversial, raising further questions in Brussels and other member state capitals over the diversification of EU supplies.

Nabucco, South Stream and the 'Southern Corridor'

In the South-East of Europe, several pipeline projects were locked in competition for several years throughout the 2000s. These include the Russian-backed South Stream that aimed to bring Central Asian and Russian gas across the Black Sea from Russia into Bulgaria (Alexeev, 2013). Further south, a number of pipelines including the EU-backed 'Nabucco', the Trans-Adriatic Pipeline (TAP), White Stream and the Interconnector-Turkey-Greece-Italy (ITGI) competed for over a decade to be the chosen pipeline project(s) to bring gas from the Caspian (and potentially Central Asia and the Middle East) to Europe.

The two most geopolitically significant were the EU-sponsored Nabucco and the Russian-proposed South Stream. Nabucco, originally envisaged in 2002, was given high-level backing by the European Commission and (although not always acted on) by member states after the gas crisis in 2006, largely due to its capacity to reduce supply dependence on Russia and Russian companies. The Nabucco pipeline was envisioned to run from the Turkish border with Georgia, across Turkey and up into South-East Europe finishing in Baumgarten in Austria. The original plan was for Nabucco to bring 30 billion cubic metres of gas to Europe relying on supplies from Azerbaijan, Turkmenistan and, potentially, Iraq and Iran.

In the final cut, the Nabucco pipeline will now not be built having lost out to two other pipeline routes: the Trans-Anatolian Pipeline (TANAP) and the Trans-Adriatic Pipeline (Hafner, 2015). Nabucco suffered from a number of factors. First, as a private project headed by a number of smaller energy companies, Nabucco struggled to attract the financing necessary for construction (Hafner, 2015). This was compounded by the fact that the Nabucco consortium, despite assistance from the EU, was unable to get assurances from foreign producer governments that could fill the pipeline. The only guaranteed supplies were from Azerbaijan, with the project relying on supplies either from geopolitically unstable Iraq, sanctioned Iran or Turkmenistan, across the Caspian Sea. The last of these was the most viable option technically and in terms of security, but geopolitically it was fraught with difficulty. Just as funders were unlikely to commit funds in the absence of guaranteed supply, the Turkmen government was unwilling to commit to the project until it knew it was to be built – especially important as agreeing to build a pipeline across the Caspian would have drawn the ire of Moscow.

Nabucco's problems were compounded by the presence of the South Stream project, which sought to cross the Black Sea from Russia landing in Bulgaria. From a Russian perspective, the pipeline made sense both as a project in its own right, but also as a challenge to Nabucco. In its own right, and to ensure minimal supply disruption risk, Russia wanted to develop another pipeline infrastructure (like the Nord Stream) that would circumvent Ukraine. Likewise, from a 'security of demand' point of view, Russia wanted to minimise the likelihood that the Nabucco pipeline would be built. The latter would reduce dependence on Russian gas and open up a non-Russian route to energy sources currently under Russian control in Central Asia and Turkmenistan in particular. Gazprom has not had it all its own way, however. The European Commission effectively vetoed the South Stream project, or at least its crossing any EU territory by ruling that the pipeline would contravene EU internal competition rules. Gazprom's response has been to rename the pipeline 'Turkish Stream' and redirect the route to finish in Turkey rather than Bulgaria. The extent to which this is still a viable project given recent Turkish–Russian tensions over Syria remains to be seen.

As mentioned, the TANAP and the TAP have beaten main rival Nabucco (and South Stream) in the competition for access to the Azeri gas essential for the project (Bryza and Koranyi, 2013). The TANAP project, rather than an EU-sponsored or supported project, was driven forward directly by the Azerbaijani and Turkish governments and financed by a mixture of Azeri oil funds and loans from international financial agencies, including potentially European ones (Hafner, 2015). However, while the TANAP and TAP pipelines do reduce European dependence on Russian supplies and have a positive impact for the small markets in South-East Europe, the overall volume of 10 billion cubic metres of gas is quite small in the context of a European market of 500 billion cubic metres.

Conclusion

The EU has had an active energy security policy towards its Eastern neighbours for nearly two decades. However, it is only since the gas crises of

2006 that this dimension of the EU's external energy has really come to the fore. Energy has been a difficult area for the EU generally, in terms of the promotion of Europeanisation. Tensions between member states and EU institutions have limited the effectiveness of EU action towards Eastern neighbours as evidenced by competition and the limited success of the EU overall in terms of pipeline diversification. The divergence between EU member states, driven in part by perceptions of relations with Russia, has hindered a more Europeanised position on the construction of pipelines to the East. The eventual outcome of the Southern Corridor is sub-optimal from the position of the Commission, but has served the interests of some member states (especially Italy) and their companies.

In terms of governance promotion, the EU's position has been more cohesive and there has been less divergence over the contours of energy governance towards Eastern neighbours. It would be a mistake, however, to see EU actions as Europeanised and even less so in the case of outcomes in the region. As the case study of the Caspian has shown, the EU's governance in the wider neighbourhood comprises institutional structures that are both European and international in scope. EU governance promotion has packaged these and promoted them through macro structures such as the ENP and the Central Asia Strategy and has contributed to a more internationalised governance situation in the Caspian. However, fully *Europeanised* (i.e. EU-ised) it is not.

Overall, the role of countries in the East in shaping events is not to be underestimated. Of course, Russia's impact on European energy policy is very significant as Russia's role in hindering developments in the Southern Corridor has shown. However, others play a big role too. Governments in the Caspian region have been slow to adopt European norms in energy for their own reasons and the huge economic imbalances between them and the EU have made little impact on this. Likewise, in terms of pipelines, the eventual Southern Corridor route was decided by Azerbaijan and Turkey, with the EU Commission unable to push through its preferred option despite trying for a decade.

Notes

1 It should be noted that this chapter does not cover the EU's relations with the (potential EU member) states in Eastern Europe and the Balkans that have joined the EU Energy Community. This is an area of more successful Europeanisation. See Deitz et al. (2007) for more information.
2 Interview with European Commission official, Brussels, July 2011.
3 Interview with European Commission official, Brussels, November 2012.

The EU and the European Other: the Janus face of EU migration and visa policies in the neighbourhood

In 1992, as war and suffering tore through the disintegrating Yugoslavia, 'Europe' faced the biggest refugee and migration crisis since the Second World War. Germany alone admitted 350,000 refugees and was processing a further 438,000 applications. It was further estimated that around 500,000 illegal migrants entered Italy via North Africa and the Balkans (Torpey in Andreas and Snyder, 2000: 44–45). 'The burden on the host countries is becoming unbearable' exclaimed the UN High Commissioner for Refugees Sadako Ogata and 'the plight of the displaced is increasingly desperate' (*The New York Times*, 1992). In 2015, an even bigger crisis was haunting the continent. With conflicts across the Middle East and ongoing instability in Afghanistan and throughout Africa, it is estimated that over one million migrants and refugees crossed into Europe by land and sea (International Organization for Migration (IOM), 2016), many seeking shelter and a new life in the EU. This prompted member states to agree on further cooperation in areas of border, migration and asylum while, at the same time, disagreeing on how such policies ought to be implemented. However, both cases highlight the major role migration – and indeed cross-border flows – play between the EU and wider Europe (hereafter referred to as the EU's Eastern neighbourhood).

The aim of this chapter is to place those relations in a wider context by historically tracing the emergence of discursive and non-discursive strategies that help us to understand the EU's migration and visa policies in the Eastern neighbourhood. As Walters and Haahr note, the aim is to understand this process in a 'much broader history of rationalities, arts and techniques of government' (Walters and Haahr, 2005: 5) not only within the institutions and the territory of the European Community (EC)/EU, but also its gradual extension into both candidate states and those states for whom EU membership is either undesirable or a distant (im)possibility.

This chapter argues that there are three primary rationales regarding the role of EU migration policies in the Eastern neighbourhood: (i) to protect the internal 'milieu' from potential external risks/insecurities (Dillon, 2007);

(ii) to extend its control into the neighbourhood through 'politics of inclusion' or 'politics of exclusion' (Smith, 1996); and (iii) to shape the neighbourhood by inhabiting the external space with rules and regulations. This chapter focuses, first, on how the European Community (and, later, the European Union) sought new means of governing the Western European 'milieu', beginning from its economic foundations and spreading into new areas for intervention. In particular, this chapter elaborates on how the removal of internal borders for the freedom of movement of goods, services and people required new means of regulating potential insecurities or risks to the internal circulation (Dillon, 2007) through the creation of common external borders and their external projection in the form of visa, migration or asylum policies.

Second, with the fall of the Iron Curtain and successive enlargements southwards and eastwards, the EU gained a new neighbourhood: on the one hand, the non-European states of the Middle East and North Africa and, on the other, countries in 'wider' Europe – some, such as Ukraine, with Euro-Atlantic aspirations. With new initiatives for creating a 'ring of friends' around the EU (Prodi, 2002), this chapter deals with attempts at closer association between the EU and its Eastern neighbours and the ongoing shift from enlargement rationalities towards 'politics of half-open doors' (Timmerman, 2003: 8). This involves making 'people-to-people contact' conditional on the neighbourhood states' ability to protect their own borders and, consequently, extending control of border management into the neighbourhood. In this sense, 'borders are inherent to logics of inside and outside, practices of inclusion and exclusion ... questions about identity and difference' (Vaughan-Williams, 2012: 1) between the EU, the European 'Other' and those Mike Smith (1996) termed the 'real outsiders'.

Third, the chapter explores how these strategies, inherent in the EU's migration and visa policies, seek to shape the Eastern neighbourhood according to the EU's agenda by inhabiting it with the EU's own rules and regulations. According to Walters and Haahr, 'it is in acts and moments of problematisation that mentalities and their forms of reason can be identified' (2005: 6). This chapter traces this problematisation and, more specifically, the 'technocratic and politically manufactured spillover of the economic project of the internal market into an internal security project' (Huysmans, 2000: 752), its harmonisation and gradual extension beyond the borders of the Union. This should assist us in understanding attempts at EU-isation (see Chapter 1) as the diffusion of the EU's governing rationalities that originally sought to secure the internal milieu are increasingly externalised, and seek to inhabit the external space through EU-set norms and regulations.

Further, it should be noted that treating this 'Eastern neighbourhood', or the EU's relations with the various states, as a homogenous Eastern 'Other' is misleading. For example, the Former Yugoslav Republic of

Macedonia (FYROM) may appear to be the EU's Eastern neighbour but it is also Greece's Northern and Bulgaria's Western neighbour. Thus, treating them as homogenous, irrespective of a state's geographic position, has implications for our perceptions of the European 'Other' and the management of cross-border mobility between the EU and these states. It is important, therefore, to stress that the states' responses to the EU's attempts at control differ, while their migration profiles vary significantly. While the Western Balkans were first to receive visa-free regimes from the EU, increased asylum claims in the EU (especially from Kosovo) coupled with the ongoing refugee and migrant crisis (along with Turkey), question the success of the visa-free regime and the EU's ability to extend border control into the neighbourhood. In Eastern Europe, on the other hand, levels of illegal migration remain in the hundreds (rather than hundreds of thousands), while cross-border mobility is increasingly based on supervisory (rather than more direct) forms of control, with Moldova being the first state to gain a visa-free regime as early as 2014.

Securing the 'milieu': cross-border mobility and internal security

According to Sandra Lavenex, the rationale of common EU policies on visas and migration can be traced to domestic member state actors attempting to circumvent internal obstacles to reforms of border management (Lavenex, 2006: 332). For Vaughan-Williams, however, questions of borders and regulation of the internal milieu have much deeper roots in changes that have taken place in the aftermath of the Second World War and the ensuing Cold War, which divided the continent between the liberal West and the command economies of the socialist East. Questions on how to govern the European space have been a historical constant and therefore the emergence of the EC/EU as an 'area of freedom, security and justice' was one particular historical response to the problematisation of 'Europe' (Walters in Larner and Walters: 2006: 156).

The post-Second World War geopolitical changes and economic developments in the means of production heralded a more visible introduction of a liberal economy into political practice, meaning that 'to govern a state', according to Foucault, 'will therefore mean to apply an economy at the entire level of the state' (in Larner and Walters, 2006: 166). As a result, the European project presented by the founding fathers had economic rationalities as the means to organise the Western European space at a time when a post-war economic recovery and the reintegration of Germany were seen as the main priorities in safeguarding the security of the Western part of the continent.

The Rome Treaty of 1957 sought to create an 'ever closer union' between the peoples of Western Europe through a gradual removal of social, economic and political boundaries to facilitate internal circulation and deepen the internal market. The freedom of movement within the internal market thus became a 'tool of government' (Walters and Haahr, 2005: 43), assisting in the recovery of post-war Western European economies and fostering closer relations (as a way of removing antagonism) through 'interventions' that regulated the above circulation and its impact within the union (2005: 45).

As such, the EC's 'freedom of movement' solution to the problematisation of Europe created the need to further compensate externally for the internal security deficit. In particular, with the increasing removal of sectoral barriers, it was necessary to regulate the side effects of the internal freedoms and to limit the exposure of individual member states and the internal circulation to external insecurities. However, with the 1968 Council Regulation Resolution 1612/68 it was possible to observe the early foundations of 'Fortress Europe', distinguishing between the right to free movement of member states' citizens and those from third countries, highlighting that free movement within the EC was to be a prerogative for member state nationals (Huysmans, 2000).

This led to an increased subjectivising (securitising) of potential external threats such as migrants from third countries (including those in wider Europe)[1] even before the subject could pose a risk. EU border management, therefore, developed by calculating risks in terms of economic predictions and probabilities, as highlighted in the EU's perception of the 2015 crisis: 'In response to the migration crisis facing the EU, the objective must be to rapidly stem the flows, protect our external borders, reduce illegal migration and safeguard the integrity of the Schengen area' (European Council, 2016a). This process has been perhaps best described by Jef Huysmans:

> The securitisation of the internal market is the key dynamic through which the European integration process is implicated in the securitisation of migration. Its central element is the assumption that, after the abolition of internal controls, transnational flows of goods, capital, services and people will challenge public order and the rule of law. This link has been constructed so successfully that it has obtained the status of common sense. (Huysmans, 2000: 758)

While the issue of risk has become powerful in the EU's discourse on internal security, it has also had a practical impact on the management of cross-border flows and the administration of the external borders. The 1985 Schengen Agreement and the 1986 Single European Act enshrined the Third Pillar of Justice and Home Affairs as an inter-governmental (competence of the member states) method of cooperation, ensuring that while the Community (the supranational Commission) held decision-making competence over the free movement of goods, capital and services, the member states, concerned about the loss of regulatory control, remained in control over issues of policing and the movement of people. For example, the monitoring of visa liberalisation with the countries of Eastern Europe and the Southern Caucasus (launched after 2009) was even further tightened by the member states following the increase in illegal migration and asylum application levels from the Western Balkans.

In this respect, the Schengen Accords became the basis for a common policy to manage cross-border mobility (and the source of ongoing tensions) and in 1996 the Council first considered matters of practical local cooperation between consulates on matters of visa issuance including 'visa shopping' (Council of Ministers, 1996). However, most importantly for the EU's relations with third countries and the management of movement of third-country nationals into the EU, there was a move towards the common short-stay (90-day) visa. Similarly, the Schengen Application Convention in 1990 highlighted the need take into account both the internal removal of borders and the potential of new external insecurities, setting a first wave of common standards for the management of common external borders at a time of new external pressures.

From the 1980s, while the member states retained administrative control, there was 'gradual incorporation' and institutionalisation of justice and home affairs to the European level in the form of new technology such as the EURODAC (European Dactyloscopy) database holding fingerprints from asylum applicants (Huysmans, 2000: 755) and including a whole array of instruments such as the Schengen Information System I and II, Schengen Visa Information System and EUROSUR (European Border Surveillance System).

In this respect, 'European cooperation has been amplified with regard to surveillance, migration, policing and asylum measures ... for the protection of European citizens from those unwanted and uninvited "others"' (Walters in Larner and Walters, 2006: 168). Securing the internal milieu from external threats consisted of developing a common legal base, investing in 'avant garde' technology, and harmonising diverging practices and views on managing cross-border flows – 'the site of safe(r) domestic inside that is juxtaposed with a dangerous and sometimes chaotic outside' (Walters and Haahr, 2005: 94).

Interestingly, the migratory pressures on the EU throughout the 1990s did not hinder the removal of internal borders. By 2015, however, the economic focus on risk management and prevention in new areas of 'intervention' was increasingly put under pressure as the EU found itself reacting to multiple migratory push and pull factors from its Southern neighbourhood and Turkey, such as the war in Syria and the socio-economic situation in parts of Africa. Discovering that harmonisation of practices alone was not enough when faced with tens of thousands of arrivals daily and diverging views on how to manage their flow, the (2016) President of the European

Council, Donald Tusk, pleaded with European leaders that member states must stop fighting over different plans for safeguarding the external border, coordinate more effectively and, crucially, respect the rules they had agreed on.

Despite the proliferation of strategies, technologies, and the focus on risk prevention, harmonised external border management alone proved to be an inadequate response to tackling the internal security deficit. Rather than representing successful securitisation in the constructivist speech act logic of Buzan et al. (1998), the member states' continuing failure to adhere to the agreed policies rather highlighted the EU's increasing failure to securitise (Neal, 2009: 334). As Neal notes: 'discursive securitisation of migration failed, producing neither urgent policy responses nor Member State solidarity in the face of what was articulated as a common threat' (Neal, 2009: 334). In this sense, these strategies and technologies instead created new subjectification of threats in the neighbourhood and beyond without adequately addressing fundamental questions such as the competencies of a European Border Guard Service.

Inclusion at the cost of exclusion: externalising EU border management

Nevertheless, while failing to adequately secure the external borders, the EU has gradually come to practise the externalisation of border management into its neighbourhood, in particular, the Western Balkans and Eastern Europe and also Turkey. Such methods are making increasingly irrelevant the concepts of bordering, de-bordering and re-bordering on a wider European scale. What has become ever more clear is that with the ongoing opening of the internal space, cross-border crime and migratory pressures, a physical external border alone is an inadequate protection from external risks. As the UK's Home Office and Foreign and Commonwealth's report 'Securing the UK Border: Our Vision and Strategy for the Future' already noted in 2007:

> the border has been traditionally understood as a single, staffed physical frontier, where travellers show paper-based identity documents to pass through … This philosophy will not deal effectively with the step change in mobility that globalisation has brought to our country … a new doctrine is demanded. (Vaughan-Williams, 2012: 17)

Alternatively, as the French philosopher Étienne Balibar argued, borders 'are no longer at the borders', calling for a new analytical rigour to challenge the old perceptions that borders are limited to the physical border of a polity (in Vaughan-Williams, 2012: 6). In this respect, we must first understand border as a whole configuration of the physical border, surveillance instruments, databases, migration and asylum policies, visas and, increasingly, the participation of third countries' institutions.

With regards to the neighbourhood, visas and migration policies have had a significant impact on the EU's relations with the countries of Eastern Europe, the Southern Caucasus and the Western Balkans. For example, the 2004 and 2007 enlargements pushed the Eastern borders of the Union eastwards building new border structures and requiring new means of managing security risks beyond the physical border. The 2004 accession of the Visegrad Four (V4) (the Czech Republic, Hungary, Poland and Slovakia), the Baltic states (Estonia, Latvia and Lithuania), followed by Romania and Bulgaria in 2007 created new realities on the EU's Eastern border, and led to a need by the EU to engage more directly with parts of the continent with which it had previously relatively limited interaction. In this sense, the European Neighbourhood Policy (ENP), introduced on the eve of the 2004 'big bang' enlargement, represented a direct response by the EU to create a new institutional platform which was dominated by issues of visas and migration.

As Malcolm Anderson notes, while creating 'Fortress Europe', European leaders have been careful not to completely close the EU's external borders – although Vaughan-Williams argues that such 'politics of exclusion' is impossible (2012) – instead relying on different intensities of exclusion. The EU's external borders have therefore become sufficiently 'porous, to filter' the wanted from unwanted migrants (Anderson in Andreas and Snyder: 2000: 22).

The EU increasingly came to stress the importance of people-to-people contact through cross-border mobility and a visa-free regime as a long-term goal. For example, FYROM, Montenegro and Serbia received visa liberalisation by 2009, followed by Albania and Bosnia-Herzegovina in 2010. With a visa-free regime concluded with Moldova in April 2014, nearly 500,000 Moldovans took the opportunity to travel to the Schengen area without a visa or on a free visa for those not in possession of a biometric passport. By May 2016, Moldovan citizens had made 4.4 million journeys between Moldova and the EU (EUBAM, 2016).

Currently, Georgia and Ukraine (after a prolonged process), have finally received visa-free travel. Armenia is currently in the process of potentially signing a Visa Liberalisation Action Plan (VLAP) agreement by the time of the 2017 Brussels EaP Summit while Azerbaijan is in the implementation stage of its visa facilitation and readmission agreements. The possibility of signing such agreements with Belarus is still being negotiated. Turkey's role in the migration and refugee crisis also raises further questions concerning its future relations with the EU. With the establishment of the Eastern Partnership initiative, it would appear that the goal of achieving greater cross-border mobility and more inclusive people-to-people contact with the countries of the Eastern neighbourhood seems on track to succeed.

However, stressing 'people-to-people' contact does not come as mere normative posturing. In fact, it is also linked with the wider rationalities of governing and extending the management of internal security beyond the borders of the Union. During the course of the 1990s, it became increasingly clear that the EU's external border, for all its efforts at harmonisation and investment in state-of-the-art technology, could not be adequately safe-guarded (filtered) without the assistance or, at the very least, the security (stability) of the neighbouring third countries. In the first instance, during the 1990s, this had come to directly involve the neighbouring candidate countries in Central and Eastern Europe, turning this area into a 'buffer zone' by prescribing high levels of pre-accession conditionality through the first wave of visa facilitation agreements (simplified visa procedures) and a series of bilateral agreements. This was based on the strengthening of the states' border management and rule of law, including the creation of more exclusionary migration strategies towards the European 'Other'.

According to Lavenex, the 2004 Eastern enlargement constituted 'an early element of extraterritorial control' (2006: 333). For example, the first readmission agreement was signed between the Schengen area and Poland in 1991. Embraced formally at the Edinburgh European Council, it was the first legally binding 'contractual engagement' between the Schengen area and a third country which highlighted the need to cooperate with countries of 'origin or transit' in order to protect the external borders of the Union (European Council, 1992).

Lavenex argues that the Central European states' position on transit routes for migrants and asylum seekers, as in the case of the Western Balkans and Turkey today, prompted member states to include them in the emerging border management system (2006: 334) as additional means of anticipating and preventing risks from reaching the borders of the Union. Thus, at one and the same time candidate countries and the new neighbour-hood 'were hence vehicles to expand the territory of immigration control beyond the circle of the Member States' (Lavenex, 2006: 335), stressing the need for 'comprehensive and tailor-made packages of incentives ... for specific countries to ensure effective returns and readmission' (European Council, 2016b). Furthermore, the EU sought to establish unofficial frame-works of cooperation, such as the Budapest Group, made up of internal ministry officials from forty countries (particularly focusing on the Eastern and Southern neighbourhoods) as a platform for external migration control.

In 2001, the EU further launched the Söderköping Process under which the EU, the candidate states and their Eastern neighbours sought to work on: a) harmonisation in migration management; b) improving border man-agement; c) the safe third-country concept and readmission agreements; and (d) practices related to the reception of aliens, asylum seekers and irregular migrants and the return of rejected asylum seekers and irregular migrants. For example, in October 2001, a meeting between the Hungarian,

Slovak and Ukrainian authorities with representatives from the Council presidency (Belgium), Germany and Sweden took place in the Subcarpathian town of Uzhgorod seeking to work on a common strategy on burden sharing and support in light of increasing irregular migration. In the second meeting in Brest (Belarus), the EU promised increasing technical assistance so that the countries on the Eastern side of the soon-to-be new EU border 'harmonise their capacities with their immediate western neighbours' (Söderköping Process, 2001) – a further move in the construction of the Eastern border rather than easing its impact. However, as Bigo notes, 'what is seen as a merging between internal and external aspects of security is mainly the expansion of the internal security dimension' (Bigo, 2006: 395). For example, while the Commission was claiming that 'the security of the external borders of the European Union is an essential subject for European citizens (European Commission, 2002), it was also quick to point out that a 'continent-wide application of the model of peaceful and voluntary integration among free nations is a guarantee of stability' (European Commission, 1997), once again highlighting the tension between internal freedoms and the need for security beyond the internal milieu.

In other words, while dialogue with wider Europe gradually came to include expansion of the EU's border management, the process was less to do with existing external insecurities than with extending and managing the internal fear of insecurity in ever wider circuits. President Hollande (2016) of France illustrated this process in the case of Turkey: 'As Turkey is making an effort to take in refugees – who will not come to Europe – it's reasonable that Turkey receive help from Europe to accommodate those refugees', or, as the Reuters Agency (2016) concluded: 'The Europeans ... are under pressure to manage the biggest influx of people since World War Two ... the crisis has helped populist opponents and set nations against each other, straining the open internal borders of the EU.'

In this sense, the EU's rhetoric of an 'open' Europe and of shared values and historical ties with the neighbourhood is secondary to the pressures of securing the internal milieu from any potential insecurities. For example, by the mid-1990s the non-candidate Eastern European states enjoyed a relatively liberal visa regime with the V4 which included a visa-free regime and significant fee reductions or waivers. This was important not only for Polish minorities in Belarus and Ukraine, Rusyns in Western Ukraine or the three million strong Hungarian minorities in neighbouring countries, including Ukraine. In 1996, 2.6 million Ukrainians were able to cross the Polish border having only to show evidence of disposable money (Freudenstein in Andreas and Snyder, 2000: 180).

However, as the EU offered the candidate countries more inclusive interaction, 'the more limited the opportunities became for our eastern neighbours' (Stefan Batory Foundation, 2009). No longer simply a buffer zone on the periphery of the EU, the very restrictions that were once applied to the citizens of Central Europe in travelling westwards were now being applied by these very states, however reluctantly, on their Eastern border.

Thus, the risk-driven impact of 'Fortress Europe' spread not only into the candidate countries but also, however grudgingly, to their neighbours and, after the 2004 and 2007 enlargements, from the 'new' neighbours on to their neighbours as countries such as Moldova and Georgia imposed new requirements on nationals of other third countries. The imposition of EU-driven migration laws was particularly contested in Georgia which sees itself as an open country for the flow of goods, services and people. As Vachudova (in Andreas and Snyder, 2000: 158) notes, Schengen visa regimes in particular became 'the most visible manifestation of the common external border and, overall, more exclusionary than the national policies they replaced. Freudenstein went further, calling it the 'Huntingdon border', bearing the increasing risk of 'marking a break between civilisation in the twenty-first century' (in Andreas and Snyder, 2000: 174) and, indeed, being symbolic of the EU's politics of exclusion of the 'real outsiders' (Smith, 1996) – the securitised unknown 'Other' beyond the borders of the buffer zone 'Other'.

Shaping the Eastern neighbourhood in the EU's image

Small technical steps taken at the European level and implemented on the border with Belarus, Moldova and Ukraine did show the first glimmer of, at least, minimising the effects of the EU's risk-dominated approach, including the lowering of visa fees (Stefan Batory Foundation, 2009). More importantly, a local border traffic system was initiated, which provided bilateral and more flexible border crossing arrangements for citizens living in the border regions of the Eastern neighbourhood countries (Council of the European Union, 2008). With the introduction of permits and the creation of special lanes on local border traffic-only crossings, simplified access within a 50-kilometre radius of the border was established bilaterally by Hungary, Poland and Slovakia with Ukraine. This was followed by Poland and Lithuania with Belarus, and Romania with Moldova.

Further changes in the management of visa issuance occurred as a result of a French initiative which began the practice whereby Schengen member states would be represented by one designated member state's consulate in third countries. Eastern Europe, where visa applications for Schengen visas rose dramatically, became a testing ground for such new approaches. Thus, in 2007 Hungary opened the first EU Common Visa Application Centre in Chisinau as part of the EU–Moldova 2006 visa facilitation agreement (Fernandez, 2006: 11). This allowed the citizens of Moldova a one-stop access to visa application at a time when only a limited number of member states had diplomatic or consular representation in Chisinau, and, crucially, encouraged reforms under EU-set conditions.

According to Grabbe (2000), this gradual form of inclusion coupled with attempts to externalise border management also provided an opportunity to extend EU rules and regulations into the wider European space. As Grabbe points out, in the early 1990s the neighbouring states did not have developed migration policies because during the period of Soviet domination the ruling regimes were less concerned to keep 'foreigners out rather than to keep their own citizens in' (2000: 529). Therefore, EU policies 'filled institutional lacunae' by developing new synergies on the regulation of access to their territory and thus closer proximity to the EU border.

In fact, questions of border management made up the greatest proportion of the elements of conditionality in the area of Justice and Home Affairs (Grabbe, 2000: 525–526). The EU explicitly linked the implementation of EU border management standards to the financial and technical assistance provided via programmes such as PHARE (Poland and Hungary: Assistance for Restructuring their Economies), TACIS (Technical Assistance for the Commonwealth of Independent States), ENPI (European Neighbourhood and Partnership Instrument) and the ENI (European Neighbourhood Instrument). In the case of Turkey, the Reuters Agency was blunter about the EU's intentions: 'Turkey promised to help stem the flow of migrants to Europe in return for cash, visas and renewed talks on joining the EU' (Reuters, 2016).

On the other hand, the Söderköping Process increasingly encouraged member states to share their Eastern neighbours' experience in 'aligning their migration and asylum related legislation, policies and practices with the EU acquis standards', including institutional and legal support, network facilitation, stressing the 'harmonisation' of border practices as part of the EU's growing policy of border externalisation (Söderköping Process, 2005). Also, from 2005, the EU launched the cross-border BUMAD initiative (Belarus, Ukraine, Moldova Anti-Drugs Programme), its Border Assistance Mission to Moldova and Ukraine (EUBAM), and provided assistance for 'study visits to the EU, training sessions on fighting corruption in various sectors, legal advice on drafting laws to protect whistleblowers, information on how to further integrity in public administration, and the role of the press in anti-corruption' (Lavenex and Wichmann, 2009: 96; Hernandez and Segrera, 2014).

In 2008, the Council agreed on the so-called 'Return Directive' which strengthened the 2004 provisions by attempting to set common standards on readmission and return, and to provide new financial incentives on readmission of illegal migrants to third countries (Council of the European Union, 2008). The Readmission Agreements signed with individual countries in the Eastern neighbourhood were connected to the Visa Facilitation Agreements, signed as the first part of a process leading up to visa liberalisation between the EU and third countries. In its Facilitation Agreements with third countries in the EaP, the Union emphasised the desire to increase people-to-people contact although under set conceptual parameters (Kurki, 2011), including the strengthening of law enforcement institutions, border management, democratic governance and the aforementioned readmission of illegal migrants.

Readmission and Visa Facilitation Agreements, therefore, were a further attempt by the EU to use migration and visa policies as tools to inhabit its neighbourhood with its own norms (Delcour, 2013), 'thereby providing an additional control zone between the refugees' countries and potential destination countries in western Europe' (Collinson, 1996: 82). To that extent, the neighbouring countries have taken greater roles in managing access to the Union.

Although the EU sought to use such strategies with its neighbours to create a new zone of safety around its borders, the ability to either create a safety zone or successfully extend its rules and regulations became ever more challenging. On one hand, in 2015 there were just 1,920 illegal border crossings from Belarus, Moldova and Ukraine into the EU, in contrast to the 69,000 crossing over from Turkey in January 2016 alone, taking the Western Balkans route into the EU (Frontex, 2016). In countries such as Serbia, the sheer volume of migrants and refugees essentially made the Readmission Agreements redundant, while FYROM Border Police only allowed access for Syrians and Iraqis (*New York Times*, 2016). As the European Council's (2016b) conclusions on migration noted: 'The full and speedy implementation of the EU–Turkey Action Plan remains a priority, in order to stem migration flows and to tackle traffickers and smugglers networks. Steps have been taken by Turkey to implement the Action Plan, notably as regards access by Syrian refugees to Turkey's labour market and data sharing with the EU.'

On the other hand, it is also worth noting the EU's somewhat different strategies pursued in the Western Balkans in contrast to the countries of Eastern Europe and the Southern Caucasus. Spurred on by the membership prospects of some countries (such as Croatia) and the need to help stabilise others (in particular Bosnia-Herzegovina), the EU employed a uniquely inclusive migration and visa policy which, despite set benchmarks noted above, led to a quick process of visa liberalisation. Although they lacked the same levels of monitoring employed in the case of Moldova or Georgia, FYROM, Montenegro and Serbia received visa liberalisation by 2009, followed by Albania and Bosnia-Herzegovina in 2010.

By 2013, however, owing to increased levels of irregular migration and asylum applications from the region, it gradually became clear that inclusive migration and visa policies, without at least some degree of control, posed a potential risk to the EU's internal milieu. According to the European Commission (2015), there were over 53,000 asylum applications in 2013 alone. The visa liberalisation process launched with the countries of Eastern

Europe and the Southern Caucasus was therefore caught between the exclusionary and controlling strategies of EU-isation and the lack of adequate control exercised in the Western Balkans. When the migration and refugee crisis reached the external borders of the EU in 2015, it became abundantly clear that the EU's attempts at externalising its border management and inhabiting wider Europe with its own rules and regulations were severely limited.

Conclusion

Given the EU's desperate attempts to stem the flows of migrants from reaching the internal milieu, it would appear that borders are once again an important feature of the European continent. In fact, as demonstrated, the relevance of borders has never disappeared. Instead, borders have been merely reconfigured, manifesting themselves in more nuanced ways by the EU's attempts at externalising its border management into the neighbourhood and inhabiting this wider European space with rules and regulations inherent in its migration and visa policies (Merheim-Eyre in Bossong and Carrapico, 2016).

Commencing with the problematisation of governance in Western Europe and the fears of potential risks arising from the internal freedom of movement, this chapter has attempted to situate EU migration and visa policies in the Eastern neighbourhood by placing them in a wider context of EU governance. The chapter has argued that there are three primary ways to understand the role of EU migration policies in the Eastern neighbourhood: (i) to protect the internal 'milieu' from potential external risks/insecurities; (ii) to extend its control into the neighbourhood through 'politics of inclusion' or 'politics of exclusion' (Smith, 1996); and (iii) to shape the neighbourhood by inhabiting the external space with rules and regulations.

In this sense, the EU's internal security project has extended outwards into neighbouring countries, seeking to diffuse its norms and regulation into ever wider circuits. While the EU sought new methods of dealing with its Eastern neighbourhood, initiatives such as the Söderköping Process were essentially dominated by a justice and home affairs agenda that promoted continental cross-border mobility but under EU-set conditions.

However, it was also shown that without incentives such as visa liberalisation, convergence with EU norms was severely limited. In other words, while the EU's instruments were being developed to project EU internal security beyond its borders, the ability to influence the EU's neighbours was limited, highlighting the need for new strategies to incentivise the Eastern countries. The case of the Western Balkans, however, highlighted the limits to inclusive forms of visa and migration policies. Therefore, when the visa liberalisation process was eventually launched with individual countries in

Eastern Europe and the Southern Caucasus, the policy in practice was caught between the exclusionary and controlling attempts at EU-isation and the lack of adequate control exercised in the Western Balkans and on the border with Turkey.

Nevertheless, the ongoing importance played by these policies in the EU's relations with its Eastern neighbours cannot be ignored. This includes the various migratory and refugee crises troubling the EU. The EU's search for new ways of dealing with these pressures merely furthered the crucial role played by the neighbourhood in stemming such flows.

In this sense, this European 'Other' – not quite the 'insider' nor the 'real outsider' (to use Mike Smith's term, 1996) – has been essential in the EU's strategies and the related countries are being rewarded by more inclusive visa and migration policies for their own citizens. For example, while the Western Balkans enjoyed visa-free travel into the EU from as early as 2009, the citizens of Georgia, Moldova and Ukraine are at last enjoying the same benefits, showing that citizens from the Eastern neighbourhood countries are facing increasingly fewer restrictions on travel, studies or doing business in the Union. The future of visa liberalisation with Turkey, however, remains contested. As the Slovak Ministry of Foreign and European Affairs (2014) made clear about the need for greater inclusion of the EU's Eastern neighbours: 'according to our own experiences – [visas] represent a definite obstacle to human relations, business, [and] cultural exchange'.

Note

1   To some extent, one can also witness the process of 'othering' in the different perceptions of migration to and from Western Europe and the member states of Central-Eastern Europe. This, however, is a research agenda of its own.

13 Maria Stoicheva

'Neighbour languages': Europeanisation and language borders

The chapter aims to explore EU/Eastern neighbourhood relations in the area of languages and language policies, with a focus on processes of Europeanisation and the reinforcement of European identity. It covers not only issues related to language management but demonstrates the importance of language practices, beliefs about language varieties, and the impact of Europeanisation on language in the Eastern neighbourhood. In many aspects, these are issues related to 'neighbour languages'. The external limits of territories (borders) and the internal delimitations within societies (boundaries) have long been thought of in different terms: nationality, citizenship, immigration and language, in particular, with its capacity for generating 'imagined' communities.

The European Neighbourhood Policy introduces another aspect in the process of making borders, in both senses, since it produces new realities concerning political and social boundaries which could have an impact on language policies in the contemporary multilingual reality. Within the European neighbourhood particular languages may be considered as 'neighbour languages' on pure linguistic terms as a category that avoids the choice between 'foreign languages' and 'dialects' while recognising the closeness and proximity at hand. However, as politics gets in the way, the conceptualisation of the EU space and its neighbours feeds into language ideology that moulds language behaviour and draws new borders. This chapter explores the aspects of language shifts and the potential for frustrations and frictions over language issues in the near neighbourhood, comparing it to issues about language and multilingualism within the EU.

Contradictions of Europeanisation

In December of 2007, the Constitutional Court of Ukraine announced that starting in 2008 all foreign-language movies shown in the country will have

to be translated into Ukrainian via dubbing, subtitles, or synchronous translation. (Pavlenko, 2008: 275)

This is how Pavlenko (2008) starts her analysis of multilingualism in post-
Soviet countries, emphasising the contradictory situation in which a language (Russian) native to 30 per cent of the population of Ukraine and
one used and understood by the majority of the remaining 70 per cent,
is officially categorised as 'foreign'. Far from being a unique instance of
language management, this announcement should be considered in the
much wider context of the implementation of new language laws and
reform of the educational systems in the post-Soviet countries. Fourteen
new independent countries emerged from the dissolution of the Soviet
Union in 1991, previously united by the same language, common educational space and political system often referred to as 'Russification'.
In this context, the potential concerns about language policies, language
status, risk of discrimination and the linguistic rights of minorities are
not limited to Ukraine. Instead, they are a marked feature of the renegotiation of the linguistic imbalance of the previous situation, of the status
planning of the titular languages and, in effect, of an imposition of a new
linguistic regime according to a radically transformed framework of beliefs
and ideologies.

Another example concerns the area of minority rights and, in particular,
linguistic rights. Although it does not come from the EU's Eastern neighbourhood, it reveals the same narrative of the past in the context of a radically changed language regime. In the case of *Podkolzina* v. *Latvia* [2002]
of the European Court of Human Rights (Application no. 46726/99), the
applicant, a Latvian national who was born in Latvia and a member of the
Russian-speaking minority in Latvia, alleged that the removal of her name
from the list of candidates at the general election for insufficient knowledge
of Latvian, the official language in Latvia, constituted a breach of the right
to stand as a candidate in an election, guaranteed by national legislation and
by European conventions on protection of minority rights. This is not the
only example of Russian speakers appealing for protection of their minority
rights and referring to the Council of Europe Framework Convention in
the post-Soviet space. On this particular occasion the European Court of
Human Rights held unanimously that there had been a violation of Article
3 of Protocol No. 1 of the European Convention of Human Rights: the
right to free elections. It should be noted that the new language legislation
already had a history of over ten years of application in the country at the
time when the decision came out. As Patten and Kymlicka (2003: 3) note
in their book on language rights and political theory, 'laws declaring the
majority language as the sole official language were often the first laws
adopted by the newly independent countries of the former Soviet Union
or Yugoslavia'.

In the late 1980s and the beginning of the 1990s, the former Soviet republics that gained independence reasserted the status of their national languages as a counteraction to the previous dominance of Russian. The six countries on the European territory of the former USSR – Ukraine, Belarus, Moldova, Latvia, Lithuania and Estonia – proclaimed, between 1988 and 1990, their titular languages as the sole state languages, thus setting new normative ground by establishing new language regimes and norms, that is the official language status, the language of instruction in schools, the language applied for administrative purposes as well as minority, regional and other languages and their status and use in society. This justifies the statement that, upon achieving their independence, the normative aspect of language policy was officially resolved and the countries had already started implementing a language policy involving a substantial shift (Pavlenko, 2008: 285). The establishing of the new language regimes was met by criticism from Russia, often accompanied by statements about language discrimination against the large Russian-speaking minorities in the post-Soviet space. Additionally, the Russian Federation introduced legislation such as the federal programme 'Russian Language' 2006–10 adopted in 2005. The external focus of the programme related to the spread of the Russian language and meeting the cultural and linguistic needs of compatriots outside Russia (Hogan-Brun and Melnyk, 2012: 596). The language policies of the EU and the Council of Europe also closely focused on this in connection with the accession of the Baltic states to NATO and the EU – a period of concentration on and meeting the criteria for EU membership.

These two cases illustrate the systematic process of bringing about change in the area of language use, involving intervention by governments and public authorities. As such, in this particular context (the post-Soviet area) language policy is only one element in a much broader policy context of gaining independence. It is often described as 'de-Russification' (Hogan-Brun and Melnyk, 2012), as a process marked by the successful outcome of a return to titular languages in all areas of public life even through measures like the above example. Instances of radical shifts were also observed in other areas of social and public life. For example, those societies in which street protests were non-existent, experienced sporadic demonstrations after 1989. In 1988 political protest had seemed impossible yet by 1989 it had become normal.

In interpreting these examples, we should note that the Court's decision came at that time not because there had been no cases or serious complaints about the linguistic rights of the minority populations before, but because international organisations had not yet developed sufficient legal ground for dealing with such complaints. However, in 1992 the Council of Europe's European Charter for Regional and Minority Language was adopted and came into force in 1998. The Framework Convention on the Protection of National Minorities was signed in 1995 and became active in 1998. In

1998 the Recommendations on Linguistic Rights of National Minorities were adopted by the Organization for Security and Cooperation in Europe (OSCE). All these international documents are considered as 'declarations of minimum standards' (Kymlicka and Patten, 2003: 3) regarding linguistic diversity and the concept of linguistic rights plays an important part in them (May, 2006). Moreover, the authors argue that their adoption was largely triggered by fears of ethnolinguistic conflict in Eastern Europe and 'were intended to guide east European countries in their effort to "rejoin Europe"' (Kymlicka and Patten, 2003: 4). Thus, they were initially intended as norms and setting standards for the Europeanisation of the applicant countries, but later from the perspective of the normative impact of the European Neighbourhood Policy. They clearly indicate the understanding of Europeanisation as value-based with its emphasis on protection and respect for linguistic diversity, multilingualism and language rights. It is also clearly in line with the general communication policy in the EU which 'requires strict adherence to the principle of equality for speakers of all the official languages of member states and rejects the idea of a lingua franca' (Wright, 2009).

Provisions related to the protection of minority and regional languages further extend these principles. The accession criteria – or so-called Copenhagen criteria – set out the conditions and principles to which any country wishing to become an EU member must conform. They include 'protection of minorities' among its first criteria, which must be satisfied in order for EU accession negotiations to be launched. This clearly indicates how high up on the political agenda the issue of protection of minorities' rights were at the time of their adoption. The normative debate which followed the establishment of new language regimes concerns the context of interaction between two or more language communities, in particular their coexistence within a political entity which is being transformed and Europeanised.

The situation of language shift

The language regimes in the EU's neighbourhood are dynamic. On the one hand, new language regimes have been established in the countries. On the other, a characteristic inertia often produces the impression that little has changed regarding the marked asymmetrical bilingualism of the former Soviet linguistic situation. This is the position in which the non-Russian population speaks Russian and is bilingual, which is not the case for the Russian population of the former republics of the Soviet Union who are practically monolingual no matter where they live. For example, the main feature of the Ukrainian sociolinguistic situation is Ukrainian-Russian bilingualism, which has a regional character and includes common individual bilingualism of this type (Masenko, 2004 in Pavlenko, 2008; Hogan-Brun and Melnyk, 2012). The dynamic of this type of language situation is often characterised as 'renegotiation of linguistic imbalance' or as a contested linguistic space (Pavlenko, 2008), or as the imposition of new linguistic regimes marked by 'identity in formation' (Laitin, 1998). For example, the Ukrainian constitution, although somewhat vague on issues of language use, ensures the comprehensive development and functioning of the Ukrainian language in all spheres of social life in the entire territory of Ukraine, but also mentions the guarantee of free use and protection of other languages of national minorities of Ukraine, among which Russian is specially mentioned. In the Moldovan Constitution, Russian is defined in Article 3 of the Language Law as a 'language of inter-ethnic communication'. Therefore, it seems to be placed in a third category between those of 'official' and 'minority' languages. Thus, a specific interaction among titular languages on the one side and Russian on the other marks clearly the language situation in the post-Soviet countries.

The de-Russification and shift in the direction of titular languages emerged as the key goals of post-Soviet language policy. It covered all components and dimensions of overt language policy requiring an increase in the teaching of the national language in all school systems, measures promoting the national languages in broadcasting, publishing and public life, special regulation in signage and the requirement that all those working with the public be able to demonstrate their competence in the national language. Tests of conversational and basic reading/writing skills in the national language have also been introduced in some cases as part of the systems of naturalisation. This, together with some restrictive aspects of the citizenship laws in Estonia and Latvia, makes this an area where international scrutiny is needed to avoid human rights abuse. There are also examples of pressure by European organisations on interpretation of what constitutes conformity with European norms and standards and the implications of normative principles of freedom and equality for language policy. This type of language policy is often justified with regulations on the use of language (even in private enterprises) in order to ensure the capacity for communication in the national language at an appropriate level and with the 'legitimate public interest' to ensure the proper functioning of the state institutional system. However, it seems clear that these issues are predominantly identity related and are there to support a substantial shift in identity (re)formation.

It has been argued by Skutnabb-Kangas and Phillipson (1994) that earlier 'linguistic imperialism' in the Baltics has had enduring consequences, changing what would seem to be the assumed status of a national language. In this view, Russian is a 'majorized minority language (a minority language in terms of numbers, but with the power of a majority language), whereas the Baltic languages are minorized majority languages (majority languages, in need of protection usually necessary for the threatened minority languages)' (Skutnabb-Kangas, 1994: 178). Similarly, it has been argued that if 'the goal is to achieve a situation where two unequal languages would finally be equal, then this cannot be achieved through granting similar rights to the languages' (Maurais, 1997: 150).

The previous situation of inequality between the languages produced a kind of 'asymmetrical bilingualism'. Russians were remaining largely mono-lingual, while non-Russians needed to become bilingual to function at any level in the Soviet system. This is different, it is argued, from a multilingual situation that has been presented as liberal best practice in European legisla-tion and conventions regarding languages and language rights. It has per-sisting implications and constitutes a major concern of the current language policies in the post-Soviet space. The expectations that Russian speakers will rapidly assimilate linguistically have not been fulfilled. The asymmetry of the past has still not been overcome or reversed as 'almost two decades after independence, levels of Estonian and Latvian language competence are still lower among Russian speakers than levels of Russian-language compe-tence among Estonians and Latvians ('Round 2000 of population and housing censuses in Estonia, Latvia and Lithuania', 2003; Rannut, 2004, 2008). In the past the Soviet Union included more than 100 ethnic groups and was one of the largest multi-ethnic states in the world. The minority problems then, including language minority problems, were related to the dominant status of Russian and to the so-called 'language safety net' drawn over Russian speakers creating an asymmetrical bilingualism. However, according to Kolstø (1995: 4), 'this does not mean that the minority prob-lems were overcome, some of them seem as big if not bigger than in the Soviet Union'.

A very brief look at the language situation in this period clearly indicates the scope of the shift that was triggered and carried out through overt language policy interventions, which resulted in significant changes in the self-identification of people as speakers of a particular language (see Table 13.1). The depiction of the language situation requires the introduction of the category L1 (first language) Russian speakers, which takes account of the above described situation of a 'majorisation' of a minority language. It is also clear that there have been major transformations in language use. These transformations are closely linked to de-Russification and European-isation of the countries in the neighbourhood.

Patterns associated with Europeanisation

The language shift in the post-Soviet space is 'part of a more general process of de-sovietisation' (Pavlenko, 2008: 282) Its main features are elimination of Russian as a language of general use, reduction of Russian language schools and the teaching of Russian in schools, and the adoption of specific

Table 13.1 Proportions of titulars, ethnic Russians and L1 Russian speakers in Soviet republics in 1989 and in post-Soviet countries in 1999–2004 (USSR Census and respective post-Soviet Censuses)

	1989	1989	1989
	Titulars	Russians	L1 Russian speakers
Armenia	93.3%	1.6%	67.5%
Belarus	77.9%	13.2%	32.3%
Georgia	70.1%	6.3%	9.0%
Moldova	64.5%	13.0%	23.3%
Ukraine	72.7%	22.1%	33.2%
	1999–2004	1999–2004	1999–2004
	Titulars	Russians	L1 Russian speakers
Armenia	97.9%	0.5%	0.9%
Belarus	81.2%	11.4%	62.8%
Georgia	83.8%	1.5%	–
Moldova	75.8%	5.9%	16.0%
Ukraine	77.8%	17.3%	29.6%

linguistic features, e.g. the replacement of Cyrillic with Latin in orthography. For example, Latinisation is interpreted as a move away from a common heritage of Soviet, and especially Slavic, countries. Supporters of Latinisation in public debates argue that it has the effect of distancing the country from the Soviet past and allows better access, and links, to the Western world (Hogan-Brun and Melnyk, 2012: 595). Moldova is a specific case, in that it shifted to the Latin alphabet and, to some degree, recognised the titular language as Romanian with one significant exception – the Transnistrian Republic, which did not acknowledge the language law and adopted a three official languages policy (Russian, Moldovan in the Cyrillic alphabet and Ukrainian). Although we cannot talk of the removal of Russian as a whole, there is a radical shift in language use and the steady emergence of new linguistic repertoires which have normative aspects. The language policy sets as a norm a repertoire that citizens should have in a new, radically changed language regime. The titular-Russian interaction and presence of Russian in the state norm of linguistic repertoires of the citizens were previously felt as unjust and inappropriate and this belief was the main driver for language policy in the changed political situation.

However, attitudes towards Russian differ in the newly independent countries. In some countries there is a normative hostility towards Russian resulting in its radical exclusion from public spaces. The Baltic states, Ukraine and Georgia are included in this group. In some countries, citizenship requires language tests thus effectively introducing restrictive citizenship legislation (Latvia and Estonia). In other countries, Russian is banned in government offices and language inspection services are introduced (Lithuania). Ukrainian law mandates the use of the titular language in schools and other areas, while in Georgia Russian language programmes are banned from many television and radio channels. These may be viewed as examples of expressions of normative hostility. In other post-Soviet countries, language policy legislation reflects mixed feelings towards Russian. In Armenia and Moldova, Russian has preserved some of its special status – the status of a semi-official language – which is largely spoken by the top state officials and is still used as a primary language in school, although sometimes on a regional basis. On the other side of the scale, in Belarus, Russian has remained an official language along with Belorussian.

Despite these differences there are visible commonalities in the (re-) building processes which these countries experience. Among these are the focus on language development and the similar approaches chosen for language management (Hogan-Brun and Melnyk, 2012). In most cases these patterns of transformations, defined very often as Europeanisation, have been justified with narratives of the past and particularly of reaching towards a pre-Soviet past. The Baltic countries referred to their pre-Soviet independent status. In Moldova there is the discourse of the reunification with Romania. As a rule, the language outcome of the drive for Europeanisation has been an official monolingualism with one language functioning as a 'state language', with the exception of Belarus. In this case a policy of two official languages was adopted after the referendum in 1995, which was generally viewed as a solution to ethnic problems in the country (de Varennes, 1996; Hogan-Brun and Melnyk, 2012; O'Reilly, 2001). However, 'the investigation conducted by Western and local scholars of the language shifts proceeded in parallel' rather than in collaboration with other research on the situation in the post-Soviet space. It focused on documenting the change of linguistic regimes and detailed sociolinguistic portrayals of the countries but 'without sufficient scholarly collaboration and without the integrative drive displayed by the political scientists' (Pavlenko, 2008: 277). This is also related to the issue of language and minority rights which also seem to be under-explored in post-Soviet scholarship (Hogan and Melnyk, 2012: 613).

The main issues of the language shift, which are closely related to Europeanisation, concern the titular–Russian divide. This is not an issue of division and distancing of languages in purely linguistic terms. The distance between the languages might have a role in the dimensions of the divide but is not a matter of specific influence on the forms of its manifestation.

The Soviet past involved a rather intensive Russification for some countries, which concerned not only the privileged position of Russian; but there were also cases where the language situation was characterised by high level maintenance of the national languages, particularly in the Caucasus. The national languages had official status under the Soviet regime in the three countries of the region – Georgia, Armenia and Azerbaijan. The categorisation of Russian is subject to a complex process of reinterpretation, which plays an important role in the implementation of the language policies. There is lack of consistency in the definition of the status of Russian in the region. It is defined in some cases, including legal documents, as a language of national minority, but also as a regional language, language of inter-ethnic communication, supra-ethnic language or even foreign language, which sets a status for the language despite the language practices in society. This is an issue both inside societies but also for legal circles from outside.

The Venice Commission in its Opinion on the 2012 Ukrainian draft law, notes that the wide range of definitions proposed in Article 1 of the Draft Law and their interrelations are 'too complex and therefore confusing' (Venice Commission, 2011: 4). The Advisory Committee of the Framework Convention for the Protection of National Minorities (FCNM) in its Opinions refers to Russian as the language of a national minority (e.g. Third Opinion on Moldova, para 136–137, 2009). Russian is defined in the 1989 Language Law of Moldova as 'language of inter-ethnic communication', though as a compromise alongside Romanian (Kolstø, 2002). Thus, it is placed in a third category between those of 'official' and 'minority' language (Prina, 2013: 8) Special status is granted to Russian in the Law on the Rights of Persons belonging to National Minorities and the Legal Status of their Organizations of 12 July 2001, where minority languages are treated separately from Russian. Similar is the case of the status of Russian in the former Ukrainian Language Law. The 2012 Law on the principles of the state language policy includes Russian in the group of regional languages.

Parallel to the re-establishment of a new language regime, as a result of the language shift, there has been a clear process of adherence to a number of UN and European agreements on political and civil rights, including issues of language rights. This was considered a mainstream Europeanisation process preparing the ground for EU accession or for establishing closer neighbourhood relations with the EU. The European Charter for Regional and Minority Languages was signed and ratified by Ukraine (2005) and Armenia (2002). The FCNM was widely acknowledged and officially adopted by most of the post-Soviet countries (Ukraine 1997; Georgia 2005; Armenia 1998; Estonia 1997; Latvia 2005; Lithuania 2000). International organisations and the EU effectively acted as agents of Europeanisation in the area of language minority rights. The UN Association of Georgia launched a four-year National Integration and Tolerance in Georgia (NITG) Programme in 2007. The OSCE High Commissioner on National

Minorities has exercised an especially important role in Georgia through its supervision of the treatment of minorities for the promotion of peace and stability.

The perception of Europeanisation through the lens of language policy was linked to the accession to NATO and the EU. It was inevitably associated with pressure from the international community to increase support for minority languages and protect minority rights (Adrey, 2005). At domestic level, the spread of the titular language is linked and viewed as acquiring a new European identity. In Ukraine, the implementation of the new language regime is related to becoming European (Bilaniuk and Melnyk, 2008; Kuzio, 1998) as opposed to becoming 'Little Russia'. The debate around Moldovan/Romanian is similarly linked to European identity as a narrative of the past and rebuilding a pre-Soviet situation. Thus, the domestic understanding of the Europeanisation process links it closely to establishing (i.e. reviving) and widening the spread of the titular language rather than one particular language – Russian. The drive to independence and Europeanisation are interpreted as a reverse picture of affirmative action – as affirmation directed towards the titular languages rather than the minority languages. The identification of the main problem to be resolved by the language policy as mentioned above – the slow progress of titular language competence among Russian speakers – is another representation of this view on the role of languages.

Policy vs practice

The language situation, however, does not always comply with the policy. 'The present as reality is a construct of past conceptions' (see Mannin, Chapter 1 in this volume), in this case of an established framework of language use. Thus, in quite a number of cases, Russian is maintained in the multilingual repertoires of the citizens and of the linguistic landscapes of the cities and countryside (Council of Europe, 2009). A number of factors complicate the reversal of Russification through language shift policies in the post-Soviet countries (Hogan-Brun and Melnyk, 2012: 594), including the large populations of monolingual Russian speakers and the Russification of members of the titular populations (Pavlenko, 2008: 283). The scene becomes even more complex because national minorities in some cases prefer Russian-medium instruction due to the codification of the minority language in the Cyrillic alphabet and the tradition of using Russian textbooks in schools and, in some cases, at higher levels of education, among other reasons. This aspect is related to Russian functioning as the language of multi-ethnic communication in the Soviet Union as a multi-ethnic and multicultural unity. Purely linguistic features also influence the narrowing of the distance between languages. Some of the functional limitations of the titular languages are reinforced by the use of the Russian language as standard practice (Pavlenko, 2008). Language contacts within the Slavic language group led to Ukrainian-Russian and Belarussian-Russian language mixing (суржик /surzhyk and трасянка/ trasyanka). However, in a situation of language shift these variations are often liable to neglect and diminishing value. The titular–Russian divide influences people's perceptions that are as significant to them, if not more so, as any scientific analysis of the linguistic patterns and links between the two languages. The language shift has significant implications on language beliefs and language practices, or on the tendency to avoid using some languages in public as well as private space.

The value of diversity becomes a somewhat distorted and politically loaded expression where language use, in particular Russian, is mirrored in the process of independent development and de-Russification. On the one hand, the 'Western' postmodern language planning model is clearly grounded in recognition and support for variation in society and the protection and maintenance of plurality (Lo Bianco, 1987; Neustupny, 2006; Ricento, 2000). The implications of this model are that practical efforts to support minority languages now form an emerging paradigm (Jernudd and Nekvapil, 2012: 30–31). This view is embedded in the concept of 'ecology' where the failure to accommodate language minorities is seen as a form of discrimination. On the other hand, there is the counter-argument that the adoption of Russian as a second state language hampers titular language revival as in Belarus. It sustains a practice of dominance of one language over another, leading to a situation where the titular language is not comprehensively developed, and perhaps endangered.

Multilingualism is a main expression of the European language policy promoted widely at the political level by all European institutions both within the EU and the Council of Europe. The Council of Europe takes the view that all linguistic diversity is enriching for countries and for individuals, and should be encouraged (Council of Europe, 2011). Multilingualism encodes the main thrust of the EU language policy in its Framework Strategy on Multilingualism from 2005 and the new strategic document *Multilingualism: An Asset for Europe and a Shared Commitment* (2007). One of the most successful programmes of the Council of Europe is the Language Education Policy Profile Programme. It analyses language education policies on the basis of a methodology of 'self-evaluation' of the policy in a spirit of dialogue with Council of Europe experts, with a view to focusing on possible future policy developments within the country/region. The *Guide for the Development of Language Education Policies in Europe* (2007) identifies 'plurilingualism' as a fundamental aspect of policies of social inclusion and education for democratic citizenship. In a similar vein, the Declaration and Programme on Education for Democratic Citizenship emphasises the significance of the preservation of European linguistic diversity. The Language Education Policy Profile Armenia states that: 'The development of plurilingualism is not simply a functional necessity: it is also an essential component of democratic behaviour'. It also notes the following:

> But even within the domain of foreign language learning there are important differences: most obviously the Russian language has a particular and not entirely 'foreign' role, but also English is fast developing a *de facto* special position as a perceived world language of communication. The point here is not to deny these differences but to examine how a common policy may take account of them. (Council of Europe, 2009)

The educational system in Armenia provides education in five minority languages, including Russian, which is still widely applied as the language of reference literature. The profile of the education language policy of Armenia demonstrates clear accomplishments in the protection of language minority rights in accordance with the European Charter. However, with regard to the radical language shift in the countries of the former Soviet Union, 'bilingualism' – with pejorative connotations – has emerged as a code word for 'Russification' (e.g. 'forked tongues' or 'double-dealing') (Pavlenko, 2008: 306; Taranenko, 2007) and devaluing the presence of Russian in the concept of bilingualism.

The changed position of Russian in education does not leave a vacuum because the language shift introduces new languages into the school curriculum and inevitably raises the status of English as a global lingua franca. These linguistic practices adopted within the EU institutions are often criticised as an instrument for the imposition of English as dominant language, while the official bilingual status of the Council of Europe gives significant preference to French and English. With some exceptions, the Council of Europe can also be considered as a largely English-speaking environment. Thus, English becomes closely associated with European-isation, as a language that allows for the opening of the countries to the West, to the European Union and to the world. This is an aspect of the language policy implementation that is the other side of the titular/Russian divide, reinforced by a significant change in the school curriculum. One example is the action of the Georgian government to change to an English curriculum. In 2011, Georgia flew in 1,000 native English speakers in a programme similar to Teach for America, with the hope that every school in Georgia would have at least one native English teacher. In this case, this programme to increase the use of English in schools is closely linked to programmes reinforcing the official language in the Georgian Language for Future Success programme. The mainstreaming of English as associated with Europeanisation is a direct side effect of some of the EU-funded programmes in the region, such as Tempus and Erasmus+ Capacity building, which support the introduction of European languages in the curriculum (mostly English) and which, as a rule, have English as the language of the established partnership of EU-based institutions and institutions from the region.

The implications of these policy actions and of the radical language shift clearly show the central role of language policy in processes of identity formation. The change of language repertoires provides the everyday outcome of identity transformation and is an expression of a repertoire of multiple identities. There are different configurations and outcomes for different post-Soviet states which reflect different pre- and post-Soviet language situations. However, the Soviet language and education policies cannot be reduced to 'linguistic Russification'. This has led to the emergence of a group of 'Russian speakers' in the countries of the EU neighbourhood. They are very difficult to categorise and describe, being viewed as 'Russian diaspora' (Kolstø, 1995), 'language minority', 'immigrants', 'non-citizens', 'aliens' and 'occupiers' (more in Laitin, 1998; Pavlenko, 2008).

Whatever the argument for the adoption of some of these names, there is one thing that most researchers agree on. It is inappropriate to call them 'Russians' because of the multi-ethnic nature of this large group. To what extent there are issues of protection of their minority rights, is not clear if we interpret the language policy of these countries as a specific case of language revitalisation of languages still perceived as under threat. The language policy thus represents an attitude towards Russian culture, the Russian demographic presence and the Russian language as the main threat to the cultural survival of the new independent countries. Within this context, the EU and all stakeholders in the process of Europeanisation lessen their normative pressure and try to avoid making mistakes, such as the anecdotal gaffe made by Gerard Stoudmann, Director of the Office of Democratic Institutions and Human Rights of OSCE, when he suggested that Latvia adopt Russian as a second official language, only to hastily withdraw his statement. The better approach is engaging in more listening and pretending to better understand the specificity of the present as a reality of past constructions and tensions.

Conclusion

After the fall of the Berlin Wall and the Eastern enlargement of the EU, the call for a 'return to Europe' has occupied the enlargement rhetoric and has also been embedded in the EU Eastern neighbourhood policy. This metaphor is understood both as a means of imagining the political outcome of a process of 'catching up with Europe' and as a means of understanding the Europeanisation process as a past and present narrative. As pointed out by Batt (2013: 15), this is the slogan that 'best encapsulated popular understanding of the meaning of the revolutions of 1989–91 in Central and Eastern Europe'. Therefore, for Central and East Europeans, 'the contradictions between "national self-determination" and joining the EU and NATO are much less obvious' than the contradictions of Europeanisation concerning the Eastern Neighbourhood. Batt (2013: 16) argues that the notion of 'returning to Europe' usually captures an essential fact of life in the Central and Eastern European region: 'the inseparability of the internal and external dimensions of politics' that is so vividly felt in the case of the Eastern Neighbourhood. It has an inevitable impact on all aspects of social life and policies, including an intensive influence on the language policies and management of the radical language shift in the newly independent countries of the post-Soviet area.

Neumann (1998: 406) argues that another essential feature of the accession rhetoric of the EU Eastern enlargement process is the constant and steady stretching of the borders between Europe and Asia by claiming that each of the joining countries is European. Very often this claim is linked with the statement that the country neighbouring with it to the East is not European or not European enough. Thus, the dichotomy between Europe/Asia and Europe/East becomes the main instrument for the self-determination of the acceding countries. Neumann (1998: 406) argues that this is the case with the discourse on the EU Eastern enlargement, whose main feature was the self/other relations in countries such as the Czech Republic, Slovenia, Slovakia, Poland and Croatia.

The enlargement discourse can thus be read as an identity discourse (Huelsse, 2006: 399). The Europeanisation process, through its various facets, introduces an internal mode of differentiation which finds contradictory manifestations and obscures straightforward solutions of issues read as identity discourses. This constitutes a powerful framework that embeds the manifestation of otherness in the very core of the Europeanisation process. However, linguistic practices and the realities of the present have the potential for a slow redefinition of identity on a territorial basis and under the pressure of the West–East divide there is a gradual reduction in referring to first and preferred language use as the basis for defining identity.

Security and democratisation: the case of the South Caucasus[1]

Since the fall of the Berlin Wall, the European Union has deepened and widened from an exclusively Western European economic bloc to an enlarged supranational entity encompassing nearly all of the continent's states, save for the non-Baltic former Soviet republics and parts of the Balkans. Created at the height of the Cold War to undergird stability by adding an economic dimension to Franco-German reconciliation (Gillingham, 1991), it subsequently redefined its purpose of ensuring stability in a 'reunited' Europe through the export of the very norms and values which successfully supported the 'European project' in its initial stages. The idea that democracy and the rule of law had been central to banishing conflict and insecurity from the West emerged as a major anchor of policy in the 1990s. Security and stability through 'Europeanisation' was central to this approach, expanding an area marked by 'a-security' to include an ever-growing number of states (Olsen, 2000; Wæver, 1998), with the expanding EU adopting a central role in promoting the rule of law and fundamental rights.

The European Community had already helped entrench democracy in post-authoritarian Greece, Portugal and Spain in the 1970s, but following the end of the Cold War, several expansion 'waves' saw the Union's outer boundaries shift eastwards, leading to the largely successful incorporation and socialisation of new members from Estonia to Bulgaria (Hoen, 2013). In terms of both democratisation and the maintenance of security, the expansion into Central and Eastern Europe (CEE) did appear to be a considerable achievement. Democracy now seems well-established throughout the region – although minority rights and corruption remain significant issues in some of them – and any fears regarding the stability of the new EU member states have not come to pass. CEE states have become part of a 'security community', a 'transnational region comprised of sovereign states whose people maintain dependable expectations of peaceful change' (Adler and Barnett, 1998: 30).

The EU's idea of securing the 'new Europe' through democratisation was at least partly informed by a broader revival in Democratic Peace Theory

(DPT) following the end of the Cold War, both in the academic and the policy-making realm. The claim that 'democracies don't make war on each other' had gained academic traction in a series of largely empirical studies and theoretical works throughout the 1970s and 1980s (Brown et al., 1999). With liberalism apparently in the ascendant, policy makers in Washington and Brussels also concluded that a more democratic world would be a more peaceful one (Carothers, 1997, 1999a, 1999b; Diamond, 1992; Kopstein, 2006; Magen and Morlino, 2009; Talbott, 1996). This logic – which lay at the heart of the European project itself – has now been extended beyond Central and Eastern Europe, towards the EU's Eastern neighbourhood: the states of the former Soviet Union.

Apart from the Baltic states, these former Soviet republics had never featured as potential members and the EU's previous peaceful expansion into CEE had always been contingent upon – depending on how one viewed it – either Russia's *weakness* or its *acquiescence* (Flenley, 2008; Trenin, 2005). Two problems now arose with the extension of Europe's 'democratising logic' to former Soviet lands. First, could the success of security and stability through democratisation be replicated in Europe's new Eastern neighbourhood in the absence of a firm membership promise? Academic research and policy analysis soon raised serious questions about the effectiveness of such an approach in the absence of this major incentive (Kelley, 2006; Magen, 2005; Popescu and Wilson, 2009; Schimmelfennig and Scholtz, 2008). These reservations were only partially allayed by the upgrading of the European Neighbourhood Policy (ENP) into the Eastern Partnership (EaP) in 2009, which was introduced as 'a step change in relations with these partners ... responding to the need for a clearer signal of EU commitment following the conflict in Georgia and its broader repercussions' and promised a greater role for the EU in a region of strategic importance (European Commission, 2008).

Second, would Moscow's acquiescence continue as, under President Putin, Russia began an economic recovery that underpinned a more active regional policy? The CEE countries' quest for membership in the Euro-Atlantic Community was partly motivated by quite recent memories of Soviet domination (Fierke and Wiener, 1999; Schimmelfennig, 1998). With the EaP now potentially encroaching on its 'sphere of "privileged interests"' – to quote former President Medvedev (Kremlin.ru, 2008) – Russia's resistance began to manifest itself (Costea, 2010; Flenley, 2008; Leonard and Popescu, 2007). An alternative vision of Eurasian integration – the Eurasian Union – was put forward by Putin (2011) and began to receive institutional expression in the development of the Customs Union into the Eurasian Economic Union. Putin spoke of a 'supranational' Eurasian Union based on the 'common strategic interests' of post-Soviet states and 'integration on new values, political and economic basis' though, in his words, there was 'no question of recreating the USSR'. The project was presented as a kind of prototype EU but without political conditionality. The idea received a mixed response from Russia's regional partners, with Moscow applying pressure on countries in the shared neighbourhood to forgo closer integration with the EU in favour of its project (Tapiola-Shumylo, 2012; Trenin, 2011), leading to dramatic U-turns by Armenia and (before President Yanukovich's departure), Ukraine, during autumn 2013.

The assumed link between democracy and security within EU policymaking towards its Eastern neighbourhood is the subject of this chapter, which focuses more specifically on the idea that democratisation may lead to peaceful relations between the states of the South Caucasus, which, through the ENP and the EaP, have long been involved in these policies, with only limited progress (Alieva, 2006; Blank, 1995; Cornell and Starr, 2006; Dekanozishvili, 2004; Delcour and Duhot, 2011; Dominese, 2005). The three South Caucasus states – Georgia, Armenia, Azerbaijan – have pursued quite different policies vis-à-vis Europe and Russia since the mid-2000s, with 'Euro-Atlantic integration' remaining a vital centrepiece of Georgia's security outlook (Kakachia and Cecire, 2013), Armenia locked in a strategic alliance with Russia even while pursuing relations with the EU (Shirinyan and Ralchev, 2013). In terms of Europeanisation/democratisation, they have all been included in the EaP despite their divergent democratic credentials, with Georgia consistently ahead of both its neighbours according to a wide range of metrics. In this chapter we pose three central questions. First, in light of the existing conceptual literature on the DPT, are the above-mentioned expectations of pacification through democracy justified? Second, how far is democratisation a realistic prospect, and to what extent do the assumptions made in the DPT concept stand up to the empirical realities in the region? Third, how does the assertive presence of Russia, and its alternative 'integration' project, affect prospects for democratisation, Europeanisation and greater security?

The following section thus centres on the system level and on the assumed link between democracy and security, providing a brief overview of those elements within the democratic peace literature that are relevant to our argument. The democratic peace literature has evolved considerably since its emergence in the 1980s and addresses issues that go far beyond the simple correlations it initially posited. More specifically, we question whether expectations of a democratic peace emerging in the South Caucasus through external efforts are justified in light of the considerable literature on the causal links between democracy and peace and on the validity of the theory in 'partially democratised' states and regions. Subsequent sections then critically assesses the long-term prospects for EU democracy promotion in this part of the former Soviet Union in view of the empirical realities at the regional and domestic levels. An additional section then examines the prospects for the EU's democracy promoting policies in light of Russia's assertive attempts to impose an alternative to Europe's normative order.

The democratic peace and its complications

Michael Doyle is widely credited with the reintroduction of the 'Kantian' notion of the democratic peace into the realm of contemporary international relations. In a series of essays (Doyle, 1983a, 1983b, 1986) he laid down the essential principles of DPT, reformulated from Kant's treatise (1795), arguably giving them the most elegant and comprehensive formulation to date. His starting point was the ample empirical historical evidence as to the absence of wars between 'liberal' states and, conversely, the relative frequency of wars within liberal/non-liberal dyads. In his words, '[e]ven though liberal states have become involved in numerous wars with nonliberal states, constitutionally secure liberal states have yet to engage in war with one another' (Doyle, 1983a: 213).

Doyle's theorising took place in a period of intense empirical inquiry into the nature of the democratic peace and, as such, did not represent the first contemporary formulation of its ideas. It occurred at a time when the dyadic correlation – between the democratic nature of two states, and their peaceful relations – had been more or less firmly established, and causal theorising on the phenomenon was about to begin. Today, while debate on the validity of its monadic counterpart continues, and those operating from the realist paradigm (Gartzke and Weisinger, 2013; Layne, 1994; Mearsheimer, 1990; Spiro, 1994) remain sceptical, the dyadic version of the DPT has become, in Jack S. Levy's (1988: 88) oft-quoted phrase 'as close as anything we have to an empirical law in international relations'. There is a firm correlation between the democratic regime type of two states and peaceful interaction between them, as confirmed by a substantial body of political science research.

The causal explanations for this correlation fall broadly into two categories: structural/institutional and normative. Those focusing on the former explanation argued that democratic states tend to interact peacefully because of the complex rationality inherent in elite coalition-building, institutional checks and balances, and public accountability in democratic states. Self-interested, rational elites in democratic states were no different from their autocratic counterparts in their objective of maintaining power; they were, however, restrained through the above mentioned factors in their ability to go to war. Normative explanations, by contrast, saw democratic elites as espousing norms and values that were qualitatively different from their autocratic counterparts and it was the transfer of the norms of compromise and negotiation underlying their pacific domestic political culture on to the inter-state level that produced peace. By the late 1990s, there was a general tendency towards normative versions of the *causal* mechanism behind the democratic peace (Chan, 1997; Weart, 1998: 43–45). While institutions and structures also played an important role, much of the literature either preferred normative explanations or collapsed the structural/normative distinction into its normative element, seeing institutions/structures as fundamentally constituted by (and therefore epiphenomenal to) norms.

The next question that emerged from this research programme was more directly policy-relevant: if democracy engenders peace, would *democratisation* result in a more peaceful world? Two groups of scholars confronted each other around this question. Both groups held that the dyadic form of DPT had been sufficiently confirmed by the evidence. They diverged, however, in their acceptance of a correlational or causal link between *democratisation* and *pacification*. This implied a disaggregation of the DPT into immature and mature (or, for Zakaria (1997, 2007), *illiberal* and *liberal*) democracies. While agreeing that mature liberal democracies were more peaceful towards each other, even if they were overall just as likely to go to war as other states, they differed in their predictions for immature, illiberal, democratising states. Di Palma (1990), Gleditsch (1995) and Diamond (1992) posited that even partial democratisation would tend to produce pacifying effects. The opposing argument – that the resulting partial, immature democracies would be more war-like than either mature democracies or established autocracies – was primarily associated with a long-running research programme carried out by Mansfield and Snyder (2002; 1995a, 1995b; see also Mansfield and Snyder, 2005; Snyder, 2000).[2]

The main insights emerging from these debates suggest caution is in order when linking 'democracy' and 'security' in 'immature' democracies. Snyder (2000: 46–83), for instance, showed how, in combination with low economic development and a malformed media landscape, the weak state institutions in such immature democracies cause elites to use varying forms of conflict-generating nationalist myth-making as a mobilising mechanism in lieu of democratic legitimacy through exclusionary politics, inaccurate strategic assumptions and pandering to veto groups in nationalist bidding wars. Mansfield and Snyder (2005) further argued that it is, therefore, highly dangerous to promote democracy in societies where a wider sequence of conditions allowing for rapid, efficient democratisation (solid institutions, economic development) are not yet in place: *partial* democratisation would increase rather than decrease conflict and instability, and it was therefore important to minimise the period a state spent in this zone between autocracy and mature democracy. Allowing an autocratic government to develop the state institutions and economic infrastructure necessary to allow for rapid democratisation – as arguably happened in East Asia – might thus end up being preferable to prematurely pressing for democratisation.

The assertion proved controversial and resulted in a vigorous debate between 'sequencers' like Mansfield and Snyder (see also Zakaria, 2007 and Chua, 2004) and 'gradualists' represented by other, less sceptical, adherents to the 'democratisation' model and its pacific effects. But even the latter theoretical group – who looked more favourably on the link between democracy and pacification – provided important caveats regarding the success of any move towards democracy. Carothers (2007), for instance, rejected Mansfield's and Snyder's prescriptions, arguing that a *non-sequential, gradualist* approach could, in fact, lead to democratisation without the pitfalls of heightened conflict. Far from complicating the rule of law and state-building, the public accountability associated with democracy enabled it, especially when assisted by established, mature democracies (Carothers 2007: 20–23). Rather than seeing successful democratisation as the result of a sequence of necessary preceding conditions, one had to view successful democratisation as a gradual process inhibited or enabled by a range of simultaneously operating 'facilitators or non-facilitators' including the level of economic development, the concentration of sources of national wealth, identity-based divisions, historical experience with political pluralism and the democratic and non-democratic nature of a state's immediate neighbourhood (Carothers 2007: 24). This, of course, implied that democratisation depended on the presence or the absence of these 'facilitating conditions' – something relevant to the EU's efforts in the South Caucasus.

The democratic peace and the Caucasus

What are the implications of the above for the questions posed in the introductory section? To start with, at least at the inter-state level covered by the democratic peace, the general approach equating democracy and security in EU policy must be qualified. The academic literature confirms, at most, a correlation – although admittedly a robust one: the democratic nature of two states *lowers the probability* of their engaging in a war. Whether democratic states are in themselves more peaceable – regardless of their adversaries' regime type – remains the subject of vigorous debate – according to Mansfield and Snyder partial democratisation increases rather than decreases the risks of conflict.

In this reading, for the democratic peace to work, all states in the region would have to become democracies simultaneously or at the very least in close chronological succession. The alternative would be the creation of mixed democratic/autocratic dyads where the presence of authoritarian states would obviate the full benefits of the democratic peace. A long delay in democratisation would make most states in the region *partial or immature democracies*, which could *heighten* rather than *reduce* the risk of armed conflict. From the point of view of the sequencer/gradualist division discussed, the presence or absence of the right sequence of prerequisites, or the appropriate facilitating conditions, becomes of the essence in accelerating democratisation (and minimising the insecurity that comes with partial democracy).

As mentioned, democratisation in the South Caucasus has been far more uneven and slower than what had been seen in CEE. Since the 2003 Rose

Revolution, Georgia has very much become the front-runner in terms of democratic governance (Freedom House, 2013c) – something reinforced by the first constitutional handover of power in the region to a successor government not approved by the incumbent (Broers, 2005; Siroky and Aprasidze, 2011; Wertsch, 2005). While also 'partly free' according to Freedom House (2013a), Armenia has consistently lagged in its democracy scores, encumbered by a succession of flawed elections (with the 2008 massacre of anti-government protesters as an infamous low point). Azerbaijan, meanwhile, has over the more than twenty years of rule by the Aliyev dynasty, descended into Freedom House's (2013b) 'not free' category. The nature of regimes in the separatist territories of Abkhazia, South Ossetia and Nagorno-Karabakh Republic (NKR) is similarly diverse (Caspersen, 2008; Kolstø and Blakkisrud, 2008). The prospects of the states of the South Caucasus turning into democracies in a coordinated and rapid way appear distant.

The most democratic state in the region, Georgia, was the only one involved in an armed conflict (with Russia in 2008). Georgia's status at the time, as a 'partly free' democratising state (Freedom House, 2009a) and Russia's as a 'not free' autocracy (Freedom House, 2009b), arguably makes the 2008 conflict conform with a 'mixed' democratic/autocratic dyad and the normative causal explanations within the DPT literature cited. The Georgian government at that time, led by Mikheil Saakashvili, certainly identified with the community of democratic states, clearly articulating a Euro-Atlantic orientation and at least a *rhetorical* adherence to liberal-democratic reform. While Georgia was, at most, a partial democracy in practice, this stated adherence to democratic and free market norms became an integral part of its foreign policy outlook. Saakashvili often linked Russia's purportedly aggressive stance to the nature of its autocratic regime (Dzieciolowski, 2008; Socor, 2005). A host of other factors were at play but it is certainly fair to ask whether, in the absence of aspirations to membership of the 'civilised community of democratic states', Georgia would have courted Western support and, consequently, incurred Russia's wrath in the run-up to 2008. The role of its adherence to democratic norms in generating conflict within the intersubjectively constituted democratic/autocratic Georgia/Russia dyad deserves scrutiny, as would the perception by Russia of democratisation and Europeanisation as a geopolitical tool and a threat to the established order of 'sovereign democracies' (Wilson, 2010).

That Georgia was only a partial, immature democracy brings our discussion to the literature's cautionary claims about the more *conflictual* nature of such regime types, and the consequent necessity for rapid democratisation. For Mansfield and Snyder, the democratic peace only applies to mature democracies. From their point of view, this would make a relatively rapid transition towards full democracy – as seen in Central and Eastern Europe – especially important. Depending on one's position within the sequencer/

gradualist debate, the rapidity of democratisation would then depend on either a pre-set sequence of factors or a number of simultaneous 'facilitating conditions' – for sequencers, a sufficiently developed institutional framework and a suitably modernised economy, for gradualists, democratisation would be helped by economic development, a wide distribution of national wealth, the absence of identity-based divisions, a historical experience with political pluralism, and the democratic nature of a state's immediate neighbourhood. In the absence of the correct 'sequence', or these facilitating factors, the region would risk remaining within the potentially conflictual limbo that comes with the partial democratisation of its states.

The recent historical experience of the region is important in understanding the questions posed in this chapter. All of the frozen conflicts in the region stemmed from Gorbachev's liberalising reforms in the dying years of the Soviet Union, which unleashed political forces specific to each new state. The movements that challenged Soviet totalitarian power – the Karabakh Committee in Armenia, the Popular Front in Azerbaijan, the Round Table in Georgia – combined their demands for democratisation with conflict-generating nationalisms as a mobilising factor (MacFarlane, 1997; Snyder, 2000: 220–235). In Armenia, the Karabakh Committee (which after its transformation into the Armenian Pan-National Movement, ruled the country until Levon Ter-Petrosyan's ousting in 1998) linked *glasnost* and *perestroika* directly to a demand for Karabakh's attachment to Armenia, based on the 'democratic' will of its majority Armenian population (Libaridian, 1999, 2004; Malkasian, 1996). Conversely, Azerbaijan's Popular Front combined its goal of an independent, democratic Azerbaijan with that of maintaining control over the territory (Cornell, 2010; Musabekov, 2005). Gamsakhurdia's rhetoric was similarly a curious combination of anti-Soviet anti-totalitarianism, aggressive Georgian ethno-nationalism and Orthodox mysticism which, for many observers, was directly responsible for South Ossetia's initial decision to secede (Jones, 1994; Nodia, 1996). Abkhazia's separation, ironically, occurred following military action initiated by Gorbachev's 'reformist' foreign minister Eduard Shevardnadze.

While the first years of independence were marked by internal turmoil in both Azerbaijan and Georgia – leading to the kind of ethnic outbidding and short-termist political entrepreneurship identified by Mansfield and Snyder (2005) – by 1994 all three states had to some extent stabilised into, at best, partial democracies. Whether ruled by members of the former Soviet elite (as Georgia and Azerbaijan were), or former anti-Soviet dissidents (as Armenia was), they all displayed flawed electoral politics, highly circumscribed civil societies, and a malfunctioning rule of law. Until the 2008 Russian–Georgian war, all conflicts in the region remained frozen (bar some ceasefire violations) without being finally resolved. Was this *because of* or *despite* the limited democratic progress in the societies involved? Several episodes in the negotiations surrounding the frozen conflicts provide an illustration as to how the (now firmly entrenched) ethno-nationalism could actually be militating for, instead of against, conflict under conditions of partial democracy – in the case of Nagorno-Karabakh, the removal from power of Levon Ter-Petrosyan in 1998 and Ilham Aliyev's reported about-turn following the Key West talks on the same subject in 2001.

In both cases, the prevailing nationalist consensus in their respective societies scuppered crucial progress in resolving inter-state conflict. The 1998 palace coup that toppled Ter-Petrosyan following his acceptance of a stage-by-stage solution of the Karabakh conflict, was supported by a broad cross-section of Armenian society which rejected his willingness to postpone any final solution to the status until *after* a withdrawal of Armenian troops from the regions surrounding NKR (Astourian, 2000; Papazian, 2006). Ter-Petrosyan's democratic legitimacy had been circumscribed by his dubious re-election in 1996, and that had made him more dependent on nationalist groups – including the 'Yerkrapah' union of Karabakh war veterans – for his political survival. Going against these elite groups and against the nationalist ideology that had put Karabakh at the centre of the Armenian political narrative since independence, ultimately proved his downfall. When, in April 2001, Azerbaijan's then president Ilham Aliyev reportedly came to an agreement with his Armenian counterpart allowing for a territorial swap and 'non-hierarchical' relations with Nagorno-Karabakh, he demurred on his return to Baku following admonitions that he would be unable to 'sell it' to his population.[3]

Both countries' regimes had compensated for a lack of democratic legitimacy through the use of nationalism as a 'substitute' mobilising factor. As a result, any required concessions made the existing regimes vulnerable to 'ethnic outbidding' by their opposition. And even today, leaders on both sides remain hostage to the mobilising nationalisms that had emerged on both countries' road towards independence, reinforcing Mansfield and Snyder's arguments on the pitfalls of partial democratisation. In both Armenia and Azerbaijan, Karabakh is now a matter of stubborn consensus. An overwhelming majority of Armenians see the matter already resolved and oppose *any* concessions on the matter, including a return of the territories surrounding Karabakh (Cooper and Morris, 2013; Toal, 2013). The restoration of sovereignty over the territory – by force, if necessary – is part of a similar consensus within Azeri society (Novikova, 2012: 558–563; Tokluoglu, 2011). Conflict and insecurity thus remain inextricably intertwined with the nationalist legacies of the imperfect democratic transition of earlier years.

If the partial democratisation of the Caucasus states hinders the emergence of a fully functioning democratic peace, what are the prospects of their transformation into mature democracies? Judging from both the sequencer and gradualist perspectives, conditions do not appear propitious. In terms of state-building, all three countries' institutions remain flawed and inefficient. Their economic indicators remain far below those of the CEE countries (World Bank, 2014). Especially in Armenia and Azerbaijan, national wealth remains concentrated in the hands of government connected clans and individuals. Any 'modernisation' has focused purely on pursuing economic gains for elites rather than promoting political and social renewal through the democratic process. Despite its economic growth, Azerbaijan remains a hydrocarbons based *rentier* economy which, as the literature amply demonstrates, is not conducive to democratisation (Franke et al., 2009; Guliyev, 2013; O'Lear, 2007). Armenia's economy, affected by an Azerbaijani– Turkish blockade, remains dominated by a small number of state-linked oligarchic cartels that make a mockery of the 'rule of law' (Hrayr Maroukhian Foundation, 2013; Petrosyan, 2013). While Georgia has opened up its economy and reformed its state institutions to a considerable degree, in rough GDP per capita terms it still falls far behind even the poorest members of the EU. Moreover, identity based divisions remain part and parcel of Caucasus politics. There is little historical experience with political pluralism and, with even Turkey in Freedom House's (2014) 'partly free' category, there are no states in the immediate neighbourhood that would unambiguously qualify as 'mature' democracies. Starting conditions for any democratisation project would appear to be much less favourable than what confronted the European Union during the initial eastward enlargement of its 'democratic zone of peace'.

The application of the democratic peace literature to the Caucasus suggests that the prospects of this region's 'pacification through democratisation' appear distant. Compared to Central and Eastern Europe, the Caucasus is far less fertile ground for a repeat of the rapid and near-synchronised move towards 'mature democracy' experienced by Europe's newest members, prompting serious doubt about the emergence of a democratic peace. The phenomenon is only robustly confirmed among dyads of mature democracies. The prolonged existence of mixed democratic/autocratic dyads, or of only partially democratised states, could postpone the beneficial effects of democracy on security – a central assumption in Europe's policies towards its neighbourhood. There is, however, one final – and major – complicating factor which may very well end up thwarting Europe's democracy promotion, one inherent to the policies employed to that effect rather than the imperfect workings of the democratic peace; more specifically, the inability of those policies to function in an environment marked by geopolitical competition.

Enter the Kremlin

For much of the post-Cold War period, the European Union has combined eastward expansion with peaceful inter-state cooperation and a deepening of its internal order. At the same time, beyond its Eastern boundary, a patchy political and security map has emerged with organisations with varying geographical and functional remits interacting with a pluralist, competitive regional security dynamic. With Eastern states locked out of EU/NATO membership, they have become subject to competing processes of regional integration and institutionalisation and divergent principles of order, with many conflicts frozen rather than resolved and others rekindled. This comes at a time when the EU faces material and ideational constraints as an international actor stemming partly from the continuing internal problems of the model of European integration – the financial crisis, a broader crisis of legitimacy, a lack of institutional coherence and of political/administrative capacity. The strengthening of the remit of the High Representative and creation of the European External Action Service provided by the Lisbon Treaty might bring improvements but it is still proving difficult to coordinate the powerful instruments of the European Commission regarding trade, aid and enlargement with the EU's foreign policy tools in support of effective external action.

This is all the more important in view of the challenges confronting the EU's 'grand project', at two levels. Internally, many of the states in the neighbourhood are less prepared to adopt EU democratic standards than their counterparts in CEE and the unwillingness of the Union to provide membership as an incentive increases the probability that this will remain so in the foreseeable future. Externally, the EU now has a geopolitical and, arguably, a normative competitor in Putin's Russia. Over the longer term, these challenges may endanger the survival of European democracy promotion which leads one to question whether it can outlive the internal (institutional and cultural) and external (security-related) realities in the former Soviet space. The EU still commands considerable 'soft power' in many of the former Soviet states but whether this can last in the face of Russia's willingness to employ the 'harder' variant of great power capacity remains an open question.

Russia's governing elite has pointedly dismissed this Western commitment to democracy as cloaking the EU's status as a 'value-empire' (Haukkala, 2008), describing its democratisation efforts with a pejorative neologism – 'demokratizatorstvo' (Averre, 2009: 1696). Foreign Minister Sergei Lavrov has argued that 'attempts to bring the OSCE [Organization for Security and Cooperation in Europe] space under the interests of one group of countries through aggressive imposition of a neoliberal interpretation of human rights are ruinous for European civilisation' (OSCE, 2013). The implication is that the EU is what Diez has characterised as a 'normative hegemon' (see Diez, 2013: 199–200 for definition). Put simply, the moulding of former Soviet states in the image of Western liberal democracies is part of a longer-term project uniting geopolitics and ideology: the securing of Europe's Eastern neighbourhood through democracy promotion would turn these states away from Moscow at the expense of Russia's own security interests (Dias, 2013b). Based on historical precedent in CEE, integration or association with Europe, accession to the EU and membership of NATO – all processes associated in some form with the establishment of a democratic community of states – fall within the same logic.

A key dilemma presents itself: how to maintain a focus on the promotion of human rights, the rule of law and democracy as key elements of building secure and stable states while dealing with weak and/or authoritarian regimes for trade and political ends in an environment which has now turned geopolitically competitive. As above, the EU's democracy promoting policies have been based on the socialisation of states – primarily their elites – through conditionality. These policies have, more often than not, been approached from a rational actor perspective with conditionality seeking to incentivise 'rational' elites towards the kind of institutional, legal and social modernisation that would lead to the adoption of 'Europeanised' – and, hence, *democratised* – modes of governance through strategic calculation, or what March and Olsen's (1989) call a 'logic of consequences' (e.g. Sasse, 2008; Schimmelfennig, 2000, 2005; Schimmelfennig et al., 2006).

But this 'rational actor' approach can only capture part of the processes behind 'Europeanisation' – what is ultimately necessary for democracies to consolidate is 'complex socialisation', the internalisation of the norms and values of democracy. A 'logic of consequences' must ultimately be superseded by a 'logic of appropriateness', with elites and societies adopting the preferences and identities associated with democracy as their own rather than merely complying with them out of a rational concern with higher-level strategic interests. The emphasis on *governance* – the EU's regulatory or technocratic approach – at the expense of *government* – domestic processes leading to locally derived political solutions – stems from the assumption that security problems can be resolved beyond the realm of the political. However, starting from ethics and norms and seeking to derive political frameworks on their basis, rather than from the clash of interests in society (Chandler, 2006), may be a flawed strategy in the case of the South Caucasus. As Mikhelidze (2013) points out, there is a potential conflict between state-building – based on the core, legitimacy enhancing function of securing territory and improving living standards – and the adoption of the norms of 'civilised state behaviour' – human rights and good governance – which would engender a self-sustaining 'positive peace' for the region.

The extensive literature on the *causal* mechanisms behind the democratic peace approaches them from rationalist or constructivist perspectives. Institutional explanations point to 'checks and balances' and posit a world populated by rational, utility-maximising elites; normative explanations use the conceptual language of norms, values and identities associated with the constructivist paradigm. Crucially, the democratic peace literature does seem to have an overall preference for normative explanations: peace emerges not just from institutional restraints and rational choices, but from the gradual emergence of the preferences and identities that sustain expectations of peaceful behaviour at the international level. This also chimes with the dyadic nature of the democratic peace – contrasting democratic in-groups with autocratic out-groups – and Mansfield and Snyder's assertion that the democratic peace is based on the emergence of 'mature' democracies, with well-established institutions and well-internalised democratic political cultures.

This necessity for 'complex socialisation' (Flockhart, 2005) and 'internalisation' (Checkel, 2005) through 'argumentative persuasion' (Checkel and Moravcsik, 2001; Risse, 1999) makes democracy promotion a long-term affair. Considering the relatively low base from which it has to be applied in the Caucasus, adequate conditionalities must be maintained to incentivise elites and engage civil society in 'deep democracy' towards engagement with Europe and its democratic norms for a long enough period for them to securely internalise these norms as their own (see Casier et al., 2013). The problem is that, as a *structure* of incentives (and disincentives), these conditionalities can also be relatively easily manipulated and distorted by an outside actor; the 'adoption costs' of democratic European norms can be increased at short notice, with (material) hard power incentives intruding upon the longer-term processes of socialisation/internalisation that would be necessary for democracies to mature.

Contrary to previous efforts at democracy promotion in CEE, the EU is now faced with a geopolitical competitor able and willing to use its resources to tilt the conditionalities playing field in its favour. Through coercion – in the form of a change in the material incentives structure surrounding local elites – Moscow may thwart continued engagement with (and socialisation into) the EU, diverting attention from the long-term processes needed for 'complex socialisation' to take effect. There may already be indications that this is happening in at least two of the countries where socialisation was already shallow to begin with. Following its reorientation towards the Customs Union (De Waal, 2013; Harutunyan, 2014), Armenia appointed a prime minister who is seen by one analyst as 'one of the more visible examples of the incestuous mix of business and politics in Armenia, with little real understanding or appreciation of reform or democratisation' (Giragosian, 2014). Azerbaijan has grown increasingly impervious to EU criticism of its deficient democratic and human rights credentials, an insensitivity exemplified by its arrest of two prominent figures involved in European sponsored civil society projects (Geybullayeva, 2014). Some observers have even speculated that Georgia could revise its Euro-Atlantic orientation in response to sustained Russian pressure in the absence of clearer incentives on the EU's (and NATO's) part (De Waal, 2014). With the greatest incentive of all – the prospect of membership for states participating in the EaP off the table, it would be more difficult for the EU to thwart attempts by Russia to shape the normative environment, neutralising Europe's conditionalities over the short term by adding its disincentives to the equation.

Conclusion

In a recent paper, Mikhelidze (2013: 13) concludes as follows: 'The interplay between normative goals in democracy development and security concerns related to conflict resolution has complicated the task of the EU's foreign policy making in the South Caucasus. The EU has opted for stabilisation rather than substantial democratic transformation in the region.'[4] States in the region are security consumers and this will not change in the near future. The EU's (and NATO's) attractiveness is likely to diminish if they are seen to have limited capacity and limited political will to act as security providers in the event of Russian military action. Low levels of socioeconomic development, limited social capital stemming in part from ethnic divisions and unresolved identity issues, a weak or at least marginalised civil society and a legacy of authoritarian political culture and informal economic ties complete the picture. Elites adopting liberal European political norms risk a loss of power and autonomy (something that Moscow is only too ready to point out) and are only ready to accept this loss in the event that external gains are forthcoming (Schimmelfennig, 2007: 129–131).

The EU does have a significant advantage in the attractiveness of its normative framework, based on a standard of liberal democratic modernity that still commands considerable 'soft power'. By contrast, Russia's Eurasian project consists of a less attractive normative framework of managed or 'sovereign' democracy and conservatism (in the recent period shading into nationalism) which has limited (if not entirely absent) long-term appeal to non-Russians (Popescu and Wilson, 2009: 27–38; Tafuro, 2014). This comparative advantage may in itself be insufficient if the EU is unable to socialise local elites into accepting its norms. In fact, the broader question arises in how far the limited democratisation that *has* actually taken place can directly be traced to Brussels' policies or in fact whether limited 'Europeanisation' – beyond the adoption of technical-legal standards – would not have occurred without the various post-Cold War EU programmes. As elsewhere in the former Soviet Union, thorough reassessments will have to be made if democracy promotion and its associated advantages are to have any relevance to regional security.

Notes

1   This chapter is based on initial research for a work package entitled 'Reconceptualising Democracy and Security in the Caucasus' on a Seventh Framework

Programme project 'Exploring the Security-Democracy Nexus in the Caucasus' [FP7 THEME SSH.2013.4.1–1 'Security and democracy in the neighbourhood: the case of the Caucasus'].

2 A similar, more qualitatively informed, discussion emerged from Zakaria's (1997, 2007) concept of 'illiberal democracy'.

3 While such reports should be approached with the necessary scepticism, they are reinforced by Aliyev's reputation as a pragmatist and statements by former high-ranking officials published in, among others, government-connected media (See Azerbaijan in the World, 2008: 2; see also BBC Monitoring, 2002; De Waal, 2003).

4 For an analysis of EU policy towards Belarus, characterised as 'institutionalized functional co-operation', with implications for its relations with the South Caucasus states, see also Bosse (2012) and Chapter 6 in this volume.

Paul Flenley and Michael Mannin

Conclusion

This volume set out to examine the factors that shape relations between the EU and those states and regions that compose its Eastern neighbourhood. In particular, we explored the context of what we have termed the 'EU-isation' of the neighbourhood to include notions of competing identities and values as well as evident contemporary national and transnational interests.

In Part I we examined each of these notions from a mainly theoretical and generic perspective, illustrating their overall relevance to EU–neighbourhood relations. In each case, Europeanisation, shared values and identities, and the EU-driven institutionalisation of (mutual) interests were analysed as both solutions to, and problems for, the establishment of secure and mutually advantageous EU–neighbourhood relations.

The chapters in Parts II and III examined the different ways in which the nexus of identity, values and interests operates between the EU and the neighbourhood such as to affect the process of EU-isation. We first considered this in the context of different country and area studies. For each of these, Europeanisation and the concept of Europe act as part of their politics and identity. However, they can be variously problematic and have different meanings and uses. We also looked at a number of key sectors and themes which are prominent in the conduct of relations between the EU and its neighbours. We found that in various ways each of these highlight the contradictions to be found in the approaches and assumptions of EU-isation. Tensions in the nexus – between interests and values, for example – emerged in areas such as energy, migration and security.

This conclusion draws together and contextualises some of the assumptions regarding the applicability of a common Europeanisation process or, more specifically, EU-isation to Eastern neighbours. Does EU-isation fit within this nexus when applied to the complexity of the Eastern neighbourhood? What factors lead to what seemed in many of our observations to be an evident 'uncomfortability of fit'? Thus, we explored the values and norms of Europeanisation itself. On the one hand, there is

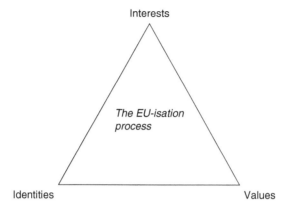

Figure 15.1 The nexus of EU/neighbourhood relations

the notion of *Europeanism* (McCormick, 2010) as a shared collection of historic and cultural values with origins in the intellectual commonality of the Enlightenment. On the other, there are evidently different interpretations of these original values that shape the assumptions surrounding Europeanisation as a unidirectional process. We note the significance of the 'present reality' – that is the EU's contribution to contemporary Europeanisation in the form of EU-isation – for the EU's members and its neighbours. However, the extent to which the EU still provides such a pathway and direction to current notions of Europeanisation is debated in subsequent chapters.

We also introduced the salience of identity and interest as conceptual ingredients that are significant in exploring this Europeanisation conundrum, as applied to the EU's Eastern neighbourhood. Chapter 2 addresses the legitimising role of identity to the normative status of the EU but also challenges the notion of European identity itself. While the notion of European identity is evident in the shape of a tangible EU citizenship and related official policies and symbols of the EU, the reality of national, regional, cultural and historic identities leads to identity choices which are described as multi-layered. Though the EU offers the notion of 'unity in diversity', an EU identity remains challenged by, first, the availability of identity choice and, second, the shifting notion of what a European 'other' is. The Cold War period, and the post-war experience of an initially benign but then a more strident Russia; Turkey, as a candidate member state, but culturally and politically perceived by some member states as an 'other' state; and the boundaries that the migration crisis have recently created are all manifestations of 'shifting otherness' that provide a challenge to the easy acceptance of a dominant 'EU-isation' of the Continent. Chapter 8 indicates this complexity in the Balkan states that are perceived as a unique cultural space, but with contrasting identity politics and attitudes towards the EU (perhaps best illustrated in the cases of Croatia and Serbia).

What seems a clear split in pro/anti EU identities is evident in Ukraine where, in Chapter 5, the authors see evidence of a 'bounded Europeanisation' that is reinforced by the East–West geopolitical identity clash. In both the Balkan and Ukrainian discussion but also in the Moldovan chapter, identification with EU norms and values is more evident among political and business elites or, more particularly, mobile sectors of the population compared with less mobile and non-elite sectors of society. A further difficulty that the notion of an EU identity faces is the inconsistency in treatment of neighbourhood states by the EU in relation to the application of the ENP and EaP. This differentiated approach mentioned in Chapters 2 and 3 and detailed in the chapters on Moldova and Belarus challenges the notion and extent of a viable European *demos* and community.

However, several authors consider the possibility of a more overarching European identity being constructed in response to the receipt of tangible benefits from the EU project. Chapter 3 discusses the extent to which neighbourhood states have responded to the ENP and EaP in terms of such interest-driven perceptions. EU-isation as an external governance approach towards the neighbourhood has been profoundly influenced by both the internal interests of recipients and the external perspectives of not only the EU but also EU member states as well. From an interest-driven perspective, a number of chapters note the differing attitudes towards 'more Europe', with Ukraine and Georgia being contrasted with Belarus and Azerbaijan. It is clear from our country studies especially that differing policy responses to EU conditionalities are dependent on the particular interest agendas of elites. It is also to be noted that the EU's reform expectations more effectively resonate with elite interests when there is a coincidence of a dominant and supportive domestic narrative. Different historical narratives that support the idea of the 'past as present reality' give legitimacy to elite objectives in both East and West Ukraine. As we see in Chapter 8 on the Balkans, historical memory can be manipulated politically to produce a narrative that mobilises popular support.

It is suggested in Chapter 3 that neighbourhood elites also dominate the implementation and application of EU civil society policies, shaping the salience of citizen-to-citizen contact, capacity building and, thus, neighbourhood or societal awareness and interaction with EU norms and values. Relatively limited EU funding towards civil society projects, their implementation by neighbourhood central authorities, and, importantly, the limited visa access for neighbourhood–EU interaction are all factors that are argued to have precluded the effectiveness of EU societal, neighbourhood and civil society programmes, and hence inhibited greater socialisation or 'thick' EU-isation. This theme of 'thin' EU-isation is common to a range of chapters. Elites in Ukraine, Belarus and Russia, for example, are shown to be more instrumental in their approaches to EU-isation, preferring more pragmatic relations with the EU. Avoidance of deeper socialisation or 'thick' EU-isation helps preserve domestic power structures and practices.

This somewhat diverse perspective on the salience of interest as a key factor in the effectiveness of the ENP/EaP is complicated by the inconsistencies that are evident between EU actors and institutions towards EU neighbourhood policies. For example in general terms, the European Parliament stresses the importance of human rights and anti-corruption (i.e. more values-based perspectives) while the Commission focuses on trade and standards. The chapters on energy, trade and migration in particular have shown the contrast between EU-isation in terms of a common EU normative approach to the neighbours and areas where member states assert their individual interests such as trade with Russia and pipelines. In the area of identity there can also be tensions between a common EU approach and the perceptions of Europe and national identity within individual member states. This is most apparent on the questions of Turkish membership of the EU and migration quotas. While in practice both member states and EU institutions can usually combine the promotion of interests in a discourse of values, in some instances there can be glaring contradictions. In the neighbourhood there is regularly a need to cooperate with states whose internal security and democratic status are often incompatible with the normative goals of EU foreign policy. The following quote from Chapter 14 raises an important question regarding this dilemma in relation to the EU's relations with former Soviet states: 'how to maintain a focus on the promotion of human rights, the rule of law and democracy ... while dealing with weak and/or other authoritarian regimes for trade and political ends' in a geo-politically competitive environment (page 206).

The geopolitical environment is inevitably a dominating factor in this volume, both in terms of interest politics and also in terms of norms and values. After the collapse of the Soviet Union in 1991 and into the millennium, a relatively benign Russian neighbour presented an EU Eastern borderland that could be included in a norms-based 'return to Europe' for ex-Soviet states. Borders could be 'pushed back' with attached conditionalities and with CEE recipients, at least at face value, sympathetic to norms and values familiar to Western liberal principles (Mannin, 1999). Thus, the Europeanisation process was operationalised within a relatively benign and unambiguous set of external circumstances within the Copenhagen Criteria. Since the turn of the century (at the time that Helen Wallace hardened the conceptual boundary of the term to 'EU-isation' (Wallace, 2000)), Russian regional resurgence has opened up other strategic, tactical and normative pathways for neighbourhood countries that have been termed the 'in-betweeners' situated between two major centres of gravity. They seek a 'balance of cooperation' with the EU and Russia and are offered choices between a 'value Empire' (the EU) and the more concrete, hard power incentives of Russia (see chapters on Moldova, Belarus, Moldova, Ukraine and Chapter 14 on the South Caucasus).

Chapter 4 outlines clearly the challenges a confident Russian voice presents to the EAP and to the assumed westward trajectory of several of the EaP member states. It also reveals the limits of any singular conceptualisation of Europeanisation. The chapter indicates the interest-based approach that current Russian governance has taken when dealing with the technical conditionalities that are necessary to facilitate trading relations with the EU and the clear rejection of those conditions which are norms-based. In effect, the distinction is made between instrumental and normative EU-isation, the latter being rejected as not in line with Russia's historical interpretation of what Europeanisation has meant. Here the arguments of Chapter 1 are revisited. The Enlightenment as a paradigmatic frame has been subject to historic interpretation and, for Russia, value-driven Western Europeanisation as modernisation was never a high priority. The EU's late-twentieth-century triumphalism and its insistence on the rightness of its legal norm-based value system has been challenged, rejected, and indeed ridiculed. The alternative model, a looser Eurasian Economic Union (see Chapters 3–7) seems to offer to the near neighbours a different Europeanised future that implies alternative norms perhaps more in keeping with their existing domestic politics and identity than EU-isation.

Russia's more hard power approach towards the near neighbourhood, manifested most evidently in its annexation of Crimea and support for East Ukraine insurgents and seeming use of its energy monopoly as a tool of foreign policy, are clearly destabilising factors for both the neighbourhood states and the EU's neighbourhood policies. Such destabilisation has both geostrategic but also internal policy consequences for the actors concerned. For example, as Chapter 14 concludes, without evidence of the EU's ability (along with NATO) as security provider in the South Caucasus, any slow progress towards democratisation through EU normative soft power is severely weakened. In this instance, as in others, the geopolitical pull of Russia is clearly in operation. In such a context the EU's normative power is only really effective if political actors in the region can see that there are evident concrete external gains. This has been further complicated by the destabilising views of the nature and future of EU–US–Russian relations that emerged with the election of the Trump administration in 2016.

The chapter on language also shows the implications of geopolitics and the 'in-betweener' phenomenon but in the area of identity. Language policies are seen to have inevitably become a salient feature of national identity formation as well as a statement of value direction. The continued existence of Russian as a functioning language within near neighbour states complicates the implementation of language policies undertaken in post-Soviet CEE countries. Where English as a foreign language is promoted (Georgia) or Russian is accepted as one half of bilingualism (Belarus), there is a clear message towards a cultural/political affinity with either the 'West' or Russia. Though complicated between and within near neighbour states, language policy can be seen as a dichotomous representation of West European and East European value sets and thus a 'powerful statement of "otherness" or belonging at the very core of the Europeanisation process'.

This theme of 'otherness' recurs throughout the volume as one of the key aspects of current EU-isation and the creation of a European identity. As we have seen this can have a range of destabilising consequences. As Chapter 4 indicates, it is at the root of the current divisions between the EU and Russia. For other neighbours, the EU-centric approach to EU-isation and its implementation through programmes such as the ENP and EaP results in a sense of their being on the periphery of Europe when instead, as Chapter 6 on Belarus indicates, they actually have a sense of being 'core European'. In addition, the practical effects of the EU's neighbourhood policies – such as the AAs, the EaP and so on, offering them a European perspective without any concrete promise of membership – is to leave them in a permanent state of irresolution in terms of their foreign policy and national identity. In the case of Turkey, the long state of limbo while awaiting a concrete prospect of membership and the continuing view of its 'otherness' in the minds of some EU member states has combined with domestic political factors plus a renewed sense of its own strategic importance to stimulate it to assert its own separate path – what Chapter 10 describes as 'a new Ottoman ambition'. The EU's second 'other', Russia, has also charted such a separate European course in the 2000s. Some suggest that this common experience as the EU's outsiders will encourage them to combine forces (Bertrand, 2016).

A major failing of academic political analysis is a temptation to be driven by the nature of current events surrounding that analysis. As our introduction states, the EU has since 2008 been subjected to political and economic storms of historic intensity, most recently the threatened loss of one of its most significant member states and the conflicting messages regarding the US stance towards the EU, NATO and Russia. This, together with the reassertion of a Russian international presence, leads to a somewhat pessimistic outlook for continued eastward Europeanisation through a successful and progressive EaP. The EU triumphalism of the 1990s and early 2000s has been replaced by existential doubts for the very survival of the EU. Our opening discussion in Part I may appear to be based on such pessimism. The earlier clarity of EU-isation as the 'current reality' of Europeanisation is now muddied by the competing notions of Euro-Asian and Euro-Atlantic perspectives. We argue, however, that this background to the development of the concept of EU-isation must be fully appreciated. EU-isation, when used or viewed through a purely political or conceptual prism, fails to include a key element as a descriptive/conceptual container – that is, its historic and cultural origins. The significance of historical constructivism for its heuristic value is therefore unappreciated, especially when attempting to unpick the complexity of EU–near-neighbour relations.

We would therefore reject McCormick's (2010) conclusion that the distinction between the EU and 'Europe' can be assumed to be increasingly meaningless. We would, however, take on board his paradigm of 'Europeanism' within which the 'current reality' of EU-isation and competing and complementary current realities of Euro-Atlanticism and Euro-Asianism operate. This helps in understanding the complexity of EU–near-neighbour relations. Without the incorporation of such a paradigm into the political and academic analysis of these relations, the opportunities for resolution of what seem dangerous and divergent notions of Europe's future security are seriously diminished.

What are the implications of our conclusions for the implementation of EU-isation in practice and the attempt to promote a European identity? First, it is clear from several chapters that the existence of 'either/or' choices for neighbours that involve them ignoring the reality of their geopolitical position or entrenched domestic power structures or external/internal threats to stability in the name of prioritising the relationship with the EU can be counterproductive. Neighbours clearly prefer 'both/and' rather than 'either/or' choices. The EU has already begun to recognise this by moving on from the 'one size fits all' approach of the EaP and recognising, for example, that countries like Belarus and Georgia have very different aspirations in terms of their relations with Russia and the EU. The EU has also recognised that it needs to have different expectations of neighbours if it is to maintain influence. Insistence on full acquiescence in areas of norms may risk 'losing' the neighbour or discourage any reform at all, especially if there is an alternative pole which can be turned to (i.e. Russia) which does not have such normative expectations. The domestic political systems and external circumstances of neighbours differ significantly. In some cases therefore (such as Belarus), what may appear to be small-scale reforms or merely technical engagement may actually have greater significance than earlier appreciated by the EU.

One dilemma emerging out of this approach, however, is how far should the EU go in diluting any promotion of norms and values and concentrate mainly on the pursuit of interests? The chapters in this volume have shown that elites in the neighbourhood tend to adopt an instrumental interpretation of EU-isation. EU regulations are adopted for specific purposes, such as modernisation or access to global markets. As suggested earlier, the emphasis is on keeping EU-isation as an elite project based on pragmatic interests to avoid the deeper, 'thicker' EU-isation or socialisation which may threaten their interests. Often lip-service is paid to norms and values. The chapters on trade and energy indicate that for many EU member states that is also what they wish to pursue – for example, in their bilateral relations with Russia – uploading normative/values issues to the EU level. For some theorists of Europeanisation this emphasis on the pursuit of interests and acquiescence in the neighbours 'Europragmatism' is not problematic as interests and values are interlinked anyway. Mere engagement with EU regulations will have a socialising effect over time. As the chapter on Belarus shows, this approach of concentrating only on technical areas of cooperation and support for non-political projects is so far the only way of influencing the system, but at least it is an opening and could have wider spiralling effects. The problem with this approach – the effective abandonment of the normative agenda, at least in any explicit form – is highlighted well in the chapter on Moldova. The EU would be in danger of being rejected by the population as effectively endorsing the status quo and being complicit in such practices as corruption. As Chapter 3 indicated and as emerges elsewhere in the volume, the EU is in an often impossible dilemma. In order to have any access it needs the cooperation of the very elites whose networks and practices are threatened by its normative agenda. If it alienates elites it may lose traction altogether. If it is too close then it risks provoking cynicism towards the EU and its normative agenda.

As Chapter 1 and several of the chapters have indicated, one key reason for resistance to EU-isation is because it is perceived in terms of the EU as 'subject' and hence the neighbours as 'object'. In addition, the 'othering' of neighbours such as Turkey and Russia and indeed the suggestion that countries such as Belarus and Ukraine are on the periphery rather than being essentially European, can mean a turn to other political poles or domestic political traditions in which other norms and cultural traditions are more attractive. One solution to this and indeed to the geopolitical 'either/or' choice of the neighbours mentioned earlier, is to move to a more inclusive definition of Europeanisation and European identity. As Chapter 1 suggests and as indicated earlier in the discussion of the usefulness of the term 'Europeanism' as a tool of academic analysis, such a redefinition should acknowledge different but equally valid paths of Europeanisation and their common roots. It would not necessarily mean the abandonment of EU norms and values such as human rights or democracy but would mean moving away from the perception that grew after the end of the Cold War that these notions were the preserve of the EU and should be pushed eastwards in a kind of 'civilising' process. It would mean recognising that such values are part of the tradition – often of resistance and revolution – across the Continent both East and West, that the end of communism and the Cold War and the process of democratisation was initiated and promoted within Russia and Ukraine rather than exported by the EU. In this sense it would mean going back to the idea of building 'a common European home' as a mutual activity rather than Europe being constructed through EU-isation as the promotion of EU values eastward. In terms of accompanying structures this may mean that rather than insisting that neighbours are seen as aligning with EU rules and regulations, there is some move to a real common European space that includes Russia, Turkey and the 'in-betweeners', as this volume has termed them. So far there has been little effort to align regulations between the EU and the EEU for reasons which Chapter 4 has indicated. However, such an approach may be the only ulti-mate solution to avoid a permanent state of instability and insecurity on the EU's eastern borders.

A final comment is perhaps in order from the editors. The volume has tended to concentrate on the problems and contradictions of the EU's exter-nal relations with its neighbours. Given the nature of academic analysis this has been highly critical. The introduction to the volume also identified the wide range of external threats and domestic crises faced by the EU. Many on the Eurosceptic wing of politics would have reason to see all this as the context for the disintegration of the EU and an indication of the failure of its external policies. However, a more optimistic observer might suggest that such threats make the existence of the EU and its transformative mission even more relevant. Thus, any persistent negative EU discourse from the Trump administration and the EU's response to Brexit may, of necessity, act as drivers for integration rather than dislocation. It is clear from the chapters in this volume that the EU does have enormous signifi-cance for its neighbours, even if EU-isation is interpreted differently and used for ends other than those intended by the EU. It could also be argued that the current challenges are – rather like previous periods of post-world-war reconstruction, Cold War division, collapse of the Soviet bloc – oppor-tunities for the EU to revisit its mission, structures and approaches. Currently, for some in the member states of the EU and among the neighbours, the alternatives to the EU may appear more attractive – Eurasian Economic Union, nationalism, populism and the apparent 'renewal of state sover-eignty' offered by a Brexit pathway. However, these alternatives have yet to prove themselves as more effective ways of meeting the myriad challenges – economic, environmental, security, migration and so on – that face the populations of the wider Europe.

Bibliography

Abdelal, R., Yoshiko, M. H., Johnston, A. I., and McDermott, R. (2009). *Measuring Identity: A Guide for Social Scientists*. Cambridge: Cambridge University Press.

Adams, T. E. (2010). Social Constructivist Approach to Political Identity. *Encyclopaedia of Identity*, 10, 74–742.

Ademmer, E. (2015). Interdependence and EU-Demanded Policy Change in a Shared Neighbourhood. *Journal of European Public Policy*, 22(5), 671–689.

Ademmer, E., and Börzel, T. (2013). Migration, Energy and Good Governance in the EU's Eastern Neighbourhood, *Europe-Asia Studies*, 65(4), 581–608.

Adler, E., and Barnett, M. (eds) (1998). *Security Communities*. Cambridge: Cambridge University Press.

Adrey, J. B. (2005). Minority Language Rights Before and After the 2004 EU enlargement: The Copenhagen Criteria in the Baltic states. *Journal of Multilingual and Multicultural Development*, 26(5), 453–468.

Advisory Committee on The Framework Convention for The Protection of National Minorities, Third Opinion on Moldova (2009). Accessed 15 December 2015 at: https://www.coe.int/t/dghl/monitoring/minorities/3_FCNMdocs/PDF_3rd_OP_Moldova_en.pdf.

Alexeev, I. (2013). *South Stream Shapes European Energy Security, Nabucco Falls Behind – Analysis*. Accessed 30 June 2013 at: www.eurasiareview.com/08042013-south-stream-shapes-european-energy-security-nabucco-falls-behind-analysis/.

Alieva, L. (2006). EU and South Caucasus. *Centrum für angewandte Politikforschung Discussion Paper*.

Aliyev, H. (2016). Assessing the European Union's Assistance to Civil Society in its Eastern Neighbourhood: Lessons from the South Caucasus. *Journal of Contemporary European Studies*, 24(1), 42–60.

Altunişik, M., and Cuhadar, E. (2010). Turkey's Search for a Third-party Role in Arab–Israeli Conflicts: a Neutral Facilitator or a Principal Power Mediator? *Mediterranean Politics*, 15(3), 371–392.

Anastasakis, O. (2005). The EU-ization of the Balkans. *Brown Journal of World Affairs* 12(1), 77–88.

Ancel, J. (1929). *Peuples et nations des Balkans: Géographie politique*. Paris: A. Colin.

Anderson, B. (1983). *Imagined Communities: Reflections on the Origins and Spread of Nationalism*. London: Verso.

Andreas, P., and Snyder, T. (eds). (2000). *The Wall around the West: State Borders and Immigration Controls in North America and Europe*. Lanham: Rowman & Littlefield Publishers.

Aral, B. (2001). Dispensing with Tradition? Turkish Politics and International Society during the Özal Decade, 1983–1993. *Middle Eastern Studies*, 37(1), 72–88.

Aras, B. (2009). The Davutoğlu Era in Turkish Foreign Policy. *Insight Turkey*, 11(3), 127–142.

Aristotle. (1946). *Politics*, trans. and ed., E. Barker. Oxford: Clarendon Press.

Astourian, S. H. (2000). *From Ter-Petrosian to Kocharian: Leadership Change in Armenia*. Berkeley Program in Soviet and Post-Soviet Studies Working Paper Series, Berkeley: University of California.

Avdonin, V. S. (2006). *Rossijskie issledovanija politiki Evropejskogo sojuza*. Rjazan: Rjazanskij gosudarstvennyj universitet.

Averre, D. (2009). Competing Rationalities: Russia, the EU and the 'Shared Neighbourhood'. *Europe-Asia Studies*, 61(10), 1689–1713. doi: 10.1080/09668130903278918.

Avery, G. (2004). The Enlargement Negotiations. In F. Cameron (ed.), *The Future of Europe: Integration and Enlargement* (pp. 35–62). London: Routledge.

Ayan Musil, P. (2014). Emergence of a Dominant Party System after Multipartyism: Theoretical Implications from the Case of the AKP in Turkey. *South European Society and Politics*, 20(1), 71–92.

Ayata, S. (1996). Patronage, Party and State: the Politicization of Islam in Turkey. *The Middle East Journal*, 50(1), 40–56.

Aydin, M., and Açikmeşe, S. (2007). Europeanization through EU Conditionality: Understanding the New Era in Turkish Foreign Policy. *Journal of Balkan and Near Eastern Studies*, 9(3), 263–274.

Azerbaijan in the World. (2008). A Conversation with Vafa Guluzade on Azerbaijan's Foreign Policy. *Azerbaijan in the World*, 1(5), 1–5. Accessed at: http://ada.edu.az/uploads/file/bw/pdf145.pdf.

Bal, P. G. (2016). The Effects of The Refugee Crisis on the EU–Turkey Relations: The Readmission Agreement And Beyond. *European Scientific Journal*, 12(8), 14–36.

Baran, Z. (2007). EU Energy Security: Time to End Russian Leverage. *The Washington Quarterly*, 30(4), 131–144.

Barbarosie, A. (2015). Unprecedented Decrease in the Support for the European Integration. Causes and Consequences (interview with Lina Grâu). *Synthesis and Foreign Policy Debates*, 3, 2–4.

Barbe, E., Costa, O., Herranz Surralles, A., and Natorski, M. (2009). Which Rules Shape EU's External Governance? The Pattern of Rule Selection in Foreign and Security Policies. *Journal of European Public Policy*, 16(6), 834–852.

Barjaktarović, M. (1970). 'Cigani u Jugoslaviji danas', *Zbornik filozofskog fakulteta* (Beograd) XI (1), 743–748.

Barth, F. (1998) *Ethnic Groups and Boundaries*. Long Grove, IL: Waveland Press.

Barylski, R. (1995). Russia, the West, and the Caspian Energy Hub. *Middle East Journal*, 49(2), 217–232.

Barysch, K. (2007). Russia, Realism and EU Unity. Accessed 12 November 2012 at: www.cer.org.uk/publications/archive/policy-brief/2007/russia-realism-and-eu-unity.

Batt, J. (2013). Introduction: Defining Central and Eastern Europe. In S. White, P. Lewis, and J. Batt (eds), *Developments in Central and East European Politics*. Durham: Duke University Press.

Bauer, M., Knill, C. and Pitschel, D. (2007). Differential Europeanization in Eastern Europe: The impact of Diverse EU Regulatory Governance Patters. *Journal of European Public Policy*, 29(4), 405–424.

BBC Monitoring. (2002). Former Azeri Official Confirms Territorial Swap Plan on Agenda for Long Time. Accessed from Nexis UK.

Bechev, D. (2004). Contested Borders, Contested Identity: The Case of Regionalism in South East Europe. *Journal of Southeast European and Black Sea Studies*, 4(1), 77–96.

Beck, U. and Grande, E. (2007). *Cosmopolitan Europe*. Cambridge: Polity.

Beichelt, T. (2008). Dimensions of Europeanisation. In F. Balfoil., and T, Beichelt (eds), *Europeanisation D'Ouest en Est* (pp. 1–14). Paris: L'Harmattan.

Belarusian Ministry of Culture. (2011). *Ab stanie, prabliemach i daliejšym razvicci sučasnaj kul̓tury Bielarusi i roli Respublikanskaha hramadskaha savieta pa spravach kul̓tury i mastactva pry Saviecie Ministraŭ Respubliki Bielaruś u kul̓turnym pracesie*. Accessed 23 March 2016 at: http://www.kultura.by.

Belarusian Ministry of Foreign Affairs. (n.d.). *Our Relations with Countries and Regions*. Accessed 23 March 2016 at: http://mfa.gov.by.

Belarusian Telegraph Agency. (2014). *Makei blames Europe for Ukraine Crisis*. Accessed 23 March 2016 at: http://belta.by.

Bellamy, J. A. (2003). *The Formation of a Croatian National Identity: A Century-old Dream?* Manchaster: Manchester University Press.

Bellamy, R. (2008). *Citizenship: A Very Short Introduction*. Oxford: Oxford University Press.

Belsat. (2015). *Usau: Karatkievič i inšyja ŭdziel̓niki hetych vybaraŭ – dadatkovy administracyjny resurs uladaŭ*. Accessed 23 March 2016 at: http://belsat.eu.

Belyi, A. (2009). EU External Energy Policies: A Paradox of Integration? In J. Orbie (ed.), *Europe's Global Role*. (pp. 203–215). Farnham: Ashgate.

Bertrand, N. (2016). Russia may be Preparing a Long term 'Game-changing move' with Turkey. *Business Insider: 5th August*. Accessed at: uk.businessinsider.com/ …oup-2016–8r=usandir=t

Betmakaev, A. M. (2014). Faktory evropeizacii vneshnej politiki gosudarstv – uchastnikov Evropejskogo sojuza. *Izvestija Irkutskogo gosudarstvennogo universiteta. Serija: politologija. Religiovedenie*, 7, 51–57.

Bigo, D. (2006). Internal and External Aspects of Security. *European Security*, 15(4), 385–404.

Bilaniuk, L. and Melnyk, S. (2008). A Tense and Shifting Balance: Bilingualism and Education in Ukraine. *International Journal of Bilingual Education and Bilingualism*, 11(3/4), 340–372.

Blank, S. (1995). Russia and Europe in the Caucasus. *European Security*, 4(4), 622–645. doi: 10.1080/09662839508407243.

Blatter, J., and Haverland, M. (2012). *Designing Case Studies. Explanatory Approaches in Small-N Research*. Basingstoke: Palgrave Macmillan.

Blavoukos, S., and Oikonomou, G. (2012). *Is Europeanisation still in academic fashion? Empirical trends in the period 2002–2012*. Conference paper: Concepts and Experiences, Athens, 14–16 May.

Blockmans, S. (2014). Seven Challenges to the Eastern Partnership. *Centre for European Policy Studies, 14 November*. Accessed 3 March 2015 at: www.ceps.eu /print/9810.

Blom, T,. and Vanhoonacker, S. (2015). The European External Action Service (EEAS). The New Kid on the Block. In M. W. Bauer et al. (eds), *The Palgrave Handbook of the European Administrative System*. London: Palgrave Macmillan.

Boian, V. (2010). *Taking Stock and Evaluation of Financial Assistance Granted to Moldova by the European Union*. Chisinau: APE.

Bolgova, I. (2014). Krizis Vostochonoi poitiki ES. *Vestnik MGIMO Universiteta*, 37(4), 133–138.

Bordachev, T. (2007). *Predely evropeizatsii. Rossiya i Evropeiskii souz 1991–2007. Teoriya i praktika otnoshenii*. Moscow:Vysshaya shkola ekonomiki.

Börzel, T. (2002). Member State responses to Europeanisation. *Journal of Common Market Studies*, 40(2), 193–214.

Börzel, T. (2005). How the EU Interacts with its Member States. In S. Bulmer and C. Lequesne (eds), *The Member States of the European Union* (pp. 1–24). Oxford: Oxford University Press.

Börzel, T., and Pamuk, Y. (2012). Pathologies of Europeanization. Fighting Corruption in the Southern Caucasus. *West European Politics*, 35(1), 79–97.

Börzel, T., and Risse, T. (2003). Conceptualizing the Domestic Impact of Europe. In K. Featherstone and C. Radaelli (eds), *The Politics of Europeanisation* (pp. 57–80). Oxford: Oxford University Press.

Börzel, T., and Risse, T. (2012a). From Europeanization to Diffusion: Introduction. *West European Politics*, 35(1), 1–19. doi: 10.1080/01402382.2012.631310/

Börzel, T., and Risse, T. (2012b). When Europeanisation meets Diffusion: Exploring New Territory. *West European Politics*, 35(1), 192–207.

Bosse, G. (2010). The EU's Relations with Moldova: Governance, Partnership or Ignorance? *Europe-Asia Studies*, 62(8), 1291–1309. doi: 10.1080/09668136 .2010.504528

Bosse, G. (2012). A Partnership with Dictatorship: Explaining the Paradigm Shift in European Union Policy towards Belarus. *Journal of Common Market Studies*, 50(3), 367–384.

Bossong, R., and Carrapico, H (eds). (2016). *EU Borders and Shifting Internal Security – Technology, Externalisation and Accountability*. Berlin: Springer Press.

Boswell, C., and Geddes, A. (2011). *Migration and Mobility in the European Union*. Palgrave Macmillan: Basingstoke.

Braghiroli, S., and Carta, C. (2009). *An Index of Friendliness towards Russia: An Analysis of Member States and Member of the European Parliament's Decisions*. Accessed 14 October 2012 at: www.utu.fi/fi/yksikot/tse/yksikot/PEI/raportit-ja-tietopaketit/Documents/Braghiroli_%20Carta%201509%20web.pdf.

Bretherton, C., and Mannin, M. (eds). (2013). *The Europeanization of European Politics*. Basingstoke: Palgrave Macmillan.

Broers, L. (2005). After the 'Revolution': Civil Society and the Challenges of Consolidating Democracy in Georgia. *Central Asian Survey*, 24(3), 333–350.

Brown, M.E., Lynn-Jones, S. M., and Miller, S. E. (eds). (1999). *Debating the Democratic Peace: an International Security Reader*. Cambridge: The MIT Press.

Browning, C., and Christou, G. (2010). The Constitutive Power of Outsiders: the European Neighbourhood Policy and the Eastern Dimension. *Political Geography*, 29, 109–118.

Brubaker, R. (1998). Myths and Misconceptions in the Study of Nationalism. In J. A. Hall (ed.), *The State of the Nation: Ernest Gellner and the Theory of Nationalism* (pp. 272–305). Cambridge: Cambridge University Press.

Brubaker, R., and Cooper, F. (2000). Beyond identity. *Theory and Society*, 29(1), 1–47.

Bruter, M. (2005). *Citizens of Europe? The Emergence of a Mass European Identity*. Basingstoke: Palgrave Macmillan.

Bryza, M., and Koranyi, D. (2013). A Tale of Two Pipelines: Why TAP has won the Day. Accessed 30 June 2013 at: www.naturalgaseurope.com/southern-corridor-strategic-importance-tap-nabucco.

Brzezinski, Z. (1997). *The Grand Chessboard*. New York: Basic Books.

Buchan, D. (2009). *Energy and Climate Change: Europe at the Crossroads*. Oxford: Oxford University Press.

Bulmer, S., and Radaelli, C. (2004). The Europeanisation of Public Policy. In C. Lequesne and S. Bulmer (eds), *Member-States and the European Union* (pp. 338–59). Oxford: Oxford University Press.

Buzan, B., Waever, O., and de Wilde, J. (1998). *Security: A New Framework for Analysis*. London: Lynne Rienner Publishers.

Całus, K. (2013). Vlad Filat: A Vote of no Confidence in Moldova. *New Eastern Europe*. Accessed at: www.neweasterneurope.eu/component/content/article/20-eastern-europe-50/621-vlad-filat-a-vote-of-no-confidence-in-moldova.

Całus, K. (2014). A Captured State? Moldova's Uncertain Prospects for Modernization. *OSW Commentary*. Accessed at: www.osw.waw.pl/sites/default/files/commentary_168_0.pdf.

Cantir, C., and Kennedy, R. (2015). Balancing on the Shoulders of Giants: Moldova's Foreign Policy toward Russia and the European Union. *Foreign Policy Analysis*, 11(4), 397–416. doi: 10.1111/fpa.12051.

Carey, S. (2002). Undivided Loyalties: Is National Identity an Obstacle to European Integration? *European Union Politics*, 3(4), 387–413.

Carothers, T. (1997). Democracy Assistance: The Question of Strategy. *Democratization*, 4(3), 109–132. doi: 10.1080/13510349708403527.

Carothers, T. (1999a). *Aiding Democracy Abroad: the Learning Curve*. Washington: Carnegie Endowment for International Peace.

Carothers, T. (1999b). Western Civil-Society Aid to Eastern Europe and the Former Soviet Union. *East European Constitutional Review*, 8, 54–62.

Carothers, T. (2007). The "Sequencing" Fallacy. *Journal of Democracy*, 18(1), 12–27. doi: 10.1353/jod.2007.0002.

Casier, T. (2011). The Rise of Energy to the Top of the EU-Russia Agenda: From Interdependence to Dependency. *Geopolitics*, 16, 536–552.

Casier, T. (2013). The EU–Russia Strategic Partnership: Challenging the Normative Argument. *Europe-Asia Studies*, 65(7), 1377–1395.

Casier, T., Korosteleva, E. A., and Whitman, R. G. (2013). Building a Stronger Eastern Partnership: Towards an EaP 2.0. *Global Europe Centre Policy Paper*. Canterbury: University of Kent.

Caspersen, N. (2008). Separatism and Democracy in the Caucasus. *Survival*, 50(4), 113–136.

Castano, E., Paladino, M.P., Coull, A., and Yzerbyt, V.Y. (2002). Protecting the Ingroup Stereotype: ingroup identification and the management of deviant ingroup members. *British Journal of Social Psychology*, 41(3), 365–385.

Çelenk, A. A. (2007). The Restructuring of Turkey's Policy Towards Cyprus: the Justice and Development Party's Struggle for power. *Turkish Studies*, 8(3), 349–363.

Central Election Commission of Ukraine. (2004). *Data on Elections of President of Ukraine in the Regions*. Accessed 9 April 2016 at: www.cvk.gov.ua/pls/vp2004 /wp0011.

Central European Policy Institute. (2013). *Second Moldova Reality Check: Success Story Before the Storm?* Accessed at: www.cepolicy.org/publications /2nd-moldova-reality-check-success-story-storm.

Cepoi, M. (2014). *Informarea societăţii moldoveneşti privind procesul de integrare europeană: între acţiuni întârziate şi manipulare*. Chisinau: IDIS "Viitorul".

Citrin, J., and Sears, D.O. (2009). Balancing National and Ethnic Identities: The Psychology of e pluribus unum. In R. Abdelal, Y.M. Herrera, A.I. Johnston and R. McDermott (eds), *Measuring Identity: A Guide for Social Scientists* (pp. 145–174), Cambridge: Cambridge University Press.

Chan, S. (1997). In Search of Democratic Peace: Problems and Promise. *Mershon International Studies Review*, 41(1), 59–91.

Chandler, D. (2006). Back to the Future? The Limits of neo-Wilsonian Ideals of Exporting Democracy. *Review of International Studies*, 32, 475–494.

Chandler, D. (2014). Democracy Unbound? Non-linear Politics and the Politicization of Everyday Life. *European Journal of Social Theory*, 17(1), 42–59.

Checkel, J.T. (2005). International Institutions and Socialization in Europe: Introduction and Framework. *International Organization*, 59(4), 801–826.

Checkel, J.T., and Moravcsik, A. (2001). A Constructivist Research Program in EU Studies? *European Union Politics*, 2(2), 219–249.

Chernikova, T.V. (2014). *Process evropeizacii v Rossii vo vtoroi polovine XV-XVII vv. Dissertacija na soiskanie uchenoj stepeni doktora istoricheskih nauk*. MGIMO-MID, Doktorate Dissertation, Moscow.

Chirila, V. (2002). The Relations Between the Republic of Moldova and the European Union. In A. Barbăroşie and V. Gheorghiu (eds), *The Republic of Moldova and the European integration* (pp. 37–67). Chişinău: Cartier.

Chizhov V. (2016) Vyderzhki iz otvetov na voprosy zhurnalistov Postojannogo predstavitelja Rossii pri ES V.A.Chizhova v hode brifinga, organizovannogo MIA 'Rossija-segodnja' v formate vedemosta 'Moskva-Brjussel'. *RussianMission.eu*. Accessed 2 April 2016 at: www.russianmission.eu/ru/novosti/россия-ес-б рифинг-вачижова-в-формате-видеомоста-москва-брюссель.

Chizhov, V. (2015). Intervju Postoyannogo predstavitelya Rossii pri Evropeiskom souse V.A. Chizhova informagentstvu 'Rossiya segodnya', *RussianMission.eu*, 15. Accessed 17 August 2015 at: www.russianmission.eu/ru/novost i/интервью-вачижова-информагентству-«россия-сегодня».

Chua, A. (2004). *World on Fire: How Exporting Free Market Democracy Breeds Ethnic Hatred and Global Instability*. London: Arrow Books.

Citrin, J., and Sides, J. (2004). More than Nationals: How Identity Choice Matters in the New Europe. In R. K. Herrmann, T. Risse, and B. M. Brewer (eds),

Transnational Identities: Becoming European in the EU (pp. 161–185). Lanham: Rowman & Littlefield Publishers.

Claes, D. (2009). EU Energy Security Between Internal Market and Foreign Policy. In G. Fermann (ed.), *Political Economy of Energy in Europe* (pp. 37–61). Berlin: BWV.

Cohen, I.J. (1995). *Broken Bonds: Yugoslavia's Disintegration and Balkan Politics*. Oxford: Westview.

Collinson, S. (1996). Visa Requirements, Carrier Sanctions, 'Safe Third Countries' and 'Readmission': The Development of an Asylum 'Buffer Zone' in Europe. *Transactions of the Institute of British Geographers, New Series*, 21(1), 76–90.

Concepția politicii externe a Republicii Moldova. (1995). Accessed at: http://lex.justice.md/viewdoc.php?action=viewandview=docandid=306955andlang=1

Cooper, A., and Morris, K. (2013). The Nagorno-Karabakh Conflict in Light of Polls in Armenia and Nagorno-Karabakh. In M. Kambeck and S. Ghazaryan (eds), *Europe's Next Avoidable War: Nagorno-Karabakh* (pp. 89–100). Basingstoke: Palgrave.

Cornell, S. (2010). *Azerbaijan Since Independence*. Armonk: E. M. Sharpe.

Cornell, S., and Starr, F. S. (2006). *The Caucasus: A Challenge for Europe*. Accessed 7 August 2017 at: http://isdp.eu/content/uploads/publications/2006_cornell-starr_the-caucasus-a-challenge-for-europe.pdf.

Costea, S. (2010). The Profound Causes of Russia's Hostility Towards the Eastern Partnership. *World Security Network*. Accessed from www.worldsecuritynetwork.com /Europe-Russia/Costea-Dr.-Simion/The-profound-causes-of-Russias-hostility-towards-the-Eastern-Partnership.

Council of Europe, European Court of Human Rights (2002). Press release issued by the Registrar, Chamber judgement in the case of *Podkolzina* v. *Latvia*, 9 April.

Council of Europe. (2009). *Language Education Policy Profile of Armenia*. Accessed 10 December 2015 at: www.coe.int/t/dg4/linguistic/Profils1_EN.asp#TopOfPage.

Council of Europe. (2011). *Language Education Policy Profile of Ukraine*. Accessed 10 December 2015 at: www.coe.int/t/dg4/linguistic/Profils1_EN.asp#TopOfPage.

Council of the European Union. (1996). Recommendation of 4 March 1996 on 'Local Consular Cooperation Regarding Visas', *Official Journal C 080*.

Council of the European Union. (2003a). *A Secure Europe in a Better World: European Security Strategy*, Brussels, 12 December. Accessed 15 July 2008 at: https://www.consilium.europa.eu/uedocs/cmsUpload/78367.pdf.

Council of the European Union (2003). *Initiative of the French Republic with a view of adoption of a Council Decision amending point 1.2 of Part II of the Common Consular Instructions and drawing up of a new Annex thereto 14701/03 VISA 184 COMIX 682 OC 710 Brussels 11 December 2003.*

Council of the European Union. (2008). *The Future French, Czech and Swedish Presidencies. 18 Month Programme of the Council* (11249/08). Accessed 23 March 2016 at: http://register.consilium.europa.eu/doc/srv?l=ENandf=ST%20 11249%202008%20INIT.

Council of the European Union. (2009). *The Future Spanish, Belgian and Hungarian Presidencies. 18 Month Programme of the Council* (16771/09). Accessed 23 March 2016 at: http://register.consilium.europa.eu/doc/srv?l=ENandf=ST%20 16771%202009%20INIT.

Council of the European Union. (2011). *The Future Polish, Danish and Cypriot Presidencies. 18 Month Programme of the Council* (11447/11). Accessed 23 March 2016 at: http://register.consilium.europa.eu/doc/srv?l=ENandf=ST%20 11447%202011%20INIT.

Council of the European Union. (2012). *The Future Irish, Lithuanian and Greek Presidencies. 18 Month Programme of the Council* (17426/12). Accessed 23 March 2016 at: http://register.consilium.europa.eu/doc/srv?l=ENandf=ST%20 17426%202012%20INIT.

Council of the European Union. (2012). *Decision of 22 June 2012 on Signing on Behalf of the European Union, of the Agreement between the European Union and the Republic of Moldova amending the Agreement between the European Community and the Republic of Moldova on the facilitation of the issuance of visas*; Official Journal of the European Union (2012/353/EU) L174/4 4.7. 2012.

Council of the European Union. (2014). *The Future Italian, Latvian and Luxembourg Presidencies. 18 Month Programme of the Council* (10948/1/14). Accessed 23 March 2016 at: http://register.consilium.europa.eu/doc/srv?l=ENandf=ST%20 10948%202014%20REV%201

Council of the European Union. (2016). *Refugee Facility for Turkey: Member States Agree on Details of Financing*; Press Release 25/16, 3 February 2016.

Cowles, M. and Risse, T. (2001). Transforming Europe: Conclusions. In M. Cowles, T. Caporasso and T. Risse (eds), *Transforming Europe: Europeanisation and Domestic Change* (pp. 217–238). New York: Cornell University Press.

Croatian Ministry of Education and Sports. (1999). *The Development of Education: The National Report*. Croatian Ministry of Education and Sports.

Cvijić, J. (1918). *La Peninsule Balkanique: Géographie Humaine*. Paris: A. Colin.

Czech EU Presidency. (2009). *Work Programme of the Czech Presidency of the Council of the EU. Europe without Barriers*. Accessed 23 March 2016 at: Www.Eu2009.Cz/ Assets/News-And-Documents/News/Cz-Pres_Programme_En.Pdf.

Dagnis Jensen, M., and Snaith, H. (2016). When politics prevails: The Political Economy of a Brexit. *Journal of European Public Policy*, 1–9.

Dangerfield, M. (2000). *Subregional Economic Cooperation in Central and Eastern Europe*. Cheltenham: Edward Elgar.

Dangerfield, M. (2013). The Czech Republic, Hungary and Slovakia. In M. David, J. Gower, and H. Haukkala (eds), *National Perspectives on Russia: European Foreign Policy in the Making*. London: Routledge.

Dangerfield, M. (2015). 'Visegrad States' Attitudes to Sanctions on Russia: 'Putinisation' or Pragmatism? Paper presented at the EUSA Fourteenth Biennial Conference, 5–7 March 2015, Boston, USA.

Davies, N. (1997). *Europe: a History*. London: Pimlico.

Davutoğlu, A. (2001). *Stratejik Derinlik: Türkiye'nin Uluslararasi Konumu (Strategic Depth: Turkey's International Location)*. Istanbul: Küre.

Davutoğlu, A. (2008). Turkey's Foreign Policy Vision: An Assessment of 2007. *Insight Turkey*, 10(1), 77–96.

De Varennes, F. (1996). Language, Minorities and Human Rights. *International Studies in Human Rights, 45*, The Hague: Martinus Nijhoff Publishers.

De Waal, T. (2003). *Black Garden: Armenia and Azerbaijan Through Peace and War*. New York: New York University Press.

De Waal, T. (2013). An Offer Sargsyan Could not Refuse. Accessed from http://carnegie.ru/eurasiaoutlook/?fa=52841andreloadFlag=1.

De Waal, T. (2014). EU Should Risk More to End Eastern Europe's Limbo. Accessed 7 August 2017 at: www.bloombergview.com/articles/2014-01-26/eu-should-risk-more-to-end-eastern-europe-s-limbo.

Declaraţie privind constituirea Coaliţiei de guvernare 'Alianţa pentru Integrarea Europeană'. (2009). Accessed at: www.e-democracy.md/parties/docs/joint/200908081/.

Reuters. (2016). Declaring a 'new beginning', EU and Turkey seal migrant deal (01/02/2016), www.reuters.com/article/us-europe-migrants-turkey-idUSKBN0TI00520151129.

Deitz, L., Stirton, L., and Wright, K. (2007). *The Energy Community of South East Europe: Challenges of, and obstacles to, Europeanisation.* Accessed 16 April 2016 at: http://competitionpolicy.ac.uk/documents/8158338/8256111/CCP+Working+Paper+08-4.pdf/acda7bff-3e3c-486f-86a6-aa4cd2cd21b6.

Dekanozishvili, M. (2004). *The EU in the South Caucasus: By What Means, to What Ends?* Accessed 6 August 2017 at: https://www.gfsis.org/media/activities/thumb1_/pub/files/publications_politics/dekanozishvili_The_EU.pdf.

Delanty, G. (1995). *Inventing Europe: Idea, Identity, Reality.* New York: St Martin's Press.

Delanty, G. (2002). Models of European Identity. *Perspectives on European Politics and Society*, 3(3), 345–359.

Delanty, G., and Rumford, C. (2005). *Rethinking Europe: Social Theory and the Implications of Europeanisation.* London: Routledge.

Delcour, L. (2013). Meandering Europeanisation: EU Policy Instruments and Policy Convergence in Georgia under the Eastern Partnership. *East European Politics*, 29(3), 344–357.

Delcour, L., and Duhot, H. (2011). *Bringing South Caucasus Closer to Europe.* Achievements and Challenges in ENP implementation, College of Europe, Natolin Research Paper 03/2011 (College of Europe Natolin Campus: Warsaw, April.

Delegation of the European Union to Moldova. (2010). The EU High Level Policy Advisors were Officially Presented. Accessed at: http://eeas.europa.eu/delegations/moldova/press_corner/all_news/news/2010/20100422_01_en.htm.

Delegation of the European Union to Moldova. (2015). EU–Moldova Relations: Deliverables. Accessed at: http://eeas.europa.eu/delegations/moldova/eu_moldova/political_relations/eu_moldova_relations_deliverables/index_en.htm.

Demenko, O. (2010). Non-Block Status of Ukraine: Realities and Perspectives. *Modern Ukrainian Politics. Politicians and Political Scientists about it*, 20, 310–315. (Деменко, О. (2010). 'Позаблоковий статус України: реалії та перспективи', *Сучасна українська політика. Політики і політологи про неї*, 20, с.310–315).

Dempsey, N., Hough, D., and Barton, C. (2016). *Energy Prices.* House of Commons Library Briefing Paper. Available at: www.parliament.uk/briefing-papers/sn04153.pdf.

Devyatkov, A.V. (2006). Perspektyvy uregulirovanija Pridnestrovskogo konflikta. *Vestnik Evrazii*, 2, 134–153.

Devyatkov, A.V. (2011). Moldova na Perekrestke otnoshenii Rossii i ES. *Aktualnye problemy Evropy*, 2, 187–202.

Devyatkov, A.V. (2012). *Pered vyzovom evropeizacii: politika Rossii v Pridnestro-vskom uregulirovanii (1992–2012 gg.)*. Tjumen: Izd-vo Tjumenskogo gosudarst-vennogo universiteta.

Di Palma, G. (1990). *To Craft Democracies: an Essay on Democratic Transitions*. Berkeley: University of California Press.

Diamond, L. (1992). Promoting Democracy. *Foreign Policy* (87), 25–46. doi: 10.2307/1149159.

Dias, V.A. (2013a). The EU's Post-Liberal Approach to Peace: Framing EUBAM's Contribution to the Moldova–Transnistria Conflict Transformation. *European Security*, 22(3), 338–354. doi: 10.1080/09662839.2012.712039.

Dias, V.A. (2013b). The EU and Russia: Competing Discourses, Practices and Interests in the Shared Neighbourhood. *Perspectives on European Politics and Society*, 14(2), 256–271.

Díez Medrano, J., and Gutiérrez, P. (2001). Nested Identities: National and Euro-pean Identity in Spain. *Ethnic and Racial Studies*, 24(5), 753–758.

Diez, T. (2013). Normative Power as Hegemony. *Cooperation and Conflict*, 48(2), 194–210.

Dillon, M. (2007). Governing through contingency: The security of biopolitical governance. *Political Geography*, 26, 41–47.

Dimitrova, A., and Dragneva, R. (2009). Constraining External Governance: Inter-dependence with Russia and the CIS as Limits to EU's Rule Transfer in Ukraine. *Journal of European Public Policy*, 16(6), 853–872.

Diplomacy and Trade. (2014). Russian Embargo: Negligible Effect on Hungary. Accessed 4 November 2015 at: www.dteurope.com/economy/news/russian-embargo –negligible-effect-on-hungary.html

Direction of the Slovak Foreign and European Policy. (2014). *Ministry of Foreign and European Affairs of the Slovak Republic*. Accessed at: www.mzv.sk/App/wcm/media.nsf/vw_ByID/ID_1E870F04753534FCC1257C7F0048B9F7_EN/$File/Direction%20of%20Slovak%20Foreign%20and%20European%20Policy%20 2014.pdf.

Ditchev, I. (2002). The Eros of identity. Accessed 10 June 2015 at: http://belintellectuals.eu/media/library/Eros_of_Identity.pdf

Dominese, G. (2005). Europe and Security in the Caucasus. *Transition Studies Review*, 12(1), 101–118.

Doyle, M.W. (1983a). Kant, Liberal Legacies, and Foreign Affairs. *Philosophy and Public Affairs*, 12(3), 205–235.

Doyle, M.W. (1983b). Kant, Liberal Legacies, and Foreign Affairs, Part 2. *Philoso-phy and Public Affairs*, 12(4), 323–353.

Doyle, M.W. (1986). Liberalism and World Politics. *The American Political Science Review*, 80(4), 1151–1169.

Dragneva, R., and Wolczuk, K. (2012). *Russia, the Eurasian Customs Union and the EU: cooperation, stagnation or rivalry?* Chatham House Briefing Paper REP BP, 1.

Duchesne, S. (2008). Waiting for a European identity … Reflections on the Process of Identification with Europe. *Perspectives on European Politics and Society*, 9(4), 397–410.

Duchesne, S., Frazer, E., Haegel, F., and Van Ingelgom, V (eds). (2013). *Citizens' Reactions to European Integration Compared: Overlooking Europe*. Basing-stoke: Palgrave.

Duijzings, G. (2000). *Religion and the Politics of Identity in Kosovo*. London: C. Hurst and Co.

Duleba, A. (2003). Slovakia's Policy towards Russia, the Ukraine and Belarus. In K. Pelczyńska-Nalęcz, A. Duleba, L. Póti, and V.Votápek (eds), *Eastern Policy of the Enlarged European Union*. Bratislava: Slovak Foreign Policy Association.

Duleba, A. (2009). Slovakia's Relations with Russia and Eastern Neighbours. Accessed 9 December 2011 at: www.fakprojekt.hu/docs/04-Duleba.pdf.

Duman, Ö., and Tsarouhas, D. (2006). "Civilianization" in Greece versus "Demilitarization" in Turkey: a Comparative Study of Civil-Military relations and the Impact of the European Union. *Armed Forces and Society*, 32(3), 405–423.

Dumka, I. (2013). Europeanization in EU External Relations after the Eastward Enlargement: Complications and Bypasses to Greater Engagement with the Eastern ENP Countries. *Review of European and Russian Affairs*, 8(1), 1–24.

Dzieciolowski, Z. (2008). Georgia's President Saakashvili, On the Eve of War. Accessed 6 August 2017 from http://pulitzercenter.org/blog/untold-stories/georgias-president-saakashvili-eve-war

Eder, K., and Spohn, W. (eds) (2005). *Collective Memory and European Identity: The Effects of Integration and Enlargement*. Farnham: Ashgate.

EITI Secretariat. (2010). *EITI National Coordinators met in Brussels to review progress*. Accessed 22 June 2013 at: http://eiti.org/news-events/eiti-national-coordinators-met-brussels-review-progress.

EITI Secretariat. (2013). *EITI Board Members 2013 -2015/2016*. Accessed 22 June 2013 at: http://eiti.org/files/EITI-Board-members-2013–2015–16.pdf.

EITI Secretariat. (n.d.). *Stakeholders: Countries*. Accessed 22 June 2013 at: http://eiti.org/supporters/countries.

Emerson M., and Movchan V. (eds). (2016). *Deepening EU–Ukrainian Relations: What, why and how?* Centre for European Policy Studies (CEPS), Brussels, Institute for Economic Research and Policy Consulting (IER), Kyiv. London: Rowman & Littlefield International.

Emerson, M., and Cenusa, D. (eds). (2016). *Deepening EU–Moldovan Relations: What, why and how?* Centre for European Policy Studies (CEPS), Brussels; Expert-Group, Chisinau. London: Rowman & Littlefield International.

Emerson, M., and Kovziridze, T. (eds). (2016). *Deepening EU–Georgian Relations: What, why and how?* Centre for European Policy Studies, Brussels; Reformatics, Tbilisi. London: Rowman & Littlefield International.

Epstein, R. A., and Jacoby, W. (2014). Eastern Enlargement Ten Years On: Transcending the East–West Divide? *JCMS: Journal of Common Market Studies*, 52(1): 1–16.

Eralp, A. (2009). The role of temporality and interaction in the EU-Turkey relationship. *New Perspectives on Turkey*, 40(2), 147–169.

Eriksen, M. (2015). EU-ization of the Balkans within an Identity-Based Framework. *Politeja*, Krakow: Jagiellonian University Press.

EU Delegation to Azerbaijan. (n.d.). Eastern Partnership. Accessed 23 March 2016 at: http://eeas.europa.eu/delegations/azerbaijan.

EU Delegation to Belarus. (2012). Launching European Dialogue on Modernisation with Belarus. Accessed 23 March 2016 at: http://eeas.europa.eu/delegations/belarus.

EU delegation to Belarus. (n.d.). Relations between Belarus and the EU – an Outline. Accessed 30 November 2015 at: http://eeas.europa.eu/delegations/belarus.

European Commission and High Representative. (2013). *European Neighbourhood Policy: Working towards a Stronger Partnership*. Joint Communication to the European Parliament, the Council, the European Economic and Social Committee and the Committee of the Regions, Brussels, 20 March, 8–9.

European Commission. (1973). *Declaration on European Identity*, Copenhagen.

European Commission. (1993). *First Report on Citizenship of the Union*, COM(93) 702 Final Brussels.

European Commission. (1997). For a Stronger and Wider Union: Agenda 2000; COM(97) 2000 Final Brussels.

European Commission. (2002). Communication from the Commission to the Council and the European Parliament – Towards integrated management of the external borders of the Member States of the European Union; COM(2002) 0233 Final Brussels.

European Commission. (2004). *European Neighbourhood Policy Strategy Paper.* COM(2004), 373 final, Commission of the European Communities. Accessed 15 July 2015 at: http://eur-lex.europa.eu/legal-content/EN/TXT/?uri=CELEX:5 2004DC0373.

European Commission. (2007). *Unity in Diversity.* Cordis News, http://cordis .europa.eu/fetch?CALLER=EN_NEWSandACTION=DandRCN=27389.

European Commission. (2008a). *Fifth Report on Citizenship of the Union*, COM(2008) 85 Final Brussels.

European Commission. (2008). Communication from the Commission to the European Parliament and the Council – Eastern Partnership. Accessed from http://eur-lex.europa.eu/legal-content/EN/ALL/?uri=CELEX:52008DC0823.

European Commission. (2010). *Promoting your EU electoral rights*, Citizens Factsheets.

European Commission. (2011). *Communication on Security of Supply and International Cooperation.* Accessed 12 January 2012, from the Europa website: http://ec.europa.eu/energy/international/security_of_supply/doc/com_2011_0539 .pdf.

European Commission. (2012). *Kazakhstan.* Accessed 17 July 2013 at: http://ec.europa.eu/trade/policy/countries-and-regions/countries/kazakhstan/.

European Commission. (2013a). *EU Citizenship Report 2013 EU Citizens: Your Rights, Your Future*, COM(2013) 269 Final Brussels.

European Commission. (2013b). Europe for Citizens: Europe for Citizens Programme 2007–2013, Programme Guide.

European Commission. (2014a). European Union Supports Key Reforms in the Republic of Moldova. Accessed at: http://europa.eu/rapid/press-release _IP-14–886_en.htm.

European Commission. (2014b). *Neighbourhood at the Crossroads: Implementation of the European Neighbourhood Policy in 2013* (SWD(2014) 99 final), Accessed 23 March 2016 at: http://eeas.europa.eu/enp/pdf/2014/regional/ eastern_partnership_report.pdf.

European Commission. (2014a). *Citizens 2014*, http://europa.eu/citizens-2013/.

European Commission. (2014b). The European Citizens' Initiative, Accessed 6 August 2017 at: http://ec.europa.eu/citizens-initiative/public/basic-facts.

European Commission. (2015). Commission Reports on Visa-Free Travel from the Western Balkans; Press Release 25 February, Brussels.

European Commission. (2015a). *Support for the Eastern Partnership*. Directorate-General for Neighbourhood and Enlargement Negotiations. Luxembourg: European Union. Accessed on 2 August 2016 at: ec.europa.eu/enlargement/neighbourhood/pdf/eastern-partnership-results-2014pdf.

European Commission. (2015b). *Review of the European Neighbourhood Policy* (JOIN(2015) 50 final). Accessed 15 March 2016 at: http://eeas.europa.eu/enp/documents/2015/151118_joint-communication_review-of-the-enp_en.pdf.

European Commission. (2015c). ENP Country Progress Report 2014 – Republic of Moldova. Accessed 8 August 2017 at: http://europa.eu/rapid/press-release_MEMO-15-4682_en.htm.

European Commission. (2015d). EU–Turkey Joint Action Plan, Brussels: MEMO/15/5860. Accessed 6 August 2017 at: http://europa.eu/rapid/press-release_MEMO-15-5860_en.htm.

European Commission. (2016a). *Managing the Refugee Crisis: EU-Turkey Joint Action Plan: Implementation Report*: Brussels.

European Commission. (2016b). International Cooperation And Development: Building partnerships for change in developing countries, http://ec.europa.eu/europeaid/home_en

European Commission. (2016c). Europe for Citizens (2014–2020), http://ec.europa.eu/citizenship/about-the-europe-for-citizens-programme/future-programme-2014–2020/index_en.htm

European Commission. (2016d). The EU motto, https://europa.eu/european-union/about-eu/symbols/motto_en

European Commission. (2016e). EU-Turkey Agreement: Questions and Answers, http://europa.eu/rapid/press-release_MEMO-16–963_en.htm

European Council. (1992). Conclusions of the Edinburgh Presidency.

European Council. (2016a). Remarks by President Donald Tusk following the first session of the European Council meeting, Statements and remarks 74/16, Brussels.

European Council (2016b). *Conclusions on migration*, Press Release 72/16, Brussels.

European Economic Community. (1963). *EEC-Turkey Association Agreement*, Official Journal L217, EIF 29 December 1964, http://ec.europa.eu/world/agreements/prepareCreateTreatiesWorkspace/treatiesGeneralData.do?step=0&redirect=true&treatyId=172.

European External Action Service. (2014). *European Neighbourhood Instrument 2014–2020, Programming Document*, http://eeas.europa-eu/enp/documents/financing-theenp/index_en.htm.

European External Action Service. (2014). *Strategy Paper and Multiannual Indicative Programme for EU support to Belarus (2014–2017)*. Accessed 23 March 2016 at: http://eeas.europa.cu/enp/pdf/financing-the-enp/belarus_2014_2017_programming_document_en.pdf.

European External Action Service. (n.d.). EU Relations with Belarus. Accessed 23 March 2016 at: http://eeas.europa.eu.

European External Action Service. (n.d.). The Eastern Partnership Multilateral Platforms. Accessed 30 August at: http://eeas.europa.eu/eastern/platforms/index_en/htm.

European Union. (1995). Partnership and Cooperation Agreement between the European Communities and their Member States and the Republic of Kazakhstan. Accessed 15 August 2011 at: http://eur-lex.europa.eu/LexUriServ/LexUriServ.do?uri=CELEX:21999A0728%2802%29:EN:NOT

European Union. (2006). Ministerial Declaration on Enhanced Energy Co-Operation Between the EU, the Littoral States of the Black and Caspian Seas and their Neighbouring Countries. Accessed 15 August 2011 at: http://ec.europa.eu/dgs/ energy_transport/international/regional/caspian/energy_en.htm

European Union. (2009). *The European Union and Central Asia: The New Partnership in Action.* Accessed 15 August 2011 at: http://www.eeas.europa.eu/ central_asia/docs/2010_strategy_eu_centralasia_en.pdf.

European Union. (2016). *Relations with Russia: EU's Guiding Principles.* EEAS, 15 March 2016. Accessed 2 April 2016 at: http://eeas.europa.eu/delegations/russia/ press_corner/all_news/news/2016/20160315_en.htm.

Eurostat. (2011). *Eurostat Statistics in Focus*, 69/2011. Brussels: European Commission.

Fadeeva, T.M. (2009). Politika evropeizatsii (svodnyi referat). *Sozialnye, gumanitarnye nauki. Otechestvennaya i zarubezhnaya literatura. Seriya 5: Istoriya. Referativnyi zhurnal*, 4, 119–126.

Fairclough, N. (2013). *Critical Discourse Analysis: The Critical Study of Language.* London: Routledge.

Featherstone, K. (2003). Introduction: In the Name of Europe. In K. Featherstone. and C. Radaelli (eds), *The Politics of Europeanisation* (pp. 3–36). Oxford: Oxford University Press.

Feklyunina, V. (2008). The 'Great Diversification Game': Russia's Vision of the European Union's Energy Projects in the Shared Neighbourhood. *Journal of Contemporary European Research*, 4(2), 130–148.

Fernandes, S. (2016). The European Union Institutional Balance: Assessment of its Impact on the Relationship with Russia. In T. Cicero (ed.), *The European Union Neighbourhood: Challenges and Opportunities* (pp. 143–171). London: Routledge.

Fernandez, A.M. (2006). The Europeanisation of Consular Affairs: The Case of Visa Policy. Discussion Papers in Diplomacy. The Hague: Netherlands Institute of International Relations 'Clingendael'.

Fierke, K. M., and Wiener, A. (1999). Constructing Institutional Interests: EU and NATO Enlargement. *Journal of European Public Policy*, 6(5), 721–742.

Finnemore, M. and Sikkink, K. (1998). International Norm Dynamics and Political Change. *International Organization*, 52(4), 887–917.

Flenley, P. (2008). Russia and the EU: The Clash of New Neighbourhoods? *Journal of Contemporary European Studies*, 16(2), 189–202.

Flenley, P. (2015). The Partnership for Modernisation: Contradictions of the Russian Modernisation Agenda. *European Politics and Society*, 16(1), 11–26. doi: 10.1080/15705854.2014.965893.

Fligstein, N. (2008). *Euroclash: The EU, European Identity and the Future of Europe.* Oxford: Oxford University Press.

Flockhart, T. (2005). Complex Socialization and the Transfer of Democratic Norms. In T. Flockhart (ed.), *Socializing Democratic Norms: the Role of International Organizations for the Construction of Europe* (pp. 42–62). Basingstoke: Palgrave.

Flockhart, T. (2010). Europeanisation or EU-ization? The Transfer of European Norms across Time and Space. *Journal of Common Market Studies*, 48(4), 785–810.

Foucault, M. (2007). *Security, Territory, Population: Lectures at the Collège de France 1977–78.* Basingstoke: Palgrave Macmillan.

Franke, A., Gawrich, A., and Alakbarov, G. (2009). Kazakhstan and Azerbaijan as Post-Soviet Rentier States: Resource Incomes and Autocracy as a Double 'Curse' in Post-Soviet Regimes. *Europe-Asia Studies*, 61(1), 109–140.

Freedom House. (2009a). Freedom in the World: Georgia, https://freedomhouse.org/report/freedom-world/2009/georgia-.U4w6KPldXKg.

Freedom House. (2009b). Freedom in the World: Russia, https://freedomhouse.org/report/freedom-world/2009/russia-.U4w5nvldXKg.

Freedom House. (2010). Nations in Transit: Moldova, https://freedomhouse.org/report/nations-transit/2010/moldova

Freedom House. (2013a). Freedom in the World: Armenia, https://freedomhouse.org/report/freedom-world/2013/armenia-.U4tZbxa1Hpg.

Freedom House. (2013b). Freedom in the World: Azerbaijan, https://freedomhouse.org/report/freedom-world/2013/azerbaijan-.U4tZpxa1Hpg.

Freedom House. (2013c). Freedom in the World: Georgia, https://freedomhouse.org/report/freedom-world/2013/georgia-.U4tYLha1Hpg.

Freedom House. (2014). Freedom in the World: Turkey, https://freedomhouse.org/report/freedom-world/2014/turkey-0-.U4yAmfldXKg.

Frontex. (2016). Migratory Routes Map: Main migratory Routes into the EU/land and Sea. Accessed at: http://frontex.europa.eu/trends-and-routes/migratory-routes-map/

Fukuyama, F. (1992). *The End of History and the Last Man.* New York: The Free Press.

Fundamental Freedoms: The Primacy of Domestic Politics, *Journal of Balkan and Near Eastern Studies*, 16(1), 86–101.

Furness, M. (2013). Who controls the European External Action Service? Agent Autonomy in the EU External Policy, *European Foreign Affairs Review*, 18, 103–126.

Galtung, J. (1973). *The European Community: A Superpower in the Making.* London: Allen & Unwin.

Gänzle, S., and Müntel, G. (2011). Europeanization 'Beyond' Europe? EU Impact on Domestic Policies in the Russian Enclave of Kaliningrad. *Journal of Baltic Studies*, 42(1), 57–79.

Gartzke, E., and Weisinger, A. (2013). Permanent Friends? Dynamic Difference and the Democratic Peace. *International Studies Quarterly*, 57, 171–185.

Gawrich, A., Melnykovska, I. and Schweikert, R. (2010). Neighbourhood Europe-anization through the ENP: the Case of Ukraine. *Journal of Common Market Studies*, 48(5), 1209–1235.

Geybullayeva, A. (2014). Azerbaijan: Treason and Other Charades, www.aljazeera.com/indepth/opinion/2014/04/azerbaijan-treason-other-charad-201443071951458121.html.

Giesen, B. (2003). The Collective Identity of Europe. In W, Spohn., and A, Trian-dafyllidou (eds), *Europeanisation, National Identities and Migration* (pp. 21–35). London: Routledge.

Gilbert, M. (2012). *European Integration: a Concise History.* New York: Rowman & Littlefield.

Gillingham, J. (1991). *Coal, Steel, and the Rebirth of Europe, 1945–1955: the Germans and French from Ruhr Conflict to Economic Community.* Cambridge: Cambridge University Press.

Giragosian, R. (2014). Armenia's "Game of Thrones", www.armenialiberty.org/articleprintview/25333731.html.

Gleditsch, N.P. (1995). Democracy and the Future of European Peace. *European Journal of International Relations*, 1(4), 539–571.

Götz, R. (2008). A Pipeline Race Between the EU and Russia. In K. Barysch (ed), *Pipelines, Politics and Power: The Future of EU-Russia Energy Relations* (pp. 93–101). London: Centre for European Reform.

Grabbe, H. (2000). The sharp edges of Europe: Extending Schengen Eastwards. *International Affairs* 76(3), 519–536.

Grabbe, H. (2006). *The EU's Transformative Power: Europeanization through Conditionality in Central and Eastern Europe*. Basingstoke: Palgrave Macmillan.

Greenberg, R. D. (2004). *Language and Identity in the Balkans: Serbo-Croatian and its Disintegration*. Oxford: Oxford University Press.

Greenfeld, L. (1992). *Nationalism: Five Roads to Modernity*. Cambridge: Harvard University Press.

Grey, J. (2015). The Sorcery of Numbers – An Essay, *The Guardian Review*, pp. 19–20. 14 March.

Gromoglasova, E. S. (2010). Koncepcija evropeizacii v zarubezhnoj politologii. *Vestnik Moskovskogo universiteta. Serija 25. Mezhdunarodnye otnoshenija i mirovaja politika*, 4, 27–43

Groszkowski, J. (2015). Czech Dilemmas over Russia and NATO. *OSW Analyses*. Accessed 25 November 2015 at: www.osw.waw.pl/en/publikacje/analyses/2015–04–01/czech-dilemmas-over-russia-and-nato.

Gülalp, H. (2001). Globalization and Political Islam: the Social Bases of Turkey's Welfare Party. *International Journal of Middle East Studies*, 33(3), 433–448.

Guliyev, F. (2013). Oil and Regime Stability in Azerbaijan. *Demokratizatsiya*, 21(1), 113–147.

Habermas, J. (2003). Towards a Cosmopolitan Europe. *Journal of Democracy*, 14(4), 86 – 100.

Habermas, J., and Derrida, G. (2003). What Binds Europe, Together? Plea for a Common Foreign Policy, *Frankfurter Allgemeine Zeitung*, 31 May.

Haddon, L., et al. (2015). *History and Policy-making – a Report*. London: Institute of Government.

Hadfield, A. (2008). Energy and Foreign Policy: EU–Russia Energy Dynamics. In S. Smith, T. Dunne, and A. Hadfield (eds). *Foreign Policy: Theories, Actors, Cases* (pp. 321–338). Oxford: Oxford University Press.

Hafner, M. (2015). The Southern Gas Corridor and the EU Gas Security of Supply: What's Next? Accessed 16 April 2016 at: www.naturalgaseurope.com/southern-gas-corridor-and-eu-gas-security-of-supply-22688

Hagemann, C. (2013). External Governance on the Terms of the Partner? The EU, Russia and the Republic of Moldova in the European Neighbourhood Policy. *Journal of European Integration*, 35(7), 767–783. doi: 10.1080/07036337.2012.732073.

Hall, P.A. (1993). Policy Paradigms, Social Learning, and the State: The Case of Economic Policymaking in Britain. *Comparative Politics*, 25(3), 275–296.

Harutunyan, S. (2014). Karabakh Linked To Armenian Foreign Policy Change. Accessed 6 August 2017 at: https://www.azatutyun.am/content/article/25375439.html.

Haukkala, H. (2008). The European Union as a Regional Normative Hegemon: The Case of The European Neighbourhood Policy. *Europe-Asia Studies*, 60(9), 1601–1622.

Haukkala, H. (2015). From Cooperative to Contested Europe? The Conflict in Ukraine as a Culmination of a Long-Term Crisis in EU-Russia Relations. *Journal of Contemporary European Studies*, 23(1), 25–40.

Headley, J. (2008). *The Europeanisation of the World: on the origins of Human Rights and Democracy*. Princeton: Princeton University Press.

Headley, J. (2012). Is Russia out of step with European norms? Assessing Russia's relationship to European identity, values and norms through the issue of self-determination. *Europe-Asia Studies*, 64(3), 427–447.

Heater, D. (2004). *Citizenship: The Civic Ideal in World History, Politics and Education*. Manchester: Manchester University Press.

Heper, M. (2005). The EU, Turkish Military and Democracy. *South European Society and Politics*, 10(1), 33–44.

Héritier, A. (2001). Differential Europe: the European Union Impact on National Policy-making. In A. Héritier, D. Kerwer, C. Knill, D. Lehmkuhl, M. Teutsch, and A.-C. Douillet (eds), *Differential Europe – the European Union Impact on National Policy-Making* (pp. 1–21). Lanham: Rowman & Littlefield.

Hernandez, I., and Segrera, R. (2014). The Impact of Visa Liberalisation in Eastern Partnership Countries, Russia and Turkey on Trans-Border Mobility; CEPS Paper in Liberty and Security, *Centre for European Policy Studies*.

Herrmann, R., and Brewer, M.B. (2004). Identities and Institutions: Becoming European in the EU. In R. K. Herrmann, T. Risse, and B. M. Brewer (eds), *Transnational Identities: Becoming European in the EU* (pp. 1 – 22). Lanham: Rowman & Littlefield.

Hett, F., Kikić, S. and Meuser, S. (eds). (2015). *Reassessing the European Neighbourhood Policy: The Eastern Dimension*. Friedrich-Ebert-Stiftung: Perspectives, http://library.fes.de/pdf-files/id-moe/11483.pdf.

Hettne, B. (1995). *Development Theory and the Three Worlds* (2nd edn). Harlow: Longmans.

Hill, C. (1993). The Capability-Expectations Gap, or Conceptualizing Europe's International Role. *Journal of Common Market Studies*, 31(3), 305–328.

Hintz, L. (2013). Identity contestation and Turkey's EU stalemate. *Turkish Policy Quarterly*, 12(1), 149–159.

Hobson. J. (2004). *The Eastern Origins of Western Civilisations*. Cambridge: Cambridge University Press.

Hodson, D. (2015). Eurozone Governance: Deflation, Grexit 2.0 and the Second Coming of Jean-Claude Juncker. *Journal of Common Market Studies*, 53(S1), 144–161.

Hoen, H. (2013). Good Governance in Central and Eastern Europe: the European Union as an Anchor for Reform. *Economic and Environmental Studies*, 13(2), 95–112.

Hogan-Brun, G (ed.). (2005). Language and Social Processes in the Baltic Republics Surrounding their EU Accession. *Journal of Multilingual and Multicultural Development (Special issue)*, 26(5).

Hogan-Brun, G., and Melnyk, S. (2012). Language Policy Management in the Former Soviet Sphere. In B. Spolsky (ed), *Language Policy*. Cambridge: Cambridge University Press.

Horky-Hluchan, O. and Kratochvil, P. (2014). Nothing is Imposed in this Policy: The Construction and Constriction of the European Neighbourhood. *Alternatives: Global. Local, Political*, 39(4), 252–270.

Hrayr Maroukhian Foundation. (2013). *Monopolies in Armenia*. Accessed 10 August 2017: http://www.maroukhianfoundation.org/english/wp-content/uploads /2013/02/Monopolies-eng-web.pdf.

Hrytsak, Y. (2002). Twenty Two Ukraines. *Krytyka*, 4, 3–6. (Грицак, Я. (2002). 'Двадцять дві України', Критика, 4, с. 3–6).

Huelsse, R. (2006). Imagine the EU: the Metaphorical Construction of a Supra-nationalist Identity. *Journal of International Relations and Development*, 9.

Hungarian Government (2015). *We have Strengthened our Cooperation with Russia (17 February 2015)*. Accessed 4 November 2015 at: www.kormany.hu/en/ the-prime-minister/news/we-have-strengthened-our-cooperation-with-russia.

Hungarian Spectrum. (2013). *Viktor Orbán in Moscow: 'Putin's New Little Kitten*. Accessed 12 January 2016 at: http://hungarianspectrum.org/2013/02/01/viktor-Orbán-in-moscow-putins-new-little-kitten/.

Huntington, S.P. (1996). *The Clash of Civilizations and the Remaking of World Order*. New York: Simon & Schuster.

Hurd, E. S. (2006). Negotiating Europe: the Politics of Religion and the Prospects for Turkish Accession, *Review of International Studies*, 32(03), 401–418.

Hutchinson, J. (2003). Enduring Nations and the Illusions of European Integration. In W. Spohn, and A. Triandafyllidou (eds), *Europeanisation, National Identities and Migration: Changes in Boundary Constructions Between Western and Eastern Europe* (pp. 36–51). London: Routledge,

Huysmans, J. (2000). The European Union and the Securitisation of Migration. *Journal of Common Market Studies*, 38(5), 751–777.

IISEPS. (2015). *Trends of Change in Belarusian Public Opinion 2015*. Accessed 23 March 2016 at: www.iiseps.org.

Ilko Kucheriv Foundation. (2014a). *Public Perception of the Foreign Policy Vector of Ukraine: Regional Distribution*. Accessed 8 April 2016 at: http:// dif.org.ua/ua/polls/2014_polls/stavlennja-gromadjan-do-zovnishnopolitichnogo-vektoru-ukraini-regionalnii-rozriz_1412015523.htm.

Ilko Kucheriv Foundation. (2014b). Foreign Policy Orientations of the Population of Ukraine: Regional, Age, Electoral Distribution and Dynamics. Accessed 8 April 2016 at: http://dif.org.ua/ua/polls/2014_polls/mlvbkrfgbkprhkprtkp.htm.

Ilko Kucheriv Foundation. (2015). What Unites and Divides Ukrainians – Public Opinion Poll in Ukraine. Accessed 8 April 2016 at: http://dif.org.ua/en/polls/2015a/ sho-obednue-ta-rozednue-.htm.

Infotag (2002). Proyekt kontseptsii vneshney politiki Moldovy opredelyaet evropey-skuyu integratsiyu v kachestve prioritetnoy zadachi, Accessed at: http://press.try.md/ item.php?id=15523.

Inotai, A. (2015). Hungary on the Way from a Liberal to Illiberal System. Introduc-tory Remarks. *Südost-Europa*, 2(63), 167–172.

Institutul de Politici Publice. (2015). *Barometrul Opiniei Publice: Dinamica răspunsurilor (aprilie 2003–martie 2015)*. Accessed at: http://ipp.md/public/files/Barometru /BOP_04.2015_anexa.pdf.

International Organisation for Migration (IOM). (2016). *Migration Flows – Europe Interactive Map*. Accessed at: http://migration.iom.int/europe/.

Ioffe, G. (2012a). Belarus Defies Clichés. *Eurasia Daily Monitor*, 9(117). Accessed 23 March 2016 at: www.jamestown.org/single/?no_cache=1andtx_ttnews [tt_news]=39514.

Ioffe, G. (2012b). Who Is Losing Belarus? *Eurasia Daily Monitor*, 9(22). Accessed 23 March 2016 at: www.jamestown.org/programs/edm/single/?tx_ttnews %5btt_news%5d=38959.

Isin, E.F. and Turner, B. (eds). (2002). *Handbook of Citizenship Studies*. London: Sage.

Jernudd, B., and Nekvapil, J. (2012). History of the Field: a Sketch. In B. Spolsky (ed.), *The Cambridge Handbook of Language Policy*. Cambridge: Cambridge University Press.

Johnson, B., and Christensen, L. (2014). *Educational Research – Quantitative, Qualitative, and Mixed Approaches*. London: Sage Publications.

Joint Declaration of the Eastern Partnership Summit, 28–29 November 2013. Accessed 23 March 2016 at: http://www.eu2013.lt/en/news/statements/-joint-declaration-of-the-eastern-partnership-summit-vilnius-28–29-november-2013.

Jones, S. (1994). Populism in Georgia: The Gamsakhurdia Phenomenon. In D. V. Schwartz and R. Panossian (eds), *Nationalism and History: The Politics of Nation Building in Post-Soviet Armenia, Azerbaijan and Georgia* (pp. 127–149). Toronto: University of Toronto – Centre for Russian and East European Studies.

Judt, T. (2004). Dreams of Empire. *New York Review of Books*, November (4), 38–41.

Kahanec. M., and Zimmermann, K.F. (eds). (2010). *EU Labour Markets After Post-Enlargement*. Berlin: Springer Verlag.

Kaina, V. (2013). How to Reduce Disorder in European Identity Research? *European Political Science*, 12, 184–196.

Kaina, V. and Karolewski, I.P. (2013). EU Governance and European Identity. *Living Reviews in European Governance*, 8(1), 1–41.

Kakachia, K., and Cecire, M. (eds). (2013). *Georgian Foreign Policy: the Quest for Sustainable Security*. Tbilisi: Konrad-Adenauer-Stiftung.

Kalan, D. (2014). They Who Sow the Wind … Hungary's Opening to the East. *Bulletin of the Polish Institute of International Affairs*, 37.

Kalicki. J. (2001). Caspian Energy at the Crossroads. *Foreign Affairs*, 80(5), 120–134.

Kalinichenko, P.A. (2013). Evropeizacija rossijskoj sudebnoj praktiki (na primere vlijanija prava evropejskogo sojuza na reshenija rossijskih sudov). *Lex Russica*, 95(11), 1224–1234.

Kambas, M. (2015). Cyprus Says Cannot Lift Veto on Turkey's EU Talks. *Reuters*, Accessed 6 August 2017 at: www.reuters.com/article/us-cyprus-turkey-cu -idUSKCN0SD0TH20151019.

Kant, I. (1795). Perpetual Peace: A Philosophical Sketch. Accessed 6 August 2017 from https://www.mtholyoke.edu/acad/intrel/kant/kant1.htm.

Kanter, C. (2006). Collective Identity as Shared Ethical Self-understanding: the Case of the Emerging European identity. *European Journal of Social Theory*, 9(4), 501–523.

Kapitonenko, M. (2015). The European Neighborhood Policy's Eastern Dimension: the Impact of the Ukrainian crisis. Neighbourhood Policy Paper, Center for International and European Studies, Kadir Has University, July, 1–8. Accessed 10 December

2015   at: www.khas.edu.tr/cms/cies/dosyalar/files/NeighbourhoodPolicyPaper
%2815%29.pdf.

Kaplan, R., and Baldauf, R.B. (eds). (2008). *Language Planning and Policy in Europe: The Baltic States, Ireland and Italy*, Multilingual Matters.

Karolewski, I.P. (2009). European Nationalism and European Identity. In *Multiplicity of Nationalism in Contemporary Europe*, Plymouth: Rowman & Littlefield, 59 – 80.

Karolewski, I.P. (2011). *The Nation and Nationalism: An Introduction*. Edinburgh: Edinburgh University Press.

Kascian, K. (2013). Grigory Ioffe's Misunderstood Belarus. *Belarusian Review*, 25(1), 8–11. Accessed 23 March 2016 at: http://thepointjournal.com/output/index.php?art_id=212andspr_change=eng.

Kascian, K. (2014). Belarus–EU Relations: Ad Hoc Actions vs Pre-developed Strategy. *Belarusian Review Working Paper*, 2, 1–10. Accessed 23 March 2016 at: http://thepointjournal.com/fa/library/brwp-02.pdf.

Kascian, K. (2016). Putinskoe pugalo rusofobii. Belorussky kontekst. *Newsader*. Accessed 23 March 2016 at: http://newsader.com/mention/tak-kto-zhe-zatevaet-rusofobiyu/.

Katzenstein, P.J. (2006). Multiple Modernities as Limits to Secular EU-ization? In T. A. Byrnes, and P. J. Katzenstein (ed.), *Religion in an Expanding Europe*. Cambridge: Cambridge University Press.

Kearns, I. (1997). Croatian Politics: Democracy or Authoritarianism? Paper presented to the Political Studies Association Conference on Eastern Europe.

Kelley, J. (2006). New Wine in Old Wineskins: Promoting Political Reforms through the New European Neighbourhood Policy. *Journal of Common Market Studies*, 44(1), 29–55.

Kennedy, R. (2010). Moldova. In D. Ó Beacháin and A. Polese (eds), *The Colour Revolutions in the Former Soviet Republics. Successes and Failures*. London: Routledge.

Keukeleire S. (2014). Lessons for the Practice and Analysis of EU Diplomacy from an 'Outside-in' Perspective. In S. Gstohl and E. Lannon (eds), *The Neighbours of the European Union's Neighbours: Diplomatic and Geopolitical Dimensions beyond the European Neighbourhood Policy* (pp. 227–241). Ashgate: Farnham.

Klimovich, A.I., and Shirokanova, A.A. (2011). Belarus i ES: Evropeizacija ili region-alizacija. *Sovremennaja Evropa*, 3, 32–45.

Klipii, I. (2002). Evolution of political framework of the European Integration problem. In A. Barbăroşie and V. Gheorghiu (eds), *The Republic of Moldova and the European Integration* (pp. 9–36). Chişinău: Cartier.

Knill, C. (2001). *The Europeanisation of National Administrations*. Cambridge: Cambridge University Press.

Kolstø, P. (1995). *Russians in the Former Soviet Republics*. Bloomington: Indiana University Press.

Kolstø, P. (1995). *Russians in the Former Soviet Republics*. London: Hurst.

Kolstø, P. (ed.). (2002). *National Integration and Violent Conflict in Post-Soviet Societies: The Cases of Estonia and Moldova*. Lanham: Rowman & Littlefield.

Kolstø, P., and Blakkisrud, H. (2008). Living with Non-recognition: State- and Nation-building in South Caucasian Quasi-states. *Europe-Asia Studies*, 60(3), 483–509.

Konoplyanik, A., and Wälde, T. (2006). *Energy Charter Treaty and its Role in International Energy*. Accessed 12 August 2012 at: http://konoplyanik.ru/ru/publications/articles/410-JENRL-11.2006.pdf.

Kopstein, J. (2006). The Transatlantic Divide over Democracy Promotion. *The Washington Quarterly*, 29(2), 85–98.

Kornienko, T.A. (2013). Evropeizacija kak normativno-politicheskij kontekst tureckoj modernizacii. *Istoricheskaja i socialno-obrazovatelnaya mysl*, 5(21), 140–145.

Korosteleva, E.A. (2010). Moldova's European Choice: 'Between Two Stools'? *Europe-Asia Studies*, 62(8), 1267–1289. doi: 10.1080/09668136.2010.504383.

Korosteleva E.A. (2011). Change or Continuity: is the Eastern Partnership an Adequate Tool for the European Neighbourhood? *International Relations*, 25, 243–262.

Korosteleva, E.A. (2012). *The European Union and its Eastern Neighbours: Towards a more Ambitious Partnership*. London: Routledge.

Korosteleva, E.A. (2014). The EU has Successfully Pursued a Strategy of Democracy Promotion by Technocratic means in Belarus. [Weblog]. Accessed 23 March 2016 at: http://blogs.lse.ac.uk/europpblog/2014/10/06/the-eu-has-successfully-pursued-a-strategy-of-democracy-promotion-by-technocratic-means-in-belarus/.

Kostanyan, H. (2014). Examining the Discretion of the EEAS: What Power to Act in the EU–Moldova Agreement? *European Foreign Affairs Review*, 19 (3), 373–392.

Kostanyan, H. (2015a). Turf Wars and Control Issues in EU Eastern Policies: Opening the Black Box of the EU Institutions and the Member States. In A. Hug (ed.), *Trouble in the Neighbourhood? The Future of the EU's Eastern Partnership?* London: Foreign Policy Centre and European Commission.

Kostanyan, H. (2015b). The European Neighbourhood Policy Reviewed: Will Pragmatism Trump Normative Values? *European Neighbourhood Watch*, 121, December. Brussels: CEPS.

Kostrigin, A.A. (2015). Osobennosti realizacii vysshego obrazovanija na sovremennom jetape razvitija obshhestva. *Nauka. Mysl*, 1, 29–39.

Kovacovska, L. (2007). European Union's energy (In)Security-Dependence on Russia. *Defence and Strategy*, 7(2), 5–21.

Kratochvíl, P. (2008). The Discursive Resistance to EU-Enticement: The Russian Elite and (the Lack of) Europeanisation. *Europe-Asia Studies*, 60(3), 397–422.

Kratochvíl, P., and Kuchyňková, P. (2010). Russia in the Czech Foreign Policy. In M. Kořan (ed.), *Czech Foreign Policy in 2007–2009: An Analysis*. Prague: Institute of International Relations.

Kremlin.ru. (31 August 2008). Interview given by Dmitry Medvedev to Television Channels Channel One, Rossia, NTV. Accessed at: http://en.kremlin.ru/events/president/transcripts/48301

Krushelnycky, A. (2013). The End of Ukraine's Balancing Act. *Foreign Policy*, 6 (February). Accessed 12 November 2015 at: http://foreignpolicy.com/2013/02/06/the-end-of-ukraines-balancing-act/.

Kubicek, P. (2016). Dancing with the Devil: Explaining the European Union's Engagement with Ukraine under Viktor Yanukovych. *Journal of Contemporary European Studies*, http://dx.doi.org/10.1080/14782804.2016

Kuhn, T. (1970). *The Structure of Scientific Revolutions*. Chicago: Chicago University Press.

Kuhn, T. (2015). *Experiencing European integration: Transnational Lives and European Identity*. Oxford: Oxford University Press.

Kurki, M. (2011). Democracy through Technocracy? Reflections on Technocratic Assumptions in EU Democracy Promotion Discourse. *Journal of Intervention and Statebuilding*, 5(2), 211–234.

Kushner, D. (1997). Self-Perception and Identity in Contemporary Turkey. *Journal of Contemporary History*, 32(2), 219–233.

Kuzio, T. (1998). *Ukraine: State and Nation Building*. London: Routledge.

Kymlicka, W. and Patten, A. (2003). Introduction. Language Rights and Political Theory: Context, Issues and Approaches. In W. Kymlicka and A. Patten (eds), *Language Rights and Political Theory*. Oxford: Oxford University Press.

Laca, P. and Tomek, R. (2014). EU Drive to Sanction Russia Bogs Down where Soviet Tanks Rumbled, *Ekathimerini.com*, 4 September. Accessed 11 March 2016 at: www.ekathimerini.com/162784/article/ekathimerini/business/eu-drive-to-sanction-russia-bogs-down-where-soviet-tanks-rumbled

Ladrech, R. (1994). The Europeanization of Domestic Politics and Institutions: The Case of France. *Journal of Common Market Studies*, 31(1), 69–88.

Laffan, B. (2006). Managing Europe from home in Dublin, Athens and Helsinki: A comparative analysis. *West European Politics*, 29(4), 687–708.

Laitin, D. (1998). *Identity in Formation: The Russian-Speaking Populations in the Near Abroad*. Ithaca, NY: Cornell University Press.

Landau, J.M. (ed.). (1983). *Atatürk and the Modernization of Turkey*. Boulder: Westview Press.

Langbein, J. (2013). Unpacking the Russian and EU Impact on Policy Change in the Eastern Neighbourhood: The Case of Ukraine's Telecommunications and Food Safety. *Europe-Asia-Studies*, 65(4), 631–657.

Langbein, J. (2014). European Union Governance towards the Eastern Neighbourhood: Transcending or Redrawing Europe's East-West Divide? *Journal of Common Market Studies*, 52(1), 157–174.

Langbein, J. and Börzel, T. (2013). Introduction: Explaining Policy Change in the European Union's Eastern Neighbourhood. *Europe-Asia Studies*, 65(4), 573–580.

Langbein, J., and Wolczuk, K. (2012). Convergence without Membership? The Impact of the European Union in the Neighbourhood: Evidence from Ukraine. *Journal of European Public Policy*, 19(6), 863–881.

Larner, W., and Walters, W. (eds). (2006). *Global Governmentality: Governing International Spaces*. London: Routledge.

Latkina, V.A. (2013). Fenomen evropeizacii v zapadnoevropejskih issledovanijah. *Mezhdunarodnye process*, 11(32).

Latkina, V.A. (2014). Politika Evropejskogo sojuza v sredizemnomor'e v kontekste "arabskoj vesny". *Vestnik MGIMO Universiteta*, 2(35), 139–149.

Latvian EU Presidency. (2015). *The Programme of the Latvian Presidency of the Council of the EU*. Accessed 23 March 2016 at: https://eu2015.lv/images/PRES_prog_2015_EN-final.pdf.

Lavenex, S. (2004). EU external governance in Wider Europe. *Journal of European Public Policy*, 11(4), 680–700.

Lavenex, S. (2006). Shifting Up and Out: The Foreign Policy of European Immigration Control. *West European Politics*, 29(2), 329–350.

Lavenex, S., and Wichmann, N. (2009). The External Governance of EU Internal Security. *Journal of European Integration*, 31(1), 83–102.

Lavenex, S., Lehmkuhl, D., and Wichmann, N. (2009). Modes of External Governance: a Cross-National and Cross-Sectoral Comparison, *Journal of European Public Policy*, 16(6), 791–812.

Lavrov, S.V. (2007). Otnosheniya Rossiya-ES: komleksnyi podkhod' Izvestiya. Accessed 14 August 2007 at: http:www.mid.ru/brp

Lavrov, S.V. (2014). Sergey Lavrov: Throwing Russia off Balance Is Ultimate Aim. Interview. *TASS, Russian News Agency*, 11 September.

Lavrov, S.V. (2015). Vystuplenie i otvety na voprosy SMI Ministra inostrannyh del Rossii S.V. Lavrova v hode sovmestnoi press-konferentsii po itogam peregovorov s Predsedatelem KMCE, zamestitelem Premier-ministra, Ministrom inostrannyh i evropeiskih del Belgii D. Reindersom, Moscow, 9 April, *RussianMission. eu*. Accessed 1 September 2015 at: www.russianmission.eu/ru/novosti/пресс-к онференция-по-итогам-переговоров-свлаврова-с-дрейндерсом

Lavrov, S.V. (2016). Russia's Foreign Policy: Historical Background. *Russia in Global Affairs*, Accessed 1 July 2016 at: www.mid.ru/en/foreign_policy/news/-/ asset_publisher/cKNonkJE02Bw/content/id/2124391

Layne, C. (1994). Kant or Cant: The Myth of the Democratic Peace. *International Security*, 19(2), 5–49.

Leonard, M., and Popescu, N. (2007). *A Power Audit of EU-Russia Relations*. London: European Council on Foreign Relations.

Levada. (2016a). Otnoshenie k organam vlasti. Accessed 3 July 2016 at: www.levada.ru/ indikatory/odobrenie-organov-vlasti/.

Levada. (2016b). Otnosheniya k stranam. Accessed 3 July 2016 at: www.levada.ru/ indikatory/otnoshenie-k-stranam/.

Levy, J.S. (1988). Domestic Politics in War. In R. I. Rotberg and T. K. Rabb (eds), *The Origin and Prevention of Major Wars* (pp. 79–100). Cambridge: Cambridge University Press.

Libaridian, G.J. (1999). *The Challenge of Statehood: Armenian Political Thinking Since Independence*. Watertown: Blue Crane Books.

Libaridian, G.J. (2004). *Modern Armenia: People, Nation, State*. New Brunswick: Transaction Publishers.

Lindstrom, N. (2003). Between Europe and the Balkans: Mapping Slovenia and Croatia's 'Return to Europe' in the 1990s. *Dialectical Anthropology* 27, 313–329.

Lithuanian EU Presidency. (2013). *Programme of the Lithuanian Presidency of the Council of the EU. For a credible, growing and open Europe*. Accessed 23 March 2016 at: http://static.eu2013.lt/uploads/documents/Presidency_programme_EN .pdf.

Lo Bianco, J. (1987). *National Policy on Languages*. Canberra: Australian Government Publishing Services.

Lomakina, I.S. (2012). Evropeizatsiya obrazovatelnoj politiki. *Pedagogika*, 3, 113–120.

Löwenhardt, J. (2005). Belarus and the West. In S. White, E. Korosteleva, and J. Löwenhardt (eds), *Postcommunist Belarus* (pp. 143–159). Lanham: Rowman & Littlefield.

Löwenhardt, J., Hill, R.J., and Light, M. (2001). A Wider Europe: The View from Minsk and Chisinau. *International Affairs*, 77(3), 605–620. doi: 10.1111 /1468-2346.00209.

Lussac, S. (2010). Ensuring European Energy Security in Russian "Near Abroad": The Case of the South Caucasus, *European Security*, 19(4), 607–625.

MacDonald, D.B. (2002). *Balkan Holocausts? Serbian and Croatian Victim-Centred Propaganda and the War in Yugoslavia.* Manchester: Manchester University Press.

Macedonia Bars Afghan Asylum Seekers, Stoking Violent Clashes. (2016). *New York Times,* 23 February. Accessed at: http://www.nytimes.com/2016/02/24/world/europe/macedonia-afghan-migrant-crisis.html?smid=tw-nytimesworldandsmtyp=curand_r=0

MacFarlane, S.N. (1997). Democratization, Nationalism and Regional Security in the Southern Caucasus. *Government and Opposition,* 32(3), 399–420.

Macmillan, C. (2016). *Discourse, Identity and the Question of Turkish Accession to the EU: Through the Looking Glass.* London: Routledge.

Magen, A. (2005). Shadow of Enlargement: Can the European Neighbourhood Policy Achieve Compliance? *Columbia Journal of European Law,* 12, 383–427.

Magen, A., and Morlino, L. (eds). (2009). *International Actors, Democratization and the Rule of Law: Anchoring Democracy?* London: Routledge.

Magnette, P. (2005). *Citizenship: The History of an Idea.* Colchester: ECPR Press.

Mahony, H., and Spongenberg, H. (2007). Turkey reacts coolly to Sarkozy win, *EU Observer,* 7 May. Available at: https://euobserver.com/enlargement/24009

Mair, P., and Zielonka, J. (2002). *The Enlarged European Union.* London: Frank Cass.

Makili-Aliyev, K. (2013) Azerbaijan's Foreign Policy: Between East and West … *IAI Working Papers.* Rome: Istituto Affari Internazionali.

Malkasian, M. (1996). *'Gha-Ra-Bagh': The Emergence of the National Democratic Movement in Armenia.* Detroit: Wayne State University Press.

Mandelson, P. (2007). The EU and Russia: Our Joint Political Challenge. *European Neighbourhood Watch,* 26(4), Brussels: Centre for European Policy Studies.

Manners, I. (2002). Normative Power Europe: A Contradiction in Terms? *Journal of Common Market Studies,* 40(2), 235–259.

Manners, I. (2006). Normative Power Europe Reconsidered: Beyond the Crossroads. *Journal of European Public Policy,* 13(2), 182–199.

Mannin, M. (ed.). (1999). *Pushing Back the Boundaries: the European Union and Central and Eastern Europe.* Manchester: Manchester University Press.

Mannin, M. (2013). Europeanisation and European Politics. In C. Bretherton, and M. Mannin (eds), *The Europeanisation of European Politics* (pp. 3–24). New York: Palgrave Macmillan.

Mansfield, E.D., and Jackson Preece, J. (2002). Democratic Transitions, Institutional Strength, and War. *International Organization,* 56(2), 297–337.

Mansfield, E.D., and Snyder, J. (1995a). Democratization and the Danger of War. *International Security,* 20(1), 5–38.

Mansfield, E.D., and Snyder, J. (1995b). Democratization and War. *Foreign Affairs,* 74(3), 79–97. doi: 10.2307/20047125

Mansfield, E.D., and Snyder, J. (2002). Incomplete Democratization and the Outbreak of Military Disputes. *International Studies Quarterly,* 46, 529–549.

Mansfield, E.D., and Snyder, J. (2005). *Electing to Fight: Why Emerging Democracies Go To War.* Cambridge: The MIT Press.

March, J.G., and Olsen, J.P. (1989). *Rediscovering Institutions.* New York: Free Press.

March, L., and Herd, G. (2006). Moldova Between Europe and Russia: Inoculating Against the Colored Contagion? *Post-Soviet Affairs*, 22(4), 349–379. doi: 10.2747/1060–586X.22.4.349

Martynau, S. (2010). Hopes and Concerns over the Eastern Partnership – the Belarus' View. *Baltic Rim Economies*, 2(5). Accessed 23 March 2016 at: www.utu.fi/fi/yksikot/tse/yksikot/PEI/BRE/Documents/BRE_2_2010_Web[1].pdf.

Masenko, L. [Пасенко, Л.] (2004) Мова I суспільство. Постколоніальний вимір [Language and society. Postcolonial dimension]. Київ Киево-Могилянська Академія.

Maurais, J. (1991). A Sociolinguistic Comparison between Québec's Charter of the French Language and the 1989 Language Laws of Five Soviet Republics. *Journal of Multilingual and Multicultural Development*, 12(1–2).

Maurais, J. (1997). Regional Majority Languages, Language Planning and Linguistic Rights. *International Journal of the Sociology of Language*, 127, 135–160.

May, S. (2006). Language Policy and Minority Rights. In T. Ricento (ed.), *An Introduction to Language Policy: Theory and Method*. Malden: Blackwell.

McCormick, J. (2010). *Europeanism*. Oxford: Oxford University Press.

McFaul, M. (2007). Ukraine Imports Democracy: External Influences on the Orange Revolution. *International Security*, 32(2), 45–83.

McGowan, F. (2008). Can the European Union's Market Liberalism Ensure Energy Security in a Time of Economic Nationalism. *Journal of Contemporary European Research*, 4(2), 90–106.

Mead, H. (1929). The Nature of the Past. In J. Cass (ed.), *Essays in Honor of John Dewey*. New York: Henry Holt.

Mearsheimer, J.J. (1990). Back to the Future: Instability in Europe after the Cold War. *International Security*, 15(1), 5–56.

Medrano, J.D. (2010). Unpacking European Identity. *Politique Européenne*, 1, 45–66.

Medvedev, D. (2015). Resheniya o sanktsiyah – kollektivnaya otvetstvennost ES. *RIA-Novosti*. Accessed 2 June 2015 at: http://ria.ru/world/20150602/1067777514.html.

Medvedev, Ts. (2008). Diskursy otchuzdeniya: "suverenitet" i "evropeisatsiya" v otnosheniyah Rossii i ES. *Mirovaya ekonomika i mezhdunarodnye otnosheniya*, 10, 23–33.

Mehta, J. (2011). The Varied Roles of Ideas in Politics: From "Whether" to "How". In D. Béland and R. H. Cox (eds), *Ideas and Politics in Social Science Research*. Oxford: Oxford University Press.

Melnykovska, I. (2008). Ukraine: Europeanization From Abroad or Inside? Chance and Challenge for the European Union. ECSA-Canada 2008 Biennial Conference, The Maturing European Union, Edmonton, 25–24 September, 1–36.

Meloni, G. (2008a). *Convergence, Best-Practice and Europeanization: a Valuable Way to Rethink EU-Russian Relations? ISPI Working Papers, 33*. Rome: ISPI.

Meloni, G. (2008b). Russia: a Case for Revising the Concept of Europeanisation. In S. Gänzle, G. Müntel, and E.Vinokurov (eds), *Adapting to European Integration: Kaliningrad, Russia and the European Union*. Manchester: Manchester University Press.

Meuller, J-W. (2014). Eastern Europe Goes South. Disappearing Democracy in the EU's Newest Members. *Foreign Affairs* (March/April), 14–19.

Migrant Crisis: Migration to Europe explained in seven charts. (2016). *BBC News*, 18 February. Accessed at: www.bbc.co.uk/news/world-europe-34131911.

Mikhelidze, N. (2013). Juggling Security, Democracy and Development in the Caucasus: What Role for the EU? *Working Paper 1322*. Rome: Istituto Affari Internazionali.

Ministry of Foreign Affairs (MID). (1993). Conceptsiya vneshnei politiki Rossiiskoi Federatsii. *Diplomaticheskiy vestnik (Special Issue)*, 1.

Ministry of Foreign Affairs (MID). (2011). *O situatsii s pravami cheloveka v ryade gosudarst mira*. Moscow: MID. Accessed 15 January 2012 at: www.mid.ru/bdomp/Ns-dgpch.nsf/03c344d01162d351442579510044415b/c32577ca00173cb244257974003e49c4!OpenDocument

Ministry of Foreign Affairs (MID). (2012). *Doklad o situatsii s obespecheniem prav cheloveka v Evropeiskom souse*. Moscow: MID. Accessed 15 December 2012 at: www.mid.ru/bdomp/ns-dgpch.nsf/03c344d01162d351442579510044415b/f400dd8cdbe26ad144257acc0035ddf3!OpenDocument

Ministry of Foreign Affairs (MID). (2013). *Report on the Human Rights Situation in the European Union*. Moscow: MID. Accessed 6 December 2014 at: www.mid.ru/bdomp/ns-dgpch.nsf/03c344d01162d351442579510044415b/44257b100055de8444257c60004a6491!OpenDocument

Ministry of Foreign Affairs (MID). (2016). Comment by the Information and Press Department on the remarks by the High Representative of the European Union for Foreign Affairs and Security Policy Federica Mogherini following an EU Foreign Affairs Council meeting. *mid.ru*, 15 March. Accessed 1 July 2016 at: www.mid.ru/foreign_policy/news/-/asset_publisher/cKNonkJE02Bw/content/id/2148856.

Mistrany, D. (1966). *A Working Peace System*. Chicago: Quadrant Books.

Molokova, E.L. (2013). Identifikacija transformacionnyh processov sistemy vysshego professional'nogo obrazovanija v uslovijah diversificirovannoj modeli integracii nacional'noj jekonomiki. *VUZ. XX1 vek*, 3(43), 126–136.

Molokova, E.L. (2014). Identifikacija transformacionnyh processov sistemy vysshego professional'nogo obrazovanija v uslovijah diversificirovannoj modeli integracii nacional'noj jekonomiki. *VUZ. XX1 vek*, 1(44), 133–142.

Moravcsik, A. (2010). Europe: The Second Superpower. *Current History*, 109(725), 91–98.

Morozov, V. (2009). *Rossiya I Drugie. Identichnost I granitsy politicheskogo soob-schestva*. Moscow: Novoe literaturnoe obozrenie.

Moscow Patriarchate. (2009). *Vystuplenie Svyateyshego Patriarkha Kirilla na torzhestvennom otkrytii III Assamblei Russkogo Mira*. Accessed 23 March 2016 at: www.patriarchia.ru.

Müftüler Bac, M. (2000). Through the Looking Glass: Turkey in Europe. *Turkish Studies*, 1(1), 21–35.

Müftüler Bac, M. (2005). Turkey's Politics Reforms and the Impact of the European Union. *South European Society and Politics*, 10(1), 16–30.

Murinson, A. (2006). The Strategic Depth Doctrine of Turkish Foreign Policy. *Middle Eastern Studies*, 42(6), 945–964.

Musabekov, R. (2005). The Karabakh Conflict and Democratisation in Azerbaijan, www.c-r.org/our-work/accord/nagorny-karabakh/conflict-democratization-azerbaijan.php Accessed from http://www.c-r.org/our-work/accord/nagorny-karabakh/conflict-democratization-azerbaijan.php

National Bureau of Statistics of the Republic of Moldova. (2014). *External Trade of the Republic of Moldova (1997–2013)*, www.statistica.md/public/files/serii_de_timp/comert_exterior/serii_anuale/eng/Com_Ext_RM.xls.

National Platform of the Eastern Partnership Civil Society Forum. (2013). *How to Increase the Transformational Potential of the European Dialogue on Modernisation with Belarusian Society?* Minsk, Belarus. Accessed 23 March 2016 at: www.eap-csf.eu.

Naviny TUT.by. (2014). *Lukashenka: Evrosoyuz i SShA, mozhet skvoz zuby, no kak-to nachinayut razgovarivat s Belarusyu.* Accessed 23 March 2016 at: http://news.tut.by.

Neal, A.W. (2009). Securitisation and Risk at the EU Border: The Origins of FRONTEX. *Journal of Common Market Studies*, 47(2), 333–356.

Nesbitt-Larking, P., and Kinnvall, C. (2013). Securitising Citizenship: (B)ordering Practices and Strategies of Resistance. *Global Society*, 27(3), 337–359.

Neumann, I. (1998). European Identity, EU Expansion, and the Integration/Exclusion Nexus. *Alternatives*, 23.

Neumann, I.B. (1996). Self and Other in International Relations. *European Journal of International Relations*, 2(2), 139–174.

Neustupny, J. (2006). Sociolinguistic Aspects of Social Modernization. In U. Ammon, N. Dittmar, K. Mattheiser, and P. Trudgill (eds), *Sociolinguistics: An International Handbook of the Science of Language and Society*. Berlin/New York: Walter de Gruyter.

Nitou, C. (2011). Reconceptualising 'Cooperation' in EU–Russia Relations. *Perspectives on European Politics and Society*, 12(4), 462–476.

Nodia, G. (1996). Political Turmoil in Georgia and the Ethnic Policies of Zviad Gamsakhurdia. In B. Coppieters (ed.), *Contested Borders in the Caucasus* (pp. 73–89). Brussels: VUB Press.

Noi (2015). *Sotsialisty: V situatsii v Moldove vinovaty Evrosoyuz i SShA.* Accessed from www.noi.md/ru/news_id/60513.

Noutcheva, G. (2009). Fake, Partial and Imposed Compliance: The Limits of the EU's Normative Power in the Western Balkans. *Journal of European Public Policy*, 16(7), 1065–1084.

Noutcheva, G. (2012). *European Foreign Policy and the Challenges of Balkan Accession: Conditionality, Legitimacy and Compliance.* New York: Routledge

Noutcheva, G., Pomorska K., and Bosse G. (2013). *The EU and its Neighbours.* Manchester: Manchester University Press.

Novak, T. (2014a). Economic Cooperation and Integration in Central and Eastern Europe. *Central Europe Now*, 5. Accessed 12 December 2014 at: www.centraleuropenow.blogspot.com.

Novak, T. (2014b). CEE at the Crossroads. What Future Awaits the Region? *Central Europe Now*, 4. Accessed 2 March 2015 at: www.centraleuropenow.blogspot.com.

Novikov, V. (2004). Obschee evropeiskoe ekonomicheskoe prostranstvo: prostranstvo vybora ili vybor prostranstve. In E. Brun, K. Greff, V. Mau, V. Novikov and I. Samson (eds), *Obschee evropeiskoe ekonomicheskoe prostranstvo. Perspektivy vzaimootnoshenii Rossii i ES* (pp. 183–194). Moscow: Delo.

Novikova, G. (2012). The Nagorno Karabakh Conflict through the Prism of the Image of the Enemy. *Transition Studies Review*, 18(3), 550–569.

O'Reilly, C. (2001). *Language, Ethnicity and the State (Volume 2): Minority Languages in Eastern Europe post-1989.* London: Palgrave.

Obydenkova, A. (2006). Democratization, Europeanization and Regionalization Beyond the European Union: Search for Empirical Evidence. *European Integration online Papers (EIoP)*, 10(1). Accessed 1 July 2014 at: http://eiop.or.at/eiop/texte/2006–001a.htm.

Official Journal of the European Communities. (2006). Regulation (EC) No 1931/2006 L 405 Of the European Parliament and of the Council of 20 December 2006 laying down rules on local border traffic at the external land borders of the Member States and amending the provisions of the Schengen Convention.

Official Journal of the European Union. (2008). Directive 2008/115/EC L 348/98 Of the European Parliament and the Council on common standards and procedures in Member States for returning illegally staying third-country nationals.

Official website of the Republic of Belarus. (2014). *Makei: The EU is Realizing the Need to Cooperate with Belarus*. Accessed 23 March 2016 at: www.belarus.by.

Oğuzlu, T. (2013). Turkey and Europeanization of foreign policy. *Political Science Quarterly*, 125(4), 657–683.

O'Lear, S. (2007). Azerbaijan's Resource Wealth: Political Legitimacy and Public Opinion. *The Geographical Journal*, 173(3), 207–223.

Olsen, G.R. (2000). Promotion of Democracy as a Foreign Policy Instrument of 'Europe': Limits to International Idealism. *Democratization*, 7(2), 142–167. doi: 10.1080/13510340008403663.

Olsen, J. (2002). The Many Faces of Europeanization. *Journal of Common Market Studies*, 40 (5), 921–952

Önis, Z. (2004). Turgut Özal and his Economic Legacy: Turkish Neo-Liberalism in Critical Perspective. *Middle Eastern Studies*, 40(4), 113–134.

OSCE. (2013). Statement by Mr Sergey Lavrov, Minister for Foreign Affairs of the Russian Federation, at the Twentieth Meeting of the OSCE Ministerial Council. Accessed at: www.osce.org/mc/109306?download=true.

OSCE/ODIHR Election Observation Mission Final Report. Accessed 23 March 2016 at: www.osce.org/odihr/elections/belarus/218981?download=true.

OSCE/ODIHR. (2016). *Republic of Belarus. Presidential Election 11 October 2015*.

Ozolins, U. (1994). Upwardly Mobile Languages: the Politics of Language in the Baltic States. *Journal of Multilingual and Multicultural Development*, 5 (2/3), 161–169.

Ozolins, U. (2003). The Impact of European Accession upon Language Policy in the Baltic states. *Language Policy*, 2.

Pachlovska, O. (2009). Finis Europae: Contemporary Ukraine's Conflicting Inheritances from the Humanistic "West" and the Byzantine "East" (A Triptych). In L. Zaleska-Onyshkevych, and M. Rewakowicz (eds), *Contemporary Ukraine on the cultural map of Europe* (pp. 40–68). New York: M. E. Sharpe Inc.

Painter, J. (1998). Multi-level Citizenship, Identity and Regions in Contemporary Europe. In J. Anderson (ed.), *Transnational Democracy* (pp. 93–110). London: Routledge.

Painter, J. (2008). European Citizenship and the Regions. *European Urban and Regional Studies*, 15(1), 5–19.

Panarin, I. (2011). Missija Rossii v evrazijskoj integracii. Ideologija i praktika. *km.ru, 12 September 2011*. Accessed 1 July 2014 at: www.km.ru/spetsproekty/2011/09/12/strategii-razvitiya-rossii/missiya-rossii-v-evraziiskoi-integratsii-ideologi.

Papazian, T. (2006). From Ter-Petrossian to Kocharian: Explaining Continuity in Armenian Foreign Policy. *Demokratizatsiya: The Journal of Post-Soviet Democratization*, 14(2), 235–251.

Pardo Sierra, O. (2010). A Corridor through Thorns: EU Energy Security and the Southern Energy Corridor. *European Security*, 19(4), 643–660.

Parker, N. (2008). A Theoretical Introduction: Spaces, Centers, and Margins. In N. Parker (ed.), *The Geopolitics of Europe's Identity: Centers, Boundaries and Margins* (pp. 3–23). Houndmills: Palgrave Macmillan.

Patton, M.J. (2007). AKP Reform Fatigue in Turkey: What has Happened to the EU Process? *Journal of Mediterranean Politics*, 12(3), 339–358.

Pavlenko, A. (2008). Multilingualism in Post-Soviet Countries: Language Revival, Language Removal and Sociolinguistic Theory. *International Journal of Bilingual Education and Bilingualism*, 11(3/4).

Petersen, A. (2008). Regions In Between: Europe, NATO and the Geopolitics of Shifting Frontiers. *Turkish Policy Quarterly*, 7(2), 59–69.

Petrosyan, D. (2013). Oligarchy in Armenia. *Caucasus Analytical Digest* (53–54), 11–18.

Petrov, R., and Kalinichenko, P. (2011). The Europeanization of Third Country Judiciaries Through the Application of the EU Acquis: the cases of Russia and Ukraine. *International and Comparative Law Quarterly International and Comparative Law Quarterly*, 60(2), 325–353.

Phinnemore, D. (2009). From Negotiations to Accession: Lessons from the 2007 Enlargement. *Perspectives on European Politics and Society*, 10(2), 240–252.

Phinnemore, M. (1993). International Institutions and Teachers of Norms. *International Organisation*, 47(4), 565–597.

Pipes, D. (2014). Who lost Turkey? *The Weekly Standard*, 13 October, http://weeklystandard.com/who-lost-turkey/article/808512.

Polish EU Presidency. (2011). *Programme of the Polish Presidency of the Council of the European Union*. Accessed 23 March 2016 at: Www.Mf.Gov.Pl/En/C/Document_Library/Get_File?Uuid=377a6c5d-76fa-4df9–98b2–54c6f3efc07eandgroupid =764034.

Polyvyannyi, D. (2015). "Balkanizacija" i "Evropeizacija" na Jugo-Vostoke Evropy. *Sovremennaja Evropa*, 5(65), 36–47.

Popescu, N. (2010). *EU foreign policy and Post-Soviet Conflicts: Stealth Intervention.* London: Routledge.

Popescu, N., and Wilson, A. (2009). *The Limits of Enlargement-Lite: European and Russian Power in the Troubled Neighbourhood*. Accessed 6 August 2017 at: https://www.files.ethz.ch/isn/101917/EU_EasternNeighborhood_June09.pdf.

Popov, N. (2000). *The Road to War in Serbia: Trauma and Catharsis*. Budapest: Central European University Press.

Popov, V. (1992). La conscience ethnique préférentielle des Tsiganes. *Études Tsiganes*, 38(2), 38–43.

Póti, L. (2003). The Good, the Bad and the Non-existent: the Hungarian Policy towards the Ukraine, Russia and Belarus, 1991–2002. In K. Pelczyńska-Nałęcz, A. Duleba, L. Póti and V. Votápek (eds), *Eastern Policy of the Enlarged European Union* (pp. 59–87). Bratislava: Slovak Foreign Policy Association.

Potocki, R. (2002). Dark Days in Belarus. *Journal of Democracy*, 13(4), 144–156.

Prague Post. (2015a). *Czech-Russian Plan Catches Babiš Unawares (28 January 2015)*. Accessed 2 March 2015 at: www.praguepost.com/czech-news/44035-czech-russian -plan-catches-babis-unawares

Prague Post. (2015b). *Czech-South Korean business talks shift relations into higher gear (3 December 2015)*. Accessed 18 December 2015 at: www.radio.cz/en/section/curraffrs/czech-south-korean-business-talks-shift-relations-into-higher-gear

Prague Post. (2016). Czech MEP Awarded Highest Russian Honour by President Vladimir Putin, Radio Prague 10 March. Accessed 11 March 2016 at: http://www.radio.cz/en/section/bulletin/daily-news-summary-2016–03–10

President of Russia. (2008). Foreign Policy Concept of the Russian Federation, Order 1440. *RussianMission.eu, 12 July 2008*. Accessed 27 January 2016 at: www.russianmission.eu/userfiles/file/foreign_policy_concept_english.pdf

President of Russia. (2013). Kontseptsiya vneshnei politikii Rossiiskoi Federatsii. *The Kremlin, February 2013*. Accessed 17 February 2013 at: http://news.kremlin.ru/media/events/files/41d447a0ce9f5a96bdc3.pdf.

President of the Republic of Belarus. (n.d.). *Belarus*. Accessed 23 March, 2016 from http://president.gov.by.

President of the Russian Federation. (1998). Mesto i rol Rossii v period formiruuschegosya mnogopolyarnogo mira. *mid.ru*. Accessed 17 June 2016 at: http://archive.mid.ru//bdomp/dip_vest.nsf/99b2ddc4f717c733c32567370042ee43/0c49f77568c6d653c3256889002a5db5!OpenDocument

President of the Russian Federation. (2000). Foreign Policy Concept of the Russian Federation, The Kremlin. *mid.ru, 28 June 2000*. Accessed 12 July 2016 at: http://archive.mid.ru//Bl.nsf/arh/1EC8DC08180306614325699C003B5FF0?OpenDocument

President of Ukraine. (2002). *European Choice: Conceptual Framework of the Strategy of Economic and Social Development of Ukraine for 2002–2011*. Accessed 12 November 2015 at: http://zakon5.rada.gov.ua/laws/show/n0001100–02.

President of Ukraine. (2014a). *Speech of the President at the Ceremony of Signing the Association Agreement between Ukraine and the European Union*, 27 June 2014. Accessed 16 December 2015 at: www.president.gov.ua/news/vistup-prezidenta-na-ceremoniyi-pidpisannya-ugodi-pro-asocia-33096.

President of Ukraine. (2014b). *President's Speech at the Session of the Verkhovna Rada in the Course of the Ratification of the Association Agreement with the EU, 16 September 2014*. Accessed 16 December 2015 at: www.president.gov.ua/news/vistup-prezidenta-ukrayini-na-zasidanni-verhovnoyi-radi-pid-33700.

Preuss, U.K. (1996).Two Challenges to European Citizenship. *Political Studies*, 44(3), 534–552.

Prina, F. (2013). *Linguistic Divisions and the Language Charter – The Case of Moldova*. Federica ECMI Working Paper 64.

Prina, F. (2015). National Minorities in Putin's Russia: Diversity and Assimilation, *Routledge Contemporary Russia and Eastern Europe Series*.

Prodi, R. (2002). A Wider Europe – A Proximity Policy as the Key to Stability. Speech given to Sixth ECSA World Conference 'Peace, Security and Stability – International Dialogue and the Role of the EU', Brussels, 5–6 December.

Programul de activitate al Guvernului Republicii Moldova 'Integrarea Europeană: Libertate, Democraţie, Bunăstare' 2009–2013. (2009), Accessed 6 August 2017 at: www.ungaria.mfa.md/img/docs/programul-activitate-guvernului.pdf

Pulišová, V. (2012). Between Europe and Russia. *New Eastern Europe*. Accessed 12 November 2015 at: www.neweasterneurope.eu/interviews/255-between-europe-and-russia.

Putin, V. (2011). *Novyi integratsionnyi proekt dlya Evrasii –budushchee, kotoroe rozhdaetsya segodnya' (New integration project for Eurasia – the future which is growing today)*. Interview 3 October. Accessed 16 August 2016 at: http://izvestia.ru/news/502761.

Putin, V. (2013). Meeting of the Valdai International Discussion Club. *The Kremlin*. Accessed 12 July 2016 at: http://en.kremlin.ru/events/president/news/19243.

Putin, V. (2014). *Address by President of the Russian Federation: Vladimir Putin addressed State duma deputies, Federation Council members, heads of Russian regions and civil society representatives in the Kremlin*. 18 March 18, The Kremlin, Moscow. Accessed 17 August 2016 at: http://en.kremlin.ru/events/president/news/20603.

Rácz, A. (2012). Hungary. In A. Lobjakas, and M. Mölder (eds), *EU-Russia Watch 2012*. Tartu: Tartu University Press.

Radaelli, C. (2000). Whither Europeanisation? Concept Stretching and Substantive Change. *European Integration Online Papers*, 3(7), htrp://eiop.or.at/eiop/comment/1999–007c.ht.

Radaelli, C. (2003). The Europeanisation of Public Policy. In K. Featherstone and C. Radaelli (eds), *The Politics of Europeanisation* (pp. 27–56). Oxford: Oxford University Press.

Radaelli, C. (2003). In the Name of Europe. In K. Featherstone, and C. Radaelli (eds), *The Politics of Europeanisation* (pp. 3–26). Oxford: Oxford University Press.

Radaelli, C. (2004). Europeanisation: Solution or Problem? *Europeanisation Online Papers*, 8 (10), http://EE IOP.OR.AT/texte2004–016.ht.

Radaelli, C., and Schmidt, V. (2004). Policy Change and Discourse in Europe: Conceptual and Methodological Issues. *West European Politics*, 27(2), 183–210.

Radio Prague. (2016a). Czech Republic's dependence on EU export has grown (28 January, 2016). Accessed 29 January 2016 at: www.radio.cz/en/section/news/czech-republics-dependence-on-eu-export-has-grown.

Radio Prague. (2016b). Czech and Chinese companies sign over 30 trade agreements at Žofín economic forum. Accessed 8 August 2017 at: www.radio.cz/en/section/news/czech-and-chinese-companies-sign-over-30-trade-agreements-at-zofin-economic-forum.

Radio Prague. (2016c). Chinese Investment in the Czech Republic comes under the spotlight. Accessed 8 August 2017 at: www.radio.cz/en/section/marketplace/chinese-investment-in-czech-republic-comes-under-the-spotlight.

Prague Daily Monitor, (2017). No big wave of Chinese investment comes to Czech Republic. Accessed 8 August 2017 at: http://praguemonitor.com/2017/04/04/hn-no-big-wave-chinese-investment-comes-czech-republic.

Raik, K. (2006). Promoting Democracy through Civil Society: How to Step up the EU's Policy Towards the Eastern Neighbourhood. *CEPS Working Document* No.237. Brussels: Centre for European Policy Studies.

Raik, K., and Dinesen, R.L. (2015). The European Union and Upheavals in its Neighborhood: A Force for Stability? *International Journal of Public Administration*, 38(12), 902–914. doi: 10.1080/01900692.2015.1015550.

Rannut, M. (2004). The Linguistic Consequences of EU Enlargement for Estonia. *Sociolinguistica*, 21.

Rannut, M. (2008). Estonianization Efforts Post-Independence. *International Journal of Bilingual Education and Bilingualism*, 11(3/4).

Ratzmann, N. (2012). Securitizing or Developing the European Neighbourhood? Migration Management in Moldova. *Southeast European and Black Sea Studies*, 12(2), 261–280. doi: 10.1080/14683857.2012.686188.

Razumkov Centre. (2005). European Integration of Ukraine: Citizens' Opinion and Assessments'. *National Security and Defence*, 44–56. Accessed 8 April 2016 at: www.uceps.org/ukr/files/category_journal/NSD67_ukr.pdf.

Razumkov Centre. (2008). What Direction of Foreign Policy Should Be Priority for Ukraine? Regional Distribution. Accessed 8 April 2016 at: www.razumkov.org.ua/ukr/poll.php?poll_id=119.

Razumkov Centre. (2012). What Integration Direction Should Ukraine Follow? Regional Distribution. Accessed 8 April 2016 at: www.razumkov.org.ua/ukr/poll.php?poll_id=666.

Razumkov Centre. (2013a). What Do You Need to Feel European. Accessed 8 April 2016 at: www.razumkov.org.ua/ukr/poll.php?poll_id=895.

Razumkov Centre. (2013b). Expectations of the Impact of the Association Agreement with the EU and Joining the Customs Union of Belarus, Kazakhstan and Russia on Different Aspects of Life (Multidimensional Graph). Accessed 8 April 2016 at: www.razumkov.org.ua/ukr/poll.php?poll_id=892.

Razumkov Centre. (2014). Do you feel European? Accessed 8 April 2016 at: www.razumkov.org.ua/ukr/poll.php?poll_id=894.

Razumkov Centre. (2015a). Foreign Policy Orientations of Citizens of Ukraine. Accessed 8 April 2016 at: www.razumkov.org.ua/upload/1429857190_file.pdf.

Razumkov Centre. (2015b). Which Foreign Policy Direction Should Be a Priority for Ukraine? (Dynamics, 2002–2015). Accessed 8 April 2016 at: www.razumkov.org.ua/ukr/poll.php?poll_id=305.

Reding, V. (2013). *Main Messages: Citizens' Dialogue in Vilnius*. Accessible at: http://europa.eu/rapid/press-release_SPEECH-13–1077_en.htm.

Regulation (EC) No 1931/2006 Of the European Parliament and of the Council of 20 December *2006 laying down rules on local border traffic at the external land borders of the Member State*s and amending the provisions of the Schengen Convention (Official Journal of the European Communities L 405 of 30.12.2006). Accessed 10 August 2017 at: http://eur-lex.europa.eu/legal-content/en/TXT/?uri=CELEX%3A32006R1931R%2801%29.

Riabchuk, M. (2003). *Two Ukraines: Real Boundaries, Virtual Wars*. Kyiv: Krytyka. (Рябчук, М. (2003). *Дві України: реальні межі, віртуальні війни*, Київ: Критика).

Riabchuk, M. (2007). Ambivalence or Ambiguity? Why Ukraine is Trapped Between East and West. In S. Velychenko (ed.), *Ukraine, the EU and Russia* (pp. 70–88). Palgrave: Macmillan.

Riabchuk, M. (2009). Cultural Fault Lines and Political Divisions. In L. Zaleska-Onyshkevych and M. Rewakowicz (eds), *Contemporary Ukraine on the cultural map of Europe* (pp. 18–28). New York: M. E. Sharpe Inc.

Ricento, T. (ed.). (2000). *An Introduction to Language Policy*. Oxford: Blackwell Publishing.

Riesenberg, P. (1992). *Citizenship in the Western Tradition: Plato to Rousseau*. Chapel Hill: University of North Carolina Press.

Risse, T. (1999). International Norms and Domestic Change: Arguing and Communicative Behavior in the Human Rights Area. *Politics and Society*, 27(4), 529–559.

Risse, T. (2003). The Euro Between National and European Identity. *Journal of European Public Policy*, 10(4), 487–505.

Risse, T. (2010). *A Community of Europeans? Transnational Identities and Public Spheres*. Ithaca, NY: Cornell University Press.

Risse-Kappen, T. (1996). Exploring the Nature of the Beast: International Relations Theory and Comparative Policy Analysis meets the European Union. *Journal of Common Market Studies*, 34(1), 53–80.

Roberts, J. (2010). *Recorded Lecture (23 September 2010) – The Caspian and Global Energy Security*, www.iiea.com/events/pipeline-politics-the–caspian-and-global -energy-security

Roberts, S. and Moshes, A. (2015). The Eurasian Economic Union: a Case of Reproductive Integration? *Post-Soviet Affairs*, published online 23 November, http:// dx.doi.org/10.1080/1060586X.2015.1115198.

Robinson, N. (2011). Russian Patrimonial Capitalism and the International Financial Crisis. *Journal of Communist Studies and Transition Politics*, 27(3–4), 434–455.

Romanova T., and Pavlova, E. (2014). What Modernisation? The Case of Russian Partnerships for Modernisation with the European Union and its Member States. *Journal of Contemporary European Studies*, 24(4), 499–517.

Romanova, T. (2012). Legal Approximation in Energy: A New Approach for the European Union and Russia. In C. Kuzemko, M. Keating, A. Goldthau, and A. Belyi (eds), *Dynamics of Energy Governance in Europe and Russia* (pp. 23–44). Basingstoke: Palgrave.

Romanova, T. (2014). Russian Energy in the EU Market: Bolstered Institutions and their Effects. *Energy Policy*, 74, 44–53.

Romanova, T. (2015a). Issledovaniya otnoshenii Rossii i Evrosouza v nashei strane i za rubezhom. *Sovremennaya Evropa*, 5, 100–114.

Romanova, T. (2015b). The Partnership for Modernisation through the Three Level-of-Analysis Perspectives. *Perspectives on European Politics and Society*, 16(1), 45–61.

Romanova, T. (2016a). Russian Challenge to the EU's Normative Power? Change and Continuity. *Europe-Asia Studies*, 68(3), 371–390.

Romanova, T. (2016b). Sanctions and the Future of EU-Russian Economic Relations. *Europe-Asia Studies*, 68(4), 774–796.

Rosecrance, R. (1998). The European Union: A New Type of International Actors. In J. Zielonka (ed.), *Paradoxes of European Foreign Policy* (pp. 15–23). The Hague: Kluwer Law International.

Ross, A. (2014). *Understanding the Constructions of Identities by Young New Europeans: Kaleidoscopic Selves*. Abingdon: Routledge.

Round 2000 of Population and Housing Censuses in Estonia, Latvia and Lithuania (2003). Accessed 19 February 2008 at: www.stat.gov.lt/en/catalog/pages_list/ ?id_1503.

Saatçioğlu, B. (2014). AKP's "Europeanization" in Civilization, Rule of Law, and

Sakwa, R. (2011). Russia and Europe: Whose Society? *Journal of European Integration*, 33(2), 197–214.

Sakwa, R. (2015). *Frontline Ukraine*. London: I. B. Taurus.

Sakwa, R. (2015). The Death of Europe? Continental Fates After Ukraine. *International Affairs*, 91(3), 553–579.

Sarigil, Z. (2007). Europeanization as Institutional Change: the Case of the Turkish Military. *Journal of Mediterranean Politics*, 12(1), 39–57.

SARIO. (2015). *Slovakia in Asia (10 October, 2011)*. Accessed 18 December 2015 at: www.sario.sk/index-old.php?newsandnews=374.

Sasse, G. (2008). The European Neighbourhood Policy: Conditionality Revisited for the EU's Eastern Neighbours. *Europe-Asia Studies*, 60(2), 295–316.

Schimmelfennig, F. (1998). NATO Enlargement: A Constructivist Explanation. *Security Studies*, 8(2–3), 198–234.

Schimmelfennig, F. (2000). International Socialization in the New Europe: Rational Action in an Institutional Environment. *European Journal of International Relations*, 6(1), 109–139.

Schimmelfennig, F. (2001). The Community Trap: Liberal Norms, Rhetorical Action and the Eastern Enlargement of the European Union. *International Organisation*, 55 (1), 47–80.

Schimmelfennig, F. (2003). *The EU, NATO and the Integration of Europe. Rules and Rhetoric*. Cambridge: Cambridge University Press.

Schimmelfennig, F. (2005). Strategic Calculation and International Socialisation: Membership Incentives, Party Constellations, and Sustained Compliance in Central and Eastern Europe. *International Organization*, 59(4), 827–860.

Schimmelfennig, F. (2007). European Regional Organizations, Political Conditionality, and Democratic Transformation in Eastern Europe. *East European Politics and Societies*, 21(1), 126–141.

Schimmelfennig, F. (2012). Europeanization beyond Europe. *Living Reviews in European Governance*, 7(1), 1–31.

Schimmelfennig, F. (2015). Europeanization beyond Europe. *Living Reviews in European Governance*, 10 (1). http://europeangovernance-livingreviews.org/Articles/lreg-2015-1/ doi:10.14629/lreg-2015-1.

Schimmelfennig, F. and Sedelmeier U. (2004). Governance by Conditionality: EU Rule Transfer to the Candidate Countries of Central and Eastern Europe. *Journal of European Public Policy*, 11(4), 669–687.

Schimmelfennig, F., and Scholtz, H. (2008). EU Democracy Promotion in the European Neighbourhood Political Conditionality, Economic Development and Transnational Exchange. *European Union Politics*, 9(2), 187–215.

Schimmelfennig, F., and Sedelmeier, U (eds). (2005). *The Europeanisation of Central and Eastern Europe*. Ithaca: Cornell University Press.

Schimmelfennig, F., Engert, S. and Knobel H. (2003). Costs, Commitment and Compliance: The Impact of EU Democratic Conditionality on Latvia, Slovakia and Turkey. *Journal of Common Market Studies*, 41(3), 495–518.

Schimmelfennig, F., Engert, S., and Knobel, H. (2006). *International Socialisation in Europe: European Organisations, Political Conditionality and Democratic Change*. Basingstoke: Palgrave Macmillan.

Schmidt, V. A. (2008). Discursive Institutionalism: The Explanatory Power of Ideas and Discourse. *Annual Review of Political Science*, 11, 303–326.

Schmidt-Felzman. A. (2008). All for One? EU Member States and the Union's Common Policy towards the Russian Federation, *Journal of Contemporary European Studies*, 16(2), 169–187.

Schmidt-Felzmann, A. (2008). Editorial: The European Union's External Energy Policy. *Journal of Contemporary European Research*, 4(2), 67–70.

Schmidt-Felzmann, A. (2011). EU Member States' Energy Relations with Russia: Conflicting Approaches to Securing Natural Gas Supplies. *Geopolitics*, 16(3), 574–599.

Second Joint Progress Report: Negotiations on the EU–Republic of Moldova Association Agreement, Chisinau. (2011). Accessed at: http://eeas.europa.eu/moldova/docs/2011_05_aa_joint_progress_report2_en.pdf

Sedelmeier, U. (2014). Anchoring Democracy from Above? The European Union and Democratic Backsliding in Hungary and Romania after Accession. *Journal of Common Market Studies*, 52(1), 105–121.

Sedelmeier, U., and Wallace, H. (1996). Policies towards Central and Eastern Europe. In H. Wallace, and W. Wallace (eds), *Policy-making in the European Union* (pp. 353–388). Oxford: Oxford University Press.

Selivanova, J. (2007). *The WTO and Energy: WTO Rules and Agreements of Relevance to the Energy Sector*. Accessed 16 March 2013 at: http://ictsd.org/i/publications/11229/?view=document.

Senior Nello, S. (1991). *The New Europe: changing relations between East and West*. New York: Harvester Pearson Education Limited.

Shapovalova, N., and Boonstra, J. (2012). The European Union: From Ignorance to a Privileged Partnership with Moldova. In M. Kosienkowski and W. Schreiber (eds), *Moldova. Arena of International Influences* (pp. 51–75). Lanham, MD: Lexington Books.

Shirinyan, A., and Ralchev, S. (2013). *U-turns and Ways Forward: Armenia, the EU and Russia Beyond Vilnius*. Policy Brief. Institute for Regional and International Studies. Accessed at: http://iris-bg.org/fls/iris-shirinyan&ralchev-Armenia-EU-Russia-Beyond-Vilnius-nov13.pdf.

Siklodi, N. (2014). Multi-level Citizenship: Labour Migration and the Transformation of Identity in the EU. In C. Rumford, and D. Buhari-Gulmez (eds), *European Multiplicity* (pp. 129–146). Newcastle upon Tyne: Cambridge Scholars Publishing.

Siklodi, N. (2015a). *Active Citizenship Through Mobility? Young and Educated Citizens' Perceptions of Identity, Rights and Participation in the European Union*, PhD thesis. Egham: Royal Holloway, University of London.

Siklodi, N. (2015b). Active Citizenship Through Mobility? Students' Perceptions of Identity, Rights and participation in the EU. *Citizenship Studies*, 6–7, 820–835.

Silander, D., and Nilsson, M. (2013). Democratization without Enlargement? The European Neighbourhood Policy on Post-Communist Traditions. *Contemporary Politics*, 19(4), 441–458.

Siroky, D.S., and Aprasidze, D. (2011). Guns, Roses and Democratization: Huntington's Secret Admirer in the Caucasus. *Democratization*, 18(6), 1227–1245. doi: 10.1080/13510347.2011.579514

Skutnabb-Kangas, T. (1994). *Linguistic Human Rights in Education. Language Policy in the Baltic States. Conference Papers*. Riga: Gara Pupa.

Skutnabb-Kangas, T., and Phillipson, R (eds). (1994). *Linguistic Human Rights: Overcoming Linguistic Discrimination*. Berlin: Mourton de Gruyer.

Slovak Ministry of Foreign Affairs. (2013). Lajcak hold [*sic*] talks with his Russian counterpart. (4 March 2013). Accessed 21 January 2016 at: www.mzv.sk/web/en/news/detail/-/asset_publisher/oLVowPO7vPxv/content/lajcak-hold-talks-with-his-russian-counterpart-lavrov-in.moscow/10182

Slovak Spectator. (2014). *Lajčák Talks Mutual Relations in Moscow* (20 May). Accessed 21 January 2015 at: http://spectator.sme.sk/articles/view/54027/10/ Lajčák_talks_mutual_relations_in_moscow.html

Smith, A.D. (1991). *National Identity*. London: Penguin Books.

Smith, A.D. (1992). National identity and the Idea of European Identity. *International Affairs*, 68(1), 55–76.

Smith, K.E. (2005). The Outsiders: the European Neighbourhood Policy. *International Affairs*, 81(4), 757–773.

Smith, M. (1996). The European Union and Changing Europe: Establishing the Boundaries of Order. *Journal of Common Market Studies*, 34(1), 6–28.

Snyder, J.L. (2000). *From Voting to Violence: Democratization and Nationalist Conflict*. London: W. W. Norton.

Socor, V. (2005). Saakashvili-Yushchenko 'Borjomi Declaration' Broadens Euro-Atlantic Vision. *Eurasia Daily Monitor*, 2(159). Accessed 6 August 2017 at: www.jamestown .org/single/?tx_ttnews%5Btt_news%5D=30785andno_cache=1-.U4w8B _ldXKg.

Socor, V. (2014). Moldova's Parliamentary Elections: European Choice Versus Russian Political Projects (Part One), *Eurasia Daily Monitor*, 11(214), www.jamestown.org/regions/europe/single/?tx_ttnews%5Btt_news%5D=43136andtx_ttnews% 5BbackPid%5D=51andcHash=fb1f0d85205ca824ea87687564227dbc#.VWw8rc -qhHw

Sokolov, S. (2007). Russia and the EU to Negotiate a New Cooperation Agreement. *Russia in Global Affairs*, 5(3). Accessed 11 July 2016 at: http://eng.globalaffairs.ru/ number/n_9135.

Soltanovsky, I.D. (2015). Interview direktora Departamenta obscheevropeiskogo sotrudnitchestva MID Rossii I.D. Soltanovskogo agentstvu «Interfaks». *mid.ru*, *27 August 2015*. Accessed 1 September 2015 at: www.mid.ru/foreign_policy/ news/-/asset_publisher/cKNonkJE02Bw/content/id/1719421.

Soros, G. (2015). A New Policy to Rescue Ukraine. *New York Review of Books*, February, www.nybooks.com/articles/archives/2015/feb/05/new-policy-rescue-ukraine.

Spief16 News. (2015). *Ministry of Industry and Trade promotes cooperation between Russia and Slovakia in high-technology industries (6 May, 2015)*. Accessed 19 November 2015 at: https://forumspb.com/en/2015/sections/22/materials/196/news/307.

Spiro, D.E. (1994). The Insignificance of the Liberal Peace. *International Security*, 19(2), 50–86.

Spolsky, B. (ed.). (2012). *The Cambridge Handbook of Language Policy*. Cambridge: Cambridge University Press.

Startin, N., and Krouwel, A. (2013). Euroscepticism Re-Galvanized: the Consequences of the 2005 French and Dutch Rejections of the EU Constitution. *Journal of Common Market Studies*, 51(1), 65–84.

Stefan Batory Foundation. (2009). *What to do with Visa for the Eastern Europeans? Recommendations from the Perspective of Visegrad Countries*. Accessed at: www.batory.org.pl/doc/Recommendations_v4.pdf.

Stegniy, O. (2011). Ukraine and the Eastern Partnership: Lost in Translation? *Journal of Communist Studies and Transition Politics*, 27(1), 50–72.

Stephens, P. (2016). Poland's threat to European Stability. *Financial Times*, *14 January 2016*. Accessed 16 January 2016 at: www.ft.com/cms/s/0/43967d14-b9f8–11e 5-bf7e-8a339b6f2164.html#axzz3yN4UAe11.

Stratfor (2016). Turkey: Foreign Minister Says Refugee Deal Will End If Terms Not Met. *Stratfor Global Intelligence*. Austin, TX.

Stråth, B. (2002). A European Identity: to the Historical Limits of a Concept. *European Journal of Social Theory*, 5(4), 387–401.

Strelkov, A.A. (2010). Tihaja evropeizacija postsovetskogo prostranstva. *Mirovaya ekonomika i mezhdunarodnye otnosheniya*, 12, 48–58.

Strelkov, A.A. (2011). Politika Evropejskogo sojuza v postsovetskom regione. *Aktual'nye problemy Evropy*, 2, 9–38.

Subotic, J. (2011). Europe is a State of Mind: Identity and EU-ization in the Balkans. *International Studies Quarterly*, 55, 309–330.

Swedish EU Presidency. (2009). *Work Programme for the Swedish Presidency of the EU*. Accessed 23 March 2016 at: www.europarl.europa.eu/meetdocs/2009_2014/documents/empl/dv/progtravpressv_/progtravpressv_en.pdf

Szolucha, A. (2010). The EU and 'Enlargement Fatigue': why has the European Union not been able to Counter 'Enlargement Fatigue'? *Journal of Contemporary European Research*, 6(1), 1–16.

Tafuro, E. (2014). Fatal Attraction? Russia's Soft Power in Its Neighbourhood – Analysis. *Eurasia Review*.

Talbott, S. (1996). Democracy and the National Interest. *Foreign Affairs*, 75(6), 47–63. doi: 10.2307/20047829.

Talina, G.V. (2014). Evropeizatsiya Moskovskoi Rusi. *Istoricheskoe obrazovanie*, 1, 135–59.

Tapiola-Shumylo, O. (2012). *The Eurasian Customs Union: Friend or Foe of the EU?* Accessed 6 August 2017 at: http://carnegieendowment.org/2012/10/03/eurasian-customs-union-friend-or-foe-of-eu/dyir.

Taranenko, O. (2007). Ukrainian and Russian in Contact: Attraction and Estrangement. *International Journal of the Sociology of Language*, 183, 119–140.

TASS. (2014). *Hungary PM to meet Putin in trade and economy push (13 January, 2014)*. Accessed 4 November 2015 at: http://tass.ru/en/economy/714434.

Taylor, C. (1989). *Sources of the Self: The Making of Modern Identity*. Cambridge: Harvard University Press.

Tema, M. (2011). European Union and the Paradox of Accession: The Conflicting Logistics of Integration and Democracy in the Case of Albania, *Western Balkans Policy Review*, 1(2), 56–84.

Thiel, M. (2012). 'European Identity in the 21st Century: Moving from External Marker to Internalized Practice. In J. Roy (ed.), *The State of the Union(s): The Eurozone Crisis, Comparative Regional Integration and the EU Model* (pp. 23–35). Dexter, MI: Thomson-Shore.

Thomson, R.W. (1973). The Regional Subsystem. A Conceptual Explication and Propositional Inventory. *International Studies Quarterly*, 17(1), 89–117, http://doi.org/10.2307/3013464

Timmermann, H. (2003). *Die EU und die 'Neuen Nachbarn' Ukraine und Belarus*. SWP Studie Berlin, Stiftung Wissenschaft und Politik.

Tischenko-Steblinskaya, S.S. (2013). Vliyanie upravlencheskih modelei ES na process evropeizatsii natsionalnyh administratsii. *Vestnik gosudarstvennogo i munitsipalnogo upravleniya*, 4, 255–262.

Tishkov, V.A. (2008). Russkiy yazyk i russkoyazychnoe naselenie v stranakh SNG i Baltii. *Vestnik RAN*, 78(5), 415–422.

TNS Social and Political. (2013). *Flash Eurobarometer 365: European Union Citizenship*.

Toal, G. (2013). Land for Peace in Nagorny Karabakh? Political Geographies and Public Attitudes Inside a Contested De Facto State. *Territory, Politics, Governance*, 1(2), 158–182.

Todorova, M. (2004). What is or is there a Balkan Culture, and Do or Should the Balkans have a Regional Identity? *Southeast European and Black Sea Studies*, 4(1), 175–185. doi: 10.1080/14683850412331321788.

Toje, A. (2008). The Consensus-Expectations Gap: Explaining Europe's Ineffective Foreign Policy. *Security Dialogue*, 39(1), 121–41.

Tokluoglu, C. (2011). The Political Discourse of the Azerbaijani Elite on the Nagorno-Karabakh Conflict. *Europe-Asia Studies*, 63(7), 1223–1252.

Tolstrup, J. (2014). *Russia v. The EU: The Competition for Influence in Post-Soviet States*. Boulder: Lynne Rienner.

Torbakov, I. (2013). The European Union, Russia, and the 'In-between Europe': Managing Interdependence. In T. Cierco (ed.), *The European Union Neighbourhood: Challenges and Opportunities* (pp. 173–190). Farnham: Ashgate.

Totul (2014). OPROS: Gagauzy schitayut, chto evrointegratsiya oznachayet ob"yedineniye Moldovy s Rumyniyey. Accessed at: http://totul.md/ru/newsitem /537142.html.

Tregubova, T.M., and Sitdikova, G. R. (2015). Formirovanie akademicheskoj mobil'nosti prepodavatelej v kontekste evropeizacii obrazovanija. *European Social Science Journal*, 9, 118–123.

Trenin, D. (2005). Russia, the EU and the Common Neighbourhood. *Centre for European Reform Essays*. Accessed 6 August 2017 at: www.cer.eu/sites/default/ files/publications/attachments/pdf/2011/essay_russia_trenin_sept05-2151.pdf.

Trenin, D. (2011). *Post-Imperium: a Eurasian Story*. Washington: Carnegie Endowment for International Peace.

Tsarouhas, D. (2012). Social Policy in the EU and Turkey: the Limits of Europeanization. In C. Nas and Y. Özer (eds), *Turkey and the European Union: processes of Europeanization* (pp. 161–80). Aldershot: Ashgate.

Tudoroiu, T. (2011). Communism for the Twenty-first Century: The Moldovan Experiment. *Journal of Communist Studies and Transition Politics*, 27(2), 291–321. doi: 10.1080/13523279.2011.564101.

Tudoroiu T. (2014). Democracy and State Capture in Moldova. *Democratization*, 22(4), 655–678. doi: 10.1080/13510347.2013.86843.

Ugrosdy, M. (2011). Money Alone Won't Buy Putin. *Centre for Strategic and International Studies, January 2011*. Accessed 10 May 2012 at: http://csis.org/blog/ money-alone-wont-buy-putin.

Umbach, F. (2010). Global Energy Security and the Implications for the EU. *Energy Policy*, 38(3), 1229–1240.

Ungureanu, O. (2002). Stability Pact for South-Eastern Europe and perspectives for the Republic of Moldova's inclusion. In A. Barbăroşie, and V. Gheorghiu (eds), *The Republic of Moldova and the European integration* (pp. 68–79). Chişinău: Cartier.

University of St Gallen. (2013). *Project: Region, Nation and Beyond: An Interdisciplinary and Transcultural Reconceptualization of Ukraine*, www.uaregio.org/en/ surveys/methodology/.

Vachudova, M.A. (2005). *Europe Undivided: Democracy, Leverage and Integration after Communism*. Oxford: Oxford University Press.

Vanhoonacker, S., and Pomorska, K. (2013). The European External Action Service (EEAS) and Agenda-Setting in European Foreign Policy'. *Journal of European Public Policy*, 20, 1316–1331.

Van Ingelgom, V. (2014). *Integrating Indifference: A Comparative, Qualitative and Quantitative Approach to the Legitimacy of European Integration*. Colchester: ECPR Press.

Vasilevich, H. (2014). Belarus–EU Dialogue: Towards more Pragmatism? *Regard sur l'Est*, 67 (Portrait du Bélarus). Accessed 23 March 2016 at: www.regard-est.com/home/breve_contenu.php?id=1527.

Vaughan-Williams, N. (2012). *Border Politics: The Limits of Sovereign Power*. Edinburgh: Edinburgh University Press.

Venice Commission. (2011). *Opinion on the Draft Law on Principles of The State Language Policy of Ukraine, adopted by the Venice Commission at its 89th Plenary Session* (16–17 December). Accessed 12 December 2016 at: www.venice.coe.int/webforms/documents/default.aspx?pdffile=CDL-AD(2011)047-e.

Verkhovna Rada. (1993). *On the Main Directions of Foreign Policy of Ukraine*. Accessed 12 November 2015 at: http://zakon4.rada.gov.ua/laws/show/3360–12?test=4/UMfPEGznhhurH.ZijI632pHI4/ws80msh8Ie6.

Verkhovna Rada. (2002). *On the Recommendations of Parliament Hearings on Relations and Cooperation with NATO*. Accessed 12 November 2015 at: http://zakon0.rada.gov.ua/laws/show/233-iv.

Verkhovna Rada. (2010). On the Foundations of Internal and Foreign Policy. Accessed 12 November 2015 at: http://zakon0.rada.gov.ua/laws/show/2411–17.

Vieira, A. (2015). Ukraine, Russia and the Strategic Partnership Dynamics in the EU's Eastern Neighbourhood: Recalibrating the EU's 'self', 'we' and 'other'. *Cambridge Review of International Affairs*, http://dx.doi.org/10.1080/09557571.2015.1093410.

Vink, M.P., and Graziano, P. (2008). Challenges of a New Research Agenda. In P. Graziano and M. P. Vink (eds), *Europeanisation: New Research Agendas* (pp. 3–20). New York: Palgrave Macmillan.

Vinogradov, V.A. (2010). Eevoljucija dogovornogo prava Evropejskogo sojuza: ot direktiv k "obshhej spravochnoj sheme". *Pravo i upravlenie. XXI vek*, 4, 120–129.

Vinokurov, E., Kulik, S., Sparak, A., Chernyshev, S., and Yurgens, L. (2015). *Konflikt dvukh integratsii*. Moscow: Ekon-Inform.

Visa Liberalisation Action Plan. (2016). http://eubam.org/what-we-do/visa-liberalisation-action-plan/.

Votápek, V. (2003). Policy of the Czech Republic towards Russia, the Ukraine and Belarus. In K. Pelczyńska-Nalęcz, A. Duleba, L. Póti, and V. Votápek (eds), *Eastern Policy of the Enlarged European Union*. Bratislava: Slovak Foreign Policy Association.

Vieira, A.V.G. (2013). The Many Patterns of Europeanization: European Union Relations with Russia, Ukraine and Belarus. In T. Cierco (ed.), *The European Union Neighbourhood: Challenges and Opportunities* (pp. 57–82). Farnham: Ashgate.

Wæver, Ø. (1998). Insecurity, Security and Asecurity in the West European Non-War Community. In E. Adler and M. Barnett (eds), *Security Communities* (pp. 69–118). Cambridge: Cambridge University Press.

Wallace, H. (2000). Europeanisation and Globalisation: Complementary or Contradictory Trends? *New Political Economy*, 5(3), 369–382.

Wallström, M. (2007). Communicating Europe in Partnership. ECAS Conference 'Is the EU really Listening to Citizens?', Brussels, 3 October, SPEECH/07/602.

Walters, W., and Haahr, J.H. (2005). *Governing Europe: Discourse, Governmentality and European Integration*. Abingdon: Routledge.

Weart, S.R. (1998). *Never at War: Why Democracies Will Not Fight One Another*. New Haven: Yale University Press.

Webber, D. (2014). How Likely is it that the European Union will Disintegrate? A Critical Analysis of Competing Theoretical Perspectives. *European Journal of International Relations*, 20(2), 341–365.

Weber K., Smith M. and Baun M. (2007). *Governing Europe's Neighbourhood: Partners or Periphery?* Manchester: Manchester University Press.

Weber, M. (1998). Citizenship in Ancient and Medieval Cities. In G. Shafir (ed.), *The Citizenship Debates: A Reader* (pp. 46–52). Minneapolis: University of Minnesota Press.

Weiner, R. (2004). The Foreign Policy of the Voronin Administration. *Demokratizatsiya*, 12(4), 541–556.

Welzel C., and Ingelhart R. (2008). Democratization as Human Empowerment. *Journal of Democracy*, 19(1), 126–140.

Wertsch, J.V. (2005). Georgia as a Laboratory for Democracy. *Demokratizatsiya: The Journal of Post-Soviet Democratization*, 13(4), 519–536.

West, R. (1985). *Black Lamb and Grey Falcon: the Record of a Journey through Yugoslavia*. Ontario: Penguin Group.

White, J. (2011). *Political Allegiance after European Integration*. Basingstoke: Palgrave Macmillan.

White, S., Light, M., and Lowenhardt, J. (2001). Belarus, Moldova and Ukraine: Looking East or Looking West? *Perspectives on European Politics and Society*, 2(2), 289–304. doi: 10.1080/1570585018458763.

Whitman, R., and Wolff, S. (2010). The EU as a conflict manager? The case of Georgia and its implications. *International Affairs*, 86(1), 1–21

Wikileaks. (2008). The Czech Republic and a Resurgent Russia. Accessed 18 February 2014 at: www.wikileaks.org/plusd/cables/08PRAGUE623_a.htm

Wikileaks. (2012). Hun/Hungary/Europe. Accessed 14 October 2013 at: www.wikileaks .org/gifiles/docs/827431_hun-hungary-europe-.html.

Wilson, A. (2009). *The Ukrainians – Unexpected Nation*. London: Yale University Press.

Wilson, A. (2011). *Belarus: the Last European Dictatorship*. New Haven: Yale University Press.

Wilson, A. (2014). *Ukraine Crisis: What it Means for the West*. London: Yale University.

Wilson, E. (1987) 'World Politics and International Energy Markets'. *International Organisation*, 41(1), 125–149.

Wilson, J.L. (2010). The Legacy of the Color Revolutions for Russian Politics and Foreign Policy. *Problems of Post-Communism*, 57(2), 21–36. doi: 10.2753/PPC1075–8216570202.

Wolczuk, K. (2007). Adjectival Europeanisation? The Impact of EU Conditionality on Ukraine under the European Neighbourhood Policy. *European Research Working*

Paper Series, 18, 1–25. Accessed 12 November 2015 at: http://is.cuni.cz/studium/predmety/index.php?do=downloadanddid=30506andkod=JPM522.

World Bank. (2014). *World Development Indicators*. Accessed at: http://data.worldbank.org/indicator/NY.GDP.MKTP.KD.ZG?page=2.

Wright, S. (1999). *Language Policy and Language Issues in the Succession States of the Former USSR*. Clevedon: Multilingual Matters.

Wright, S. (2009). The Elephant in the Room: language Issues in the European Union. *Journal of European Language Policy*, 1 (2), 93–119.

Yarovoy, G. (2010). Europeanization of a Russian Region: Republic of Karelia on the Way to New Regionalism? *Working Papers, WP 2010–06* (Bielefeld / St Petersburg: Centre for German and European Studies (CGES).

Yesilada, B.Y. (2002). Turkey's Candidacy for EU membership. *Middle East Journal*, 56(1).

Youngs, R. (2007). *Europe's External Energy Policy: Between Geopolitics and the Market*. Accessed 24 September 2009 at: www.ceps.be/book/europes-external-energy-policy-between-geopolitics-and-market.

Youngs, R. (2009). *Energy Security: Europe's New Foreign Policy Challenge*. Abingdon: Routledge.

New York Times. (1992). Yugoslav Refugee Crisis Worst Since 1940s (24 July). Accessed 6 August 2017 at: www.nytimes.com/1992/07/24/world/yugoslav-refugee-crisis-europe-s-worst-since-40-s.html

Yuval-Davis, N. (2007). Intersectionality, Citizenship and Contemporary Politics of belonging. *Critical Review of International Social and Political Philosophy*, 10(4), 561–574.

Zabortseva, Y. (2012). From the 'Forgotten Region' to the 'Great Game' Region: On the Development of Geopolitics in Central Asia. *Journal of Eurasian Studies*, 3(2), 168–176.

Zakaria, F. (1997). The Rise of Illiberal Democracy. *Foreign Affairs*, 76(6), 22–43.

Zakaria, F. (2007). *The Future of Freedom: Illiberal Democracy at Home and Abroad (Revised Edition)*. London: W. W. Norton and Company.

Zhurzhenko, T. (2002). Language Politics in Contemporary Ukraine: Nationalism and Identity Formation. In A. Bove (ed.), *Questionable Returns, Vienna: IWM Junior Visiting Fellows Conferences*, vol. 12 (pp. 1–24). Accessed 16 December 2015 at: www.iwm.at/wp-content/uploads/jc-12–02.pdf.

Zielonka, J. (2001). How the New Enlarged Borders will Reshape the European Union. *Journal of Common Market Studies*, 39(3), 507–536.

Zielonka, J. (2006). *Europe as Empire: The Nature of an Enlarged European Union*. Oxford: Oxford University Press.

Zielonka, J. (2013). Europe's New Civilizing Missions: The EU's Normative Power Discourse. *Journal of Political Ideologies*, 18(1), 33–55.

Zlenko, A. (2012). Neutrality or Non-Block Status: is it in Ukraine's Interest, *Viche. Scientific library*. Accessed 12 November 2015 at: www.viche.info/journal/1418/. (Зленко, А. (2012). 'Нейтралітет чи позаблоковість: чи це в інтересах України?', *Віче. Наукова бібліотека*, переглянуто 12 листопада 2015 року з www.viche.info /journal/1418/).

Zubrytska, M. (2009). Mirrors, Windows and Maps. In L. Zaleska-Onyshkevych, and M. Rewakowicz (eds), *Contemporary Ukraine on the Cultural Map of Europe* (pp. 157–61). New York: M. E. Sharpe Inc.

Index

Armenia 34, 173, 197, 201–204, 207, 213
  relationship with EU 40–43, 46, 49
    language policy 187–192
Association Agreements 40–47, 51
  Belarus 88
  Moldova 103, 106–112
  Turkey 126, 129–130
  Ukraine 43, 67, 76–77, 79–82
Azerbaijan 34, 201–204, 207, 212–213
  relationship with EU 40–44, 46, 49
    energy policy 159–166

Balkans 47–48, 50, 52, 114–125, 174, 178–180, 212
  EU-isation 114–115, 116–125
  identity 114–122
    Balkan 117–122
    Croatian 119–120
    European 124
    Serbian 120–121
Belarus 86–98, 212–217
  EU-isation 92–94, 96–98
    domestic reform 95
  foreign policy 91–92
  in-between-ness 84, 94
    identity 96–97
    language policy 183, 187–191
  relationship with EU 34, 38, 40–41, 44, 86–88
    EaP 89–94
    energy policy 155, 159
    migration and visa policy 173, 178

relationship with Russia 86–88, 91–92
  relationship with Ukraine 94–96
Bosnia-Herzegovina 48, 114, 166, 120, 173, 178

Copenhagen Criteria 12, 38, 135, 184, 213
Council for Mutual Economic Assistance (CMEA) 21, 142–143
Council of Europe 20, 21, 130, 183, 191–192
Croatia 119–122, 125, 178, 194, 211–212
Czech Republic 142–145, 148–153, 194
  C-RICEISC (Czech-Russian Intergovernmental Commission for Economic, Industrial and Scientific Cooperation) 145–146, 148, 151
  ČSSD (Česká strana sociálně demokratická – Czech Social Democratic Party) 150
  ODS (Občanská demokratická strana – Civic Democratic Party) 150–151

Deep and Comprehensive Free Trade Area (DCFTA) 40–41, 45, 51, 107, 109, 111
democratisation 195–208
Democratic Peace Theory (DPT) 5, 20–24, 195–199, 201

Eastern enlargement 33, 39
Eastern Partnership (EaP) 34–35,
   39–41, 212–216
   Belarus 86, 88–93, 96, 98
   energy 160–161
   migration 173, 178
   Moldova 103, 107–109, 111, 113
   security 196–197, 207
   Ukraine 71, 76
Energy Charter Treaty (ECT) 43, 162
Estonia 163, 183, 185–186, 188–189,
   195
European Union (EU)
   energy policy 155–166
      Caspian region 158–166
      dependence on Russia 156–166
      Europeanisation 159–166
      relationship with Russia 155–158
   in crisis 1, 10, 23, 34, 148, 218
   language policy 181–194
      Europeanisation 181–190
      role of Russia 181–194
   migration and visa policy 167–180
      security 169–173
      Visa Liberalisation Action Plan
         (VLAP) 173
   normative agenda 41–42, 213–214
   relationship with Russia 21, 50,
      214
      trade 142–143
   relationship with US 20–21
   security 38, 51–52, 155–166,
      169–173, 195–208
   self-interest 41, 43, 216–217
EU Border Assistance Mission
   (EUBAM) 102, 108, 177
EU-isation 1–6, 21, 24, 210–218
   conditionality 12–13, 38–42
   domestic reform 45–47
   ENP 39
   as Europeanisation 11, 16, 46–47
Eurasian Customs Union (ECU) 22,
   35, 106
Eurasian Economic Union (EEU) 3, 22,
   43–45, 214, 218
   Belarus 87–88, 98
   Moldova 110–111
   Russia 57, 64–66, 68–70

security 196
   Ukraine 71
Eurasianism 23, 24, 44, 215–216
Euro-Atlanticism 15, 20–24, 71,
   74–76, 168, 215–216
European Commission 2, 12, 25–26,
   28–31, 36, 50–51, 64–65, 90,
   102, 109, 121, 149, 158, 161,
   163–166, 170, 175, 178, 205,
   213
   Directorates Generales (DGs)
      DG Communication 29–31
      DG Development and Cooperation
         29
      DG Energy 158
      DG Justice 29
      DG for Neighbourhood and
         Enlargement Negotiations 51
      DG Trade 51
European Council 158, 174, 178
European External Action Service
   (EEAS) 41, 50–52, 89, 205
European identity 19, 21, 25–37,
   211–212, 216
   as 'bottom-up process' 29–32
   civil society 31
   as component of European
      integration 27, 28
   definitions 26–28, 37
   EU citizenship 29–32
   European Commission 26
      discourse 28–30, 34
      policy 29–32, 34
   European neighbourhood policy
      33–36
   language policy 181–194
      Europeanisation 181–190
      role of Russia 181–194
   'otherness' 11, 16, 18, 21, 26,
      34–35, 168–169, 215, 217
   as top-down process 29–32
   Russia 35, 36
   Turkey 33, 35, 36
Europeanisation 1–6, 210–218
   alternatives to 20
   asymmetry 42–43
   as 'bottom-up process' 47–48
   civil society 48–49

definition 11
domestic reform 45–47
Enlightenment 14, 15, 18–19, 23
as EU-isation 11, 16, 46–47
    challenges 23
historic Europeanisations 14–22
norms and values 16, 33, 213–214
as 'top-down' process 47–48, 212–213
as Westernisation 14, 17–18
Europeanism 13, 18, 23, 210–211, 216
European Neighbourhood Instrument
    (ENI) 48, 177
European Neighbourhood and
    Partnership Instrument (ENPI)
    104, 177
European Neighbourhood Policy (ENP)
    25, 34, 39–42, 48–53, 212–213,
    215
  Belarus 88, 92
  energy 160–161, 166
  language 181, 184
  migration 173, 177
  Moldova 102
  South Caucasus 196–197
  Ukraine 71, 73
European Parliament (EP) 29, 145, 213

Former Yugoslav Republic of
    Macedonia (FYROM) 118, 169

Georgia 34, 201–204, 207, 212–216
  relationship with EU 39–47, 52
    language policy 187–192
    migration and visa policy 176,
      178, 180
    security policy 196–197
  relationship with Russia 150–151

Hollande, François 52, 95, 135
Hungary 35, 141–153, 176–177
  H-RICEC (Hungarian-Russian
    Intergovernmental Commission
    on Cooperation in the Economy,
    Science and Technology)
    145–148, 151
  MSZP (Magyar Szocialista Párt
    – Hungarian Socialist Party)
    150

Kazakhstan 41, 44, 148, 159–162
Kosovo 48, 114, 120, 122, 169

Latvia 182–183, 185–186, 188–189,
    193
Lavrov, Sergei 44, 147
Lithuania 183, 186, 188–189
Lukashenka, Aliaksandr 87, 95

Merkel, Angela 52, 95
Moldova 51, 97, 99–113, 212, 214,
    217
  in-between-ness 99
  PCRM (Party of Communists of the
    Republic of Moldova) 101–105,
    110–111
  PDM (Democratic Party of
    Moldova) 106, 109, 112
  PL (Liberal Party) 106
  PLDM (Liberal Democratic Party of
    Moldova) 106
  relationship with EU 34, 39–41, 43,
    45, 99–113
    decline in support for membership
      110–111
    language policy 183, 185,
      187–190
    migration and visa policy 169,
      173, 176–180
  relationship with Germany 108
  relationship with Romania 99–101,
    107–108, 111, 187–190
  relationship with Russia 103,
    110–111

Nagorno-Karabakh Republic (NKR)
    201, 203
Non-governmental organisations
    (NGOs) 31, 48–49, 66
North Atlantic Treaty Organization
    (NATO) 20–22, 44–45, 52, 153,
    205–208, 214–215
  Balkans 120
  influence on language policy 183,
    190, 194
  Russia 61
  Turkey 130
  Ukraine 75–76

Organization for Security and
    Co-operation in Europe (OSCE)
    21, 52, 184, 189, 193, 205

Partnership and Cooperation
    Agreements (PCAs) 42, 61, 65,
    75, 88, 100, 161
PHARE (Poland and Hungary:
    Assistance for Restructuring
    their Economies) 177
Poland 142, 150, 153, 155, 163, 174,
    176–177, 194
Putin, Vladimir 22, 42, 43–44, 52, 61,
    68, 151, 153

Romania 99–101, 107–108, 111,
    187–190
Russia 57–70
    as alternative to the EU 1, 62–64, 68
    civil society 66
    as the EU's 'other' 35
    EU-isation 61–69
    definitions 58–61
    Europeanisation 57–71
    definitions 58–60
    historical Europeanisations 57, 60
    MID (Ministry of Foreign Affairs of
        the Russian Federation) 61,
        65–67
    relationship with EU 50, 61–69
    relationship with Eastern European
        states 43–45
    Ukraine 67
    Visegrad Four 141–154

Sarkozy, Nicholas 22, 52, 135
Serbia 47–48, 115–122, 125, 173, 178,
    212
Single European Act (SEA) 11, 170
Slovakia 141–145, 147–150, 152, 176,
    194
    SDKÚ-DS (Slovenská demokratická
        a kresťanská únia –
        Demokratická strana – Slovak
        Democratic and Christian
        Union-Democratic Party) 150
    Slovak–Russian Intergovernmental
        Commission on Cooperation in

    the Economy, Science and
        Technology (S-RICCEST)
        146–148
    SMER-SD (Smer–sociálna
        demokracia – Direction–Social
        Democracy) 150

Technical Assistance for the
    Commonwealth of Independent
    States (TACIS) 104, 160, 177
Treaty of Lisbon 12, 13–14, 34
Turkey 3–6, 148, 210–211, 215–218
    AKP (Justice and Development
        Party) 132–133, 136–137
    CHP (*Cumhuriyet Halk Partisi*
        – Republican People's Party)
        131
    EU membership 40–41
        alternatives 131–133
    European identity 33–36
    Europeanisation 128–129
        conditionality 129, 133–134
        as Westernisation 130
    relationship with EU 38–40, 43, 48,
        50, 126–138
        deterioration 135–137
        energy policy 159, 164–166
        migration and visa policy 169–
            175, 177–178, 180
Turkmenistan 159–165

Ukraine 5–6, 70, 87, 102, 108–109,
    197, 212, 214, 217
    in-between-ness 71–84
        domestic policy 77–80
        energy policy 155, 157, 159,
            164–165
        foreign policy 77–78
        identity 34–35, 81–83
        language policy 181–185,
            187–190
    NATO membership 75–76
    relationship with EU 38–52, 71–85,
        94–95
        migration and visa policy 168,
            173, 175–178
    relationship with Russia 74–75,
        94–95, 144–145, 147, 149, 152

Union of Soviet Socialist Republics
    (USSR) 21, 142, 183, 196

Visegrad Four (V4) 141–154, 173, 175
    alternative political party
        perspectives on Russia 150–152
    trade relationship with Russia
        142–153

World Trade Organization (WTO)
    162–163

Yanukovych, Viktor 43, 47, 76, 80
Yushchenko, Viktor 76, 79, 80